1971

Church of England/Methodist reunion fails.

1977

NEAC II: 'Seeing ourselves and Roman Catholics as fellow Christians, we repent . . .'

Billy Graham at Notre Dame: 'I have no quarrel with the Catholic Church.'

1978

'Only a few more divine miracles will bring us to that day of unity in truth and holiness, total unity in the Mass' (*Michael Ramsey*).

1995

EVANGELICALS AND CATHOLICS TOGETHER

D. MARTYN LLOYD-JONES

1963

Declines to chair BGEA first *World Congress on Evangelism*.

1966

Calls for Evangelical Unity at *Evangelical Alliance Conference*: 'We should be asking: What is a Christian? How can we get forgiveness of sins? and What is a church?'

1970

Breaks with James I. Packer over evangelical/Anglo–Catholic commitment.

ANGLICAN EVANGELICALS

1960

'Co-operation without Compromise'

1967

NEAC 1 (Keele): Evangelical *and* Comprehensive.

1977

NEAC 2 (Nottingham): The end of the evangelical 'party' in the Church of England?

1982

New editorial board for *Churchman* breaks with the popular policy.

1986

Proclamation Trust founded to strengthen expository preaching.

1988

NEAC 3 (Caister): 'The Church must give a firm lead against rigid thinking' (*Robert Runcie*).

WORLD CONGRESSES ON EVANGELISM (BGEA)

Berlin 1966

Lausanne 1974

'We must practise the truth we say we maintain. We must practise this truth in the area of religious co-operation where it is costly (*Francis Schaeffer*).

Evangelicalism Divided

Evangelicalism Divided

*A Record of Crucial Change
in the Years
1950 to 2000*

Iain H. Murray

THE BANNER OF TRUTH TRUST

THE BANNER OF TRUTH TRUST
3 Murrayfield Road, Edinburgh EH12 6EL, UK
P.O.Box 621, Carlisle, Pennsylvania 17013, USA

*

© Iain H. Murray 2000
First published 2000
ISBN 0 85151 783 8

*

Unless otherwise indicated, all Scripture quotations
are taken from the New King James Version
© 1982 by Thomas Nelson, Inc.

*

Typeset in 12/13 pt Bembo at
The Banner of Truth Trust
Printed in Great Britain at
The University Press, Cambridge

With thankfulness for the memory of
DOUGLAS JACK WAYTH CULLUM
1910-1971

Contents

APPENDICES

W here money is the great *want*, *numbers* must be sought; and where an ambition for numbers prevails, doctrinal purity must be sacrificed. The root of evil is the secular spirit of all our ecclesiastical institutions. What we want is a *spiritual* body; a Church whose power lies in the truth, and the presence of the Holy Ghost.

JAMES HENLEY THORNWELL, 1846
The Life and Letters of J. H. Thornwell, B. M. Palmer
(repr. Edinburgh: Banner of Truth, 1974), p. 291.

T he Protestant world will be soon educated to set inordinate store by that of which God makes least account − formal union; *at the expense* of that which he regards as of supreme value − doctrinal fidelity . . . It is obviously the 'tidal wave' of modern sentiment, the *'zeit geist'* of our day, as truly as it was of the days of Leo the Great; and it is as vital to the life of Christianity now as it was then, that it be exposed and resisted.

ROBERT L. DABNEY, 1876
Discussions: Evangelical and Theological, vol. 2
(repr. London: Banner of Truth, 1967), p. 538.

T he secularisation of Christianity and the Church is one of the evil tendencies of the day, and is one phase of the universalism which the church is now called upon to oppose. It is the repetition within the province of doctrinal theology of an attempt often made in former ages in practical propagandism. The Papal Church once sought to make Christianity a universal religion by adopting Pagan rites and ceremonies. Charlemagne would provide universal salvation for Saxons, by forcing them to be baptized at the point of a sword. Now, the attempt is to make the Christian religion a universal religion by emptying it of its distinguishing tenets, flattering it into a system of morality, and converting 'the righteousness which is of faith' into 'the righteousness which is of the law'.

WILLIAM G. T. SHEDD
The Presbyterian Review, January 1886
(Edinburgh: T. & T. Clark; and New York: Presbyterian Review
Association), p. 187.

The chief dangers to Christianity do not come from the anti-Christian systems. Mohammedanism has never made inroads upon Christianity save by the sword. Nobody fears that Christianity will be swallowed up by Buddhism. It is corrupt forms of Christianity itself which menace from time to time the life of Christianity. Why make much of minor points of difference between those who serve the one Christ? Because a pure gospel is worth preserving; and is not only worth preserving, but is logically (and logic will always work itself out into history) the only saving gospel.

BENJAMIN B. WARFIELD, 1894
Selected Shorter Writings, vol. 2
(Nutley, NJ: Presbyterian & Reformed, 1973), p. 665–6.

We are undoubtedly living at one of the great turning-points of history. I sometimes have a fear that we who are Evangelical, of all people, are most guilty of failing to recognize this.

D. M. LLOYD-JONES, 1969
The Puritans: Their Origins and Successors
(Edinburgh: Banner of Truth, 1987), p. 217.

I am convinced that this is only the beginning of a rather larger movement which is going to continue to escalate. This is happening because of the reigning cry for tolerance, because of the abysmal lack of discernment in the church, and because of the tremendous impetus which the unity movement has.

JOHN F. MACARTHUR, 1996
Speaking of *Evangelicals and Catholics Together* at Orlando.

I

Setting
the Scene

EVANGELION (that we call the gospel) is a Greek word; and signifieth good, merry, glad and joyful tidings, that maketh a man's heart glad, and maketh him sing, dance and leap for joy.[1]

So William Tyndale wrote in 1525, and at the same period all who so thought became described as 'gospellers' or, less commonly, as 'evangelicals'. Over two hundred years later it was the latter term that was to pass into more permanent usage at the time of the 'Evangelical Revival'. That it did not do so earlier is largely due to the fact that all the churches of the Reformation were 'of the gospel' in their creeds and confessions. By the eighteenth century, however, while the profession of the national churches in England and Scotland remained orthodox there were many pulpits from which no gospel was heard and when the evangel was recovered a term was necessary to distinguish its preachers from others: they were the 'evangelicals'.

---

[1] Tyndale, *Doctrinal Treatises* (Cambridge: Parker Society, 1848), p. 8.

By the nineteenth century the Church of England especially was noted for its 'evangelical party' and its members, together with those who held to the same gospel priority in other Protestant denominations, became identified as adherents to 'evangelicalism'. The Evangelical Alliance, founded in 1846, brought such men together on both sides of the Atlantic in a federation which had no pretensions to being a church organization. The unity was one of fellowship and belief, not of shared denominational structure.

But if nineteenth-century evangelicals were content to support a wider spiritual unity while remaining committed to different views on the organization of the church, this does not mean that they had no cause for concern. In almost all of the main-line denominations theological liberalism had entered before the end of the century and a gap was widening between the biblical creeds which were still officially professed and the teaching which was gaining acceptance. In this situation, while apprehensive for the future, evangelicals generally saw no grounds for leaving their denominations provided their formal constitutions remained unchanged.

It was also during the nineteenth century that another influence arose which was to bring unease to evangelicals. This was the movement for 'the reunion of Christendom', and at first evangelicals were among those interested. After all, the New Testament says nothing of different denominations, all to be found in the same location. For the first time since the Reformation it was now seriously proposed that churches should forego traditional distinctives and separate structures in order to fulfil at last, as it was said, the prayer of Christ 'that they all may be one'. Certainly there was evangelical representation at the World Missionary Conference at Edinburgh in 1910 – an event often regarded as the start of the ecumenical movement. But time was to show that the main inspiration for reunion came from the lowered need for fidelity to Scripture which liberalism had introduced. Years before 1910, orthodox Christian leaders had foreseen that it would be from an indifference to doctrine that the reunion movement would gain its momentum.[1] By the mid-twentieth century the correctness of that conviction was amply confirmed. The first assembly of the World Council of Churches in 1948 offered membership to 'churches which accept our Lord Jesus Christ as God and Saviour', but expressed no concern whatever about how these few words should be interpreted. Rather there was the assurance, 'the basis is not a creedal test to judge churches or persons'. The only belief which appeared to be sacrosanct was that the Christian standing of all participants should not be open to doubt.

Such, in brief, is the background to twentieth-century evangelicalism. But to understand how subsequent issues arose as they did, and why their development has come to threaten the unity of evangelical Christianity, we must first take up a crucial part of the story in more detail. In a recent book entitled *Crisis in the Church,* Dr John H. Leith has written:

> Contemporary theologians have, since Schleiermacher, been subject to the temptation to understand the Christian faith in the light of the *dogmas* of the Enlightenment, rather than the Enlightenment in the light of the dogmas of the Christian faith.[2]

At first sight it may appear a strange thing to link *contemporary* theology with the Enlightenment of the eighteenth century and with a name almost unheard of in ordinary Christian circles today – Friedrich Schleiermacher (1768-1834), who was in his prime almost two hundred years ago. But in this chapter I want to show why Leith is correct in this identification and in his belief that 'the crisis . . . has been long in the making.'[3]

---

[1] See the quotations from R. L. Dabney and W. G. T. Shedd on p. ix above.

[2] John H. Leith, *Crisis in the Church: The Plight of Theological Education* (Louisville, Ky: Westminster John Knox Press, 1997), p. 36.

[3] *Ibid.,* p. 9.

Schleiermacher was born in the age of unbelief which, in Germany, took the name of 'Enlightenment' (*Aufklärung*) and, according to its spirit, rationalism had captured the universities and many of the pulpits of that nation.[1] Human reason was held up as the only means whereby truth can be known and proved. Born into a home of contrary persuasion, his father, a minister in the German Reformed Church, sent him away to study at Moravian centres where piety and faith in Scripture as divine revelation were still maintained. But even there, through books and companions, the spirit of the age reached the youth. 'God and immortality disappeared before my doubting eyes', Friedrich was later to write.[2] A crisis came when he disclosed his change to his father in a letter of 1787:

> I cannot believe that He, who called himself the Son of Man, was the true, eternal God: I cannot believe that His death was a vicarious atonement, because He never expressly said so Himself: and I cannot believe it to have been necessary, because God, who evidently did not create men for perfection, but for the pursuit of it, cannot possibly intend to punish them eternally, because they have not attained it.[3]

Schleiermacher left the Moravian seminary at Barby and, despite his unbelief, became in due course a Reformed minister in Germany. It is a commentary on the state of the times that such a position was open for him. Across the country few made any real distinction between the church and the world. It was commonplace for all to be baptized at birth and for

[1] *The Shorter Oxford English Dictionary* (Oxford: Clarendon Press, 1934) represents the standpoint of a past age in defining 'Enlightenment' as 'shallow and pretentious intellectualism, unreasonable contempt for authority and tradition, etc.; applied *esp.* to the spirit and aims of the French philosophers of the 18th c.' The translation of the German word passed into general use in the United States but was less used in Britain.

[2] Schleiermacher, *On Religion: Speeches to its Cultured Despisers*, trans. R. Crouter (Cambridge: Cambridge University Press, 1988), p. 84.

[3] *Life of Schleiermacher*, trans. F. Rowan, vol. 1 (London: Smith, Elder, 1860), pp. 46–7.

admission to the communion service to be universal before adulthood. Discipline to exclude any from the Lord's Table was virtually unknown. Frederick II of Prussia, who reigned at the time of Schleiermacher's youth, well illustrates the prevailing conditions. Although he had been brought up in a nominal Reformed faith, Frederick the Great (as he became known) was a thorough rationalist and patron of 'free thought'. The sight of a cross, it was said, was enough to make him blaspheme. On one occasion when he was declaiming against Christ and the Christian religion during a dinner he observed an apparent lack of sympathy on the part of one of his guests, Prince Charles of Hesse. To an enquiring question from the king, the prince replied: 'Sire, I am not more sure of having the honour of seeing you, than I am that Jesus Christ existed and died for us as our Saviour on the cross.' After a moment of surprised silence Frederick declared, 'You are the first man who has ever declared such a belief in my hearing.'[1]

With unbelief thus favoured by leaders in the court and in the church it is not surprising that the masses of the people

> *Were blinded with doubt,*
> *In wildering mazes lost.*

But Schleiermacher was not to be a spokesman for rationalism, as was clear when he sprang to fame with his first book, *On Religion,* in 1799. This was a defence of religion in the face of materialism and the general scepticism. His approach was new: adopting the Romanticism of Rousseau and the pantheism of other contemporary philosophers, Schleiermacher came forward to assert that religion is primarily not a matter of doctrine but rather of feeling, intuition and experience. The religious instinct is an element in man's nature independent of thought, and by it all men are united to the 'spirit of the universe'. In relation to other faiths, he believed, Christianity is 'sublime', yet it claims no

---

[1] Quoted in James I. Good, *History of the Reformed Church of Germany, 1620–1890* (Reading, Pa.: Miller, 1894), p. 416.

exclusiveness, for, by the religious element in man, God is united with all people. So while previous controversies had concentrated on whether the way to salvation lies in the resolution of intellectual questions, or by moral attainments, Schleiermacher saw no need of a salvation from outside man himself.

From this early position, however, Schleiermacher appeared to progress closer to orthodox Christianity. In 1805, when he was a professor of theology at Halle, he wrote to a friend: 'Through my lectures on doctrinal theology, my views in regard to separate points of Christianity are developing themselves more clearly, but I am persuaded that when, in a couple of years hence, I shall publish a little handbook on the subject, it will be an offence to the Jews and foolishness to the Greeks.'[1] More, certainly, was to come from his pen until in 1821 he published the capstone of his writings, a large volume on dogmatics which was intended, he wrote, to 'contribute to an ever clearer understanding as to the meaning of our Evangelical Faith.'[2]

Schleiermacher's move in the direction of orthodoxy had to do chiefly with the prominence which he came to give to the person of Christ and to the need for dependence upon him. The Reformers of the sixteenth century, he wrote, were not creators, merely instruments

> to bring forth in renewed glory the Evangelical Church, which is guided and governed by Jesus Christ, the eternal Son of God. He is the quickening centre of the Church; from Him comes all, to Him all returns: He is the Beginning and End: in Him we believe, and through Him alone we are blessed.[3]

Devotion to Christ, he taught, is the essence of true religion, and in order to come to feel devotion all that is

[1] *Life of Schleiermacher,* vol. 2, p. 43.
[2] Schleiermacher, *The Christian Faith,* trans. H. R. MacIntosh and J. S. Stewart (Edinburgh: T. & T. Clark, 1928), p. vii. The word 'evangelical' in Germany was used as synonymous with Protestant.
[3] *Life of Schleiermacher,* vol. 2, p. 207.

needed is faith. Yet faith, as he understood it, does not arise from truth and knowledge received from without; it springs rather from man's own intuition, from his own consciousness. To have faith, therefore, requires no revealed truths, no authoritative Bible. But how can men discover such truths as Christ's virgin birth, his atoning death and resurrection, unless they receive them from an objective revelation outside of themselves? To this Schleiermacher would reply that, whether these statements are truths or not, they are not necessary to evangelical devotion.[1] In other words, he remained committed to the starting point of his first book: the supposition that true religion belongs essentially to the realm of experience – religion is a matter of a well-disposed heart and devout feelings.

Thus, while ready to use high-flown language about Christ, and often to employ the language of traditional Christian teaching, Schleiermacher's thoughts of Christ remained essentially the same as those with which he dismayed his father in 1787. There is no sign that he ever returned to the faith he had been taught in his childhood. In the words of Daniel Edward, German-speaking pastor at Breslau:

> The Christ of Schleiermacher was a mere man. There was a gorgeous drapery of incomparable attributes and functions thrown around him for the benefit of those who were prepared not to look further than the surface, and a flimsy veil of subtle and glozing expressions to prevent offence on the part of such as were willing to be deceived . . . The false Messiah set up by Schleiermacher only differs from the false

[1] In fact, Schleiermacher's rejection of fundamental truths is clear in his dogmatics. On the atonement, for instance, he writes: 'We cannot say that Christ fulfilled the divine will *in our place* or *for our advantage* . . . Indeed, Christ's highest achievement consists in this, that He so animates us that we ourselves are led to an ever more perfect fulfilment of the divine will' (*Christian Faith*, p. 456).

Messiahs about the time of Christ – the Theudas and Barcochbas – as the nineteenth century differs from the first.[1]

Instead of providing, as some thought, a 'bridge for rationalism to return to Christianity,'[2] Schleiermacher disposed of the need for the revelation given in Scripture. Instead of the belief that 'faith comes by hearing and hearing by the word of God' (*Rom.* 10:17), here was a faith which depended neither on hearing nor Bible. Questions of orthodox belief were thus instantly reduced to matters of secondary moment; not what we *think* but what we *experience* is the important thing. So when a friend confessed to him to being 'a thorough heathen as to the understanding, but in point of feeling entirely a Christian', Schleiermacher was content to approve such a tension. Understanding, he replied, is not necessary: 'My Christian feeling is conscious of a divine spirit indwelling me, which is distinct from my reason.'[3] Referring on another occasion to his own experience, he could say, 'With my intellect I am a philosopher, and with my feelings quite a devout man; ay, more than that, a Christian.'[4]

So instead of a straight denial of Scripture truths Schleiermacher simply did away with the need for revealed truths and for an authoritative rule of faith. Christian experience consists of life, not doctrine. It derives from Christ, to be sure, but it is Christ within, not Christ revealed in Scripture and by the Holy Spirit. The Bible is simply 'the original interpretation of the Christian feeling', and by means of our own feeling we are free to add further 'interpretation'.

Schleiermacher faced opposition from a few but his teaching proved to be astonishingly successful in its influence. In part this arose from his genius. His surpassing gifts as a

[1] Daniel Edward, 'Schleiermacher Interpreted by Himself and the Men of his School', *British and Foreign Evangelical Review*, vol. 25 (London: Nisbet, 1876), pp. 610, 625. [Gloze: 'to veil with specious comments; to palliate; to explain away'.]

[2] Good, *Reformed Church*, p. 532.

[3] *Life of Schleiermacher*, vol. 2, pp. 280–1.

[4] Edward, *British and Foreign*, vol. 25, p. 609.

linguist, philosopher, writer and preacher captivated many and placed him on a pedestal above any criticism. In part his popularity arose from the support of undiscerning Christians who, confused by his language, supposed he had rescued religion from intellectual attack by showing that it stood on a different foundation.[1] Many more of those who praised him were simply happy to be confirmed in the idea natural to the human heart, that beliefs are not vital to a relationship with God. A definition of Christian which holds that creed and character have no necessary connection – that it matters not what we believe so long as our hearts are right – was bound to be popular. 'That one axiom of his, that religion stands in no need of doctrine and rigid precepts, or of revelation from another world – that certain pious and devout sentiments towards God and Christ are all that is necessary for salvation, was well calculated to carry along with him the majority of those who still inclined to have no religion at all.'[2]

The German public read with approval in Schleiermacher such words as these: 'Many who believe [that is, in an orthodox way] are manifestly not freer from faults than others, but on the contrary; and I see many unbelievers who are the best of men.' Or again: 'A religion without God may be better than another with God'; 'Christianity sets up no claim to be the only true religion.'[3]

The teaching that unbelief does not exclude anyone from heaven was welcome news in a country where the great men of culture had made no pretence to being orthodox. 'In Germany,' Edward observed in 1876, 'the Humboldts and Goethe, and a thousand men who in their lifetime despised the name of disciples of Christ, nay, avowed themselves heathens, are canonized, and have their place assigned to

[1] There is often an obscurity in Schleiermacher's language which veils rather than clarifies his meaning. There were some who saw this as consistent with his name which meant 'a maker of veils'.

[2] Edward, p. 632.

[3] *Ibid.*, pp. 629–30.

them in funeral sermons among those who are now behold-
ing the face of that Lord whom they never confessed, whose
truth they could not, "from very greatness of intellect,"
perceive while on earth.'[1]

Nominal religion had made a country ripe for the acceptance of such teaching on a large scale. By 1857 Charles
Hodge believed that the radical ideas of Schleiermacher and
his school 'are the life-blood of two-thirds of what passes for
orthodoxy in Germany, and of the affiliated systems in this
country'.[2] What Hodge could not know at that date was just
how pervasive the idea advanced by Schleiermacher was to
become throughout the English-speaking world. The
German's work, *The Christian Faith,* published in a complete
edition in Edinburgh in 1928, was heralded by its editors as
being, 'with the exception of Calvin's *Institutes,* the most
important work covering the whole field of doctrine to
which Protestant theology can point'.[3] Books on his theological thought filled shelves in all the theological libraries of
the world, or in all but the most backward.[4] Such at least was
the opinion of Ernest Trice Thompson, historian of Southern
Presbyterianism, when he wrote of Union Theological Seminary, Virginia: 'The student at Union, through the early
1920s, underwent his preparations for the ministry without
really hearing the names of Schleiermacher, Ritschl, and
other great theologians who were so profoundly influencing
the thought of the age.'[5]

[1] *Ibid.,* p. 632.

[2] Charles Hodge, 'The Inspiration of Holy Scripture, its Nature and
Proof', *Biblical Repertory and Princeton Review,* vol. xxix (Philadelphia:
Walker, 1857), p. 689.

[3] Schleiermacher, *Christian Faith,* p. v. Much more recently, against his
name in *New Dictionary of Theology* (Leicester: IVP, 1988), it is strange to
read, 'Commonly thought to be the founding father of liberal Protestantism, though he transcends that movement and is more properly ranked
with the great Reformation divines.'

[4] The library of New College, Edinburgh, for instance, catalogues over
140 items relating to Schleiermacher.

[5] E. T. Thompson, *Presbyterians in the South,* vol. 3 (Richmond, Va.:
John Knox Press, 1973), p. 208.

Schleiermacher is correctly viewed as the chief source of the massive change which has occurred in the historic Protestant denominations during the last two hundred years. Eighteenth-century rationalism rejected all truths which could not be squared with human reason. In reacting against that standpoint, he proposed another which still left authority in man himself. Yet while Schleiermacher's scheme was fundamentally similar to what it was supposed to displace, it was far more amenable to appearing in Christian dress. After all, the heart is basic to Christianity and devotion to Christ is a pre-eminent Christian characteristic.

In his separation of the intellectual content of Christianity (the objective biblical revelation) from Christian 'feeling', Schleiermacher seemed to provide a means whereby the essence of Christianity could remain unaffected, no matter how much of the Bible was rejected. Hostile criticism of Scripture need not therefore be seen as a threat to the 'faith', and so a sense of security was bred in many who might otherwise have awakened to the danger. Christianity, it was concluded, could be successful irrespective of whether Scripture were preserved as the Word of God, and this thought was the more appealing as the theological scholarship of the nineteenth century became increasingly destructive.

Further, it followed that, if it is the 'eternal verities' known to the human consciousness which constitute the essence of Christianity, then the 'dogmas' of Scripture do not need to be preached. Indeed Schleiermacher barred doctrinal preaching from the pulpit. Experience, not teaching, has to be the object of the preacher, 'the real thing in the religious discourse is an imparting of the religious consciousness'.[1] From this supposition there resulted the conditions about which R. B. Kuiper wrote in the 1940s: 'It is hardly an exaggeration to say that the Protestant ministry is today working as hard at keeping the laity in doctrinal darkness as

[1] Schleiermacher, quoted by R. B. Kuiper in *The Infallible Word* (1948; repr. Phillipsburg, N.J.: Presbyterian and Reformed, 1978), p. 224.

was the Roman Catholic clergy before the dawn of the Reformation.'[1]

Yet liberal theology very rarely presented itself as being in opposition to Scripture. On the contrary, its exponents claimed the authority of the New Testament for the view that Christianity is life, not doctrine. What happened in the first century, they claimed, was that the first disciples began with an *experience* of Christ and then, not content with that, they tried to express that experience in the form of beliefs. The church then sought to carry on these beliefs and gave them a finality − a 'mental framework' − which they were never meant to have. The real life of the church, it was argued, must not be made dependent upon the beliefs we may formulate, for they are only 'transient phrasings of permanent convictions and experiences' (to use the words of Harry Emerson Fosdick).

This opened the way, as it had done in Germany, for the idea that *belief* is no essential part of being a Christian. True experience can exist irrespective of belief. A different definition of Christian thus spread through English-speaking Protestantism, as innumerable examples could show. William Temple (1881–1944), for instance, who became Archbishop of Canterbury, wrote that 'an atheist who lives by love is saved by his faith in the God whose existence (under that name) he denies'.[2] Similarly, John Baillie (1886–1960), professor of theology at the University of Edinburgh, said that it was not what was consciously in the minds of men that determined what they were, for 'belief need not be conscious of itself'. So people may believe in God, he supposed, without knowing that they believe in him; and they may deny God with the 'top of their minds' yet believe in the bottom of their hearts. Along with this goes the usual denial of any Christian exclusiveness: 'How can we hold that the pagan or

[1] *Ibid.,* p. 228.

[2] William Temple, *Nature, Man and God* (London: Macmillan, 1934), p. 416. He proceeds to say that Article XIII of the Thirty-Nine Articles is 'unfortunately, even calamitously, expressed'.

the Jew who has had a solemn experience of conversion within his own religious tradition is as little in a state of grace, and as completely in a state of nature, as he was before?'[1]

A very public illustration of this popular teaching occurred when Aneurin Bevan, a notable British politician, died in 1960. Despite Bevan's avowed atheism, and public indifference to Christianity, a memorial service was held for him in Westminster Abbey. The following year Michael Ramsey, the newly appointed Archbishop of Canterbury, defended such action with the words, 'Heaven is not a place for Christians only . . . I expect to see some present-day atheists there.'[2] In harmony with this pronouncement, Archbishop Ramsey considered that members of the Church of England who did not believe in the virgin birth or in the resurrection of the body might properly continue to recite the Apostles' Creed.

* * * *

I turn now to consider how this departure from historic Christianity was addressed by evangelicals. The position in Britain can be briefly stated. Until the 1950s the evangelicals upon whose leadership gospel witness depended took a clear position on liberalism. Outnumbered in the denominations to which they belonged, they could not take action against error at that level; instead they stood together and supported one another in societies and various organizations of an inter-denominational character where they could control the teaching and where no one of different belief was given any influence. Among the most prominent and influential of these organizations was the Inter-Varsity Fellowship (IVF, later renamed UCCF – Universities and Colleges Christian Fellowship) which saw to it that all its affiliated Christian Unions in the universities upheld Scripture as the Word of

[1] See the review of John Baillie in *The Knowledge of God: Collected Writings of John Murray,* vol. 3 (Edinburgh: Banner of Truth, 1982), pp. 295–300.
[2] *Daily Mail,* 2 October 1961.

God and stayed apart from contrary influences. It was characteristic of prevailing evangelical convictions that, when the Cambridge Inter-Collegiate Christian Union sought the use of the University Church of Great St Mary for a mission with Billy Graham in 1955, they also proposed to exclude its liberal vicar, Mervyn Stockwood, and the bishop of the diocese, from any of the proceedings.[1]

A refusal to co-operate in evangelism with non-evangelicals was a common characteristic of all evangelical endeavour, from student witness in the universities to missionary outreach throughout the world. The same outlook also meant that evangelical leaders often advised against the study of academic theology in the universities, since the universities were feeding the unbelief which had found entrance into the churches. One missionary statesman, who did not follow that advice, talked about 'this miserable theology' which he studied at Cambridge and believed that it specialized in 'undermining faith in the Bible as the Word of God'.[2]

This response to the prevalence of error in the churches inevitably made evangelicals unpopular among the leaders of the denominations. It meant that as far as the denominations were concerned they were comparatively isolated and their influence curtailed. At best, the church authorities left evangelicals to themselves and commonly did nothing to encourage their promotion to positions of prominence.

In the United States the reaction to liberalism was broadly the same as in Britain. There were some who were unsure what to think, and in their uncertainty they erred on the side of neutrality and false charity. It was probably the attitude of

[1] Michael De-la-Noy, *Mervyn Stockwood: A Lonely Life* (London: Mowbray, 1996), p. 81.

[2] Quoted by Oliver Barclay, *Evangelicalism in Britain, 1935–1995: A Personal Sketch* (Leicester: Inter-Varsity Press, 1997), p. 20. Barclay also provides the significant fact that the leaders who gave their names to the infant Inter-Varsity Fellowship as vice-presidents 'were nearly all scientists, medicals, soldiers and missionaries, with a few working ministers' (p. 19).

this group which eventually allowed the new teaching to become so general. Others, however, were in open opposition, and prominent among them was the faculty of Princeton Theological Seminary. In an article already referred to, Charles Hodge wrote in 1857:

> The idea that Christianity is a form of feeling, a life, and not a system of doctrine, is contrary to the faith of all Christians. Christianity always has had a creed. A man who believes certain doctrines is a Christian. If his faith is mere assent, he is a speculative Christian; if it is cordial and appreciating, he is a true Christian. But to say that a man may be a Christian, without believing the doctrines of Christianity, is a contradiction. A man may be amiable or benevolent, without any definite form of faith, but how is he to be a Christian? The idea ... that a man may be a Christian although an atheist or pagan, destroys all distinction between truth and falsehood; between God and idols; between good and evil ... It is one of the fundamental principles of the Bible, that truth is as essential to holiness as light is to vision. Hence, on the one hand, the reception of truth is made essential to salvation, and, on the other, false doctrine is denounced as the source of sin, and the precursor of perdition.[1]

When the crisis came in the Presbyterian Church USA in the 1920s, it came precisely on the fault line of Schleiermacher's teaching. In the words of Fosdick, a chief spokesman for liberalism in 1924: 'To-day there are two parties in the churches. They are active in controversy now, and every day their consciousness of difference becomes more sharp and clear. The crux of their conflict lies at this point: one party thinks that the essence of Christianity is its original mental frameworks; the other party is convinced that the essence of Christianity is its abiding experiences.'[2]

---

[1] 'The Inspiration of Holy Scripture', *Biblical Repertory and Princeton Review*, 1857, p. 693.
[2] Harry Emerson Fosdick, *The Modern Use of the Bible* (London: SCM, 1924), p. 102. Quoted by Kuiper in *The Infallible Word*, p. 225.

J. Gresham Machen of Princeton Theological Seminary was Fosdick's main opponent. His convictions had been forged through a personal struggle during his own days of study in Germany. Wilhelm Herrmann, a professor of divinity in the Schleiermacher tradition whom he heard at Marburg, 'made liberalism wonderfully attractive and heart-gripping'.[1] At length Machen was to restate the position taken by Hodge: 'Christian doctrine, according to Paul, was not something that came after salvation, as an expression of Christian experience, but it was something necessary to salvation. The Christian life, according to Paul, was founded upon a message.'[2] In his book *Christianity and Liberalism* (1923), Machen put this case: 'Modern liberalism not only is a different religion from Christianity but belongs to a totally different class of religions.' No church therefore could be faithful to Scripture and allow the presence of teachers of liberalism.[3]

But the tide was flowing the other way, even at Princeton Seminary. Machen and others left in 1929 and formed a new seminary at Philadelphia which they named 'Westminster'. In the succession of events which followed Machen was suspended from the ministry of the Presbyterian Church USA and, with others, formed 'a true Presbyterian church' in 1936 – the Orthodox Presbyterian Church (OPC), as it was subsequently to be known.

Not all evangelicals in the Presbyterian Church agreed with Machen, but allied with him on the main issue were a

---

[1] N. B. Stonehouse, *J. Gresham Machen* (Grand Rapids: W. B. Eerdmans, 1955), p. 105.

[2] J. Gresham Machen, *What Is Christianity?* (Grand Rapids: W. B. Eerdmans, 1951) pp. 277–8.

[3] His understanding of the threat to the churches was the same as that expressed by Paton J. Gloag in an article on Ferdinand Christian Baur, another German teacher in the Schleiermacher tradition: 'The danger is much greater in our days than in those of our fathers. Then the citadel of faith was attacked from without; now the enemy is within. Then the attacks were open, now they are insidious' ('Ferdinand Christian Baur', *British and Foreign*, vol. 24, 1875, p. 108).

number more commonly known as 'fundamentalists'. The term had risen to sudden prominence in the 1920s. It had come to be employed both by some who wished to designate themselves as orthodox, 'Bible-believing' Christians – upholders of the 'fundamentals' – and by others who found it a convenient pejorative label for those they regarded as obscurantists. Liberals generally used the term for all evangelicals. Those who took the word to describe themselves usually belonged to a narrower number and were commonly adherents to a fundamentalist movement, organized round Bible Institutes, conferences, and evangelistic programmes, and all set to resist attacks on supernatural Christianity. In its adherence to basic beliefs, and in its use of non-denominational agencies, fundamentalism resembled evangelicalism in Britain, but the numbers were larger.

There were things, however, about fundamentalism which kept Machen and others from being ready to adopt the word. Instead of being simply the defender of Protestant orthodoxy, the fundamentalist movement had itself unwittingly adopted ideas of more recent origin. Its statements of belief were brief and lacking the doctrinal coherence to be found in the churches at an earlier date.[1] Its evangelism, while often praiseworthy for its earnestness, was generally Arminian. Its policy was too occupied with war on modernism and, sometimes, with war on denominations. Most who took the name of fundamentalist gave a high priority to separatism and advocated a policy of 'come-out-ism'. This was fuelled by popular nineteenth-century teaching on unfulfilled prophecy which saw the church as having already entered upon 'the end-time apostasy'. That same view left little incentive to work for change in the contemporary culture. Society must inevitably

---

[1] 'The substitution of brief, skeletal creeds for the historic confessions tends to shatter the organism of revealed truth into isolated and meagre fragments and to promote lack of concern with the precise formulation of Christian doctrine. Oftentimes pietistic and perfectionist vagaries have come to be accepted as the hallmark of fundamentalism' (Stonehouse, *Machen,* p. 337).

go down, and winning the souls of individuals was sometimes treated as though it was almost the only Christian duty.

While these were reasons for serious reservations on the part of Machen, he was thankful for all who stood with him 'in defense of the Word of God', and fundamentalist influences found a place in his new denomination of 1936. From that quarter, however, there soon came a challenge to the programme envisaged by the denomination's leaders in Westminster Seminary, and in 1937 the new denomination was split on that account. There was too large a difference between old-school Presbyterianism and the fundamentalist ethos. Thereafter the Seminary and the OPC pulled back from any alliance with fundamentalism and concentrated on providing Reformed pastors for Reformed churches. The leadership were convinced that, in the prevailing religious conditions, any attempt to secure wide support for their cause was bound to entail a dilution of their convictions. In the words of Paul Woolley, one of the founding members of Westminster Seminary's faculty:

> Does the OPC want to have a growing revival of the preaching, teaching and application of the biblical and Reformed Faith in these United States . . . Or does the Orthodox Presbyterian Church want to have many members and much money and read about itself in the newspapers? It can have either one, but it cannot have both.[1]

Woolley and his colleagues were in no doubt about the answer and they settled for working quietly, content with a low profile and with the long-term in view. With this position, however, some of Westminster Seminary's graduates were not to remain comfortable, and two of these men, in particular, were to play a major part in what became a new departure. They were Harold John Ockenga (1905–85) and Edward John Carnell (1919–67). Ockenga began his studies

---

[1] *Pressing Toward the Mark: Essays Commemorating Fifty Years of the Orthodox Presbyterian Church,* C. G. Dennison and R. C. Gamble, eds. (Philadelphia: OPC, 1986), p. 345.

for the ministry at Princeton, left there with Machen in the crisis of 1929 and graduated from Westminster the following year. After service in Pittsburgh he was called to Park Street Congregational Church in Boston, a church with Calvinistic origins which had more recently been under fundamentalist leadership. Carnell was a student at Westminster in the years 1941–4 and only came to know Ockenga when he undertook work and further studies in Boston. The two men became friends and had much in common. Both came from general evangelical backgrounds, Ockenga from Methodism and Carnell from the Baptists. Both put a premium on good scholarship. Ockenga earned a doctorate at Pittsburgh and Carnell at Harvard and at Boston University. Together they valued the doctrine they had heard at Westminster, but they had come to question whether their teachers (and the OPC denomination to which they belonged) had not needlessly narrowed the influence which they might have exercised. Their view was probably close to that stated by another Westminster graduate:

> We have been content, with only a few conspicuous exceptions, to regard our confessions as a barricade keeping out the world rather than as a manifesto for the marketplace ... Whatever insiders and those close to the OPC may think of it, the religious world at large has treated it casually or, with even greater disdain, paid it no heed at all.[1]

Carnell was ordained to the Baptist ministry in 1944 and served a Baptist church in Massachusetts (1945–6). After that his links were with the congregation at Park Street, Boston, where Ockenga was already known as an evangelical leader. Ockenga had served as president of the National Association

---

[1] Mark Noll in *Pressing Toward the Mark*, pp. 242, 245. The same book quotes the stronger words of an OPC minister: 'We are no longer fighting shoulder to shoulder with other Bible-believing Christians ... Instead of leading the Christian forces of our country, we have assumed the position of an isolationist porcupine' (p. 345). For a sympathetic view of the policy being followed at Westminster Seminary, see my 'Life of John Murray' in *Collected Writings of John Murray*, vol. 3.

of Evangelicals which he and others had formed in 1942. Such was his reputation that, after he had helped found Fuller as an independent theological seminary in Pasadena, California, in 1947, he was appointed its president even though his home continued to be in Boston on the other side of the country. With Ockenga's backing, Carnell became a faculty member at Fuller in 1948, when he was still under thirty years of age, and, when it was finally decided in 1954 that the minister of Park Street could no longer continue as president *in absentia*, it was Carnell who was given the post. Ockenga meant Fuller Seminary to stand for a new policy and he was confident that his younger friend shared the same vision. It is probably from Carnell's pen that we know most of what that vision was.

The 'new evangelicalism' was the name first employed to describe what was proposed at Fuller. When its intended meaning was misrepresented by critics Carnell instructed the faculty to drop the term, but by that time it had passed into wider use. Originally the name was employed interchangeably with orthodoxy, and Carnell defined the latter as 'that branch of Christendom which limits the ground of religious authority to the Bible. No other rule of faith and practice is acknowledged.'[1] By 'the authority of the Bible' its full inspiration and inerrancy was understood. Christ himself believed in the infallibility of Scripture, and, if he was wrong in that belief, by what means can we know he was right in any other? 'The evidences that support the plan of salvation are precisely the same in quantity and quality as those which support the plenary inspiration of the Bible.'[2] So Fuller Seminary meant to allow no concessions to liberalism, nor to ecumenism. Carnell rejected the experience-centred

[1] E. J. Carnell, *The Case for Orthodox Theology* (1959; repr., London: Marshall, Morgan and Scott, 1961), p. 13. For a sympathetic account of Carnell as an apologist, see, John A. Sims, *Missionaries to the Skeptics, Christian Apologists for the Twentieth Century: C. S. Lewis, Edward John Carnell, and Reinhold Niebuhr* (Macon, Georgia: Mercer University Press, 1995).   [2] *Ibid.*, p. 140.

definition of a Christian which said that a personal encounter with Christ 'is valid whether or not the Bible is inspired. Not only is the contention void of proof, but it reduces Christian commitment to a variety of religious experience . . . Religion becomes an exercise in personal feeling.'[1]

'Only propositional revelation', Carnell insisted, 'can clarify the state of a sinner before a holy God.' The World Council of Churches statement of faith 'is not praiseworthy enough to suit orthodoxy, for the only heresy it catches is unitarianism. The holes in the mesh are so wide that a sea of theological error can swim safely through. This proves that the ecumenical movement is more concerned with unity than it is with truth.'[2]

With all this a fundamentalist would be in agreement, and, indeed, Fuller's chief patron, Charles Fuller, was himself a fundamentalist, as were some of its first faculty members. But while Fuller, unlike Westminster Seminary, meant to include fundamentalists in a broader unity, the controlling policy guided by Ockenga and Carnell was to ease the new witness away from some of the fundamentalist distinctives. In the words of the former:

> Fundamentalism too often has been identified with peripheral emphases on doctrine and method, thus forfeiting the right to being a synonym with evangelical. For decades fundamentalism has proved itself impotent to change the theological and ecclesiastical scene. Its lack of influence has relegated it to the peripheral and subsidiary movements of Protestantism.[3]

If the Fuller policy was different from that of Westminster Seminary in its inclusion of fundamentalists, it differed still more in its aim to see a renewal of evangelical witness in the mainline denominations. 'We want our men', said Ockenga,

[1] *Ibid.,* p. 140.

[2] 'Orthodoxy and Ecumenism' in *Christianity Today,* 1 September 1958, p. 17.

[3] *Bulletin of Fuller Theological Seminary,* October–December 1954, quoted in George Marsden, *Reforming Fundamentalism: Fuller Seminary and the New Evangelicalism* (Grand Rapids: Eerdmans, 1987).

'to be so trained that when they come from a denomination they will go back into their denomination adequately prepared to preach the gospel and to defend the faith and to positively go forward in the work of God.'[1] This meant a move away from the separatist attitude which saw no hope of reforming the mainstream denominations from within and it also led the seminary to use a curriculum which would obtain the accreditation of the American Association of Theological Schools. In the words of George Marsden, the historian of Fuller Seminary:

> Carnell hoped to lead Fuller to full acceptance by the largely nonevangelical American theological establishment . . . Recognition by the national agency was a crucial step in putting the new-style evangelicalism solidly on the map of respectable American Protestantism.[2]

Taken by themselves these words could be read simply as an attempt to win influence in the larger religious scene. That would be unjust. Carnell at the same time as he held the above aim could also write: 'Under *no* conditions should truth be subordinated to unity . . . Our divisions will continue to scandalize the natural man, but this should not unhinge us. The message of the cross is also a scandal.' But in the same article he went on to say: 'I am sorry that orthodoxy hesitates to take an active part in the modern dialogue about unity. I should think that the possession of truth would issue in a passionate desire to guide, rather than chide, the groping efforts of a tragically divided church.'[3]

This greater openness Carnell justified in terms of principle. What he pleaded for was not a merging of

[1] Quoted by Carl F. H. Henry, *Confessions of a Theologian* (Waco, Texas: Word Books, 1986), p. 118. Henry adds: 'Ecumenically oriented denominations nonetheless perceived Fuller as an impediment to pluralistic ecumenism and in rivalry with denominational institutions.'

[2] Marsden, *Reforming Fundamentalism,* pp. 174-5.

[3] *Christianity Today,* 1 Sept. 1958, pp. 18, 24.

denominations but a recognition that 'God has true believers in *every* professing church. Whenever there are genuine signs of faith and repentance, we must presume that the gospel is at work.'[1] Our duty, then, he argued, is to love Christians everywhere, not simply those who can agree with us.[2] Nor are we permitted to abandon interest in denominations because liberals and false teachers are to be found in them. And such persons, too, are to be loved (although they may be our enemies) even as Christ loved those who slew him. In that connection he criticized the Reformers who 'occasionally entertained the fallacy that love for a dissenter carried with it approval of the dissenter's error'.[3] 'The law of love may not be taken lightly, as if we have the privilege of deciding whether to be loving or unloving.'

We have gone far enough to prepare the way for what is still before us. From Schleiermacher in Berlin, to liberal Protestantism in Britain and the United States, and on to Fuller Seminary in California, may seem a circuitous route but it is a real one. And the main issue raised in the course of that route will reappear as other events unfold.

---

[1] Carnell, *The Kingdom of Love and the Pride of Life* (Grand Rapids: Eerdmans, 1960), p. 119.

[2] He quotes Spurgeon's words: 'We must not hastily condemn men for lack of knowledge . . . The Holy Spirit makes men penitents before he makes them divines.' *Ibid.,* pp. 109–10.

[3] Carnell, 'Conservatives and Liberals Do Not Need Each Other', *Christianity Today*, 21 May 1965, p. 6.

2

Billy Graham:
Catalyst for Change

Fuller Seminary at Pasadena, California, proved to be only the starting point for a series of new agencies. Two years after its inauguration, an evangelist by the name of Billy Graham led a campaign in nearby Los Angeles in 1949. It was the moment when the thirty-year-old southerner first came into national prominence. No one could recall such crowds gathered to hear preaching since Billy Sunday in 1917. Harold Ockenga had already noticed Graham and, at his invitation, the evangelist's next campaign was to be in Ockenga's Park Street Church in Boston. The building proved to be far too small, and even the thirteen thousand seats in the Boston Garden could not contain the numbers who sought to attend a final meeting on 16 January 1950. 'New England is in the midst of a great awakening', fellow-worker Cliff Barrows wrote excitedly to a friend.[1] Ockenga

[1] John Pollock, *Billy Graham: The Authorized Biography* (London: Hodder and Stoughton, 1966), p. 97.

[24]

did not express himself so strongly but his earlier impression of Graham's gift was more than confirmed and from this date the two men were to share together in a wider cause.

While Ockenga had a plan to redefine Christian thinking through Fuller Seminary, he had never thought that scholarship alone could bring the needed change. In the end the best defence for the gospel would be its proclamation, and so Ockenga was whole-heartedly behind the formation of the Billy Graham Evangelistic Association (BGEA) in that same year (1950). Ockenga was to become one of its directors while Graham became a Board member at Fuller.

Ockenga was also involved in another development which was to be of major help to the new alignment. In June 1954 he addressed a business men's luncheon in New York and, as he wrote to Charles Fuller beforehand, he had a special interest in one man who had accepted an invitation to be there. This was J. Howard Pew (1882–1971), the business magnate who was president of the Sun Oil Company and a member of the Presbyterian Church in the USA. Conservative in belief and possessed of vast private resources, Pew was a prospective supporter of major significance. There were reasons in addition to sympathy with evangelism which drew Pew's interest. For, in common with many American business leaders of that era, he saw communism and socialism as a threat to free enterprise and the future of the nation. He knew that such men as Ockenga and Graham not only shared the same apprehension but had a public platform on which they could alert attention to it. The Boston pastor and president of Fuller (as he still was) knew what he had to say to secure the support of the distinguished luncheon guest, and he emphasized 'the Christian answer to the international challenge of communism and the insidious internal threat to our heritage of liberty'.[1]

---

[1] *Bulletin of Fuller Theological Seminary* (July–September 1954), quoted by Marsden, *Reforming Fundamentalism*, p. 156.

Ockenga's hope was fulfilled. Pew was to endow a chair at Fuller and about this time wrote to Graham proposing that they should meet in Philadelphia. Concerning this proposal Graham has written: 'I had never heard of him, and I declined. Then he sent me a check for our work in the amount of $25,000, along with a message: "When you come and spend a night with me, I'll have another check for $25,000 for you." Needless to say, *that* got my attention.'[1] Pew became a key supporter and without him, Graham has recorded, the next step could not have succeeded. The new evangelical alignment needed a major paper to advance its cause. No existing periodical, it was judged, could serve the need and so, with Pew's resources, *Christianity Today* was launched as a fortnightly journal on 15 October 1956. While the founders were Billy Graham and his father-in-law, Dr Nelson Bell, the influence of Fuller Seminary was present from the start. Ockenga became president of the board of the new journal's board and Dr Carl F. H. Henry (1913–) was brought to Washington from his Fuller professorship to be its first editor-in-chief.

Carl Henry was another key-player in the history which was in the making. Following early work in journalism, his conversion took him into the Baptist ministry, after training at Wheaton College. He had been on the Fuller faculty from the beginning and was a significant contributor to the policy which Ockenga had laid down. Some have thought that it was he, rather than Ockenga, who first coined the term 'new evangelicalism'. Certainly Henry was among the first to come from a fundamentalist background to stress in print the wider social responsibility which ought to mark Christians over against an exclusive interest in 'soul winning'. Henry's friendship with Carnell had begun in the days when they were both completing their doctorates in New England. 'Periodically,' he has recalled, 'we walked the Boston streets

[1] Billy Graham, *Just As I Am* (London: Harper Collins, 1997), p. 288. 'I came', Graham adds, 'to have great affection for him, not because he had a great deal of money but because he was a man of God and a man of wisdom.'

and talked philosophy. Except for odd moments of humor and banter, Carnell was almost always serious and intellectually engaged . . . For Carnell systematic theology was not a semantic game but a matter of life and death.'[1]

Henry was equally serious over the purpose of *Christianity Today*. He told his readers:

> 'The Bible says' is not a mere Graham platitude nor a fundamentalist cliché; it is the note of authority in Protestant preaching, lost by the meandering modernism of the past generation, held fast by the evangelical movement.[2]

Henry was the right man for the Washington post although, as we shall see, the alignment behind the public presentation of the new evangelicalism was not as united as it appeared. When plans for *Christianity Today* were still in the making, Dr Nelson Bell wrote to Graham in April 1955, 'I do not believe anyone but yourself can bring these very strong-minded people into the homogeneous group that we must have.'[3] But Bell did not mean that it was Graham's *thinking* which was forging the unity; it was rather the public status that he had come to possess.

Graham was probably one of the last to share a policy which entailed some departure from the thinking of fundamentalism and therefore from his own background. At the beginning of his ministry in strongly fundamentalist circles Graham could never have thought as he did at the inception of *Christianity Today* in 1956. Referring to that event, he has recalled: 'It was my vision that the magazine be pro-church and pro-denomination and that it become the rallying point of evangelicalism within and without the large denominations.'[4] At the earlier date the mainstream denominations where liberalism was to be found had no place in his thinking.

---

[1] Henry, *Confessions,* p. 121.
[2] 'The Resurgence of Evangelical Christianity', *Christianity Today*, 30 March 1959, p. 5.
[3] Quoted in *Just As I Am*, p. 290.
[4] *Ibid.,* p. 291.

This is illustrated by an episode noted by one of his biographers concerning the young lady who came home from China with her missionary parents in 1941. It was soon after that date that Billy Graham met Ruth Bell at Wheaton, and they were married in 1943. But during their courtship Graham had a difference with his strong-minded Presbyterian fiancée which almost threatened their engagement. Marshall Frady writes: 'Billy, who still affected a blunt fundamentalist disdain of all the establishment denominations, once advised Ruth, she says, that "Daddy couldn't be in the will of God because he was a Presbyterian. I almost gave him his ring back right there."'[1]

Ruth Graham's admiration for her father and his principles is relevant to our subject. For Nelson Bell was not only an effective missionary doctor, he was also a leader with convictions, as his increasing influence as a ruling elder in the Southern Presbyterian Church (PCUS) would show. Dr Bell had no time for any thought of evangelicals withdrawing from his own broad denomination. His vision was for a reviving of the Southern Presbyterian Church and he believed the same opportunity existed for renewal in the other major denominations, provided the evangelical cause was presented in less strident and negatives tones.

The steps by which Graham moved away from his former exclusiveness have not been recorded, but it is certain that his father-in-law played an important part in the change which had taken place by 1955. Graham has said that he 'never took a major step without asking [Nelson Bell's] counsel and advice . . . Dr Bell showed me that the strength of my future ministry would be in the church'.[2] By the late 1950s, as Marsden says, 'the Graham forces were raising a chorus against separation as a test of faith.'[3]

[1] Marshall Frady, *Billy Graham: A Parable of American Righteousness* (Boston/Toronto: Little, Brown, 1979), p. 143.

[2] Patricia Cornwell, *Ruth, A Portrait: The Story of Ruth Bell Graham* (New York: Doubleday, 1997), p. 153.

[3] Marsden, *Reforming Fundamentalism*, p. 189.

In 1955, the year before *Christianity Today* was launched, another far-reaching decision was taken: Graham accepted an invitation to hold a crusade in Manhattan, New York, in 1957. It was not the venue which made this projected crusade unusual, important although the location undoubtedly was. It was rather that this would be the first Graham crusade in North America to accept the sponsorship of non-evangelicals. 'I had already turned down two previous invitations, in 1951 and 1954', Graham writes. 'This invitation, however, was different, since it represented a much broader base of church support than the previous ones had.'[1] The sponsors for 1957 were the Protestant Council of the City of New York which meant, in the words of one impartial commentator, 'cooperation with a group that was predominantly non-evangelical and even included out-and-out modernists. It also meant sending converts back to their local churches, no matter how liberal those churches might be.'[2]

This was a change indeed for, not many years earlier, when Graham was the youthful president of Northwestern Schools (a fundamentalist college in Minneapolis), he had said, 'We do not condone nor have any fellowship with any form of modernism.'[3] Now his position was to be, 'We should be willing to work with all who were willing to work with us. Our message was clear, and if someone with a radically different theological view somehow decided to join with us in a Crusade that proclaimed Christ as the way of salvation,

[1] *Just As I Am*, p. 299.

[2] Marsden, *Reforming Fundamentalism,* p. 162. At the time of the crusade several newspapers reported Graham to say of those who would come forward, 'We'll send them to their own churches – Roman Catholic, Protestant or Jewish . . . The rest is up to God' (W. Martin, *A Prophet With Honor: The Billy Graham Story* [New York: William Morrow, 1991], p. 223). Martin's book is currently the primary source on Graham's life, being much fuller than the evangelist's own autobiography. Martin was invited to write by Graham but only took on the task when he had the assurance that there would be no conditions. For thoroughness of documentation it far exceeds other biographies of Graham.

[3] *Pilot*, the magazine of Northwestern Schools, April 1951.

he or she was the one who was compromising personal convictions, not we.'[1]

We have called this change far-reaching and, as subsequent developments will show, that assessment is justified. For the present we need to consider how the BGEA decision to go for co-operation with non-evangelicals came to be made. In part it was a logical consequence of the belief that the mainline denominations could still be recovered for the gospel. How could that hope be implemented if no association with leaders of these denominations was accepted in crusades? In this connection Ruth Graham evidently followed her father's thinking. Cliff Barrows has spoken of Mrs Graham as 'probably Billy's greatest teacher', and it is significant that it is only his wife that Graham mentions in connection with his decision to go for the broader sponsorship which the New York invitation offered. Referring to the 'final break' which the New York Crusade brought between him and 'some of the leading fundamentalists', of whom many 'had been among our strongest supporters in the early years of our public ministry,' Graham writes:

> I studied and prayed over their criticisms, wanting to accept their indictments if they were right. But I came to the firm conclusion that they were not, and that God was leading us in a different direction. Ruth likewise studied the whole matter; we discussed the issue and prayed over it frequently. Her conclusion was the same as mine.[2]

In a few areas of major fundamentalist influence opposition to the change in BGEA policy was united, in others opinion was divided. The latter was the case among Conservative Baptists. Dr Vernon Grounds, President of the Conservative

[1] *Just As I Am*, pp. 303–4.
[2] *Ibid.*, pp. 302-3. 'Jerry Beavan recalled that he resented Billy's treating Ruth and her father as his chief advisers' (Cornwell, *Ruth Graham*, p. 154). Dr Bell also helped to defend what became BGEA policy (*Just As I Am*, p. 303). Ruth Graham's published poetry has indicated something of her spirituality and her gifts.

Baptist Theological Seminary at Denver, favoured the change and believed that the new evangelicalism was 'really the old fundamentalism' at its best: 'The fundamentalism they aspire to rehabilitate is a fundamentalism marked by an unequivocal orthodoxy, topflight scholarship, permissible breadth, vital relevance, and commendable graciousness.'[1]

The magazine of the Central Conservative Baptist Theological Seminary at Minneapolis took a very different view. It believed that the concern to avoid controversy with liberals, and the new 'ecumenical evangelistic technique' which united men of opposing beliefs for evangelism, represented a serious downward turn: 'This new evangelicalism approaches the liberal bear with a bit of honey instead of a gun.'[2] Major blame was laid on Harold J. Ockenga: 'Mr Ockenga has propagated the principles of the new evangelicalism for some years, but not until fairly recently has he been successful.'

Critiques of this kind and tone were probably too strident and unfair to have much effect. In an article 'Resurgent Evangelical Leadership', written at this same period, Ockenga did not hesitate to say that modernists and evangelicals do not belong together. On the other hand:

> The evangelicals and the fundamentalists could sign the same creed. Moreover, they have a common source of life, for they belong to one family. Christian life comes from Christian faith and cannot be divorced from it. The repudiation of Christian truth cannot eventuate in a Christian life. In this the evangelical stands with the fundamentalist.

In the same article, the pastor of Park Street, Boston, insisted that the aim was not any change in evangelical doctrine. It was 'to retrieve Christianity from a mere eddy of the main stream into the full current of modern life.' 'All branches of theological thought have felt the impact of mass

---

[1] I quote from a photocopied address without date.
[2] Ernest Pickering, 'The Present State of the New Evangelicalism', in *Central C. B. Quarterly* (Minneapolis), Spring 1959.

evangelism under Billy Graham. In him we have seen the
phenomenon of an evangelical who crossed all theological
lines in his work while maintaining a strictly orthodox position.'[1]

A confirmation of 'no change in doctrine' came from a
very different source. The *Christian Century* was liberal in
position and probably the most widely read of the Protestant
journals at the time when *Christianity Today* appeared in 1956.
For four months the *Century* disdained to notice its new rival
but, with its own circulation overtaken within a year and
Graham's New York crusade in the process of gaining national
attention in the Spring of 1957, it judged that it must speak out:

> Behind the methods and message of Billy Graham, behind the
> revivalistic phenomenon which has just extended its lease on
> Madison Square Garden and emerged on national television,
> is a portentous development to which the nation's press and
> most of its churches are curiously blind. It is the attempted
> revival of fundamentalism as a major factor in Protestant life.
> The narrow divisive creed which the churches rejected a
> generation ago is staging a comeback. Through skillful
> manipulation of means and persons, including a well
> publicized association with the President of the United States,
> fundamentalist forces are now in a position aggressively to
> exploit the churches. If their efforts succeed, it will make
> mincemeat of the ecumenical movement, will divide
> congregations and denominations, will set back Protestant
> Christianity a half century.[2]

How far Ockenga was involved in the BGEA move to co-
operative evangelism is not on record. Ten years after the
New York crusade Graham was known to say that whenever
he faced a difficult problem he always consulted his friend
Harold Ockenga,[3] and he was also known to refer to him as

[1] Ockenga, 'Resurgent Evangelical Leadership', *Christianity Today*,
10 October 1960.

[2] A. W. Hearn, 'Fundamentalist Renaissance', *Christian Century*,
30 April 1958.

[3] Said by Graham in introducing Ockenga at the World Congress on
Evangelism in 1966. See Erroll Hulse, 'Berlin in Retrospect', *Banner of
Truth*, Issue 48, May/June 1967, p. 6.

'the spokesman of the convictions and ideals of the new evangelicalism'.[1] It is however clear that some of the Fuller Seminary thinking was influential for Graham. One of Graham's most frequently repeated sayings from 1957 onwards was, 'The one badge of Christian discipleship is not orthodoxy, but love.' This seems to have come directly from Carnell's, 'Jesus names *love*, not defense of doctrine, as the sign of a true disciple.' It was at this same period that Carnell, president at Fuller from 1954, was drawing attention to dangers he perceived in fundamentalism. These dangers included such things as the following:

The confusion of courtesy with compromise; the idea that believing the gospel makes a person omniscient, with a monopoly on truth; treating all beliefs as of equal importance as though 'the time of the rapture is as crucial to faith as the substitutionary atonement'; entertaining the illusion that the possession of the Word of God is the *same* as the possession of virtue; using the Bible as an instrument of self-security but not for self-criticism; enlisting the canons of orthodoxy 'in the service of self-love'; and the propensity to turn minor issues into major battles.

These, and other criticisms rarely heard in fundamentalist circles, Carnell was to publish in his book *The Case for Orthodox Theology* in 1959. As we shall see, Graham did not take all Carnell's thinking on board but he certainly endorsed the repudiation of belligerence and hostility as the only possible way to meet the liberal and the neo-orthodox.

It would appear to be the case, however, that the strongest influence which led to the broader Graham policy came from events which occurred three thousand miles away in the United Kingdom in 1954. Graham had preached in Britain as early as 1946–7 but the Greater London Crusade which began at the Harringay arena on 1 March 1954, was to be very different, and it did for the evangelist on the world stage

[1] Marsden, *Reforming Fundamentalism*, p. 167. Harold Lindsell's biography of Ockenga, *Park Street Prophet* (Wheaton: Van Kampen, 1951), was published too early. A definitive biography is anticipated from Dr Garth M. Rosell.

what the Los Angeles Crusade of 1949 had done in the USA. Preceded as it was by massive publicity, and soon after its commencement winning major press-coverage and support, attendance was said to have topped two million by the time of the final meeting on 22 May.

The London Crusade was the more remarkable in view of the fact that at the outset it was backed only by a private body, the Evangelical Alliance, with the denominations (Anglican and Nonconformist) all standing to one side and declining to endorse it. One British critic, representing liberal beliefs, wrote during the crusade that Graham 'is completely out of step with the majority of ministers and pastors'.[1] Yet it was from this very majority that a surprising interest in evangelism suddenly appeared and within weeks the one-time critics in the mainline denominations were to be found expressing their admiration for what was happening at Harringay. Such was the turn-round during the three months' crusade that John Pollock believed that in the end 'nearly eighty per cent of London churches co-operated'.[2] Even such a pronounced liberal minister and author as Leslie Weatherhead – 'the world-famous Methodist minister', as Graham calls him – became a Crusade supporter and Archbishop Fisher of Canterbury (who had previously declined to give his approval) pronounced the benediction at a final London gathering estimated to number more than one hundred thousand.[3]

Here for Graham was proof that church leaders, initially suspicious of fundamentalism and evangelicalism, could be won to the cause of a more biblical Christianity. Surely men who were so ready to befriend him and his work were basically one in heart. The implications of this for BGEA work in his own country could not be missed. It was no

[1] Dr Brian Welbeck, *Reynold's News*, 22 May 1955, quoted by William Martin, *Prophet With Honor,* p. 174.
[2] Pollock, *Graham,* p. 179.
[3] *Just As I Am,* pp. 233–4.

accident that the decisions taken in 1955 were what they were. As Marsden observes:

During his campaigns in England in 1954 Graham received broader church support than his fundamentalist supporters would have allowed him in the United States. Such successes in culturally influential religious circles were leading Graham toward the conviction that he could make marvellous inroads into America's major denominations if he could jettison the disastrous fundamentalist image of separatism, anti-intellectualism, and contentiousness.[1]

On the same point, William Martin, Graham's most authoritative biographer, has written:

He doubtless intended to keep himself and his crusades free from Modernist contamination, but success weakened his resolve. As non-Evangelicals watched the streams of people who responded to his invitation, they wanted to channel at least a trickle of them into their own churches. As they saw it was possible to co-operate with his crusades without having him attack their beliefs from the pulpit, they began to join in the invitations, and when he agreed to come to their cities, to volunteer for committees . . . Increasingly, and particularly after extensive co-operation with liberal state churches in England, Scotland, and on the Continent, Graham came to accept, then to welcome, then virtually to require, the co-operation of all but the most flagrantly Modernist Protestant groups, such as Unitarians, or such bodies as Mormons and Jehovah's Witnesses, whose teachings excluded them from both Evangelical and mainline circles.[2]

Clearly the new evangelical alignment was prepared, if need be, to lose the support of 'extreme fundamentalists'. And in this alignment, as we have noted Nelson Bell observing, Graham was the visible centre of unity. Yet from the

[1] Marsden, *Reforming Fundamentalism,* p. 159. The same author quotes from Graham how his travels abroad had affected his thinking (p. 163).

[2] Martin, *Prophet With Honor,* p. 218.

outset this unity was under strain, as can be learned from sources, such as Carl Henry's autobiography, which were to be published some years later. These show, for instance, that at the very start of *Christianity Today* there had been some difficulty in settling on an editor who would fit the policy which Bell and Graham wanted.

While the paper was still at the planning stage, Graham wrote to Harold Lindsell (a professor at Fuller Seminary) of their aim. It was to 'plant the evangelical flag in the middle of the road, taking a conservative theological position but a definite liberal approach to social problems. It would combine the best in liberalism and the best in fundamentalism without compromising theologically.'[1] Henry was told 'that the new magazine's prime objective would not be to reach or please American fundamentalists but to lead confused and and bewildered American liberals to accept the authority of Scripture'.[2] To that end the proposed strategy was apparently, in Marsden's words, 'that for the first two years they would emphasize points of commonality with ecumenical Christians, thus establishing the widest possible readership.'[3]

Carl Henry raised objections to significant parts of the strategy, including the proposal that the new journal 'introduce a sturdy theology only by degrees'. 'It carries with it', he wrote to Graham on 18 August 1955, 'if not a compromise of principle, at least a sufficiently perilous strategy as to render its ultimate effectiveness insecure and uncertain . . . At the beginning of our century, the question raised by the sponsors of that fine series, *The Fundamentals,* was, Have we told the whole truth? We seem to be wondering when we may dare to tell some of it.'[4]

More particularly, Henry feared that what was envisaged 'offers no clear and decisive criticism of that false doctrine of

[1] Graham to Harold Lindsell, 25 January 1955. Quoted by Marsden, *Reforming Fundamentalism,* p. 158.

[2] Henry, *Confessions*, p. 141.

[3] Marsden, *Reforming Fundamentalism,* p. 161.

[4] Quoted in Wilbur M. Smith, *Before I Forget* (Chicago: Moody Press, 1971), p. 181.

ecumenical unity which only treasures a minimum of doctrinal agreement'. And he warned: 'Liberalism and Evangelicalism do not have equal rights and dignity in the true church.'[1] Whether a strict definition of the inerrancy of Scripture should be upheld in the journal was also part of the preliminary discussions.[2]

By the 1960s these private discussions and differences were to surface as public issues, with Fuller Seminary closely involved. The faculty had been so racked by disagreements that it became too much for the gentle Carnell and, oppressed by sleeplessness, he stood down from the president's office in 1959. Along with medical treatment for depression, and with his former confidence greatly weakened, Carnell continued as a popular professor at Fuller until April 1967 when he was present at a Roman Catholic National Ecumenical Workshop at Oakland, California, to speak on 'The Conservative Protestant: Who is he and what is his relation to the ecumenical movement?' The address was never given for, on the day scheduled for its delivery, the forty-seven-year-old professor was found dead in his hotel bedroom. The cause, it would seem, was an accidental overdose of the medication upon which he was dependent.

It would be a serious mistake to conclude from the circumstance of this last engagement that Carnell was drifting into doctrinal indifference. On the contrary, it is clear that he was no party to the accommodation with deviant forms of Christianity which was becoming a part of the new evangelical movement. When the Fuller faculty was seriously split (in the early 1960s) over whether inerrancy applied to all Scripture or only to those parts relating to redemption, Carnell argued strongly for the traditional conservative belief, and at the time of his death he was thirty-six pages into writing a book upholding orthodox belief in Scripture. Lindsell,

[1] Marsden, *Reforming Fundamentalism*, p. 161–2.

[2] Graham favoured the view of Bernard Ramm who did not think that the accuracy of Scripture had to do with matters of science. *Ibid.*, pp. 158–9.

his colleague at Fuller, could write that at the end of his life Carnell 'saw clearly what the issue was and was right back where he had started years before'.[1]

In his criticisms of fundamentalism Carnell was careful to make a distinction which Graham seemed to miss. Carnell distinguished between the 'mentality' which was too often associated with fundamentalism and the *truths* for which, as a movement, it had done well to stand. In seeking 'to prove that modernism and biblical Christianity were incompatible', Carnell believed that the movement was right. 'In this way the fundamentalist movement preserved the faith once for all delivered to the saints.'[2] The perils of fundamentalism, he believed, were nothing to do with the great truths to which it adhered, they arose rather out of the failure adhering to all fallen men:

> The mentality of fundamentalism comes into being whenever a believer is unwilling to trace the effects of original sin in his own life. And where is the believer who is wholly delivered from this habit? This is why no one understands fundamentalism until he understands the degree to which he himself is tinctured by the attitudes of fundamentalism.[3]

So when Christians display a wrong spirit, he went on to argue, 'The Word of God is *not* voided by the frailties of those who come in the name of the Word of God.' Parallel with

[1] Quoted in Rudolph Nelson, *The Making and Unmaking of an Evangelical Mind: The Case of Edward Carnell* (New York: Cambridge University Press, 1987), p. 205. Nelson is a liberal and his treatment of his subject involves much misrepresentation. He writes: 'What an immense and crippling burden it was for Edward Carnell to carry around the doctrine of biblical inerrancy.' He had 'an anachronistic theology tied to an inerrant Bible', and this rendered any genuine 'openness of mind' impossible.

[2] *Case for Orthodox Theology*, p. 113.

[3] Carnell, 'The Case of Orthodox Theology', in *Christianity Today*, 27 April 1959, p. 13. This emphasis is similar to that of Thomas Scott, the eighteenth-century evangelical leader, who wrote, 'Calvinists, as well as others, may be proud of their notions and supposed privileges, and we all have too much, far too much, of this remaining.' *Letter and Papers of Thomas Scott* (London: Seeley, 1824), p. 326.

this in his thinking was the fact that while 'the law of love' is
imperative, it is never to be stated as an endorsement of the
ecumenical principle that a man's spirit is more important
than what he believes. Rather:

> Love and truth must be simultaneously respected. Christian truth
> accounts for the Church's time-tested conviction that God
> inspired holy men to declare the plan of salvation on
> divine authority . . . Unless our religious convictions grow out
> of a divinely revealed system of truth, we shall have no means by
> which to be certain that *anything* is holy, not even love itself.[1]

The above quotation comes from Carnell's last
contribution to the columns of *Christianity Today* in which he
opposed a case put forward by Egil Grisles that 'Conservatives
and Liberals Need Each Other'. The uniqueness of liberalism,
he wrote, lay in its repudiation of 'all claims to fixed and
final truth as indispensable elements in the Christian faith',
while that very claim is of the essence of orthodox Christianity. Liberalism is not committed to truths which are the
same in all generations but to a quest for progress and relevance to present needs. For the evangelical, on the other
hand:

> If the Church has been entrusted with a plan of salvation that
> is true on divine authority, then the relevance of Christianity
> is automatically established by the fact that it is true. To try to
> impose any other standard of relevance is manifestly wrong.
> What God says is final; even the slightest mishandling of
> Scripture is altogether out of order.

Here, then, was a major difference over the assessment of
liberalism and other forms of belief which had become
increasingly inherent in the Graham platform. As Marsden
writes, 'The death of Carnell was a signal that the new
evangelicalism was near its end as a unified and progressive
enterprise.'[2]

[1] Carnell, 'Conservatives and Liberals Do Not Need Each Other',
Christianity Today, 21 May 1965, p. 7
[2] *Reforming Fundamentalism,* p. 259.

We turn now to note how the differences which had emerged in the United States also led to serious division among evangelicals in Britain. The same apparent lesson that Graham took back to the States with him after the London Crusade of 1954 had been observed by a number of evangelicals in Britain, not least by a number of clergy who belonged to the Church of England and had been active in supporting the crusade. For men who had long felt it necessary to remain apart from the prevailing denominational influences, and to stand only with other evangelicals when it came to evangelism, it had been a near-stunning sight to see the readiness of non-evangelical clergy and ministers to join in the crusade. Was it possible that the comparative isolation that British evangelicals had been experiencing, and the smallness of their influence (compared with the 38,000 who made decisions in the 1954 meetings), had been largely brought upon themselves? This disturbing possibility was the more credible as evangelical leaders became conscious that Graham was clearly able to strike up friendships with church figures with whom they had never known any such relationship. Among that number, for instance, was Mervyn Stockwood who at first had taken pains to distance himself from the evangelist's beliefs when his church had been used by the Cambridge Inter-Collegiate Christian Union in 1955. A decade later, when Stockwood, as Bishop of Southwark, was making his diocese the most *avant-garde* in the country, he would be found on the council supporting another BGEA crusade in London.

No less surprising was the relationship which Graham was able to establish with Archbishop Michael Ramsey. We must pause for a moment with Ramsey whose name has already arisen in these pages and will appear again. He was born in Cambridge in 1904, the second son of 'a pious Congregationalist father' whose home observed family worship every day. But, following education at Repton and Cambridge, Ramsey became an Anglo-Catholic priest in the Church of England and then a professor of divinity at

Durham. In the latter role he combined his churchmanship[1] with a considerable element of liberal belief. He did not hold all Scripture to be the authoritative Word of God, nor did he believe such doctrines as the penal, substitutionary atonement. From the academic life of Durham he moved on to its bishopric, then to the archbishopric of York, before his appointment to Canterbury in 1961.

At first Ramsey opposed Graham's beliefs as heretical[2] but he seems to have been charmed by the American's amicableness when the two met at the New Delhi Third Assembly of the World Council of Churches. The evangelist has recorded how their friendship began on that occasion when he asked the archbishop, 'Do we have to part company because we disagree in methods and theology? Isn't that the purpose of the ecumenical movement, to bring together people of opposing views?'[3] Thereafter there was no more opposition.

A. T. Houghton, veteran Anglican missionary and evangelical leader, has also written of the influence which Graham was able to exercise as a distinguished guest at New Delhi (1961) and noted, as a sign of a happy change, that the

---

[1] In Ramsey's view bishops continued the work of the apostles and were necessary to the validity of 'sacramental acts': 'Church order is of the gospel.' This case, he argued, was not to be countered by an appeal to the New Testament for, 'To burrow in the New Testment for forms of ministry and imitate them is archaeological religion.'

'Protestantism, lacking the universal Church order and the liturgical structure, has made central in worship what really belongs to the circumference.' See A. M. Ramsey, *The Gospel and the Catholic Church* (London: Longmans, 1961), pp. 69, 198.

[2] 'He has taught the grossest doctrines and flung his formula "The Bible says" over teaching which is emphatically *not* that of the Bible. He has gone. Our English fundamentalism remains. It is heretical.' 'The Menace of Fundamentalism', *British Weekly*, 9 February 1956. For Ramsey's own view of how Christianity should be presented, see his *Introducing the Christian Faith* (London: SCM, 1961): '*Baptism* was from the beginning the means whereby the convert died to the old life . . . I commend to you what is called "going to confession" . . . whereby you confess audibly in the presence of the priest and receive from him audibly Christ's absolution' (pp. 54–5).

[3] *Just As I Am*, p. 695.

evangelist was 'directly invited by the World Council'.[1] Formerly, Houghton observed, 'Evangelicals who spoke the truth as they saw it were neither welcomed nor tolerated. Today, in the changed climate of opinion concerning relationships the definite Evangelical can express his views without compromise.'[2] There was therefore reason to heed the view heard at the council that the ecumenical movement remained impoverished because 'a large number of Evangelical Churches and organizations remain aloof.'[3]

In the early 1960s in England the opinion that their former aloofness had been a mistake steadily gained ground among evangelicals, and when some of them joined in ecumenical occasions they were quick to report to others that they had been given a respectful hearing. Finally, when the first National Evangelical Anglican Congress (NEAC 1) met at Keele in April 1967 the former evangelical stance was publicly disowned. Prior to the congress, the Rev. John R. W. Stott, its chairman, had said:

> It is a tragic thing, however, that Evangelicals have a very poor image in the Church as a whole. We have acquired a reputation for narrow partisanship and obstructionism. We have to acknowledge this, and for the most part we have no one but ourselves to blame. We need to repent and change.[4]

What was to be involved in the proposed change was clear enough when the honour of giving the opening address at the Congress was allocated to a guest specially invited, Archbishop Ramsey. With echoes of Schleiermacher, the archbishop reminded his hearers that 'experience' goes before 'theology', and he made it clear to the congress that

[1] A. T. Houghton, *What of New Delhi?* (London: Bible Churchmen's Missionary Society, 1962), p. 47.

[2] *Ibid.*, pp. 22–3. To be fair to Houghton it should be added that he adds at one point: 'One cannot but feel some disquietude as to how far the WCC is ready to secure [evangelical beliefs] in its inner councils' (p. 51). [3] *Ibid.*, pp. 48–9.

[4] *Keele '67: The National Evangelical Anglican Congress Statement*, ed. P. Crowe (London: Falcon Books, 1967), p. 8.

if evangelicals were really prepared to play a full part in the life of the Church of England they must turn their back on their old exclusiveness, 'We are all called as Christians and as Anglicans to be learning from one another.'[1]

The Congress went on to set out a good statement of evangelical doctrine but coupled with it was a confirmation of the ground rule for all ecumenical dialogue, namely, that so long as anyone confessed Jesus Christ as 'God and Saviour' there must be an acceptance of their Christian standing. It was of course well known to the organizers of the Keele Congress that Archbishop Ramsey was a liberal Anglo-Catholic. Henceforth that was to be no bar to fellowship and co-operation and the principle was to be that all engaged in ecumenism 'have a right to be treated as Christians'.[2] John Lawrence, who had long worked for such an outcome, rejoiced:'Now this wall is down Evangelicals will be heard in a new way, but this would not have happened if they had not shown that they are now ready to listen to others.'[3] And Lawrence had already reached an opinion on the main cause of this change of mind among evangelicals:

> In retrospect it looks as if the Conservative Evangelical movement in Britain crossed the ecumenical watershed at Dr Billy Graham's Crusade at Harringay in 1954.[4]

[1] For fuller documentation see my *David Martyn Lloyd-Jones: The Fight of Faith, 1939–1981* (Edinburgh: Banner of Truth, 1990), p. 539.

[2] *Keele '67*, p. 37

[3] *Ibid.*, p. 16. Another observer present, Canon D. M. Paton, asked: 'Have Evangelicals fully grasped that to play a real part in the corporate life of the Church of England involves taking very seriously (positively as well as negatively) the existence and views of those in the Church of England who are not Conservative Evangelicals?' The fact that comments by such observers as Lawrence and Paton were printed in *Keele '67* underlines how eager the evangelicals were to concede that, in words they quote from the *Church Times,* 'Their new image has been beaten into shape' (p. 12).

[4] Lawrence, *Hard Facts of Unity* (London: SCM, 1961), p. 68. D. M. Lloyd-Jones was of the same opinion (*Knowing the Times: Addresses Delivered on Various Occasions 1942–77,* Edinburgh: Banner of Truth, 1989, p. 310).

There was only one senior evangelical voice raised in Britain on the danger facing evangelicals. It was that of Martyn Lloyd-Jones, one-time medical doctor, who had been minister of Westminster Chapel in the centre of London since 1938.[1] The one occasion, regrettably, when his words drew widespread attention, was a public meeting convened by the Evangelical Alliance on the evening of 18 October 1966 as the opening of a two-day 'National Assembly of Evangelicals'. The date is significant, for it was only six months before the Anglican evangelicals assembled at the Keele Congress and plans for that congress had been in preparation since 1964. In other words, there is no way that the direction taken at Keele in April 1967 can be explained as a reaction to what Lloyd-Jones had said in the preceding autumn. The Lloyd-Jones address of 18 October 1966 has repeatedly been described as 'dividing evangelicals', but the division was already there. And when the chairman – John Stott – intervened to disagree with the speaker he was presumably aware that what he had been hearing ran counter to the thinking which Keele would seek to justify.

John Stott had long enjoyed a friendly association with Dr Lloyd-Jones, twenty-one years his senior, and was, like him, serving a leading church in central London and working to restore expository preaching. In 1945 Stott had gone straight from Cambridge to All Souls, Langham Place, where he became the rector in 1950. The two men frequently shared together in the work of Inter-Varsity and it was in that connection that the rector of All Souls quickly became known both as a missioner and as an author. The difference between them which became public at the 1966 Evangelical Alliance assembly was not, then, of a personal nature. Both preachers respected and esteemed one another.[2]

It is regrettable that the real nature of their disagreement became confused as others subsequently joined in the debate.

[1] Until 1943 as the colleague of Dr G. Campbell Morgan.
[2] See Timothy Dudley-Smith, *John Stott: The Making of a Leader* (Leicester: IVP, 1999), pp. 233–4, 260.

It was not that one of them was for holding to tradition while the other was proposing change. Both men could see that neither evangelicalism nor the denominations were standing still. Stott might have agreed with Lloyd-Jones' words at the Evangelical Alliance meeting when he said: 'The situation is indeed so novel that I am afraid that many of us as evangelicals do not yet quite realise it and are not aware of what is happening.'[1] What was at issue was how the situation was to be interpreted. Stott believed that a new opportunity was occurring both for the advance of evangelicalism (given its much higher national profile since 1954) *and* for a renewal of evangelical influence within the major denominations.

Lloyd-Jones believed that both of these objectives could not be achieved at the same time. He saw that for evangelicals to gain ecumenical and denominational acceptance they would have to pay a price which would imperil the very legitimacy of their distinctive beliefs. If evangelical belief is, in essence, *gospel* belief, how can Christian fellowship exist independently of any common commitment to such belief? How can a right belief on fundamentals retain the primary importance which Scripture gives to it if, after all, it is not necessary to salvation? How can evangelicalism be said to represent biblical essentials if one regards as Christians and works alongside those who actually deny these essentials? The effect of such broad co-operation, he argued, would be bound to promote the doctrinal indifferentism characteristic of the ecumenical movement.

This was the heart of the case which Dr Lloyd-Jones presented at the Evangelical Alliance meeting. As a consequence of that case he also said that for evangelicals to be consistent with their doctrine, they should give higher priority to the unity which that doctrine entailed than to denominational relationships which required no such allegiance to Scripture. An evangelical, he argued, is a person who believes truths essential to salvation and has experienced their power in his own rebirth. 'Here is the great divide. The

[1] Lloyd-Jones, 'Evangelical Unity: An Appeal', in *Knowing the Times*, p. 249.

ecumenical people put fellowship before doctrine. We are evangelicals; we put doctrine before fellowship (Acts 2:42).' He pointed out that the contemporary discussion across the denominations was not about preserving their independence but about the hope of reunion in an ultimately national, ecumenical church which (many hoped) would include the Roman Catholic Church. The question therefore was, Should evangelicals be prepared to think of themselves as a wing in such a church? To the argument that non-participation in ecumenism meant being content with a state of schism, he replied that schism is division among *Christians* and that the biblical definition of a Christian (the very thing ignored by the ecumenical movement) ought to be the starting point in their thinking:

> I argue that people who do not believe the essentials of the faith, the things that are essential to salvation, cannot be guilty of schism. They are not in the church. If you do not believe a certain irreducible minimum, you cannot be a Christian and you are not in the church. Have we reached a time when one must not say a thing like that? Have evangelicals so changed that we no longer make an assertion like that?[1]

To be true to the evangelical heritage, he concluded, the need of the hour was to honour the Word of God and to make biblical unity the first priority. Thus the thrust of his address was an appeal for unity. But it was *not* an appeal to accept any particular form of Protestant church government, still less to 'join him in a pure Reformed Church' – the view which he was misquoted as wanting. He knew as well as anyone that questions of denominational structures were not fundamental truths. His point was that if evangelical belief is what it claims to be then those who held it should make corporate action and unity with one another their first concern; they should 'stand together as churches, constantly together, working together'.

This message could not be congenial to those who believed that a broader policy of inclusivism towards non-

[1] *Ibid.*, p. 254.

evangelicals had brought on 'a remarkable period of renaissance within evangelicalism in England'.[1] For them this was no time to be redrawing lines between evangelicals and others. They saw it as far too negative. The Graham crusades had created an unbounded optimism and, in this new atmosphere, what could be wrong with asking Ramsey to open the Keele Congress? Given the patronage being shown to evangelicals, why was it necessary to continue the old days when Bible-believing men had only known isolation and disfavour? But Lloyd-Jones' Evangelical Alliance address cut right across this new policy and the outcome was that he was blamed for disrupting an evangelical unity which, it was said, would otherwise have continued as it had always done.

The charge widely laid at Lloyd-Jones' door following his address was that he was dividing evangelicals because he was making church issues a test of a man's evangelicalism and in so doing, it was said, he was introducing a new condition for evangelical unity and one bound to 'wreck' the interdenominational unity which evangelicals had hitherto enjoyed. Some no doubt sincerely misunderstood Dr Lloyd-Jones, but it can scarcely have been an accident that the Christian press which belonged in part or whole to the Graham organization represented his case as they did. *The Christian*, the London evangelical weekly owned by BGEA, led its front-page report of the Alliance meeting under the heading:

EVANGELICALS – LEAVE YOUR DENOMINATIONS,
Says Dr Martyn Lloyd-Jones.[2]

[1] A. McGrath, *To Know and Serve God: A Biography of James I. Packer* (London: Hodder & Stoughton, 1997), p. 99.
[2] *The Christian*, 21 October 1966. This paper, one of the foremost evangelical weeklies in Britain, was owned by BGEA from 1962 until its sudden closure in 1969. Its editor, the Rev. J. D. Douglas, clearly favoured Graham's broad-church policy. When a replacement for Carl Henry as editor of *Christianity Today* was being discussed by its board in 1968 the name of Edmund P. Clowney (President of Westminster Theological Seminary) was raised as a possibility but objected to on the grounds that he would not support an inclusivist policy: 'Westminster Seminary exists

He had said no such thing, and to summarize his address in such a fashion was inevitably to mislead those who had not heard him. A quarter of a century later the same thing was being repeated. Lloyd-Jones appealed, R. T. France believed, 'to evangelical members of the main-line denominations to secede and join a "pure" evangelical church'.[1]

The *Church of England Newspaper (CEN)*, in which the Graham organization had earlier come to purchase a controlling share, gave the same slant to the address and described it as 'nothing short of hare-brained'.[2] What Lloyd-Jones had said was to state a case which, if true, would justify some ministers in leaving their denominations – an action which he well knew was no light nor easy matter: 'There are great problems confronting us if we act on these principles.' But, instead of addressing his main case, unsympathetic reporters ignored it and represented him as calling for instant separation, as though he was an advocate of extreme 'come-out-ism'.[3]

It was not the address of Lloyd-Jones which fractured evangelicalism but the new policy which had already been adopted by those who so keenly disagreed with him. Neither that policy nor Dr Lloyd-Jones' response to it was ever discussed at the two-day Evangelical Alliance conference of 1966. The big issue, as he had kept saying, was not about church unity at all: 'We should be asking, "What is a Christian? How can we get forgiveness of sins?" and "What is a church?"'

But such questions went almost unheard in the public debate. It was the editor of another Anglican evangelical paper who addressed the real issue when he wrote: 'In certain respects Dr Martyn Lloyd-Jones and the Archbishop

___
on the premise that the United Presbyterian Church is apostate' (Henry, *Confessions*, p. 294).

[1] R. T. France and A. E. McGrath, *Evangelical Anglicans* (London: SPCK, 1993), p. 55.

[2] *CEN*, 28 October 1966. Speaking of his purchase of *CEN*, Graham has written, 'We didn't publicize our involvement at the time' (*Just As I Am*, p. 293).

[3] For the full, unedited text of the Lloyd-Jones address see *Knowing the Times*, pp. 246–57.

[Ramsey] are saying the same things. It is on the question of defining the word "Christian" that they differ, but what a difference this makes.'[1]

Before we close this chapter we must note a feature of particular relevance for the course of later events. Adrian Hastings, who has attempted perhaps the fullest church history for this period, goes too far when he writes: 'The modern Anglican Evangelical belongs internationally on the one hand to the Anglican communion, but on the other he belongs to a movement dominated by the immensely rich Billy Graham Evangelistic Association.'[2] Yet there is no doubt that from the mid-1950s the connection between the two became very close. The evangelist's main support at Harringay came from the evangelical Anglicans belonging to the Evangelical Alliance. At that time John Stott had acted as an 'informal pastor to the team' and a warm friendship had developed between him and Graham – the two being of similar age.[3] Hastings writes that Stott 'reconciled, better than almost anyone else, Establishmentarianism with crusading', and that he 'became the very hinge of this double belonging':[4]

> Within the world Evangelical movement of the second half of the century he [Stott] played to Billy Graham a role not altogether unlike that which J. H. Oldham had played fifty years before to John R. Mott. In each case the less flamboyant but more intellectual Englishman was endeavouring to guide the movement into new, less simplistic vistas.[5]

These words anticipate what we have yet to consider in more detail. In the next chapter we shall see Graham's evangelicalism widening very considerably. Hastings' view is that the thinking which, under Stott's leadership, prevailed at the Keele Congress brought on the change which would be

---

[1] *English Churchman*, 2 February 1968, following a sermon on unity preached by Ramsey in the Roman Catholic Westminster Cathedral.

[2] Adrian Hastings, *A History of English Christianity 1920–1985* (London: Collins, 1986), p. 456.

[3] Dudley-Smith, *John Stott*, p. 297.

[4] Hastings, *English Christianity*, pp. 456, 458.   [5] *Ibid.*, p. 617.

seen in Graham's Lausanne Congress of July 1974. Keele, he writes, 'made it possible for non-Evangelicals to be on the same wave-length as Evangelicals . . . What Keele did was to offer Evangelicals a viable way forward in line with Christendom as a whole'.[1] For proof that Stott led Lausanne in the same direction Hastings draws on the history given by Arthur P. Johnston. Johnston, an admirer of Billy Graham and a participant at Lausanne, conceded that while 'the basic theology of Lausanne was sound and clear', the congress 'opened the door to broad evangelical viewpoints'.[2] He believed that the Congress made concessions to those who did not want to affirm the verbal inspiration of Scripture, and to ecumenical theology in the statements on social action and on the need for 'church unity'.[3]

Hastings believes that Stott was leading Graham and evangelicalism away from the older convictions, and says: 'What is remarkable is how far Stott was able to go without losing the confidence of Graham.'[4] Johnston makes no such observation, although his misgivings are clear. Perhaps the next volume of the Stott biography will give more light on the way the Englishman's thinking contributed to further change in Graham. About one thing the two men were already certain in the 1960s: the future of evangelicalism was within 'the great denominations'.[5]

[1] *Ibid.,* p. 554.

[2] Arthur P. Johnston, *The Battle for World Evangelism* (Wheaton: Tyndale House, 1978), p. 300.   [3] *Ibid.,* p. 325–9.

[4] Hastings, *English Christianity,* p. 617.'For Johnston,' Hastings asserts, Stott 'was leading the movement back on to the slippery slope which was believed to have been so fatal half a century before in the days of the SCM' (p. 616).

[5] Pollock, *Billy Graham,* p. 47. The Lausanne Covenant's section on 'Cooperation in Evangelism' ignored the appeal made by Francis Schaeffer: 'We must practice the truth we say we say we maintain. We must practice this truth in the area of religious cooperation where it is costly . . . If we say that Christianity is truth, yet for any reason, including evangelism, we blur the line between liberal theology and biblical Christianity in the area of religious cooperation, we lose credibility.' *Let the Earth Hear His Voice: International Congress on World Evangelization,* ed. J. D. Douglas (Minneapolis: World Wide Publications, 1975), pp. 361–2.

3

High Aims,
Wrong Priorities

We have seen that the new evangelicalism, launched with such promise, had lost its way in the United States by the late 1960s. In this chapter I will argue that this happened because there was an element of pragmatism inherent in the movement, an element which was to override biblical principles with disastrous consequences.

American fundamentalism had combined historic Christian beliefs with some ideas and practices which were new to the Christian churches. One of the foremost of its innovations concerned evangelism. In the nineteenth century it came to be believed that the most successful soul-winning belonged to the 'revival' meeting where many are seen to come to Christ as the evangelist calls them to a visible, public decision. Walking the aisle in response to the 'altar call' was so closely identified with conversion that coming to Christ and coming to the front were treated as one and the same thing. Behind the practice lay the fallacy that saving faith is of the same nature as a physical decision, and that if only sinners will answer the evangelist's invitation then grace will secure their rebirth.

This thinking was inherited by Billy Graham and it is clearly expressed in the way he has spoken of conversion: 'We do not know Christ through the five physical senses, but we know Him through the sixth sense that God has given to every man – which is the ability to believe.'[1] 'Don't let distance keep you from Christ. Christ went to the Cross because he loved you. Certainly you can come these few steps. Come right now.'[2] Or again: 'I'm very much opposed to general invitations that call people forward for anything in order to get a move. We try to make our invitations straightforward so that a person knows he is coming for conversion and salvation.'[3]

While it departed in various respects from fundamentalism, the Billy Graham Evangelistic Association (BGEA) retained this basic practice. There was some change of vocabulary: 'revival meetings' became 'crusades', and the one-time 'personal workers' were now called counsellors, but the idea that conversions are best secured by the requirement of a public decision remained as it had been since the time of Finney. It was defended, as it had been before, on the grounds that it

[1] Graham, *Peace with God* (Kingswood, Surrey: World's Work, 1954), p. 134. I do not, of course, mean that no human decision occurs in conversion but it is *grace,* not our act, which is the determining cause (*John* 1:13; *Eph.* 2:8) and a *moral* change of nature is needed before the will is free to exercise the repentance and faith which God commands (*Acts* 16:14; *Rom.* 8:7; *1 Cor.* 2:14, etc.). Hence the danger of representing what is needed to become a Christian in terms of a *physical* action which is within the ability of all at any time. I have dealt with the historical and theological origins of 'the altar call' in *Revival & Revivalism: The Making and Marring of American Evangelicalism* (Edinburgh: Banner of Truth, 1994).

[2] Quoted in Curtis Mitchell, *God in the Garden: The Official Story of the Billy Graham New York Crusade* (Kingswood, Surrey: World's Work, 1957), pp. 148–9.

[3] Quoted in C. Catherwood, *Five Evangelical Leaders* (London: Hodder and Stoughton, 1984), p. 211.

was only a matter of method and that, after all, the New Testament itself requires an 'open confession' of Christ. But Scripture nowhere teaches that it is *by* a 'confession' that anyone *becomes* a Christian.

The dangers in the invitation system are many. It creates the impression that compliance with it is part of becoming a Christian. Speaking of the Greater London Crusade of 1954, John Pollock can slip into writing: 'As the weeks wore on, Billy Graham put less and less force into his closing invitation; there was no need to press when so many were waiting to accept Christ *as soon as he stopped preaching*.'[1] Further, what are individuals to think who obey the instruction to come to the front and who experience no spiritual change?[2] In fact the BGEA is well aware that many respond to the 'public invitation' who in reality never become Christians. 'I've always thought that in any group that comes forward,' Graham says, 'a fourth of them will be there in five years from now.'[3] He also knows that others, hearing the gospel, come to repentance and faith without ever going to the front in an evangelistic meeting.

Why then retain the practice? It would appear that the fundamental reason is practical and pragmatic. When numbers can be *seen to respond* to the invitation there is a visual demonstration of the effect of the message. The evangelism is validated as the work of God. In Graham's words:

> When the average American, moral, respectable . . . sees thousands of respectable, normal people listening to all he

---

[1] Pollock, *Graham,* p. 170, my italics.

[2] Even those who gave the invitation could become confused about what it meant, as happened with Charles Templeton, the vice-president of Youth for Christ who first hired Graham as an evangelist and later lost his faith altogether. 'Billy', he recalled, 'would invariably have more people come forward than anyone else would . . . we were all getting along by personal magnetism, just on speaking abilities.' Frady, *Billy Graham,* pp. 163, 179. On this whole subject see D. M. Lloyd-Jones, 'Conversions: Psychological and Spiritual', in *Knowing the Times,* pp. 86–9.

[3] David Frost, *Billy Graham in Conversation* (Oxford: Lion, 1998), p. 65.

hears and then sees hundreds voluntarily get up and walk to the front in response ... he'll begin to consider the message.'[1]

The numbers seen making their decisions, and quickly publicized, are thus important for the projection of success. Pollock, however, as Graham's authorized biographer, gave a different explanation of why the number of those making a decision was announced. He wrote that 'Graham personally dislikes statistics ... They are kept only for the sake of accuracy and to prevent exaggeration by pressmen who do not appreciate that the crowd they see come forward is partly formed of counsellors.'[2] Leaving aside the question why counsellors need to be so organized that they also come forward, one is astonished that Pollock can offer this as *the main* reason why decision figures were announced at each crusade. Pollock himself, in repeating decision statistics so long after the newsmen of the day had lost interest in them, is showing that they had another purpose. He tells us of more than thirty-eight thousand who came forward in the Greater London crusade of 1954; of sixteen thousand decision cards at Berlin; of 56,780 and 28,105 in Sydney and Melbourne respectively; and of one night alone in Los Angeles when 3,216 people came forward. According to Pollock, 'Just short of one million (by the end of 1965) have "come forward".'[3]

The publicity value of such figures is clearly of importance to Pollock as it is to the Graham organization. Prior to Harringay, 1954, Graham directed, 'No amount of money should be spared to awaken and stimulate the consciences of London's eight millions.'[4] Jerry Beavan, his public relations director, was ready to see this done. 'In our crusades and work,' he would say, 'we need every instrument of modern mass communications. We've got the greatest product in the world to sell – salvation for men's souls through Christ. Why shouldn't we sell it as effectively as we promote a bar of soap?'[5]

[1] Frady, *Billy Graham*, p. 287.
[2] *Ibid*, p. 327.
[3] Pollock, *Graham*, pp. 178–9, 184, 255, 272, 324, 327.
[4] *Ibid.*, p. 152.
[5] Quoted in Frady, *Billy Graham*, pp. 285–6.

This is not the place to discuss the place of publicity in Christian work, or whether Reinhold Niebuhr was fair to speak of Graham's 'Madison Avenue' methods of promoting crusades,[1] but it is certainly arguable that some of the advantage of the publicity was only of short-term duration. We saw, for instance, the great impression which the numbers attending the Greater London Crusade made upon British church leaders. The sheer numbers of those making 'a decision for Christ' had a near-irresistible appeal for men concerned to see a rise in church membership. We quoted earlier the opinion of William Martin that this new support for Graham from non-evangelical clergy and ministers was not, however, due to a change of mind on their part; it was rather that they wished to channel some of the streams of people 'into their own churches'.

Lest this should seem to be a cynical judgment it needs to be noted that a number of these unexpected Graham supporters made no secret of the reason for their out-of-character alignment. Leslie Weatherhead, for instance, pronounced liberal that he was, had a ready justification for his participation in the crusades: 'What', he asked, 'does fundamentalist theology matter compared with gathering in the people we have all missed and getting them to the point of decision? Theology comes much later.'[2] Archbishop Ramsey told his clergy the same thing. He advised them to receive those referred to their churches by Graham's London crusade of 1966, 'whatever one thinks of the theology'.[3] Along the same lines an official of the World Council of Churches is alleged to have said: 'We do not agree with Billy Graham's theology, but we are using him to build our churches.'[4]

[1] Richard Fox, *Reinhold Niebuhr* (Waco, Texas: Word Books, 1977), p. 266. Quoted by Sims, *Missionaries to the Skeptics*, p. 188.

[2] *Moody Monthly*, October 1954, quoted by Martin, *Prophet With Honor*, p. 181.

[3] *Canterbury Diocesan Notes*, April, 1966, p. 2.

[4] Martin, *Prophet With Honor*, p. 656. Lloyd-Jones understood this ploy back in May 1954. See my *The Fight of Faith*, p. 340.

The apparent enthusiasm of non-evangelicals for evangelism was however to fall away when time revealed that the numerical success was far less than they had first believed. An analysis of 'decision' figures has repeatedly revealed that the majority who endure in their commitment are already either church members or attenders and that many who come forward, having no such connection, are never heard of again. The *British Weekly,* which had supported Graham's 1954 London crusade, eventually concluded that 'the main impact was among already sympathetic church members. The effect outside the Church, speaking generally, appears to have been very little indeed in terms of figures.' Archbishop Fisher, whose benediction at the close of the Greater London Crusade of 1954 was so widely reported, three years later 'reluctantly concluded "there is very little to show" for the Harringay crusade'.[1]

If Fisher meant that there were few real conversions I do not agree with him, but it would be hard to dispute that the number was far less than the thirty-eight thousand decisions announced at the time. In this regard the initial publicity was ultimately injurious in the critical reaction which it produced.

Nor should it be thought that such critical later assessments came only from non-evangelicals. In 1968 the Evangelical Alliance, BGEA's first sponsor in Britain, published a report on evangelism that included a survey of eighty-five churches which had participated in Graham's shorter London crusades of 1966-67. Its authors (a large committee) concluded:

[1] *Ibid.,* pp. 184-5. For similar comment on US decision figures, see Frady, *Billy Graham,* p. 220, 309–310. Seven months after the Harringay Crusade the London *Evening Standard* took a poll of London's twenty largest Anglican parishes and found that two thirds of the 336 inquirers referred to them were already members or regular attenders of these churches, while 'of the remaining 110 people, only thirty-five were still attending church'. Pollock, *Billy Graham,* pp. 327-32, argues that the converts did last. That is not in dispute; the issue is how many of the decisions announced were real conversions.

On mass evangelism generally, the recurring theme was that the crusade did not make a lasting effect on the complete outsider. Even when they went, they either made no response, or made no lasting response ... Church members, whether they went forward or not, found blessing and encouragement from the services, but the complete outsider tended to go back outside again. In the words of one comment, 'If they asked, "What shall we do?" they seem to have been given little answer beyond "to decide for Christ" ... On inquiry they were unable to give any real answer as to what this meant, other than they desired to live a better life.'[1]

While believing that 'many have come to faith in Christ' through crusades, the authors of this report considered that they accounted for 'only a small proportion of all conversions taking place', and they reported 'a declining confidence among churches and ministers in this method'. It was even suggested that the invitation system would be better dropped.[2]

Unaccustomed to any criticism from such a quarter, Maurice Rowlandson, Director of the London office of the the BGEA, complained that the report of the Evangelical Alliance 'put back the clock on evangelism for at least the next ten years' in Britain.[3] Graham was not to return to the UK until 1984 when his meetings would be called 'missions'. 'The last crusade meetings in Britain', comments Rowlandson, 'were held in 1967.'[4]

[1] *On the Other Side*, the report of the Evangelical Alliance's Commission on Evangelism (London: Scripture Union, 1968), p. 143.

[2] *Ibid.*, pp. 167–9. In his second volume of Graham biography, Pollock was overlooking these opinions when he seemed surprised that Graham's Lausanne Congress of 1974 was 'opposed' by 'Britons of judgment and integrity'. He noted that 'more than half' of the invitations sent to Britishers were refused, *Billy Graham, Evangelist to the World: An Authorised Biography of the Decisive Years* (Sydney: Harper, Row, 1979), p. 211.

[3] Maurice Rowlandson, *Life With Billy, An Autobiography* (London: Hodder & Stoughton, 1992), p. 95.

[4] *Ibid.*, p. 115. Rowlandson says that he 'found the critique on mass evangelism very hard both to understand and to accept'. He offers no response to the main points of concern. The BGEA London office closed in 1987 (*ibid.*, p. 156).

My present point, however, has to do with the changed perception of liberals in relation to the events of 1954–55. In the immediate wake of those events Weatherhead could tell the Methodist Conference: 'Graham is helping to fill our churches. We can teach people theology when we have got someone to teach.'[1] Such words were not to be heard ten years later. The optimism over filling churches had been illusory. No one now thought as Bishop Hugh Gough had done in 1955 when he said, 'Quite clearly we are witnessing the beginning of another Evangelical Revival.'[2]

* * * *

The reason why the BGEA decided to co-operate with liberals and other non-evangelicals was never set out in terms of principle. The fact is that the policy was seen as a necessary expedient designed sincerely for the best end, namely, to gain a wider hearing for the gospel. Crusades depended upon crowds and in the Graham story there is an almost ever-present concern for maintaining and increasing numbers. 'Keeping a customary eye for maximum public impact' and 'trying always for the largest possible crowds' was

[1] Kingsley Weatherhead, *Leslie Weatherhead: A Personal Portrait* (London: Hodder and Stoughton, 1975), p. 199. What Weatherhead's theology was is very clear in this biography by his son. For example: 'Of a text in Hebrews, "Without shedding of blood is no remission of sin," Les has said, "In our modern view this is simply not true." ' (p. 61). What he surmised on the virgin birth is unprintable.

[2] Pollock, *Graham*, p. 201. In *Billy Graham: Evangelist to the World*, Pollock explains the lack of subsequent advance by saying: 'Too many churches, however, held back, debating the pros and cons of this evangelism instead of recognizing their opportunity. Had they grasped it, the sixties might have been different for Britain nationally' (p. 315). In fact the problem with the churches was far deeper. Too many had lost or denied the evangel.

a settled part of the Billy Graham Association's strategy.[1] In Frady's opinion, 'Graham and the press co-acted out of much the same appreciations and excitements, the same sensibilities. He lived in their world: the journalistic reality of polls, trends, public personages, public commotions.'[2]

This is surely part of the explanation for an eagerness to cultivate connections with the famous whose names would catch attention. Friendship was sought with all whose high profile could reflect with advantage on the message he preached. The furtherance of the gospel was undoubtedly the aim, and in his big-heartedness he was too often ready to assume that individuals favourable to him must have sympathy for his work. But in many cases such friendships were not built on a common commitment to Christ and the Bible and therein lay their danger.

A Graham crusade in Rio de Janeiro, Brazil, in 1974, coincided with a visit of Michael Ramsey to that country. Learning of this fact, the BGEA hurriedly invited the archbishop to speak briefly at the opening meeting. As Ramsey's good relations with the Pope were known, it can only be assumed that his platform presence was meant to impress a country still largely Roman Catholic. 'Ramsey', writes his biographer, 'did not believe in crusades', but he accepted the invitation and Graham wrote to say he was 'overwhelmed

---

[1] The words quoted are those of Martin, *Prophet With Honor*, pp. 251, 458. T. W. Wilson, one of Graham's closest aides, recalled how 'he was a super salesman' (*Ibid*. p. 289). 'When he was asked, as he always was, why he found it necessary to advertise himself and his campaigns so extensively, he said, as if the matter were out of his hands, "I've wondered about that many times. I don't have the answer" '(*Ibid*., p. 321). There is an ambivalence in Graham on this subject. He can also say: 'Everytime I'm praised and patted on the back, it makes me cold at heart. It fills me with horror. Because God said he will share his glory with no man.' 'There are times now when I feel like I'm being devoured. By the adulation as well as the hostility.' Frady, *Billy Graham*, pp. 228, 493.

[2] Frady, *Billy Graham*, p. 223.

with gratitude . . . we come from such diverse religious backgrounds and yet . . . this glorious unity.'[1]

But an unexpected difficulty arose immediately before the meeting when Ramsey had to meet the man who was to be his interpreter. He proved to be an old Presbyterian pastor and, when he heard from the archbishop the gist of what he was to interpret, he objected. 'The interpreter', records Ramsey's biographer, 'said he could not translate all that on grounds of conscience. They took the problem to Billy Graham who said the archbishop was his guest and that the translator would interpret every word.' The same writer reports how surprised many Protestants in the crowd were to hear a man, looking like a cardinal and known for his prominence in the ecumenical movement, speak before Billy Graham. They heard Ramsey say:

> You cannot come to Christ unless you bring your Roman Catholic brother with you . . . If you are asked to come forward to testify to Christ, don't come unless you bring with you a resolve to be more charitable to your Roman Catholic brothers. Don't come unless you resolve from now on to be doing something about poverty.[2]

In the 1960s Malcolm Muggeridge, a celebrity journalist and one-time womanizer, had suddenly become a notable religious spokesman against moral decadence. When Muggeridge was invited (at the suggestion of Ruth Graham[3]) to be a main speaker at the Billy Graham Lausanne Congress in 1974 Graham records that another speaker objected when he saw his name on the programme: 'One speaker threatened

---

[1] Owen Chadwick, *Michael Ramsey: A Life* (Oxford/New York: OUP, 1991), p. 335.

[2] Ramsey's biographer says that he 'was astonished to find himself speaking from one of Billy Graham's platforms' (*Ibid.*, pp. 235–6). He also says that the interpreter interfered with Ramsey's message, for instance: 'When he talked of the need for Christian unity, the interpreter explained that he did not wish all Protestants to submit to the Pope.'

[3] Pollock, *Billy Graham: Evangelist to the World,* p. 211.

to pull out', because Muggeridge, 'a fairly recent convert to the Christian faith, was not as versed on theological distinctions as this speaker felt that he should be.' The outcome, in Graham's view, proved the rightness of their staying with their choice, for Muggeridge 'received the only standing ovation of the Congress'.[1] But the real question here is not alluded to at all. It was not whether the ex-journalist understood theological details, it was whether he was an evangelical who understood the meaning of conversion. Time was to show that the objector was right. Conversion for Muggeridge meant a turn from the 'flesh' to the 'spirit', and thus, writes his biographer, 'it was no surprise to anyone who had followed Malcolm's career' when, at the age of seventy-nine, he and his wife were received into the Church of Rome on 27 November 1982. Mother Teresa wrote to him of her thankfulness 'to God and his Blessed Mother for giving you the joy of his coming into your hearts on 27th November'.[2]

Similar to this is Graham's willingness to appear alongside Sir David Frost on television and in print.[3] Unlike Muggeridge, Frost has professed no conversion. In his latest public discussion with the evangelist, subsequently published, he said nothing of the decision he made at Harringay in 1954. Frost does not speak as a Christian and remains unsure of what happened to him and others who go to the front: 'Is the explanation mass hysteria and hypnotic techniques, or is the explanation that he is a messenger from someone who speaks through him?'[4] Whatever the explanation, Frost avers that

[1] *Just As I Am*, p. 570.

[2] Richard Ingrams, *Muggeridge: The Biography* (London: Harper Collins, 1995), pp. 234–6. In old age, Ingrams comments, 'their new-found faith seemed to offer little comfort' (p. 243). 'Having read his last book, which is called *Jesus Rediscovered*, I would not hesitate to say that Malcolm Muggeridge is not a Christian at all.' Lloyd-Jones, *Knowing the Times*, p. 311.

[3] Frost, *Billy Graham in Conversation*.

[4] Words quoted in the *Church of England Newspaper* review of the Frost title, 17 April 1998.

Graham is one of his heroes, along with Robert Kennedy and Nelson Mandela.

This cultivation of connections with celebrities came to its fullest expression with political leaders in the United States. Irrespective of his beliefs, Graham's command of numbers and influence appealed to them. 'Aside from the intrinsic value of his message,' wrote Curtis Mitchell, 'he represents a cultural, even a national asset.'[1] For his part, Graham would praise any religious leanings in presidents in the hope of adding to the status of the gospel in national life. Thus he pronounced Eisenhower to be 'a spiritual leader'.[2] President Lyndon Johnson was qualified, Graham declared, to 'provide moral leadership for the country. The President is a very religious person.'[3] The facts of Johnson's life, with its 'bawdier Rabelaisian gustos', proved the opposite. 'I almost used the White House as a hotel when Johnson was President', Graham was to say, apparently unconscious of nothing worse than the fact that his host 'might have said "hell" or "damn" a couple of times' in his presence.[4]

In the presidency of Richard Nixon, begun in 1968, the evangelist gave cautious support to the war in Vietnam and full support to the man under whose presidency the disastrous war continued. 'Tricky Dick', as opponents called the president, was, in Graham's eyes, 'a devout person'. 'There is no American I admire more.' 'You have given moral and spiritual leadership to the nation', he wrote to Nixon.[5] Part

---

[1] Mitchell, *Billy Graham: Saint or Sinner?* (Old Tappan, NJ: Fleming Revell, 1979), pp. 24–5. Thus, as Frady argues, Graham might be conscripted by the great 'to serve what they themselves may have considered the national interests, but ends somewhat apart from his own gospel purposes', *Billy Graham*, p. 242.

[2] Frady, *Billy Graham*, p. 257.

[3] *Ibid.*, p. 259.

[4] *Ibid.*, p. 260.

[5] *Ibid.*, pp. 352, 354, 371. Charles Colson, who had a better understanding of the reality of Nixon's spiritual position, noted that he did not believe in the resurrection of Christ and 'wished he could be a Catholic because they had a set of beliefs' (*Ibid.*, p. 359).

of Nixon's response was to affirm his admirer to be 'the top preacher in the world'.[1] Carl Henry, no hostile critic, observed, 'Billy Graham had amiable ties with the Nixon White House and during one crusade in Tennessee he and Nixon traded tributes.'[2]

But with the Watergate scandal of 1973–4, and its revelation of the corruption which Nixon had supported to help gain his re-election as president, it was found that the president's opponents were not so wrong after all. Graham, who in 1972 was insisting Nixon 'would never, *never,* try to use me', was compelled to admit that the Watergate tapes 'revealed a man I never knew.'[3] When he discovered how far he had been misled by Nixon he said, 'I felt like a sheep led to the slaughter.'[4] Similarly, in later years, answering criticism of his earlier views on the Vietnam war, Graham was to say, 'I would listen to General Westmoreland, Abrams, Zumwalt – I was like a babe in the woods, I didn't know what was really going on.'[5]

Nor did Graham know what was going on in the sad life of the last president with whom his autobiography draws to a close. He writes of an afternoon with Bill Clinton at the White House: 'It was a time of warm fellowship with a man who has not always won the approval of his fellow Christians but who has in his heart a desire to serve God and do His will.'[6]

Curtis Mitchell plays down Graham's association with the

---

[1] Part of Nixon's speech at a Billy Graham day at Charlotte, October 1971 (*Ibid.,* p. 460). The mutual praise is paralleled by earlier words of President Johnson: 'I told him he was the greatest religious leader in the world and he said I was the greatest political leader' (Martin, *Prophet With Honor,* pp. 320–1).

[2] Henry, *Confessions,* p. 386.

[3] Martin, *Prophet With Honor,* p. 431.

[4] *Ibid.,* p. 399 n. Said to Martin in 1991 when the manuscript of *Prophet With Honor* was sent to Graham to permit him to check for factual errors.

[5] Frady, *Billy Graham,* p. 432.

[6] *Just As I Am,* p. 656.

'high and mighty', and comments: 'Billy spends very little time golfing with presidents or with movie stars, but if he does, it makes news.'[1] But this defence is undermined by Graham himself in his autobiography. The proportion of space which he gives to relations with the famous (including eight chapters on presidents) gives some weight to Frady's critical words:

> Graham's vulnerability was that, while he contended that he looked on all his associations now in government and commerce as mere openings for a fuller propagation of his ministry, at the same time he also was given to a compulsive entrancement with all those larger affairs and offices of the world. He seemed helplessly infatuated by the various appointments of earthly importance.[2]

* * * *

'Softness and hardness', Martin Luther once wrote, 'are the two main faults from which all the mistakes of pastors come.'[3] Graham was right in his concern to avoid 'hardness'. He was right, too, to believe, as he said in the 1950s, that there are 'godly men who hold to the essentials of the Christian faith but who for various reasons do not want to be identified with modern-day evangelicalism, its organisations and institutions'.[4] But in repudiating one danger he fell into the other. It was a serious mistake to think that the many non-evangelicals who showed him friendship must be real Christians and that they therefore agreed with him on essentials. The consequence of that assumption was that he saw no need to endanger the friendship of such men by opposition to matters on which they might differ.

Graham was right, also, in his concern to love all men, but to 'present an ecumenical spirit of love toward those of all stripes' is not necessarily the same thing. 'Beware of men'

[1] *Billy Graham,* p. 301.

[2] Frady, *Billy Graham,* pp. 243–4.

[3] 'Lectures on Romans', *Luther's Works,* vol. 25 (St Louis: Concordia, 1972), p. 139.

[4] Martin, *Prophet With Honor,* p. 240.

(*Matt.* 10:17) is also a Christian duty. The generosity of spirit which was Graham's strength was also his weakness. 'Billy won't believe anything bad about a person,' says his associate, Robert Ferm.[1] An old friend of Graham's expressed the opinion, 'He's a popular and pleasant fellow who doesn't like to offend his hosts, whether in Washington or Moscow.'[2] President Nixon's aide, H. R. Haldeman, who saw something of Graham and the VIP treatment he was given at the White House, spoke of him as possessing 'a talent for seeing the best of everything that is happening – not choosing to see the bad'.[3]

The danger of this feature in Graham's temperament was compounded by his apparent innocence and ignorance with regard to the destructive theological views of the religious leaders whose recognition and approval he often sought. Orthodox ministers who knew him were alarmed at his naivety in this respect.[4]

Instances of this naivety are far more numerous than the examples already given above. When he spoke at Cambridge University in 1955 the following exchange took place, as William Martin recorded:

> At one address a divinity professor who introduced him pointedly noted that he 'could not agree with his doctrinal views'. Graham countered this chill-inducing remark with a smile and observed that he did not pay great attention to theological differences. 'We are all Christians,' he said, 'and we love one another.'[5]

---

[1] *Ibid.*, p. 568.   [2] *Ibid.*, p. 518.

[3] *Ibid.*, p. 394. Martin writes of 'Graham's remarkable ability to overlook or trivialize the unpleasant, particularly when it involved powerful friends whose favour he curried' (p. 387).

[4] Carnell, for instance, in a letter to Ockenga in 1957, wrote: 'After Billy Graham has reviewed the plan of salvation, he has very little to add. Billy Graham has not been to a seminary. He has no criteria by which to measure the shades of better or worse in the complex systems that vie for the modern mind. And his weakness pretty well sums up the weakness of orthodoxy itself.' Quoted by Nelson, *Making and Unmaking of an Evangelical Mind*, pp. 217–8.

[5] Martin, *Prophet With Honor*, p. 190.

Had he known what was actually being taught by such divinity professors he could hardly have spoken with such confidence. John Pollock records that before Graham, during the All-Scotland Crusade of 1955, was televised preaching on Good Friday

> he invited the foremost theologian in Scotland, Dr James S. Stewart, Professor of New Testament Language, Literature and Theology in the University of Edinburgh, and a future Moderator, to spend much of Sunday with him. 'Most of our talk and discussion was of a theological nature,' writes Dr Stewart, 'especially relating to the doctrine of the Atonement.' Dr Stewart did not realise at the time that Graham was working over with him the theme of the TV sermon, determined that nothing should be theologically unsound.[1]

Yet the fact was that Stewart, great preacher though he undoubtedly was, held neither the orthodox doctrine of Scripture nor that of penal, substitutionary atonement. In 1928 it had been Stewart who had given new currency to Schleiermacher by co-editing the English publication of his doctrinal work, *The Christian Faith*.

Subsequent history was to show that a lack of apprehension of danger, a determination only to be charitable, and an increasing commitment to ecumenism, were to corrode the convictions which had initially been part of Graham's leadership in the new evangelicalism. The drift was already present by the time of Carnell's death in 1967.[2] When the German

---

[1] Pollock, *Graham*, p. 196.

[2] Other deaths were no doubt still more significant in the removal of restraints. J. Marcellus Kik had died in 1965. He had ceased to be on the staff of *Christianity Today* in 1959 and thereafter exercised an important influence behind the scenes as the full-time theological adviser to Howard Pew. His differences with the prevailing policy of the BGEA can be understood from his book *Ecumenism and the Evangelical* (Philadelphia: Presbyterian and Reformed, 1958) where he writes: 'Minimizing theology will produce a weak and spineless religion that has little resemblance to the strong and valiant Christianity that conquered pagan Rome and heathen nations . . . How can the church tolerate differences of belief

Lutheran bishop Kurt Scharf hesitated over an invitation to bring greetings at the opening of the Berlin Congress of 1966 on the grounds that he supposed it would be 'anti-ecumenical', his mistake, writes Graham, was easily 'cleared up'.[1]

An acceleration was to follow. William Martin (by no means a 'fundamentalist') has noted Graham's 'diminishing dogmatism' and 'ever widening acceptance of others who professed to be Christians'. In the late 1950s the duty of Dr Robert O. Ferm, one of the BGEA staff workers, included writing a defence of broader co-operation in his book *Co-Operative Evangelism*. With various arguments Dr Ferm repudiated any compromise on Graham's part. He insisted, for instance, that there was 'a firm baseline' and that Roman Catholic participation in their work was excluded. Referring to crusade services, he replied to the inquiry of a Kansas minister, 'Certainly Catholic priests do not attend . . . [They] have not been invited to participate in any way. Nor would they do so if they were invited.'[2]

This was all to change. When Graham had the ear of Richard Nixon, during Nixon's years as president, he

---

concerning that which the New Testament has declared vital for salvation?' (pp. 14–15). Mr Pew, who died in 1971, remained the chief financial backer of *Christianity Today*. He 'wanted more aggressive denunciation of ecumenical perspectives', and believed that Carl Henry, the editor, 'should criticize Church involvement "more fully and more often"'; but Henry warned, 'On that basis we would soon forfeit dialogue with the ecumenical leaders and churches.' Henry was to retire from the journal in 1968 as a result of Pew's pressure. Henry, *Confessions*, pp. 290, 293. Nelson Bell died in 1973, the year when his hopes of renewal in the PCUS failed with the major secession from his denomination which became the PCA. Bell can hardly have anticipated that the new evangelicalism would embrace Roman Catholicism. 'Rome', he believed, 'never changes', 'it threatens basic freedoms and those constitutional rights for which our forefathers died.' Martin, *Prophet With Honor*, p. 275.

[1] *Just As I Am*, p. 562.

[2] Martin, *Prophet With Honor*, p. 295. But Ferm was not facing facts, as the Graham quotation concerning the directing of converts in the 1957 New York Crusade, given above, shows.

could recommend the Roman Catholic Archbishop H. E. Cardinale to speak at a White House service. To offset criticism which Nixon was receiving in 1970 for appointing an unofficial emissary to the Vatican, Graham advised the president that a prominent Southern Baptist lay preacher be invited to another of these services. Graham himself shared a White House service with Rabbi Edgar Magnin and John Cardinal Krol.[1] In his autobiography he refers to such meetings in terms of his 'ecumenical strategy'.[2]

What Ferm had formerly called his 'emphatically Protestant theology' was clearly no longer operative in 1977 when he shared with Graham in a crusade on the campus of Notre Dame, the premier Catholic university in the United States. The same year Graham meetings were televised to a Catholic church in Asheville.[3]

This change with regard to Roman Catholicism had been preceded by the existence of cordial personal relations with Catholic leaders. Well before he went to Notre Dame, Graham tells us, he 'enjoyed good rapport with Cardinal Richard J. Cushing'. He had also become 'good friends' with Bishop Fulton Sheen, 'with whom I felt a special affinity'.[4] Quotations from Sheen were specially introduced into Graham's Notre Dame crusade sermons. Years earlier he had said, 'I have no quarrel with the Catholic Church',[5] and now it was plain for all to see. Speaking of the difference between evangelicalism and Roman Catholicism he could further say, 'I don't think the differences are important as far as personal salvation is concerned.'[6] Graham could now say:

[1] Martin gives details of these White House religious services (*Ibid.*, pp. 356–60).

[2] *Just As I Am*, p. 450. [3] *Ibid.*, p. 460. [4] *Ibid.*, pp. 390, 692–3.

[5] Quoted by Martin, *Prophet With Honor*, p. 223.

[6] *Ibid.*, p. 461. When an evangelist expressed the belief that Catholics were not Christians, T. W. Wilson, Graham's 'chief lieutenant', as Martin calls him, declared him 'absolutely wrong . . . to say they are not Christians – man alive! Anybody that receives Jesus Christ as their Lord and Saviour is converted! They're born again. I believe the Pope is a converted man. I believe a lot of these wonderful Catholics are Christians' (*Ibid.*, p. 461).

I feel I belong to all the churches. I am equally at home in an Anglican or Baptist or a Brethren assembly or a Roman Catholic church . . . Today we have almost 100 per cent Catholic support in this country. That was not true twenty years ago. And the bishops and archbishops and the Pope are our friends.[1]

In 1987 Graham agreed to share a service in Columbia, South Carolina, with Pope John Paul II.[2] He was already on record as affirming, 'He's a wonderful pope.'[3] Yet Curtis Mitchell rejected the idea that Billy Graham has 'gone Catholic' with this reply:

I would say that the Catholics have 'gone Billy Graham' . . . The charge against Billy Graham comes from some of the more extreme fundamentalist groups, who object to the fact that Billy has permitted priests to be included among crusade counseling staffs and has permitted those who come forward to designate a Catholic church if that is their choice.[4]

From all this it is clear that, while Graham has professed no change in his doctrinal beliefs, he had come to accept the primary idea of ecumenism that there is a shared experience of salvation in Christ which makes all differences of belief a very secondary matter. Whereas the co-operation had first begun out of a desire to gain an entrance for the gospel in other religious circles, it was now discovered that the saving gospel had been with the non-evangelicals all the time. A defence from any suggestion of compromise was no longer needed; the intrinsic rightness of co-operation with non-evangelicals was now regarded as obvious: 'The ecumenical movement has broadened my viewpoint.'[5]

---

[1] Frost, *Billy Graham in Conversation,* pp. 68, 143. The first of these quotations was part of an answer to the question, 'Are you in favour of the ordination of women?' After the words 'equally at home', Graham continued with reference to that question, 'I would identify with the customs and the culture and the theology of that particular church.'

[2] *Just As I Am,* p. 599. He regretted that an unexpected invitation to China made his participation in the service impossible.

[3] Martin, *Prophet With Honor,* p. 577.

[4] Mitchell, *Billy Graham: Saint or Sinner,* p. 272. [5] *Ibid.,* p. 220

The tragedy of this is that, while the vision of the 1950s had been to see a restoration of evangelical convictions in the main denominations, all these convictions save one had been whittled down. 'We discovered', Graham writes, 'that the only word that would bring some of them together was *evangelism*.'[1] He elaborated on this point at his Amsterdam 'school for evangelists' held in 1986. When asked by a correspondent of *Foundation* magazine how he justified the theological diversity of the participants, he replied: 'Evangelism is about the only word we can unite on . . . Our methods would be different and there would be debates over even the message sometimes, but there is no debate over the fact that we need to evangelize . . . I think there is an ecumenicity here that cannot [be gotten] under any other umbrella.'

So an undefined 'evangelism' remained the great priority. In this connection Carl Henry has written of his regret that a unity was not built among evangelicals, but he saw that it was impossible for Graham to work for evangelical unity while acting as though ecumenical unity was of more importance:

> In the early 1970s Graham was still the one charismatic personality who might have rallied evangelicals for a long, hard look at their need of more comprehensive unity and at the neglected issue of evangelical ecclesiology. But interest on Graham's part in a new and larger non-NCC movement would have seriously complicated relationships of his crusades to ecumenically oriented churches, since he exacted their endorsement as the price of city-wide meetings.[2]

Preaching which had begun with 'The Bible says' had given way to a policy in which almost everything seemed to be subservient to the desire for numerical success in evangelism. Back in the New York crusade of 1957, Niebuhr

[1] *Just As I Am*, p. 560.

[2] Henry, *Confessions*, p. 384. 'Non-NCC' refers to evangelical churches not aligned with the ecumenical National Council of Churches.

thought there was a 'frantic pursuit of religious success'. In later years it would be hard to dispute the observation of one commentator who wrote:

It is a peculiar brand of American evangelism that Billy Graham offers – an evangelism eager above all to be popular. It seeks the friendship of all political parties, supports all churches, bids for the goodwill of intellectuals, and refuses to have anything to do with bigotry. It provides a simple answer to all problems, with the assurance that 'surrender' will not affect the convert's status in the community – indeed, will not even make him lose his friends in the crowd.[1]

The common answer to such criticism is to point to the success which Graham has achieved. This is the line taken, for instance, by Mark Noll in 'The Innocence of Billy Graham', a review of the Graham autobiography. Noll drew attention to the vast number of people the evangelist has addressed, his 'access to the top levels of political decision-making', and the unifying effect of a 'witness that has knitted together an incredibly far-flung network of Christian believers from all over the world'. He considered the view that 'Graham's nose for the powerful took some of the edge off his message', and that his 'strategies of access and ecumenicity undermine his message', but defended the basic policy. By minimizing offence and 'reducing friction', Graham 'traded angularity for access', yet, Noll believed, he did not lose anything essential in the process: 'The reason that Graham's message, though admittedly soft at the edges, remains solid as a rock is that at its centre is the Cross.'[2]

It is beyond doubt that eternal good was done by the message which Graham preached and thankfulness for that should not be forgotten. But whatever the success has been – and the full reality has to await a future day – the Bible

[1] Weiner, quoted by Frady, *Billy Graham*, pp. 248-9.
[2] In *First Things*, edited by Richard John Neuhaus, 19 January 1998, pp. 34–40. That this Catholic magazine should have produced a major defence of Graham is not without significance.

never makes success the criterion of truth. Noll's words do not face the fact that the developing BGEA ministry has been accompanied by a disastrous weakening of evangelical belief.

The change in Dr Graham has been reflected in the other institutions from which the new evangelicalism was launched in the 1950s. Fuller Theological Seminary no longer stands where it once did in relation to historic evangelicalism.

Christianity Today is the journal whose first editor, as noted above, was concerned lest there should be 'no clear and decisive criticism of that false doctrine of ecumenical unity which only treasures a minimum of doctrinal agreement'. In 1980 one of its senior board members resigned in protest because '*Christianity Today* is no longer the magazine it was founded to become'.[1] Today the same paper regards the support of ecumenism as something which is so acceptable that it no longer needs defending. Thus a recent Graham crusade – *Festival '98* – at the University of New Mexico in Albuquerque was reported in these terms:

> The neutral university location of *Festival '98* and ecumenical appeal of the Grahams attracted an ethnic cross-section that churches in New Mexico struggle to achieve. The crusade also helped to break down barriers between Protestant and Catholic churches, which historically have not worked together. 'The Catholic diocese here had been very much in favour and even wrote a letter to every one of their parishes recommending that they get involved', says festival director Herb McCarthy. 'If we're really honest, the things that divide us are small in comparison to the things we hold in common.'[2]

---

[1] Henry, *Confessions,* p. 379. Further on the change in *Christianity Today,* see David Wells, *No Place For Truth, or, Whatever Happened to Evangelical Theology?* (Grand Rapids: Eerdmans, 1993), p. 209 where he points out that between 1959 and 1989, 'the biblical and doctrinal content was reduced from 36 to 8 percent of the paper's content'.

[2] *Christianity Today,* 15 June 1998, p. 14. William Franklin Graham was working with his father in this crusade.

Achieving 'common ground' with Roman Catholicism is one of the things for which Mark Noll commends Graham.[1] But agreement with non-evangelicals has gone still further. In 1978 *McCall's* magazine quoted Graham as having said, 'I used to believe that pagans in far countries were lost if they did not have the gospel of Christ preached to them. I no longer believe that.'[2] The statement alarmed supporters of BGEA and *Christianity Today* was quick to claim that the evangelist had been misquoted. Subsequent disclosures would appear to show that it was Graham's paper rather than *McCall's* which was inaccurate, for a Graham interview with Dr Robert Schuller on 31 May 1997 put the matter beyond doubt. Schuller has attained fame as the promoter of a liberal 'self-esteem' gospel which he preaches in his Crystal Cathedral in California. In the course of his discussion with Graham, conducted by means of a television link-up, Schuller asked for the evangelist's view on the future of Christianity. Graham answered by giving his belief about the final make-up of the body of Christ. That body would be made up, he affirmed,

> from all the Christian groups around the world, outside the Christian groups. I think that everybody that loves or knows Christ, whether they are conscious of it or not, they are members of the body of Christ. And I don't think that we are going to see a great sweeping revival that will turn the whole world to Christ at any time. I think James answered that – the Apostle James in the first Council in Jerusalem – when he said that God's purpose for this age is to call out a people for his name. And that is what he is doing today. He is calling people

[1] 'He was one of the first Protestants, evangelical or mainline, to exploit the common ground of the Apostles' Creed ("My own basic creed", he calls it here) with Roman Catholics and the Orthodox' (*First Things*, 19 January 1998, pp. 37).

[2] Martin, *Prophet With Honor*, pp. 576, 712. The Graham quotation was in an article by James Beam in the January 1978 issue of *McCall's*; the disclaimer followed swiftly in 'Graham's Beliefs: Still Intact', *Christianity Today*, 13 January 1978.

out of the world for his name, whether they come from the Muslim world, or the Buddhist world or the non-believing world, they are members of the Body of Christ because they have been called by God. They may not know the name of Jesus but they know in their hearts that they need something they do not have, and they turn to the only light they have, and I think that they are saved and they are going to be with us in heaven.

Surprised by this, Schuller was anxious for clarification: 'What, what I hear you saying, that it's possible for Jesus Christ to come into human hearts and soul and life, even if they have been born in darkness and have never had exposure to the Bible. Is that a correct interpretation of what you are saying?'

'Yes, it is', Graham responded in decided tones. At which point, his television host tripped over his words in his excitement, and exclaimed, 'I'm so thrilled to hear you say this: *"There's a wideness in God's mercy".'* To which Graham added, 'There is. There definitely is.'[1]

We do not dispute the well-known line from Faber's hymn but Scripture does not authorize the sense given to it here. Graham's concessions are sad words from one who once spoke on the basis of biblical certainties. It is not merely truth 'at the edges' which has gone soft, the whole ethos in which Graham once lived has changed. The practice of seeking

---

[1] This interview was conducted by television and the quotations above are confirmed by a recording of the event which I have seen. On Schuller's book *Self-Esteem: The New Reformation* (Waco, Texas: Word, 1982), David F. Wells comments that Schuller's theology is little else than humanism employing the language of self-improvement. 'The parallels with Harry Emerson Fosdick's *On Being a Real Person* indicate how close Schuller is to liberalism and how far he is from evangelicalism' (*Evangelicalism and Modern America,* ed. George Marsden (Grand Rapids: Eerdmans, 1984), p. 194). See also Wells, *Losing Our Virtue: Why the Church Must Recover Its Moral Vision* (Grand Rapids: Eerdmans, 1998), pp. 199–200. For a full recent treatment of the question, 'Must people hear the gospel of Jesus Christ in order to be saved?', see John Piper, *Let the Nations Be Glad: The Supremacy of God in Missions* (Grand Rapids: Baker, 1993), pp. 115–166.

accommodation and acceptance with exponents of error has dimmed the light. Contending for unpopular truth is no longer a duty and the doctrine supposedly necessary for evangelicalism has become so minimal that it has ceased to be distinct.

Perhaps the most poignant quotation of all comes from the time when the divide was first opening between Graham and fundamentalists in America. William Martin records 'one prominent fundamentalist' making this observation:

> Those who know Billy best say that it is his amiable personality that makes him believe that he can become a sort of pontiff – or bridge-builder – between Bible-believing Christians and those attractive personalities who are the proponents of the non-redemptive gospel. [At a recent breakfast], he pleaded with us to recognize that many of the liberals were good men, loved the Lord, and perhaps could be won over to the conservative position . . . Billy spreads himself too thin; he tries not to offend anybody in any way . . . Not making war on some things he has gone to the other extreme, and made peace, not with the doctrines of apostasy, but with those who preach the doctrines of apostasy. This, I believe, is deadly and will one day defeat the whole cause for which this man of God is laboring.[1]

* * * *

It would be wrong to suppose that no one apart from American fundamentalists urged Dr Graham to reconsider the direction in which he and others were leading a large segment of evangelicalism. At least two notable evangelical leaders urged him to think again. One was Martyn Lloyd-Jones, whom Graham was anxious to have as chairman at the World Congress on Evangelism, planned for a European venue in the mid-1960s (Berlin was finally favoured over

[1] W. W. Ayer, quoted by Robert Dunzweiler, *Billy Graham: A Critique* (Elkins Park, Pa.: Faith Theological Seminary), p. 30, and Martin, *Prophet With Honor*, p. 223.

Rome). It was well-known that Lloyd-Jones, although personally friendly towards Graham, had been the only British evangelical leader who had not given his support to the crusades in 1954–5 – a fact which undoubtedly troubled the BGEA. In the summer of 1963 the two men talked in the vestry at Westminster Chapel on the subject of the World Congress and, after explaining his position, Lloyd-Jones put this proposal:

> I said I'd make a bargain: if he would stop the general sponsorship of his campaigns – stop having liberals and Roman Catholics on the platform – and drop the invitation system, I would wholeheartedly support him and chair the Congress. We talked for about three hours, but he didn't accept these conditions.[1]

'I have been giving much thought and prayer to our discussion', Graham wrote to Lloyd-Jones on 18 July 1963.[2] But to have followed the counsel he had been given would have meant a very major reversal of policy. One can only assume from the outcome that he concluded that his work would lose more than it could gain if he cut off the liberal and the developing Catholic support, together with the public call for decision.

The other leader who expressed the same concerns to Graham was Francis Schaeffer. Schaeffer went further than Lloyd-Jones in his co-operation with the evangelist and accepted an invitation to be one of the main speakers at the Berlin Congress which met in 1966. He made use of the occasion to give warning in public of what he had also said in private:

> Let us never forget that we who stand in the historic stream of Christianity really believe that false doctrine, at those crucial

[1] Murray, *D. M. Lloyd-Jones: the Fight of Faith 1939–1981*, p. 440. Lloyd-Jones knew a good deal of the situation in the United States. He had been both at Fuller Seminary and at Park Street, Boston. Marcellus Kik had also spoken at the Westminster Fellowship (a monthly fraternal at Westminster Chapel) on the merits and the dangers of the new evangelicalism.

[2] *Ibid.*, p. 441

points where false doctrine is heresy, is not a small thing. If we do not make clear by word and practice our position for truth as truth and against false doctrine, we are building a wall between the next generation and the gospel. And twenty years from now, men will point their finger back at us and say of us, this is the result of the flow of history . . . Evangelism which does not lead to purity of life and purity of doctrine is just as faulty and incomplete as an orthodoxy which does not lead to a concern for, and communication with, the lost.[1]

Schaeffer was not heard. In one of his last books, written in 1984, he pleaded: 'What is the use of evangelicalism seeming to get larger and larger if sufficient numbers of those under the name evangelical no longer hold to that which makes evangelicalism evangelical?'[2]

It is a painful illustration of the Graham concern to pass over the uncomfortable that in his lengthy autobiography Schaeffer's name receives no mention at all. With Lloyd-Jones it is perhaps worse. Although the two men met and were in touch on several occasions, the minister of Westminster Chapel gets only one brief reference in *Just As I Am*. Graham's serious discussion with Lloyd-Jones in 1963 is wholly passed over and all that readers are told is that the latter, 'one of Britain's outstanding preachers', stood in line to greet Graham at a luncheon in London in 1952.

[1] Quoted by Erroll Hulse in 'Berlin in Retrospect', *Banner of Truth*, Issue 48, May/June 1967, p. 8. Schaeffer drew attention to his Berlin address in his book, *The Church at the End of the Twentieth Century* (London: Norfolk Press, 1970), p. 49, and emphasized: 'We must practise the truth even when it is costly. We must practise it when it involves church affiliation or evangelistic cooperation. There is a difference between having a discussion with a liberal theologian and inviting him to pray in our programme.' In correspondence he writes to an unnamed person of the danger that the unattractiveness of 'cold fundamentalism' may lead him to think liberalism 'less of hell than it is . . . liberalism is so completely destructive in the finding of truth that I would not for a moment even seem to equate fundamentalism and liberalism as equal dangers' (*Letters of Francis Schaeffer*, ed. Lane T. Dennis, Westchester, Ill.: Crossway, 1985, p. 72).

[2] F. Schaeffer, *The Great Evangelical Disaster* (Westchester, Ill.: Crossway, 1987), p. 64.

The Graham evangelistic methods do not seem to have been openly questioned by evangelicals in the United States until after the publication of his biography by Marshall Frady in 1979. Frady did not dispute Graham's Christian devotion. But, while some of his comment was ill-judged, it was most damaging where he questioned what the planners, fund-raisers and TV experts had built around the evangelist. In his view the BGEA was not so much a spiritual force as a con-flux of the kind of American techniques which are well calculated to gain results. *Christianity Today* (16 November 1979) gave eleven columns to answering Frady, but *Eternity,* an evangelical monthly with no reputation for opposing the kind of evangelism followed by Graham, was far more discriminating. In a review article, 'The Billy Graham Books', Bob Cleath wrote for the November 1979 issue:

> In view of Frady's criticisms, Graham needs to consider afresh whether his methods in mass evangelism based on the tried and tested American evangelistic formula really gain the results ostensibly shown by his altar calls . . . In Graham's recent Milwaukee Crusade little emotion was shown by inquirers. It seemed so easy for so many to come forward. While one can-not judge the intents of the heart, one is not merely being a cynic when questioning the worth of a standardized formula intended as the vehicle for the most drastic decision in the lives of a multitude of complex individuals . . . evangelicals need to ponder deeply Frady's most significant questions: (1) Is the standardized American mass evangelism procedure the best means to win people to Christ? (2) Have Graham and middle-class evangelicals failed in their prophetic role to society? (3) Have Graham and evangelicals lacked discernment of the depth of evil in our nation? (4) Are we all going to go about innocently doing the work of Christ in the same old American way even though the results show limited success? (5) Are we going to listen for the voice of God in critical judg-ments as well as in comforting words of assurance?

The course of history would appear to indicate that these questions were not taken seriously.

4

The New Anglican
Evangelicalism
Versus the Old

The extent to which many saw the 1960s as a time of new beginnings is remarkable. For the religious world at large the Second Vatican Council meeting at Rome from 1962 to 1965 led the way. In the new Roman Catholicism, Latin rites gave way to the languages of the people, the Bible was to be made accessible to all and, for the first time, the possibility of there being Christians – 'separated brethren' – who were not yet able to accept the papacy was officially recognized. Where this would lead to no one knew, but Pope Paul VI certainly did not hide his own opinion when, welcoming the Anglican bishops of Salisbury and of Southwark to the Vatican in April 1964, he told them, 'You have always been awaited and expected.' Two years later Michael Ramsey, Archbishop of Canterbury, made a more official visit, and left wearing the Pope's episcopal ring with its emeralds and diamonds.

Ramsey was already on record as supporting the opinion that the Pope 'has a primacy among all the bishops of Christendom; so that without communion with him, there is no prospect of a reunited Christendom'.[1] In 1968 'Ramsey said he was very willing to recognize the Pope as chief of a united Church.'[2] For the present, leaders of the British Council of Churches left that controversial issue to one side and the Church of Rome was not included in the vision of 'one Church . . . not later than Easter Day, 1980' for which they covenanted at Nottingham in 1964.

For evangelicals in England in the early 1960s, as we have already seen, the main hope for a new beginning arose out of the vast success of the Graham crusades. If only what had been begun could be sustained, then, it was believed, a national revival seemed in prospect. Almost overnight 'evangelical renaissance' became a familiar term.

But another influence of which we have not yet spoken was also at work within evangelicalism at this date. Without name or distinct organization, a new tide of opinion was rising which, in its understanding of the situation, differed widely from the crusade ethos. The visible origins of this influence can be traced to such agencies as the Inter-Varsity Fellowship (with its books and student conferences),[3] the annual Puritan Conference, the Evangelical Library, and publishers who had begun to reprint long-forgotten authors in the older evangelical and reformed tradition. From small beginnings, with the reissue of works by John Calvin and

---

[1] A. M. Ramsey, *The Gospel and the Catholic Church*, p. 228.

[2] Chadwick, *Ramsey*, p. 325.

[3] This is not to say that thought among the leaders of Inter-Varsity was homogeneous or that their publications all represented the same theological outlook. F. F. Bruce who edited the *Evangelical Quarterly*, when it belonged to the IVF, has noted the embarrassment caused to the organization in 1955 when J. I. Packer compared the Keswick doctrine of sanctification, 'to its great disadvantage, with the historic Reformed teaching on the same subject' (F. F. Bruce, *In Retrospect: Remembrance of Things Past*, London: Pickering & Inglis, 1980), p. 188.

J. C. Ryle, a near flood of books in that older tradition was to be found in Christian bookshops by the 1960s. These agencies were separate streams which overlapped with one another in their common influence. The name of only one man appeared in connection with them all, and it was that of Martyn Lloyd-Jones.

A lone voice at first when he came to the pulpit of Westminster Chapel in 1938, through the years Lloyd-Jones had shown increasing numbers a different way of looking at things. A 'devotional' attachment to Scripture was not enough: Christians needed the theology and doctrinal understanding which come from serious exposition of Scripture. At a time when pragmatism was prevalent in evangelicalism, he taught that what we *believe* about God has more consequence upon church life and Christian living than anything else. Man-centredness and trust in human expedients are the outcome of low views of God. Instead of all the popular emphases to be heard in the churches, he preached that a recovery of the consciousness of the greatness of God and of his glory was the first need of the times.

This is not to imply that the minister of Westminster Chapel was primarily a teacher, intent upon deepening the intellects of his hearers and readers. Rather, in the first place, as his wife once said, he was a man of prayer and an evangelist. His concern was for a spiritual awakening which he believed would come as the truth is honoured, lived and preached under a larger anointing of the Spirit of God. When a younger generation in the 1950s began to discover the depth of former evangelical and reformed writers it was inevitable that they would begin to look for contemporary examples of such ministry and this led them to Westminster Chapel. As Cambridge students once went to Dedham to 'catch fire' under the preaching of John Rogers, so a new generation went to Westminster Chapel. Lloyd-Jones did not believe in 'movements'; he wanted something authentically of God and yet, without any design on his part, he was looked to for leadership in all the agencies which I have mentioned.

[81]

Of the younger men who gathered round Lloyd-Jones probably the most significant was James I. Packer. Born in 1926, Packer became a Christian while at Oxford, where he graduated in 1948. He remained in that city to study at Wycliffe Hall and to follow up his recent discovery of the Puritans with doctoral research on Richard Baxter. Ordained to the Church of England in 1952, he served a Birmingham curacy from that year to 1954 and then moved to training others for the Anglican ministry at Tyndale Hall, Bristol. At the Puritan Conference (which, in conjuction with Lloyd-Jones and others, he started at Westminster Chapel in 1950) he was second only to Lloyd-Jones in the appeal of his addresses, and by the 1960s, as a conference speaker and through his titles, *'Fundamentalism' and the Word of God* and *Evangelism and the Sovereignty of God,* he was the best-known of the younger exponents of what some onlookers called 'neo-Puritanism'.

Writing of his near twenty-years' relationship with Lloyd-Jones, Packer has said, 'We were together in thinking that the Puritan spirit is in essence New Testament Christianity.'[1] But elsewhere he also comments, 'Over questions of churchly responsibility we were never on the same wavelength, and this led eventually to a parting of the ways.'[2]

As this 'parting' is so closely related to the theme of these pages we must turn to it. For some fifteen of their twenty-years' relationship the two men found no problem in working together despite the fact that Dr Lloyd-Jones was twenty-six years Packer's senior and a Congregationalist (Independent) in his view of church polity. Their thinking was the same on issues bigger than denominational relationships. But those issues had implications for denominational questions and the 1960s were to bring them to the fore. If the evangelical belief that it is faith in the gospel which brings

[1] Packer, 'A Kind of Puritan' in *Martyn Lloyd-Jones: Chosen by God,* ed. C. Catherwood (Westchester, Ill.: Crossway, 1986), p. 50.

[2] Packer, 'David Martyn Lloyd-Jones' in *Chosen Vessels: Portraits of Ten Outstanding Men,* ed. C. Turner (Ann Arbor, Mich.: Servant Publications, 1985), p. 110.

spiritual unity is true, then it follows that where the gospel ceases to be believed there unity ceases to exist. Therein lay a long-standing problem for evangelicals who found themselves in denominations where many ministers and people did not believe that gospel. In such circumstances, how could they give the commitment to denominational unity which Scripture gives to the unity of Christians? They could not do so, and therefore, while serving within denominations, they found their real spiritual unity with those of all denominations who shared the same saving faith. For acting in this way, evangelicals (and those in the Church of England especially) were accused by others of their denominations of putting their 'party' before the Church. They endured the complaint, believing that a measure of isolation within their denominations was a price worth paying for believing that the gospel takes priority over denominational affiliation.

If anyone asked these evangelicals why they continued in their uncomfortable denominational relationship the answer generally given was that it was *their* faith which the constitution of the denomination upheld; and, further, they thought that they saw biblical features in their denomination which could not readily be found elsewhere. For such reasons they remained where they were, but in doing so they never supposed that their denominational affiliation exemplified the New Testament ideal for unity. Rather their outlook was that of Canon Richard Hobson of Liverpool who wrote: 'I earnestly desire, and devoutly pray, that all Evangelical churches may be drawn together: that is the only unity I believe in or dare advocate.'[1]

On this understanding of the priority of spiritual unity evangelicals had never disagreed, however much their views varied on questions of church government. This was Dr Packer's position just as much as it was that of Dr Lloyd-Jones. In his book *'Fundamentalism' and the Word of God*,

[1] Richard Hobson, *What Hath God Wrought: An Autobiography*, (London: Thynne, 1907), p. 180.

published in 1958, Packer did not hesitate to oppose the views of such Anglican dignitaries as Gabriel Hebert and Michael Ramsey. He wanted, he wrote, 'real unity, that fellowship of love in the truth which Christ prayed that His disciples might enjoy', not 'sham unity':

> The more one probes the differences between Roman and Protestant, Liberal and Evangelical, the deeper they prove to be; beneath the cracks on the surface lie fissures which run down to the very foundations, broadening as they go.[1]

So Packer wrote in 1958. Three years later he returned to the same issue, with added application to the current scene, in a booklet entitled *The Thirty-Nine Articles*. The purpose of articles of faith, he pointed out, was to preserve doctrinal unity. Every Anglican clergyman had professed his acceptance of their teaching at his ordination and yet the leaders of the Church of England were now engaged in the pursuit of unity without any reference to the standards they were pledged to uphold. 'The Articles', he observed, 'play no part whatsoever in the conception of that unity.'[2] The Church of England was looking for alignments with others when her 'own house is in a state of complete and seemingly inveterate theological disorder . . . She suspects at times that she ought to be preaching a clearer gospel; but she cannot for the moment do anything about it, because she is not clear herself as to what the gospel is . . . And it needs to be said quite categorically that the Church of England has no hope whatever of recapturing our country for Christ till the theology of the Articles possess her mind once more.'[3]

The Church of England was 'comprehensive', Packer continued, in the sense that the Articles only demand assent on fundamental matters which are 'indispensable if the gospel as the Church of England understands it is to be preserved and the Church's order maintained'. 'There was never meant to be room in the Church's ministry for persons who could not

---

[1] *'Fundamentalism'*, p. 45. On ecumenical theology, see pp. 17–18.

[2] Packer, *The Thirty-Nine Articles* (London: Church Pastoral Aid Soc., 1961), p. 4.

[3] *Ibid.*, pp. 12, 46.

assent to as much as this.'[1] In these words he was stating the classic evangelical Anglican position. Although evangelicals might seem to be 'no more than a dissentient minority in the present-day Church', in holding to the Articles they were the true upholders of the Church of England. They were the 'constitutionalists'. Those who truly subscribed to the Articles, wrote Packer, were

> resolved to preach the gospel which they define, and to oppose all doctrines, however popular and fashionable, which, specifically or in principle, they condemn. It seems impossible to maintain that a man who could not commit himself in this way would be in his right place in the ministry of the Church of England.[2]

When he wrote his booklet *The Thirty-Nine Articles,* Packer knew that the Anglo-Catholic, or so-called 'Catholic', wing of the Church of England possessed major influence. That was clear enough to all in February 1964 by the manner in which a measure to legalize pre-Reformation mass vestments went through Church Assembly. All 31 bishops present voted in favour, while in the House of Clergy there were 214 in favour and only 30 against. The same sympathy was at work in the developing ecumenical discussions and notably in the Anglican-Methodist Report of 1963 which set out the way for the Church of England and the Methodist Church to unite. The Report was clearly intent upon securing Anglo-Catholic support and it therefore contained a belief in sacramental grace ('the child baptized is *regenerate*'[3]) and

---

[1] *Ibid.,* pp. 10–11.   [2] *Ibid.,* pp. 45–6.
[3] *Conversations between the Church of England and the Methodist Church: A Report to the Archbishops of Canterbury and York and the Conference of the Methodist Church* (London: Church Information Office and the Epworth Press, 1963), p. 31. The italics belong to the original. A statement of the Lambeth Conference in 1958 included the words: 'It must . . . be recognized as a fact that Anglicans conscientiously hold that the celebrant of the Eucharist should have been ordained by a bishop standing in the historical succession and generally believe it to be their duty to bear witness to this principle by receiving Holy Communion only from those who have been thus ordained.'

based the legitimacy of the 'priesthood' on 'the historic episcopate' and its supposed authority derived from the apostles. The signatories to the Report believed that there could be no question of excluding the 'Catholic' presence in the projected union of the two denominations, nor was there any need for such an exclusion for, although Methodism had once had an evangelical tradition, the signatories now believed:

> [the fact] that there are increasing numbers today for whom the words *evangelical* and *catholic* are not mutually exclusive, points the way forward to a wider catholicity, to which Methodists will contribute and from which they have much to receive.[1]

Upon the publication of this Report, Packer, along with four other Anglican evangelicals, entered directly into the ongoing unity debate with a publication of their own, *The Church of England and the Methodist Church*. Packer's objection to the proposed way to reunion with Methodism was definite and clear cut. The whole approach was wrong and typically ecumenical in ethos. He wrote:

> The Church [of England] is represented (pp. 49f.) as containing 'evangelicals' and 'catholics' side by side on an equal footing, without mention of the fact that its authorised formularies exclude some things for which Anglican 'Catholics' stand, and which, indeed, have intruded into this report. There is no recognition that reunion should involve reformation by the word of God, and no sign of a quest for such reformation on either side, only a pragmatic mutual adjustment that sometimes looks very much like bargaining ... This resolute double-mindedness – in the service of the God of truth! – is really frivolous and irreverent.[2]

[1] *Ibid.*, p. 50.
[2] *The Church of England and the Methodist Church: A Consideration of the Report*, ed. J. I. Packer (Abingdon, Berks: Marcham Manor Press, 1963), pp. 10, 62.

When six other Anglican evangelicals, including more senior men such as A. T. Houghton and M. A. P. Wood, also went into print, but in support of the Anglican-Methodist Report, Packer at once took them up:

> They view their evangelicalism as simply a party view in the Church of England, and do not object in principle to the Church's official ecumenical actions being determined by Anglo-Catholic convictions about the ministry . . . their readiness to justify a seeming unprincipled comprehension, leaves one wondering whether 'Broad Church pietists' would not be a better description of some of them than 'Evangelicals'.[1]

It is significant to note that the very issue which Packer was here highlighting was the same point upon which he and Lloyd-Jones were repeatedly attacked by the ecumenical side. Packer, argued Gordon Rupp (Methodist supporter of reunion), was 'putting the interests of an ecclesiastical party before the welfare of the whole church of Christ'.[2] 'If we do not agree with their reckoning of what Scripture amounts to, we are only questionably Christians', complained John Huxtable, the Congregationalist leader.[3] Douglas Jones, Lightfoot Professor of Divinity at Durham, censuring the minister of Westminster Chapel in particular, declared:

> There is no greater scandal in this complex situation than the refusal of Christians to accept their fellow Christians . . . The Church is the emergence within the body of mankind of the unity to which not only Christians but all men are called – more than that, in which they already exist in Jesus Christ. Christ is the head of every man . . . the Church . . . is never possible to define.[4]

[1] Packer, 'An Evangelical Approach?' *Church of England Newspaper*, 17 July 1964.
[2] Gordon Rupp, *Consideration Reconsidered: An Examination of* The Church of England and the Methodist Church *edited by J. I. Packer* (London: Epworth Press, 1964), p. 58.
[3] Quoted by J. D. Douglas, *Evangelicals and Unity* (Abingdon, Berks: Marcham Manor Press, 1964), p. 14.
[4] D. Jones, *Instrument of Peace* (London: 1965), pp. 69–74.

All the Packer quotations given above are pre-1965. By that date a shift in his thinking was taking place, as it was in that of many other Anglican evangelicals. This change has never been explained nor, indeed, is it even noticed by Alister McGrath, Packer's recent biographer. Enough evidence exists, however, to trace the reason for it as follows. In 1962 Dr Packer moved from Bristol to become Warden of Latimer House, Oxford. Latimer House was a 'think-tank' newly set up by Anglican evangelicals 'to expound and defend evangelicalism within the Church of England'.[1] John Stott chaired its governing body.

The ecumenical debate was in full swing at this time. In the opinion of *The Times*: 'Just about the most unfashionable attitude to take inside the Church of England today is to cast doubt on the movement towards Christian unity. Ecumenism has become the Anglican passport to probity.'[2] Given that evangelical Anglican opinion on the subject was being largely ignored by the leaders of the denomination, an involvement in the current debate seemed essential if evangelicals were not to be wholly isolated. The Packer-led critique of the Anglican-Methodist report of 1963 was the beginning, and it was followed by an appeal to Anglican leaders that evangelicals should not be excluded from discussions as hitherto. The request was heeded with the result that, in McGrath's words, 'Packer found himself increasingly in demand as a member of various official church bodies, including the Archbishop's Doctrine Commission (chaired at this stage by Bishop Ian Ramsey), the Faith and Order Advisory Group, and the dialogue groups between Anglicanism and other churches.'[3]

This apparent willingness of church leaders to include evangelical spokesmen in their deliberations came as surprising news to a number of evangelicals within the Church of

[1] John Wenham, *Facing Hell: An Autobiography 1913–1996* (Carlisle: Paternoster Press, 1999), p. 140.

[2] *The Times*, 24 May 1966.

[3] McGrath, *Packer*, p. 115.

England. In the light of 'some severe defeats' for their beliefs in Church Assembly, R. T. Beckwith writes, 'Many evangelicals began to wonder whether a deliberate attempt was being made to drive them out of the Church of England.'[1] Beckwith joined Latimer House staff in 1963 and he has recorded how the team there were concerned to counter this misapprehension and to reassure evangelical clergy. Accordingly a conference entitled 'Facing the Future' was held at Swanwick:

> It was explained by Dr Packer at the conference that we were living in a time when all theological convictions were regarded as relative, not absolute: no one was going to force us out deliberately, when what they wanted us to do was to *contribute our insight* – one among many. Reassuring though this was in the circumstances, it may perhaps have led some evangelicals into accepting other people's evaluation of evangelical theology.[2]

The new policy was now in the making. Evangelicals would enter into the wider relationships which ecumenism had made so popular. They would also commit themselves to greater involvement in the structures of the Church of England but they meant to keep to their own ground rules. Despite the criticism to which A. T. Houghton had been exposed by Packer, it was Houghton's phrase 'Co-operation without Compromise'[3] which best described the new aim. Such was the background to the National Evangelical Anglican Congress held at Keele University in 1967, upon which we have already commented (pp. 42–3).

[1] 'Keele, Nottingham and the Future' in *The Evangelical Succession in the Church of England,* ed. D. N. Samuel (Cambridge: James Clarke, 1979), p. 102.

[2] Samuel, *Evangelical Succession,* p. 104. The significance of *'contribute our insight'* will be more apparent in the next chapter. If 'making a contribution' was not the evangelical intention, that should have been made plain at the outset. But to have done so would have been to dash the hopes of gaining wider acceptance in the denomination.

[3] A. T. Houghton, *Evangelicals and the World Council of Churches* (London: World Dominion Press, 1962), p. 7.

The opinion seems to have been reached that it was no longer realistic to insist on the Thirty-Nine Articles as normative for Anglican belief and that evangelicals would gain advantage from the new openness only if they put to one side their former conviction that other 'views' besides the evangelical had no legitimate place in the Church of England. The first signs of this change appeared in another publication edited by Packer and published in 1965, *All In Each Place: Towards Reunion in England, Ten Anglican Essays With Some Free Church Comment*. The old evangelical Anglican position was still to be found in these pages but with a new blurring. The ecumenical idea of full respect for the opinions of others is present with an oft-repeated regard for the need to 'safe-guard' the Anglo-Catholic conscience.[1] It was argued that the union between the two Churches (Anglican and Methodist) needed to be creedal and that a confession of faith should come first. But whatever the confession that might be agreed, evangelicals now said that they did not want it to be a 'disciplinary stick with which to beat any body of sincerely held opinion.'[2] 'Sharply as we dissent from historic Anglo-Catholicism, we do not wish a union scheme to become a concealed instrument for doctrinal discipline'.[3] On the contrary, the evangelicals wanted Anglo-Catholic agreement in any reunion plan. The ecumenical language of 'mutual recognition based on trust between all concerned' had entered Packer's vocabulary.[4]

Several things were disturbing about this book. It still said that the gospel must control unity, yet what this gospel is – as distinct from the rampant confusion about which Packer had previously often spoken – was not elaborated. The elaboration found in *All In Each Place* has much more to do with the questions of episcopacy, ordination and such like. The

---

[1] *All In Each Place: Towards Reunion in England, Ten Anglican Essays With Some Free Church Comment*, ed. J. I. Packer (Abingdon, Berks: Marcham Manor Press, 1965), pp. 10–13, 30–31, 36–37, etc.

[2] *Ibid.*, p. 13.   [3] *Ibid.*, p. 30.   [4] *Ibid.*, p. 37.

statement that the 'authorised formularies' of the Church of England 'exclude some things for which Anglican "catholics" stand',[1] has gone. Further, of the three 'Free Church friends' invited to contribute a section of 'Discussion' at the end of the book all were non-evangelical and one of them, John Huxtable, was decidedly opposed to evangelicals and especially to their belief in Scripture and a substitutionary atonement. It was Dr Huxtable who, in 1962, when the Congregationalists were supposedly commemorating Puritan faithfulness in 1662, wrote: 'Our fathers declared that all was to be done agreeably to the Word of God. We often use the same formula; but we often hide from ourselves the fact that we think of the Word of God very differently from our fathers.'[2] No doubt he was surprised to be asked to contribute to *All In Each Place* and he counted it 'one of the happier signs of the times' that evangelicals were now displaying 'a real, lively, and committed concern for Christian unity'.[3]

Here in 1965 was the first stage of a development which would lead to Archbishop Ramsey opening the Keele Congress two years later. When that occasion had passed, the evangelicals' own report on Keele drew attention to the fact that on the first evening of the congress 'the Rev. Dr J. I. Packer took up the often-repeated phrase of Dr Ramsey: "Our concern must be as wide as God's"'.[4] It was almost as though Packer's penitence for having ever criticised Ramsey had to be registered. 'There had never been anything remotely like it before', says Randle Manwaring, and, referring to 'one major change of stance', he quotes the words of Anthony Thiselton, 'For some it has been a rude shock to discover that a large Congress of Evangelicals has declared itself

---

[1] Packer, *The Church of England and the Methodist Church* (1963), p. 10.

[2] *1662 and its Issues* (London: Congregational Hist. Soc., April 1962), p. 3.

[3] *All In Each Place*, p. 228.

[4] *Keele '67*, p.10.

ready to learn from other Christians.'[1] 'The National Evangelical Anglican Assembly at Keele', Packer later wrote, 'was a milestone in twentieth-century evangelical history, for it broke with a long-prevalent pietist and sectarian mood.' The intention, he says, was, that Keele would see the image of 'ecclesiastical isolationism . . . swept away'.[2]

One practical consequence of the new comprehensiveness was that over the next five years the work on Anglican-Methodist reunion had to be abandoned by its powerful advocates and that, in part, as a result of evangelical Anglican opposition.[3] This is not to say that Anglican evangelicals had suddenly come to power. The explanation is more strange. Once inside reunion and other ecumenical discussions, and able to take stock of the relative strength of different parties, Packer and others had decided that of their differences with liberals and traditional Anglo-Catholics the former were the more serious. Those Anglo-Catholics who had resisted liberalism did at least believe in fundamental articles of the faith.[4]

---

[1] R. Manwaring, *From Controversy to Co-Existence: Evangelicals in the Church of England, 1914–1980* (Cambridge: Cambridge University Press, 1985), pp. 177, 185. Manwaring was a London business man and a Vice-Chairman of the Church Society. His autobiography was published by Howard Baker in 1992.

[2] 'Taking Stock in Theology' in *Evangelicals Today: Thirteen Stock-Taking Essays,* ed. John C. King (Guildford: Lutterworth Press, 1973). pp. 15–16.

[3] When it came to voting for the union in 1969, the Methodists voting for approval amounted to 77.4 per cent, but only 69 per cent of the Anglicans approved – short of the 75 per cent previously agreed as necessary. A renewed vote in 1971 met with no more success. Ramsey, after secret talks with the Church of Rome to ensure that the form of the reunion plan with the Methodists was not contrary to 'apostolic succession' and would not therefore prevent a future reunion with the Papacy, had been a strong advocate of the plan. Shocked by its final rejection, the archbishop concluded that the Church of England was not, after all, 'the best of all churches' (Chadwick, *Ramsey,* p. 346).

[4] 'Now that which chiefly endangers the gospel is the humanitarian Christology which denies us a living divine Saviour; and our allies against it are chiefly our catholic brethren, whose views of Christ are in step with the Creeds.' *Celebrating the Saving Work of God: Collected Shorter Writings of J. I. Packer,* vol. 1 (Carlisle: Paternoster, 1998), p. 81. From an address in 1978.

As they were apprehensive of the theological liberalism prevalent in the Methodist Church, the opportunity existed for a combination between some of them and evangelicals led by Packer who wanted to stop the union scheme. This is what occurred.

If this alignment was not surprise enough – given that evangelicals had previously pointed to the way the Thirty-Nine Articles denied Anglo-Catholics any legitimate place in the Church of England – more was to follow. Instead of regarding this new front with Anglo-Catholics as a temporary expedient, Packer with another Anglican evangelical, Colin Buchanan, went into print with two well-known Anglo-Catholics (E. L. Mascall and Graham Leonard, Bishop of Willesden) to assert that it was going to be permanent. In the Introduction to *Growing Into Union* the four men 'pledged' themselves in all further union discussions 'to stay together, to work together, and not at any stage to settle for a way through which would satisfy one "side" whilst hurting the other . . . we are all four committed to every line in the book (except the signed Appendixes), and we are determined that no wedge should be driven between us.'[1] As though to show the solid basis on which they were to build together the whole book is preceded by this quotation from the Archbishop of Canterbury's book, *The Gospel and the Catholic Church*:

> 'Catholicism' and 'Evangelicalism' are not two separate things which the Church of England must hold together by a great feat of compromise. Rightly understood, they are both facts which lie behind the Church of England and, as the New Testament shows, they are one fact.

Instead of presenting itself as a symposium in which the views of the different contributors might be identified,

---

[1] *Growing Into Union: Proposals for Forming a United Church in England* (London: SPCK, 1970), pp. 17, 19. In his report to the Latimer House Council in October 1969 Packer referred to the coming book in less high-flown language. It was to be 'a mixed Willesden-Mascall-Buchanan-Packer grill, on unity and union in England' (McGrath, *Packer*, p. 155).

Growing Into Union was written as one piece of work with each author owning responsibility for the whole. While seeking to show that both Anglo-Catholics and evangelicals held legitimate 'emphases', it appeared to give sanction to errors which evangelicals in the Church of England had hitherto always opposed. The following points were agreed: Both Scripture *and* tradition derive from Christ and confront men with him (p. 34). Tradition . . . is the handing on to each Christian of the riches of the Father's house to which he became entitled by his baptism (p. 34). Scripture keeps the Church true to its historical roots as nothing else, except perhaps the Eucharist (p. 36). The bishop is the sacramental expression of the headship of Christ (p. 79). The gospel makes us one in the Second Adam by baptism (p. 58).

In all this there was no warning of the 'magical views' of the sacraments (against which Packer had protested in 1961 when he was asserting the position of the Articles[1]), nor was anything said to clarify the nature of regeneration, saving faith and conversion. How this book could ever be seen as a way towards bringing Christians possessed of biblical convictions into a 'united Church in England' is a mystery. The truth is that the book was rather a justification for the alliance with Anglo-Catholics and was not intended for Nonconformist evangelicals. Inevitably the latter read it, and it brought to breaking point the link between Packer and Lloyd-Jones. The practical fall out from this was perhaps worse than from the disagreement at the Evangelical Alliance meeting of 1966. It not only ended such common endeavours as the work of the Puritan Conference but also the fruitful cooperation between Packer and many non-Anglican evangelicals in Bible rallies and in the ministry of the *Evangelical Magazine*.[2]

---

[1] *Thirty-Nine Articles*, p. 43. 'One's view of the sacraments is determined by one's whole theology of grace . . . The test of any theological system is its sacramental teaching' (p. 36).

[2] Not a little of Dr Packer's most valuable published work came out of this co-operation, especially his *Evangelical Magazine* articles published as

Dr Packer's words that he and Dr Lloyd-Jones were 'never on the same wavelength' on church issues and that this caused the parting do not meet the facts. The break did not come because Packer remained an Anglican, for Lloyd-Jones continued his relationships with many such until his death in 1981; but the Anglicans with whom he continued, although regarded by most as 'old fashioned evangelicals', were men who did not support the new policy of full co-operation with non-evangelicals launched so publicly at Keele.

Packer has argued that the case which Lloyd-Jones presented to fellow-evangelicals in the mid-1960s was rejected by Anglican evangelicals because it rested on 'two bad arguments':

> He was a great man, but great men can be enmeshed in bad arguments. Bad argument number one was that if we stay in the Church of England we're guilty by association of all the theological errors that any Anglican may be propagating anywhere at all.[1]

Where men challenged error, they could not be condoning it. But this number-one argument attributed to Lloyd-Jones (as Packer believed he remembered it in 1995) is not to be found in the major addresses with which Anglicans had finally disagreed at Keele thirty years earlier.[2] In fact, had

---

Knowing God (London and Chicago: Hodder & Stoughton and Inter-Varsity Press, 1973), and his Puritan conference addresses, published as *A Quest for Godliness* (Westchester, Ill.: Crossway, 1991), and in the UK as *Among God's Giants* (Eastbourne: Crossway, 1991).

[1] Address at meeting of Reform, June 1995, quoted in Roger Steer, *Guarding the Holy Fire: The Evangelicalism of John R. W. Stott, J. I. Packer and Alister McGrath* (Grand Rapids: Baker, 1999), p. 225.

[2] The key addresses – *The Basis of Christian Unity*, *'Consider Your Ways': The Outline of a New Strategy* and *Evangelical Unity: An Appeal* – are printed, as first given, in *Knowing the Times*. Only after Keele, in Dr Lloyd-Jones' Luther address of 1 November 1967, is there a passing reference to 'the question of guilt by association'. See Lloyd-Jones, *Unity in Truth: Addresses given under the auspices of the British Evangelical Council*, ed. Hywel R. Jones (Darlington: Evangelical Press, 1991), p. 41.

Lloyd-Jones rested on that argument he would himself have become 'guilty by association' for, as I have said, he continued to associate with some Anglicans. Packer went on to present the Lloyd-Jones case in these words:

> Secondly, he said, 'Don't you see the times call us to leave all the doctrinally mixed denominations and form a pure new one?' And I and others looked around and couldn't see the times called us to do any such thing.

These words pass over the heart of the matter which, in a different context, can be well-stated in Packer's own words. In an address on 'The Doctrine and Expression of Christian Unity' in 1966, Packer referred to the way in which Dr Douglas Jones of Durham University had dismissed the addresses given for the IVF by the minister of Westminster Chapel. These addresses argued that if the question of unity is to be approached scripturally and theologically it must begin with regeneration and belief of the truth:

> Professor Douglas Jones attacked Dr D. M. Lloyd-Jones for saying that Christian unity only exists where the central doctrines of Paul's Gospel are believed . . . in principle Dr Lloyd-Jones' position is unchallengeable. Integral to the Pauline concept of the one church is the notion of a Pauline commitment, confessed in worship, witness and life, to Jesus Christ as set forth in the Pauline Gospel.[1]

Further, Dr Packer's own statements affirmed that it was not this gospel commitment which constituted the unity of the Church of England. For the majority it was a very different gospel: 'The Gospel of the Anglican mainstream says: though every one is fundamentally good, what we need and what Christ gives us is help and enrichment to fulfil our human potential and to become the people in our hearts we are seeking to be.'[2]

[1] *Serving the People of God: Collected Shorter Writings of J. I. Packer,* vol. 2 (Carlisle: Paternoster, 1998), p. 36.
[2] *Ibid.,* p. 46. Address on 'The Gospel and the Lord's Supper' (1990). He adds: 'This doctrine, which the new Anglican liturgies of our day clearly reflect, relativizes the absolutes of biblical teaching.'

Here indeed was the real issue for Lloyd-Jones. He was asking why, when the ecumenical endeavour to merge denominations was admittedly wrong at its very starting point, should not evangelicals themselves address the true nature of church unity and put *that* unity first? How could the very ground rule of participation in ecumenism – that all participants 'have a right to be treated as Christians', as conceded at Keele – be compatible with the admission that the mainstream of participants showed no commitment to the Pauline gospel? How was a determination to challenge error consistent with such a concession?

Dr Lloyd-Jones could understand the desire of Anglican evangelicals to win back a historic denomination for the truth, and accordingly to want to remain in the position they had inherited. But his argument that the denominational situation *had changed* had more force to it than others seemed to recognize. Ecumenism (with its doctrinal indifferentism) was the prevailing spirit in all the mainstream denominations. That meant that evangelicals could never gain approval and influence in these denominations if they remained apart.

But to be welcomed to discussions by fellow denominationalists they would need to act *as though they did not believe* the very thing they were rightly accused of believing, namely, that there is no real unity without biblical and evangelical belief. Evangelical Anglicans professed to hold that conviction as much as Lloyd-Jones. Packer can write: 'What makes an evangelical will be that which in the eyes of the New Testament writers makes a Christian.'[1] Yet for the new policy introduced at Keele to succeed they would have to act as though they did not believe this. Certainly non-evangelicals would welcome 'contributions' to denominational and ecumenical discussions, but it would be unthinkable for evangelicals to say that those who deny Paul's gospel are no Christians at all. What was 'unchallengeable' in evangelical

---

[1] *Celebrating the Saving Work of God,* p. 75.

circles was the cause of deepest offence elsewhere.[1] The great argument, then, for Lloyd-Jones was about the gospel itself.[2] It was about what a Christian is, and how anyone becomes a Christian. So for him the questions at the heart of his appeal in the 1960s were these:

> Is it right to tolerate in the same church people whose views on the essentials of the faith are diametrically opposed? Is it right in the light of New Testament teaching that we regard such people as 'brethren'; that we refer to people who never darken the doors of a place of worship as 'lapsed Christians' simply because they have been baptized when infants? Is that compatible with the New Testament teaching with regard to the church, and her unity, and her discipline, and her life?[3]

As Dr Lloyd-Jones saw it, the biblical doctrine of the church was inevitably affected by the change upon which Anglican evangelicals had embarked. If they were to be consistent, the broad ecumenical view of 'Christian' would require a change in their ecclesiology. Hitherto all evangelicals had thought that no one should be regarded as belonging to Christ simply because they were outwardly connected with a church. James Barr complained: 'Conservative evangelicals hardly suppose, and certainly no

[1] See, for instance, James Barr, *Fundamentalism* (London: SCM, 1977 and Philadelphia: Westminster Press, 1978), p. 362, where the author holds up as 'harsh and rigid' the position of Lloyd-Jones which Packer defended over against Douglas Jones. Among the allegedly harsh words quoted by Barr from Lloyd-Jones on 'The Basis of Christian Unity' are these: 'If people question or query the great cardinal truths, "to regard them as brethren is to betray the truth".'

[2] D. A. Carson, a trans-Atlantic observer of this controversy, has written that Lloyd-Jones 'perceived that many were shifting from a view in which evangelicalism, at its best, is the locus of where the gospel is defended and proclaimed, to a view in which evangelicalism is one form of the gospel, within the cherished diversity of other equally valid forms in the national church. What was at stake for him was the gospel . . . his reading of trends was both accurate and prophetic.' *The Anglican Evangelical Crisis*, ed. Melvin Tinker (Fearn, Ross-shire: Christian Focus, 1995), p. 217.

[3] Lloyd-Jones, *The Puritans: Their Origins and Successors* (Edinburgh: Banner of Truth, 1987), p. 69.

fundamentalist supposes, that these bodies [the denominations] are conterminous with the community of true believers.'[1] After NEAC 1 change on this point was not long in coming and the proposal that church membership should be treated as *enough* to justify a person's Christian status gained increasing support. It is true that this change was not thought out at Keele. Colin Buchanan (the evangelical associated with Packer in a number of published items) refers to it as 'an unconscious shift of ecclesiology'; 'a half-underground doctrine was evident at Keele and was motivating this wide swathe of people'.[2]

The fact was that the new commitment to a wider comprehensiveness could not be defended by the earlier evangelical convictions. A new theory would have to be found to justify it, and by the 1970s it was being confidently announced that just such a theory had been found. If, it was argued, 'baptism is the visible sign of a Christian', then a New Testament ecclesiology requires us to practise unity with all the baptized. This was forcefully presented by Gervase Duffield, Anglican layman, writer and publisher, who was also, for a time, the manager of the London office of *Christianity Today*.[3] In John King's book *Evangelicals Today*, published in 1973, Duffield claimed that the only alternative to the 'Anabaptist' view of church membership was the position of 'those who held a multitudinous view of the Church as the company of the baptized'.[4] Evangelicals outside the Church

[1] *Fundamentalism*, p. 30.

[2] Colin Buchanan, *Is the Church of England Biblical? An Anglican Ecclesiology* (London: Darton, Longman and Todd, 1998), pp. 11, 13.

[3] Opened on Fleet Street in 1961. 'In view of Graham's enlarging ministries in Britain, both Graham and Jerry Beavan encouraged the possibility' (Henry, *Confessions*, pp. 201–2).

[4] Duffield, 'Involvement', in *Evangelicals Today*, p. 163. These words appear in the same book in which Packer stresses the *spiritual* nature of the church: 'The Church is essentially a community of believers, chosen in Christ and united to him by the Spirit through faith' (p. 23). This apparent disagreement did not seem to trouble King, the editor, who forewarned the reader that the work is not 'sweetly harmonious' (p. 9), and that 'evangelicalism today is a tumultous, surging youthful, inquiring phenomenon.'

of England, he wrote, 'wondered why on earth fellow Evangelicals hobnobbed with Anglo-Catholics and Liberals many of whom appeared to be very nominal Christians and some of whom actively disliked Evangelical enthusiasm.' The reason was simple: 'The doctrine of the church was rediscovered', and, 'Rediscovering ecclesiology inevitably meant church involvement'. This new understanding, he added, 'went against the narrow parish pump mentality which still dominates many Evangelical clergy'.[1]

Duffield regretted that the old brigade in the Church of England followed such men as the eighteenth-century leader John Berridge who 'seems to have held an inadequate doctrine of baptism and the Church, and went round insisting that admission to the Church was not baptism but conversion'.[2] He also regretted that evangelical Nonconformists had not made the same 'discovery' of the true doctrine of the church and he tells us loftily, 'One simply cannot do serious theology when there are major divides on basic matters like the sacraments and the Church.' He goes on to commend Billy Graham for his recognition of the need to send converts to all churches, although that 'has caused division among Evangelicals, between the separatists and the multitudinous church Evangelicals (mainly Anglicans in England)'.[3] This statement, from someone as well placed as Duffield in evangelical circles, confirms what we have said above on the effect of Graham's policy on the thinking of Anglican evangelicals.

This was the thinking which found formal expression in the Statement of the second National Evangelical Anglican Congress which met at Nottingham in 1977. While John Stott, again the chairman, said that 'a new doctrine of the church was needed',[4] a younger generation of clergy had already made up their minds on the subject. Their number included such men as Colin Buchanan, David Watson and

---

[1] *Ibid.*, p. 162.   [2] *Ibid.*, p. 172.   [3] *Ibid.*, p. 173.

[4] John Capon, *Evangelicals Tomorrow: A Popular Report of Nottingham '77, the National Evangelical Anglican Congress* (Glasgow: Collins, 1977), p. 18.

Michael Saward. Buchanan – 'the whizz-kid of the time' as Michael Smout called him[1] – amply confirmed that Duffield had not simply been speaking for himself. Watson deplored the division of the church at the Reformation and spoke of 'the profound grief that God must feel at the separation of his body'.[2] Saward has written of his changed views on the same subject and of his commitment from the mid-sixties 'to the doctrine of the church which has increasingly been at the root of Evangelical Anglican ecclesiology in the ensuing quarter of a century'.[3] The leading idea in this doctrine begins the section 'The Church and Its Identity' in the published Statement of the Nottingham Congress. It reads: 'The church on earth is marked out by Baptism, which is the complete sacramental initiation into Christ and his body'.[4]

In his book, *Is the Church of England Biblical?*, published in 1998, Colin Buchanan – by that date Bishop of Woolwich – elaborated on this change in understanding and said why he believed the older evangelical or 'constitutionalist' position had become impossible to maintain. His main reason is that

[1] M. Smout, 77 *Notts Untied* (London: Lakeland, 1977), p. 36.

[2] Capon, *Evangelicals Tomorrow*, p. 61. The statement was repeated and explained in Watson's *I Believe in the Church* (London: Hodder & Stoughton, 1978), p. 348. Michael Harper, also a speaker at Nottingham, believed that the ministry of David Watson (1933–84) 'helped forward proper ecumenism more than perhaps anyone else's in Britain during that time'. *David Watson: A Portrait by His Friends*, ed. Edward England (Crowborough: Highland Books, 1985), p. 57–8.

[3] Michael Saward, *A Faint Streak of Humility: An Autobiography* (Carlisle: Paternoster, 1999), p. 219.

[4] *The Nottingham Statement* (London: CPAS, 1977), p. 19. A vital qualification that baptism is not efficacious without faith, which was proposed at draft stage, was omitted (*Evangelicals Tomorrow*, p. 157), in stark contrast to the older Anglican and Protestant teaching. William Beveridge, Bishop of St Asaph, in his *Discourse Upon the Thirty-Nine Articles Agreed Upon in the Convocation held at London 1762*, commented on how faith preceded baptism in Acts 2:41, 'And therefore the church must needs be a congregation of faithful [i.e. believing] men, for until they be faithful men they cannot be of the church', vol. 2, (repr., Oxford, 1840), p. 104. This is not to deny infant baptism, but the New Testament does not treat infant baptism as the norm. Baptism is to strengthen faith, not to create it.

as evangelicals represented only ten per cent of the Church of England they had 'lost touch with reality' in viewing *themselves* as the true Church of England.[1] And, further, he reasons at length that the former evangelical exclusivism was untenable because it meant ignoring that 'baptism incorporates the candidate into the Church and *treats* him or her as Christian.'[2]

This case for a new ecclesiology presented since Keele fails to address a very major consideration. It is the fact that the doctrine of the church which was now being approved was not a new discovery at all. It was basically the very doctrine against which the Reformers had protested. Buchanan argues that it was *not* Scripture but 'a product of Western Protestantism' which saw the church as 'individual converts' rather than as a 'body', entered by baptism; and he attributes this perceived error to the way Protestantism, 'having seized upon a doctrine of individual justification by faith, then so enthrones that individualistic doctrine as to make all other scriptural truths function as servant to it'.[3]

But the argument which the Reformers used against equating 'church' with 'Christian' is the same argument to which Buchanan himself appeals in a different context, namely, that it was out of touch with reality. Before the Reformation, 'All were necessarily Christian', Buchanan writes.[4] Precisely so, if it is meant that being baptized and belonging to the 'church' equals 'Christian'. In protest against such an assumption the Reformation asserted a gospel which had at its heart the justification of the believing, repentant

---

[1] Buchanan, *Is the Church of England Biblical?*, p. 8.

[2] *Ibid.,* p. 81. It is by no means clear how Buchanan can argue this when he concedes that the baptism so commonly practised in the Church of England is not in accord with Scripture. The New Testament, he holds, only warrants the baptism of believers' children, not 'children from unbelieving homes' (p. 83). Instead of treating the baptized millions who rarely go near a church as 'really members of the Church' he suggests they can be seen as 'self-excommunicate' (p. 285), but the truth is that the vast majority should never have been baptized in the first place.

[3] *Ibid.,* pp. 142–3.   [4] *Ibid.,* p. 281.

sinner by Christ alone, and this message they held to be so paramount that, *without it*, church and sacraments are all of no avail for salvation. This was the gospel which threw the organized church into uproar in the sixteenth century – just as it had done in the Jewish church of the first century. The Reformers would have had to shut their Bibles before they could have regarded all their baptized contemporaries as Christians.

The question why the Church of England has so often possessed comparatively few of evangelical (gospel) belief is beyond our present discussion,[1] but this was the case in the sixteenth century and in the eighteenth. John Newton, for instance, could write in 1801: 'I am told there are about ten thousand parishes in England; I believe more than nine thousand of these are destitute of the gospel.'[2]

More to our purpose is the fact that much the same situation prevails today. It is said that out of some twenty-six million baptized members of the Church of England, less than one million go regularly to church.[3] For those who do attend there is by no means the assurance that they will hear the truth for, to quote Dr Packer again, 'In many parish churches today something quite other than the gospel of the Articles is preached and taught.'[4] He could affirm this from experience for it is on record that he was baptized and then confirmed in an apparently Anglo-Catholic context without knowing anything of a saving experience of Christ.[5]

[1] One reason is given by Ryle: 'Our Reformers themselves were not perfect men, and the characteristic jealousy of Queen Elizabeth prevented their perfecting the work of the English Reformation.' *The Upper Room* (repr. London: Banner of Truth, 1970), p. 331.

[2] *Letters and Conversational Remarks by John Newton During the Last Eighteen Years of His Life* (London: Burditt, 1809), p. 146.

[3] This was an estimate in 1999. As in all mainline denominations, the attendance figures fell in the Church of England, it is said, by 15 per cent in the 1980s (*Churchman*, vol. 107, no. 2, p. 155).

[4] *The Thirty-Nine Articles*, p. 12.

[5] See McGrath, *Packer,* pp. 7, 17–20. When he entered into new life, says McGrath, 'Packer was angry with the Church of England . . . Why had it not told him of the need for conversion?'

In language stronger than we would wish to use, Buchanan himself has written of his own denomination: 'One suspects that many congregations do indeed have the half-converted and the half-believing attending preaching services in a half-hearted way ...The sheer undiluted, unmitigated theological ignorance of virtually every worshipper is breath taking.'[1]

If, then, gospel belief and gospel preaching is not the norm in the Church of England, how can those who refused to treat the twenty-six-million baptized as Christians be put down as 'out of touch'? And what is to be thought of the many clergy who have baptized these millions and yet have never preached the gospel? With the New Testament as the guide it is clear that it was the older evangelicals who were in touch with *spiritual realities* and that it was faithfulness to Christ which often required them to stand apart within the Church of England. They believed it was vital for the gospel's sake to do so. To have given the impression that there were no fundamental differences between their message and practice and that of many fellow Anglicans, would have been to disown their mission. They held, in the words of one writer, that 'they and they alone [that is, among Anglicans] were charged with bringing the gospel to a benighted nation'.[2] They did not believe that belonging to the Church of England required them to treat all those baptized as Christians. Their position was rather that of Dr Isaac Milner, an evangelical leader at the end of the eighteenth century who was President of Queen's College, Cambridge, and Dean of Carlisle. Milner's biographer wrote:

> He was decidedly of opinion, that whatsoever difficulties might exist in ascertaining the exact benefits accompanying baptism, we ought boldly and unshrinkingly to designate by the term Regeneration, the inward change and conversion of the heart to God, by whatever means it might be effected, and to address those as unregenerate who were evidently without

[1] *Evangelicals Today,* pp. 70, 72.
[2] Gerald Bray, reviewing McGrath's biography of Packer, *Churchman,* vol. 111, no. 4 (Watford, Herts: Church Society, 1998), p. 359.

The New Anglican Evangelicalism Versus the Old

any spiritual life. This, he apprehended, had been uniformly the language of all our greatest divines, from the time of the Reformation.[1]

Ryle was equally against treating the baptized as necessarily regenerate and against the confirmation of those who gave no evidence of conversion. In the same connection he viewed the Anglo-Catholic teaching on the sacraments as imperilling the souls of men:

> There is, I am afraid, a sad disposition to give way and recede from Protestant truth in this direction. Partly from a fear of not honouring the sacraments enough, partly from the pressure of modern ritualistic teaching, there is a strong tendency to exalt baptism and the Lord's Supper to a place never given to them in Scripture . . . Multitudes live and die in the secret belief that they were 'born again', and received the grace of the Spirit in baptism, though from their infancy they have known nothing of what the Church Catechism calls 'a death unto sin and a new birth unto righteousness'. They are not 'dead to sin', but actually live in it! Multitudes more are continually receiving the Lord's Supper under the belief that somehow or other *it must do them good,* though they are destitute of the Catechism standard, and neither 'repent of sin', nor 'purpose to lead a new life', nor 'have a lively faith in God's mercy in Christ'.[2]

[1] Mary Milner, *The Life of Isaac Milner* (London: Parker, 1842), p. 642. For his thoughts on 'some confusion' in the language of the Prayer Book see p. 376. It was well for Britain and Africa that Milner treated worldly churchmen as unregenerate or he would never have been the means of the conversion of William Wilberforce. It was in the home of Wilberforce that he died in 1820. In his latest book John Stott says : 'We strongly insist that baptism must never be confused with the new birth', *Evangelical Truth: A Personal Plea for Unity* (Leicester: IVP, 1999), p. 109. But it *was* confused at NEAC 2 and thereafter.

[2] Ryle, *Principles for Churchmen* (London: Hunt, 1884), pp. 20–22. Clergy unfaithful to the 'doctrinal evangelicalism' of the Thirty-Nine Articles were the problem: 'I do not want to unchurch them, so long as they honestly and *ex animo* subscribe to the Thirty-Nine Articles. Papists, Socinians, and infidels are certainly in the wrong place in the Church of England, and I cannot tolerate them' (*Principles for Churchmen,* p. 24).

When Duffield alleged that a choice must be made between the 'Anabaptist' view of church membership and the 'multitudinous view of the Church as the company of the baptized', he was utterly ignoring the Anglican evangelical literature of former years which presents a very different position. William Goode, a leading Anglican evangelical theologian of the last century, characterized the opinion that there is 'no distinction between the members of the nominal church, but that all who are baptized are alike regarded by Christ as members of his body' as the very teaching which the Reformers denied: 'The modern "high Church" notion of all the baptized receiving indiscriminately the full baptismal blessing was opposed by them all.'[1] Edward A. Litton likewise wrote his magisterial book, *The Church of Christ*, from the standpoint of 'evangelical Protestantism, the Protestantism of Luther, Calvin, and our own reformers, as distinguished from the political, eclectic, and rationalistic systems which, at different times, have taken its place.'[2] On how that standpoint differs from the Roman Catholic he writes:

> The Romanist, while admitting that there is, or ought to be, in the Church an interior life, not cognisable by human eye, yet regards this as a separable accident, and makes the essence of the Church to consist in what is external and visible: the Protestant, on the contrary, while admitting that to be invisible is an inseparable property of the Church, makes the essence thereof to consist in what is spiritual and unseen; *viz.* the work of the Holy Spirit in the hearts of Christians.[3]

Non-evangelicals of Catholic persuasion have always complained that 'evangelicals have no doctrine of the church'. What they mean is that evangelicals 'demean the

---

[1] W. Goode, *The Doctrine of the Church of England as to the Effects of Baptism in the Case of Infants*, 2nd ed. (London: Hatchard, 1850), p. 26.

[2] E. A. Litton, *The Church of Christ, in Its Idea, Attributes and Ministry* (London: Longman, 1851), p. ix.

[3] *Ibid.*, p. 70.

church' by holding that an external connection with a church saves no one. The evangelical reply to the charge was that it is the presence of spiritual life and not names, organization or external unity which make the church, and only where this is to be found does the church exist. Thus Article XIX of the Thirty-Nine Articles begins: 'The visible Church of Christ is a congregation of faithful men, in which the pure word of God is preached and the Sacraments duly administered according to Christ's ordinance.' It is no wonder that Anglo-Catholics laboured for years to have the exclusive authority of the Articles set aside in the Church.

* * * *

This deviation from former evangelical teaching on the nature of the unity of the church was to have another consequence. If Christian unity was no longer to be defined in terms of evangelical belief, then the former evangelical boundaries of fellowship had to be regarded as needlessly exclusive and sectarian. And if this was so, what need remained for the continuance of a distinct evangelical 'party' in the Church of England? On what grounds could a party be justified – especially as its existence ever created suspicions among non-evangelical Anglicans that their new associates did not quite mean what they said about unity? The logical consequence of the Keele commitment to church unity was that the previous so-called evangelical party could disappear or at least become so indistinct that its survival would be no great concern. So in 1969 the Rev. John King, a former editor of the *Church of England Newspaper* and an apologist for Keele, was pleased that that 'monolithic evangelical unity' had given way to a new 'church consciousness'.[1] 'The outstanding effect of Keele', he wrote, 'was to deal a death-blow to the idea of an Evangelical unity existing as a kind of alternative to the ecumenical movement.'[2] Evangelical Anglicans

[1] John C. King, *The Evangelicals* (London: Hodder & Stoughton, 1969), pp. 122, 150.
[2] *Ibid.*, p. 120.

were now to think of themselves as being first of all Anglicans, 'not Evangelicals who happen to be Anglicans'.[1] Those who continued to speak of themselves as 'Christians first, and Church of England Christians in the second place'[2] risked being described as adherents to 'separatist elements' within the Church and supporters of 'evangelical exclusiveness'.[3] In King's book of 1973, from which we have already quoted, 'traditional evangelicalism' was criticized for such things as the way it dealt with the question, 'What is a Christian?', and for its policy of encouraging attendance at 'only strictly evangelical churches'. 'Evangelicals,' it was affirmed, 'recognize other Anglicans as fellow Christians however critical they are of Evangelicalism.'[4] The idea that Anglo-Catholic or other beliefs endangered the gospel itself was now regarded by many as archaic and the product of ignorant bigotry.

By the time that the second National Evangelical Anglican Congress met at Nottingham in 1977 the continued existence of an evangelical party within the Church of England was a matter of discussion. Colin Buchanan wrote: '*The* great question-mark which had to be hung against the proposal that "we" should hold another Congress in 1977 was whether there existed any identifiable "we" to do it.'[5]

---

[1] *Ibid.*, p. 146.

[2] The words are those of Canon A. M. W. Christopher, long-time rector of St Aldates, Oxford, and spoken in connection with his belief that evangelical Anglicans had more in common with Nonconformist Christians than with the Anglo-Catholic ritualists in his own denomination. J. S. Reynolds, *Canon Christopher of St Aldates, Oxford* (Abingdon: Abbey Press, 1967), p. 251.

[3] See Randle Manwaring's use of the phrase, *Controversy to Co-Existence,* p. 208.

[4] *Evangelicals Today,* p. 169.

[5] *Church of England Newspaper*, 11 March 1977. David Bebbington, who draws attention to this quotation, also quotes a *CEN* reviewer who asked 'whether the traditional evangelical understanding of the Gospel is in fact as biblical as it is often assumed to be.' *Evangelicalism in Modern Britain: A History from the 1730s to the 1980s* (London: Unwin Hyman, 1989), p. 269.

Donald Coggan and Stuart Blanch, the Archbishops of Canterbury and York respectively, were both asked to speak at Nottingham, being assured when the invitation was given 'that most Evangelicals were anxious that they should not appear to be entrenching themselves as a party'.[1] The assurance was important for two men who had themselves once been evangelicals. A few years before Blanch had confessed that while he was still prepared to be thought of as an evangelical, 'I no longer find this distinction the slightest bit meaningful.' It was hardly surprising that ordinands leaving the traditionally evangelical Anglican theological colleges began to speak in the same way. In the opinion of John Capon, the Nottingham Congress was leading to the 'end of the evangelical "party" in the Church of England. Some would say it has come to an end already'.[2] David Wells has commented on the Nottingham milestone:

> Although this transition in English Anglicanism was a matter of complexity, it is difficult to resist the conclusion that at its heart was the change from an essentially confessional movement to one that, on its own terms and through its own ecclesiastical culture, had become transconfessional [that is, ready to embrace divergent beliefs].[3]

Michael Smout was surely right in identifying the issue which Nottingham left unresolved. He wrote at the time:

> Evangelicals need to pray for an outstanding theologian on the doctrine of the Church to arise soon, very soon in fact. Unless this happens the tension between being an Evangelical and also a member of a comprehensive Church could split the movement wide open. The more Evangelicals commit themselves to the Church of England the more of a problem this tension becomes.[4]

[1] Margaret Pawley, *Donald Coggan* (London: SPCK, 1987), p. 224.

[2] Capon, *Evangelicals Tomorrow*, p. 181.

[3] *Evangelicalism: Comparative Studies of Popular Protestantism in North America, the British Isles and Beyond, 1700–1990*, eds. M. A. Noll, D. W. Bebbington, G. A. Rawlyk (New York: OUP, 1994), pp. 397-8.

[4] Smout, *77 Notts Untied*, p. 65.

As I close this chapter a caution needs to be added. Because Anglican evangelicals with the highest profile as speakers and writers, such as Stott and Packer, all appeared to speak for the Keele policy it could seem that there was no divergence of opinion among Anglican evangelicals. This was not the case. Canon Colin Craston could write in the *Church of England Newspaper* (21 February 1969): 'The great divide among evangelicals – the question of evangelical involvement – is increasingly apparent despite valiant attempts by many to hold the two sides together.'

There were clearly clergy with a less public profile who continued in the convictions with which the evangelical party had always been identified. One of these was the Rev. Alan Stibbs, long-time Inter-Varsity leader and a tutor at Oak Hill Theological College, London. From 1960 Stibbs had served with Oliver Barclay and others on the Church of England Evangelical Council, a policy-making group chaired by John Stott. Dr Barclay has written: 'When Alan Stibbs and I were invited to attend a meeting in 1971, he left almost in tears at what he felt was its departure from his hopes for it.'[1]

Nor was the grief only amongst Anglicans. For Lloyd-Jones the public parting with John Stott in 1966 and, finally, Jim Packer in 1970, marked the saddest period in his life. McGrath is mistaken to talk about the 'bitterness' which marked this separation on the Nonconformist evangelical side; and he is no less wrong to say that 'it was those who advised Lloyd-Jones, rather than the "Doctor" himself, who appear to have been responsible for this hard-line attitude.'[2] Lloyd-Jones was never 'advised' by men thirty years his

---

[1] Barclay, *Evangelicalism in Britain 1935–1995*, p. 85. Stibbs in 1942 was one of the first members of what became known as the Westminster Fellowship, a monthly fraternal of ministers which met at Westminster Chapel under the chairmanship of Lloyd-Jones. Of the controversy resulting from *Growing Into Union* in 1970 Lloyd-Jones commented, 'Stibbs is very upset about it all'. *D. Martyn Lloyd-Jones:Letters 1919–1981* (Edinburgh: Banner of Truth, 1994), p. 182.

[2] McGrath, *Packer*, pp. 160, 158.

junior, and the younger men closest to him were often slow to accept a break with Packer because, unlike Lloyd-Jones, they had some personal indebtedness to him in the recovery of Reformed and Puritan beliefs. They could see that a division with Packer would weaken a unity of Calvinistic belief. But for Lloyd-Jones evangelical unity took a definite priority over that consideration and it was that unity which, he believed, had broken down at Keele.

The parting of Anglican and non-Anglican evangelicals was a parting of friends yet the recognition that the division was over principles, not personalities, did not lessen the sadness on all sides. 'We must remember', Lloyd-Jones emphasized, 'that men who are equally honest may differ.'[1] Some time after the public disagreement at Westminster Central Hall in October 1966, writes John Stott, 'I called on Dr Lloyd-Jones to apologize – not for what I had said (which I still believe) – but for misusing the chair and almost turning the meeting (as he put it) into a "debate". . . . But we continued to have a warm personal relationship.'[2]

[1] Murray, Lloyd-Jones, *Fight of Faith*, p. 567.
[2] 'An Appreciation' in *Martyn Lloyd-Jones: Chosen by God*, p. 207.

5

How the Evangelical
Dyke Was Broken
in England

'The beginning of strife', says the book of Proverbs, 'is like the releasing of waters' (17:14), for there are certain things which, once started, cannot be stopped. To that order belongs the debate opened at Keele in 1967. The flood that followed showed that a dyke had been broken. It is said that one embankment breached in the great Mississippi flood of 1927 inundated an area fifty miles wide and one hundred miles long, and left towards 200,000 people homeless. The spiritual consequences of the breach of 1967–70 were to have still wider consequences.

The evidence that Anglican evangelicals had come to accept a new kind of comprehensiveness is now part of history. In 1976 Packer and Michael Green, were signatories to a joint publication by the Church of England's Commission on Christian Doctrine entitled *Christian Believing*. The chairman of this Commission was Professor Maurice Wiles, well known for his subsequent denial of the deity of Christ in his book *The Myth of God Incarnate*. The liberalism for which Wiles stood was very evident in the document. A review of *Christian Believing* in *The Times* (26 August 1974) asserted that it 'makes doubt respectable', and was 'an endorsement of those . . . who have turned their backs on church-made dogma'.

Christian Believing was a mishmash which did not require its signatories to endorse its contents; it was descriptive, Packer would say, of what *was* rather than of what *ought to be*, yet while the two evangelical participants elsewhere disowned some of its unbelief, they were party to its intro-ductory statement which spoke of the benefit resulting to the church from the allowance of 'conflict between followers of our common Lord'. Together all the participants 'did not rule out' what they called 'competing attitudes' (that is, beliefs), for, they wrote, 'we are convinced that any such decision would be disastrous to the health of the church'. The dis-agreements were said to represent a 'creative tension': 'It is not simply an intellectual debate, but an unceasing effort of brothers in Christ.'[1] In other words, the ground rule of all ecumenical discussion was being followed and the promoters of unbelief, who played the main part in *Christian Believing,* were accorded the same right to the name of Christian as anyone else.

The recognition of liberal clergy as having a legitimate place in the Church of England followed on from the wider principles accepted at Keele. The words of Randle Manwaring on the Anglican evangelicals who supported Keele can hardly be disputed: 'They see other traditions as

---

[1] *Christian Believing* (London: SPCK, 1976). Packer has defended his participation in *Christian Believing* in *The Evangelical Anglican Identity Problem: An Analysis* (Oxford: Latimer House, 1978), pp. 4–5. The Doctrine Commission's report, he said, was intended to do no more than provide information on differing doctrinal views in the Church of England.

[113]

fully part of the Anglican Church, as indeed they must do, if they aspire to office within their Church.'[1] How this new outlook contrasted with the earlier one was common knowledge. Explaining history, John Stott could say: 'Evangelicals have dared to maintain that they are the Church of England in its purest form.'[2] In 1966, before Keele, *The Times* could say of the 'conservative evangelicals': 'With their strict adherence to scripture and the 39 Articles they are like no other part of the Church of England, and regard themselves as the true church . . . When the conservative evangelical talks of unity (and wants it) he means unity on his terms.'[3] Jim Packer's statements before 1965, and quoted above, confirm these words.

The way in which the Keele policy would change the way evangelicals understood evangelicalism had not been foreseen by Stott and Packer. Buchanan appears to be right in writing that at Keele 'the evangelical consitutency at large was ready to move, ready to move out of the last ditch, ready even to move without being absolutely sure what the point of arrival would be'.[4] Nor when the 'point of arrival' began to emerge did the two best-known leaders seem to recognize it. Both men continued to speak of the Christian faith and the evangelical faith as one and the same thing, and of gospel unity as the only unity.[5] In 1982 Stott could still assert, 'The evangelical faith is nothing other than the historic Christian faith.'[6] 'The Church of England', Packer wrote in 1977, 'is not a multi-faith Church; its Articles commit it to evangelical essentials.'[7] At the same date he said, in a preface to a reprint

---

[1] *Controversy to Co-Existence,* p. xi

[2] Dudley-Smith, *John Stott,* p. 219.

[3] 'Scant Hope for Establishment with Complete Spiritual Autonomy', *The Times,* 25 May 1966.

[4] Buchanan, *Is the Church of England Biblical?* p. 10 n.

[5] See Stott, *Christ the Controversialist* (London: Tyndale Press, 1970), p. 33. In the same book a fine chapter is entitled 'A Plea for Evangelical Unity'. 'The evangelical's sincerely held belief', Dr Stott writes, 'is that his very loyalty to Christ requires him to hold evangelical views.'

[6] Dudley-Smith, *John Stott,* p. 15.

[7] R. T. Beckwith, G. E. Duffield, J. I. Packer, *Across the Divide* (Abingdon, Berks: Marcham Books, 1977) p. 31.

of a volume by W. H. Griffith Thomas, 'Real Anglicanism is evangelicalism in pure form', and he continued, with apparent approval, to say of Griffith Thomas: 'Within the Anglican fold he saw himself and those whose views he shared not as party eccentrics who needed to beg for toleration, but as mainstream churchmen recalling their benighted brethren to a true Anglican identity.'[1]

On the basis of such words, McGrath affirms that Packer continued 'following his own consistent reforming agenda'.[2] But how was this consistent? If true Anglicanism *means* being evangelical then the Keele policy of embracing all clergy as fellow-labourers could only be interpreted in one of two ways: it had to mean either a retreat, *in practice,* from an insistence on evangelicalism, or that there had been a discovery that the 'benighted brethren' were themselves evangelical after all. The first of these interpretations is the one which Packer himself was finally to concede.

In a publication of 1978 Packer puts the issue:

> Is Anglican comprehensiveness a matter of not insisting on more than the gospel as a basis of fellowship, or of not insisting on the gospel at all? No outsider could be blamed for concluding that it is the second, for that is what you see when you look at the church today.[3]

At that point he did not answer the question himself. His answer came in his subsequent paperback, *A Kind of Noah's Ark? The Anglican Commitment to Comprehensiveness,* published in 1981, where he concludes that Anglican comprehensiveness cannot be limited by gospel believing:

> I submit that evangelicals were right to approve the older type of comprehensiveness, based on common acceptance of the fundamentals of the creed, but that they cannot and, for a fact, do not commend or condone what that historic

---

[1] Preface to 1977 reprint of W. H. Griffith Thomas, *The Principles of Theology* (London and Grand Rapids: Vine Books and Baker, 1977).

[2] McGrath, *Packer,* p. 127.

[3] *Identity Problem,* p. 35.

comprehensiveness has now turned into. They accept it reluctantly and with sorrow.[1]

So the gospel could no longer be insisted on as the basis of fellowship for, facing the realities of the situation, evangelicals now had to take what Packer calls 'the hard-made decision' and, despite regrets, support something broader.

Here was plain acknowledgement that the policy adopted since Keele had forced a retreat from earlier convictions. Instead, however, of treating this change as a temporary expedient, justifiable perhaps in terms of long-term gain, Packer surprisingly proceeded to argue that the decision 'is one of principle – namely, that the way in which Anglican tolerance obliges you to cope with Anglican doctrinal disorder is, though taxing, the best way both for you and for the Church as a whole'.[2]

This sounds like a commendation of the very change which Packer has just said evangelicals 'do not commend or condone'. The impression is deepened as he tells us of those evangelical Anglicans, 'a generation back', who were guilty 'of an unlovely intellectual perfectionism and self-sufficiency': 'When they listened to other professed Christians, it was not so much to learn from them as to controvert them and put them straight'; that generation did not expect 'new insights into the meaning of Scripture' from 'non-evangelical partners'.[3]

In contrast with such an attitude, he sees real benefit in 'accepting Anglicanism's present doctrinal plurality . . . The risks of this procedure (unending pluralism, constant muddle, public vacillation and embarrassment) are high; however, its benefits (ripe convictions emerging from a long hard look at alternatives) make the risks worth taking.'[4]

[1] Packer, *A Kind of Noah's Ark? The Anglican Commitment to Comprehensiveness* (Oxford: Latimer House, 1981) p. 35.   [2] *Ibid.*, p. 39
[3] *Identity Problem*, pp. 11, 31.
[4] Packer, *A Kind of Noah's Ark?*, p. 34. An early use of Noah's ark as an illustration is found in Callistus who became pope at Rome in 217. Hippolytus reported him to say: 'Let the tares grow to the harvest, that is, let the sinners remain in the Church . . . the ark of Noah was made

Setting aside the question whether this reason for acceptance of the change is consistent with approving 'the older
type of comprehensiveness', I want rather to question the
ambiguity of his criticism of former evangelicals. Dr Packer
does not say that they should have been willing to learn about
'the gospel' from their non-evangelical fellow churchmen.
We should like to assume that he does not mean that.[1] Does
he mean then that evangelicals once held the view that they
could learn nothing about anything from others, that they
had arrived at all light on everything? He can hardly mean
such a thing. This was not what the generation of Griffith
Thomas implied when they regarded non-evangelical clergy
as 'benighted'. The great argument between evangelicals and
others had never been about knowledge or scholarship in
general. The divide then (as now) was over the gospel itself;
it was evangelical 'exclusiveness' over the gospel which had
always drawn the opposition of others and the fundamental
issue had not changed.

In a denomination which, by Packer's admission, was in
'doctrinal disarray', *the* question which non-evangelical and
ecumenical churchmen wanted evangelicals to answer was
whether or not they stood by their old exclusiveness. To that
question Keele had given an emphatic answer in 1967, and if
it had not done so it would never have satisfied the non-
evangelicals as it did. But what Keele left unexplained was
how evangelicals could hold to the uniqueness of their

---

into an image of the church wherein were dogs and wolves and crows
and all clean and unclean things' (quoted in S. L. Greenslade, *Schism in
the Early Church*. London: SCM, 1964, p. 112).

[1] His ambiguity leaves some uncertainty here. He does say elsewhere,
'Catholics have helped evangelicals to see Christianity as the baptismal
life' (*A Kind of Noah's Ark?*, p. 25). In that case, evangelicals have more to
learn about the gospel from others and Packer is in major disagreement
with the older evangelicalism. Catholic teaching on the relation of
baptism to the gospel is radically different from the evangelical: the
former teaches that sacraments convey grace 'by their own power': the
latter (with the Thirty-Nine Articles) that there is no grace *without faith*.

gospel message and yet profess brotherhood with those whose teaching subverts that gospel. As I have said, the new policy had to mean that evangelicals would be forced to deny in practice what they taught in theory. It was the recognition of this fact which in due course led to the change in theory as we have seen in Packer's words on his 'hard-made decision'. A number who followed him were to go further. Gervase Duffield's 'rediscovery' we have already quoted. Alister McGrath, a major critic of the older evangelicals, says outright: 'I have no intention of claiming that evangelicalism is the only authentic form of Anglicanism. My concern is simply to insist that evangelicalism is . . . a legitimate and respectable option.'[1]

From a different standpoint Dr Gerald Bray, another Anglican evangelical, has written, 'As evangelicals work their way into the structures of the Establishment, so they are forced to compromise.'[2] The hope of the 1960s that they could both enter into fuller involvement and keep their own ground rules was unfulfilled. 'Co-operation without compromise' had proved an illusion. Whatever the initial hopes, evangelicals, after all, had found themselves in the position of 'contributing insights' and displaying the 'open mind' so approved by ecumenism.

Non-evangelical Anglicans saw the change and highly approved. Mervyn Stockwood, liberal Anglo-Catholic Bishop of Southwark, was one of many who welcomed the 'new school of evangelicals which while continuing to make a distinctive contribution was open-minded and flexible'.[3] Traditional evangelical beliefs, says Stockwood's biographer, 'he did not particularly admire'. That is an understatement. Stockwood made a practice of 'wooing evangelicals' by all means, including mockery: 'I know you Tyndale men,' he

[1] *Evangelical Anglicans: Their Role and Influence in the Church Today*, eds., R. T. France and A. E. McGrath (London: SPCK, 1993), p. 13.

[2] *Churchman*, vol. 110, no. 1, p. 3.

[3] Stockwood, *Chanctonbury Ring*, p. 154, quoted by Manwaring, *Controversy to Co-Existence*, p. 145.

would say to young clergy from the denomination's most conservative college, 'all out in the garden with your telescopes, looking for the second coming'.[1] Evangelicals who became 'open-minded' could get on well enough in Southwark.

Another worker for a change in evangelicals was David Edwards who in 1977 complained that James Barr, the hostile critic of fundamentalism, had failed to notice that 'Mr Stott has, like the rest of us, gradually changed his mind or at least his emphasis.'[2] Edwards, in due course Provost of South-wark and himself a liberal, was to demonstrate the existence of evangelical change in a book co-authored with John Stott in 1988 entitled, *Essentials: A Liberal-Evangelical Dialogue.* Edwards rejected most of the essentials of the Christian faith, including the fall of man, the need for atonement by a divine redeemer and Christ's physical resurrection. Yet in this dialogue Dr Stott held to the new inclusiveness. Those who deny the virgin birth and the bodily resurrection of Christ, he affirmed, do not 'forfeit the right to be called Christians'.[3] This he underlined by a gratuitous reference to David Jenkins, Bishop of Durham, who had made headlines with his denial of the physical resurrection of Christ. Even although an archaeologist should find bones which could reasonably be proved to be the bones of Christ, such a discovery would not disprove the 'resurrection', according to Jenkins. Had there been no physical resurrection, it would make no difference to Christianity. Yet there was room, John Stott supposed, for evangelicals to agree even with Jenkins:

> A year or two ago Bishop David Jenkins kindly spent a couple of hours with five of us Evangelicals who wanted to

---

[1] De-la-Noy, *Stockwood,* pp. 144–5. Evangelicals in his diocese who were not 'open-minded' could experience his rage. Under Stockwood the Southwark diocese became what he called the centre of 'South Bank Religion'.

[2] *Church Times,* 15 July 1977, quoted by Manwaring, *Controversy to Co-Existence,* p. 115.

[3] David L. Edwards with John Stott, *Essentials: A Liberal-Evangelical Dialogue* (London: Hodder and Stoughton, 1988), p. 228.

engage in questioning and discussion with him . . . He was willing to concede that the bodily resurrection of Jesus, although in his view 'historically unverifiable' (because the story of the empty tomb was probably not written until twenty years or more after the event), could nevertheless be termed 'theologically appropriate'. There I think, was a man speaking out of his catholic tradition, but we Evangelicals endorsed it.[1]

This dialogue between Stott and Edwards was reviewed by the IVP magazine *Themelios,* a periodical which had once given theological students a definite lead in faithfulness to Scripture and was still formally committed to Inter-Varsity's strictly evangelical basis of faith. Yet in 1988, David Wenham, the editor of *Themelios,* commented as any liberal theological journal would have done fifty years earlier. Wenham deplored 'a tendency among evangelicals' to treat 'liberal Christians . . . virtually as non-Christians'. He was 'impressed by David Edwards' sincere Christian profession' and believed it was unworthy of evangelicals to entertain 'a lurking suspicion that this cannot be genuine Christianity . . . If it is a question of priorities, we should remember that for Jesus it was a priority that his followers should live in love and unity.'[2]

This attitude was so established among Anglican evangelicals by the 1990s that it had become commonplace and needed no defence. In *Evangelical Anglicans* a symposium edited by two reputed evangelicals, the fashion of asking a

[1] *Ibid.,* p. 233. 'Theologically appropriate' because, the bishop thought, Christ 'survived . . . death had not put a stop to Jesus and his mission'. The sheer unbelief of Jenkins' teaching is plain in his writings; he denies the fall of man, the virgin birth, the resurrection, etc. See David and Rebecca Jenkins, *Free to Believe* (London: BBC Books, 1991), pp. 42–44, 85. If we are only to accept as much of Christ's work and words as *we can verify* 'historically' how much is left? Yet Jenkins claimed that his view of the Bible 'does not destroy its validity, it releases its power from the deep freeze, sets it in motion, allowing it to live' (*Ibid.,* p. 37).

[2] Editorial on 'Evangelical and Liberal Theology' in *Themelios,* Religious and Theological Students Fellowship, a constituent part of UCCF (formerly IVF) and IFES, October/November 1988.

non-evangelical to contribute, led the editors to approach Richard Holloway, the Bishop of Edinburgh, who is a liberal Catholic and a teacher who denies the physical resurrection of Christ. ('Why', asked one reviewer of this book, 'do evangelicals have to look constantly over their shoulder to see if their new clothes are being admired?'[1]) A piece from the bishop thus closed their book, under the title 'Evangelicalism: An Outsider's Perspective'. Holloway professed to see no relevance in the evangelical faith for the question how anyone becomes a Christian for 'we are incorporated into Christ by baptism and grace', but he conceded evangelicalism can help with how the Christian life is lived. He went on to spell out again what Ramsey had told the Keele Congress of 1967. Where evangelicals were prone to go wrong was in failing to see the theological differences between them and the liberal and the Catholic 'not as weaknesses, but as necessary aspects of the type of spiritual system we call a catholic church as opposed to a protestant "sect".'[2] Anglicans represent 'a very wide continuum of practice and belief', and the genuine Anglican 'will seek not only to acknowledge, but to understand and affirm expressions of the common faith that may not be entirely sympathetic to his or her own tastes and convictions.'[3]

As one of these 'tastes' Holloway instanced 'the evangelical preoccupation with the sin and redemption model of Christ's work'. He preferred what he called the New Testament's way which 'offered a series of metaphors to describe the Christian experience of salvation through Christ'. What was utterly inadmissible was making 'the substitutionary theory of the atonement one of the prime tests of doctrinal purity', and he deplored the practice of evangelical organizations who still sought to impose such tests.[4]

Once again, as with Michael Ramsey at Keele, this kind of lecture from a non-evangelical was left entirely unanswered

---

[1] Christopher Idle, *Churchman*, vol. 107, no. 3, p. 280.
[2] *Evangelical Anglicans*, p. 176.   [3] *Ibid.*, p. 178.   [4] *Ibid.*, pp. 179, 181.

by the editors of *Evangelical Anglicans*; instead they were anxious that their readers should know that they did not approve of the outlook of their namesakes of an earlier generation – the men of the 'narrow parish pump mentality'.[1] Christopher Idle, the Anglican reviewer of this book already quoted, says of the authors:

> They all seem committed to the myth of Keele. Before 1967 all was chaos and darkness; pietism, parochialism and isolation reigned unchallenged. Then a thousand evangelicals met, and there was light! . . . Like most myths, this cartoon has just enough truth to make it plausible. Writer after writer now passes it on, with no suggestion of anything lost in the process and no trace of the shudder among Free Church evangelicals. One day someone will write the story differently.[2]

* * * *

Given the importance of the change in Anglican evangelical thinking which we have outlined above, it might be expected that a well-argued defence for it is somewhere to be found. This does not appear to be the case. Colin Buchanan can write in 1998, 'The underlying shift in ecclesiology which Keele represented has never been properly charted'.[3] The truth seems to be that effective disagreement with the new policy was so small that it probably did not seem to need answering. Anglo-Catholic teaching was now so peacefully and generally accepted as a legitimate expression of the biblical gospel that the kind of convictions expressed by Packer in 1961, when upholding the Thirty-Nine Articles, were unthinkable. Packer himself was confident that a 'happy' change had taken place in the

---

[1] At one point, in relation to literary criticism, the question is raised whether the 'resurgent evangelicalism' (for which the authors were speaking) was not endorsing 'the slide towards a liberal position'. In response it is said, 'If evangelicalism were to be defined in terms of historical continuity, that might be so.' But for the new approach they claimed the authority of the Bible itself, not 'human traditions' (*Ibid.*, pp. 51–2)!

[2] *Churchman*, vol. 107, no. 3, p. 279.

[3] *Is the Church of England Biblical?*, p. 12.

convergence of Anglo-Catholicism and evangelicalism and
even on such an issue as 'the efficacy of baptism towards
salvation'.[1] He saw no problem in recognizing an essential
spiritual unity between the adherents of the two systems:

> Most evangelicals perceive that the faith which catholics
> inculcate looks to the Christ whose salvation the sacraments
> display, and not to the sacraments without the Saviour . . .
> Catholics have helped evangelicals to see Christianity as the
> baptismal life; evangelicals have helped catholics to see it as a
> life of joyful assurance and expectant prayer.[2]

By 'catholic' here Packer means 'Anglo-Catholic',[3] yet the
difference has little major significance for, in all but church
affiliation, the basic belief is the same. It was therefore logical
for the *Nottingham Statement* of the second National
Evanglical Anglican Congress to say, 'Seeing ourselves and
Roman Catholics as fellow-Christians, we repent of attitudes
that have seemed to deny it . . . We believe that the visible
unity of all professing Christians should be our goal.'[4]

Different issues were here being dangerously confused. No
one doubts that the grace of God may enable an individual
Anglo-Catholic or Roman Catholic to see beyond a dangerous ritualism and grasp enough of the gospel to be a
Christian. But it is another thing to say that the catholic
system *teaches the way of salvation truly,* that its priests are
colleagues in New Testament ministry, and that its adherents
are all entitled to be regarded as Christians. If, as it was said
by Packer in 1963, the way to a wider unity has to be
confessional, beginning with clergy and the ministers, then
the issue of *belief* must come first. What is the use of 'uniting'

---

[1] *A Kind of Noah's Ark,* p. 25.   [2] *Ibid.,* p. 25.
[3] The wording is changed to read 'Anglo-Catholic' in the reprint given
in *The Anglican Evangelical Crisis,* ed. Melvin Tinker, p. 118.
[4] The draft wording on Roman Catholics as fellow Christians was
changed after an objection from a Roman Catholic observer present who
complained that it contained 'no mention of repentance by Anglicans for
past misunderstanding of Roman Catholicism' (Capon, *Evangelicals
Tomorrow,* p. 91).

Christians if those who teach them disagree on the gospel? But whereas the Thirty-Nine Articles clearly ruled out any legitimacy for Catholic or Anglo-Catholic teaching, now it was thought wrong to doubt the Christian standing of its advocates.

When it comes to relations with liberal clergy, the evangelical thinking I am addressing holds that, while *in theory* they may not be Christians, in practice, as we have seen above, they are to be treated as colleagues and no effort is to be made (as it was before the 1960s) to stand apart. Inevitably this stance leads to a toning down of the New Testament warnings on the destructive character of unbelief. Such phrases as 'muddle headedness', 'intellectual besetting sin', and 'well-meant misbelief', do not do justice to what Scripture says on the seriousness of error within the church. Referring to the attitude of evangelicals to liberals who deny the very facts of the gospel, Packer says: 'Only by an agnostic judgment of charity can they treat exponents of non-incarnational Christianity as Christians.'[1] But what warrant is there in Scripture for thinking in this way? The possibility that such men may hold office in the church and be allowed to teach error and unbelief is utterly foreign to the New Testament. It is true that individuals may have saving faith in Christ and yet be babes in understanding. That is not, however, relevant to the present discussion, for ecumenical unity is chiefly pursued among those who claim to be the leaders and teachers of others. Scripture plainly leaves no room for leaders being babes.

Just how entrenched liberalism was in the leadership of the Church of England can be seen from the case of Robert Runcie. Runcie was trained in the 'elitist liberalism of Westcott House', Cambridge. It was there and at Cuddesdon that he prepared men for the ministry before he was made

---

[1] *A Kind of Noah's Ark*, p. 29. This section is reprinted in *The Anglican Evangelical Crisis*, but, without section 3, 'Anglican Comprehensiveness – The Hard-Made Decision', it does not adequately represent Packer's position.

Bishop of St Albans in 1970. By that date he had learned that
'promotion is in the hands of certain crucial people, who
have enormous amounts of power'.[1] Having moved further
into that circle he was appointed Archbishop of Canterbury
in 1980. At his enthronement he declared, 'The Church must
give a firm lead against rigid thinking.' One of his friends and
colleagues was Hugh Montefiore (Bishop of Birmingham),
whose remarks to him on the publication of John Robinson's
book *Honest to God* tell us much. Far from being pleased to
see such radical liberal theology published, with its rejection
of the supernatural, Montefiore was alarmed. 'My God,' he
swore to Runcie, 'John Robinson's written a book which is
going to cause mayhem – he's going to tell the world the sort
of things *we* really believe.'[2] E. L. Mascall commented: 'One
might be pardoned for supposing that Robinson had
despaired of trying to convert the world to Christianity and
had decided instead to convert Christianity to the world.'[3]
For his own religious opinions Runcie was indebted to
Kierkegaard who 'thought religion had nothing to do with
the rational part of your mind'. This led him, Runcie tells us,
to 'a way in which I could hold together a fundamental
scepticism with religious devotion'.[4] As a result the Archbishop could say such things as this: 'Jesus Christ is not frozen
in the first century . . . he is part of an infinite variety of
human experiences, which alter from age to age. To imitate
him will be to find what the contemporary age is like.'[5]

The great problem for Anglican evangelicals, under such
leadership, was how to combine their policy of collaboration
with all parts of the Church with opposition to manifest
unfaithfulness. There had been no call for the discipline of
clergy unfaithful to Scripture at Keele or at Nottingham. As

[1] Humphrey Carpenter, *Robert Runcie: The Reluctant Archbishop*
(London: Hodder and Stoughton, 1977), p. 165. Carpenter was Runcie's
authorized biographer.   [2] *Ibid.,* p. 159.
[3] Mascall, *The Secularization of Christianity* (London, 1965), p. 109.
Quoted in K. Hylson-Smith, *The Churches in England from Elizabeth I to
Elizabeth II*, vol. 3 (London: SCM, 1998), pp. 234–5.
[4] Carpenter, *Runcie,* p. 88.   [5] *Ibid.,* pp. 303–4.

though to rectify the omission, John Stott, at a meeting of the
Evangelical Alliance in November 1977 urged that clergy
who denied the divinity of Christ should have their licence
to teach withdrawn by their bishops. Such discipline, he
believed, 'would demonstrate our intense care for the truth,
and increase the church's credibility'.[1] But how could this be
done when bishops themselves were a large part of the
problem? Packer wrote 'that the best way to serve a church
infected by error is to refute the error cogently in public
discussion and debate, as Paul refuted the Galatian and
Colossian errors'.[2] He had done that himself in 1957 and
1963,[3] but how could it be done after Keele without blow-
ing apart the whole policy? The 'liberal-evangelical dialogue'
of Stott and Edwards illustrated what the pressure of that
policy could do even to the best.

* * * *

It would seem that the main argument for broader
evangelical collaboration within the Church of England, and
in the larger ecumenical scene, was not a biblical or doctrinal
one at all; it consisted of an appeal to the successful results
which the change had achieved. Not to have taken the new
course, it was repeatedy argued, would have been to consign
the Anglican evangelicals to a wilderness of ineffectiveness. It
would have meant staying 'in a ghetto' and letting the world
go by. In accordance with this thinking, McGrath tells us that
Lloyd-Jones lost influence by wrongly protesting as he did in
1966. After that date:

> Lloyd-Jones retained wide respect as a spiritual guide, but he
> was no longer seen as an evangelical statesman who could

[1] Stott was also chairman of the the Church of England Evangelical
Council which produced a pamplet on the subject, *Truth, Error and
Discipline in the Church of England* (London: Grove Books, 1978).
[2] Packer, *A Kind of Noah's Ark*, p. 17.
[3] I refer to Packer's writings, *'Fundamentalism' and the Word of God*, and
Keep Yourselves from Idols: A Discussion of the Book Honest to God (London:
Church Book Room Press, 1963).

speak for the movement as a whole . . . He became increasingly a voice in the wilderness, as the move to regain the high ground in the denominations gathered momentum.[1]

Referring to the late 1960s the same author affirms: 'There was now no doubt that a major evangelical revival was under way within the national church, and that Packer was seen as one of its leading figures.'[2] McGrath also points out that Packer's successful 'policy of collaboration' was parallel to 'the co-operative mode of evangelism adopted by Billy Graham, which brings together all Christian churches in a given area'.[3]

This argument from supposed success is widely and repeatedly stated. It is said that the one thousand delegates (clergy and lay) present at Keele represented seven hundred parishes, and the two thousand at Nottingham, ten years later, 'served to highlight the contrast between a declining liberalism and a growing evangelicalism'. 'Evangelicalism', says McGrath, 'seemed to be coasting along on an upward spiral.'[4] Manwaring writes in the same vein. So does Packer in places, for instance: '"Definite" evangelicalism in the Church of England has made a come-back, under God, and looks as if it is here to stay.' 'They [evangelicals] see . . . God has been increasing their stake in the Church of England quite dramatically.'[5]

One of the most common proofs advanced for the alleged success has been the number of men from the evangelical side who became diocesan bishops; there were about a dozen by 1993, including George Carey, the present Archbishop of Canterbury. 'If numbers are to count,' writes Gerald Bray, 'then the "open evangelicalism" of the post-Keele era has been an outstanding success.' But as the same writer goes on to show, the word 'evangelical' had changed its meaning in the process:

---

[1] McGrath, *Packer*, p. 127.   [2] *Ibid.*, p. 133.   [3] *Ibid.*, p. 275.   [4] *Ibid.*, p. 213.
[5] Packer, *Identity Problem*, p. 26.

It is typical of the new breed of evangelical bishop that in the recent debate on the ordination of women, not a single one of them voted against it . . . To be an Evangelical Bishop, you must be 'open': others need not apply. The recent debates over the future of theological training have revealed 'openness' in yet another light. Of the six Evangelical training colleges, it was the one which was perceived to be the least 'open' which was slated for closure, and the response of the college authorities was both quick and revealing. Elements suspected of being resistant to 'openness' were purged in a particularly nasty and brutal manner, and when the Church authorities took a second look they gratefully announced that the teaching of the college was not as 'narrow' as they had been led to believe. It is now apparent that Evangelicals who put conviction before career are likely to be victimized, not merely by those outside their own ranks, but even more by those who would claim to be within them. Convinced Evangelicals are now derided as 'narrow' by those who are more 'open', and are being consistently marginalized within their own constituency . . . It is worth reflecting that if Jesus had been an 'open evangelical' there would not be a Church at all today.[1]

These words from 1993 have since needed no revision. Mark D. Thompson, Anglican lecturer at Wycliffe Hall, Oxford, said more recently: 'We are supposed to have more evangelical bishops in the House of Bishops than ever before, and yet the episcopal attack upon Evangelicalism continues unabated.'[2]

The success of post-Keele Anglican evangelicalism has also been challenged from a surprising source. While in the 1970s it *appeared* to have Packer's endorsement, he is now a principal witness on the other side. In a short and poignant

[1] Editorial, *Churchman,* vol. 107, no. 4 (1993). How the numbers argument looked to non-evangelical Anglicans is also significant. According to a *Church Times* study, conservative evangelical membership in the General Synod stood at only 6.0 per cent. Quoted by Roger Steer, *Guarding the Holy Fire,* p. 227.

[2] *Churchman*, vol. 111 (1997), no. 2, p. 101.

piece of autobiography written in 1984, and looking back on his previous twenty-seven years in the ordained ministry of the Church of England, Dr Packer speaks of the change between what he saw in his early and later years in England in this way:

> Having met the Church of England's Reformed and Puritan heritage in the writings of such men as J. C. Ryle, I saw that the healthiest discipleship, the truest maturity, the worthiest worship and the weightiest witness flow from deep acquaintance with God's revealed truth, deeper than was generally thought in the circles I knew. So I with others campaigned specifically for more study of the biblical faith, more use of the mind in loving God, more theological alertness among Anglican evangelicals generally. We hoped to further both reformation and revival through letting God's word loose in this way . . . For over a decade up to about 1965 I thought that in theological education, parish programmes, clergy vision and lay interest, significant ground was being gained. Since then, however, my impression is that due to a combination of factors, some distracting and some opposing, anti-intellectual pietism, fed and watered by the book trade, has largely gained control . . . theological concern – by which I mean, the passion to know everything coherently and thoroughly in terms of God's word, will and work – has ebbed.[1]

In 1996 Packer spoke more fully of the failure of his early hopes:

> For fifteen years I worked to fulfill a vision of evangelical quickening in England through theological education, spiritual formation, pastoral enrichment, profound preaching, wise evangelism, functional Christian unity and every-

---

[1] Packer, *The Thirty-Nine Articles: Their Place and Use Today* (Oxford: Latimer House, 1984), p. 19. In part this is a reprint of his material from 1961, but with significant omissions. If 'pietism' has to be blamed for post-Keele failure, this has to put a question mark on the author's earlier statement that Keele 'broke with a long-prevalent pietist and sectarian mood' (see above, p. 92).

member ministry in local congregations – a vision generated by the type of pure biblical theology that some label Calvinism. Put like that, of course, this vision sounds grandiose to a fault, and though I retain my hold on it – or rather, it retains its hold on me – I am not here concerned to defend it against its critics. I simply record that after fifteen years of actively promoting it came several years during which, through what people with other visions did in perfectly good faith to block, more or less directly, the things I was after, I lost all the vantage points I had for implementing the purposes that the vision dictated. I found myself marginalized, isolated, and required to work to unfulfilling and, I thought, flawed agendas, in a manner that made me think of the Israelites having to make bricks for Pharaoh; and for political reasons I was not free to say what I thought about this state of affairs. Outwardly appreciated, at least by some, as a useful Christian performer, I lived, like Moses in Midian, with frustration in my heart, wondering what God, who, as I believed, gave me the vision in the first place, could possibly be up to.[1]

'Fifteen years' from the date of his ordination brings us approximately into the same mid-1960s period noted as '1965' in the first quotation. In other words, the change came with the beginning of the very era about which McGrath writes so enthusiastically as a 'revival'. Packer who, unlike his biographer, knew events first-hand, evidently saw it differently and came to entertain less hope of revival than in his early ministry. It would seem that, before his emigration to Canada in 1979 at the age of fifty-two, Packer found himself in the Church of England like Moses in 'the backside of the desert' (*Exod.* 3:1, AV), comparable, at the very least, with the 'wilderness' supposedly suffered by Lloyd-Jones. Some, even among Anglicans, seemed to think that, of the position of the two men, Packer's was the worse. Michael Smout, writing of Anglican evangelicalism in the 1970s, speaks of the demise of the era in which 'the lightweight

---

[1] Packer, *Truth and Power* (Guildford: Eagle, 1996), pp. 203–4.

Arminian theology of the Keswick movement' had been challenged by a revived interest in the Puritans: 'The passing of this era has left its leader, Jim Packer, sitting a trifle uneasily among the wreckage, as the main course of evangelicalism has gone off in another direction.'[1]

This is an important part of Dr Packer's life which is unexplained by his biographer. Packer has given us hints of what happened in the autobiographical quotations given above and from them we can draw the fuller picture. The upsurge among Anglican evangelicals in the 1950s, he believed, was mainly due to three different influences:

(1) The work of Inter-Varsity conferences and publications at the student level.

(2) The Graham crusades which multiplied numbers and brought high optimism as already described. Graham has said of a 1966 crusade in London, 'We had fifty-two Anglican clergymen sitting on the platform one night, all of whom had been converted in the Harringay meetings twelve years before.'[2] 'World-wide evangelicalism in all denominations drew together impressively,' Packer writes, 'with men like Billy Graham, John Stott and Carl Henry spearheading the process.'[3]

(3) The resurgence of an older doctrinal evangelicalism or, as Packer called it, 'Puritan Calvinism'.[4]

---

[1] Michael Smout, 'What is an Evangelical Anglican?' in *77 Notts Untied* (London: Lakeland, 1977), p. 35–6.

[2] *Just As I Am*, p. 227.

[3] Packer, *Identity Problem*, p. 26.

[4] Buchanan has written of several phases in evangelical Anglican history since World War II. The first was the growth in scholarship and in the number of ordinands. The second was the 'neo-Puritan movement', and the third 'the ecclesiology people' who 'took over the Keele Congress in 1967'. He also says, 'The charismatic phase took its origin with the ecclesiology people': this is one reason why charismatic ideas were no longer resisted by the time of the Nottingham Congress ('Anglican Evangelicalism: The State of the Party', *Anvil*, vol. 1, no. 1, 1984).

These influences were all represented in the evangelical Anglicans who set the new policy at Keele in 1967 but they were far from being present in equal strength, nor were they harmonious. While Inter-Varsity influence overlapped the three groups, (2) and (3) differed considerably, as we have already seen in connection with Dr Lloyd-Jones and the Graham crusades. Packer, also critical of Arminian evangelism,[1] was almost alone in that respect among leading Anglicans. Most of the younger generation of Anglicans, Packer was later to regret, were far more interested in 'evangelism' than in doctrine and simply saw the Church of England as

> the best boat to fish from. The renewed interest during the fifties in Reformed theology and devotion touched only a few of them at anything more than a surface level. Being activists rather than intellectuals (which is not to deny that many of them had good brains) they were more impressed by practical shrewdness than by theological strength.[2]

Packer could see this when he published these words in 1978. Whether he saw it amidst the euphoria which surrounded the first National Evangelical Anglican Congress at Keele in 1967 is more doubtful. Instead of the Keele policy leading to a strengthening of biblical convictions, it had unwittingly contributed to the opposite and by the time of the second Congress in 1977 Packer had evidently moved from the centre to the edge of the proceedings. In his own words, already quoted, 'I found myself marginalized'. The reference is clearly to his diminished influence within

---

[1] See chapters 8, 10 and 18 in Packer, *A Quest for Godliness* (Wheaton: Crossway, 1990). These chapters were first published in 1959, 1960 and 1956 respectively. As a wise balance to the strength of the recovery of Calvinistic belief in those years, his *Evangelism and the Sovereignty of God* followed (London: Inter-Varsity, 1961). He also contributed significantly to the work of the Banner of Truth Trust whose reprint programme, he believed, was a major influence at this date. *Celebrating the Saving Work of God*, p. 214.

[2] *Identity Problem*, pp. 25–6.

Anglican evangelicalism. 'The Congress was a great thrill to
all the delegates', writes Manwaring.[1] It clearly was not so for
Packer. While the criticism he expressed at the way things
were going was guarded at the time ('for political reasons I
was not free to say what I thought'), he wrote enough in
1978 (the year after the second Congress at Nottingham) for
us to know something of its nature. Evangelical Anglicans,
he believed, had lost their 'common purpose' in the ten years
since Keele:

> while the total number of evangelicals in the Church
> increases, the number of campaigning evangelicals declines
> . . . There was more passion for the renewing of the church
> to be seen in the sixties than can be detected now. Are the still
> waters running deep, or are they simply stagnant? . . . It may
> be that in the euphoric years since Keele some of us attended
> more to secondary things than was good for us; maybe our
> failure to reaffirm those basics at Nottingham testifies to this.[2]

In the pages from which this quotation come there is an
ambivalence over the state of evangelicals in the Church of
England; some things are said to balance the critical notes and
no doubt they were intended to keep up spirits. 'Plainly,' he
wrote, 'this is a time for renewed effort, not for contracting
out.'[3] Yet the next year, 1979, he was gone.[4]

It is an Anglican theologian who has probably put most
succinctly the misjudgment which was at the heart of Keele
and which explains the breach between what it represented

[1] Manwaring, *Controversy to Co-Existence*, p. 198.
[2] Packer, *Identity Problem*, pp. 30–1, 37.
[3] *Ibid.*, p. 30.
[4] In a tribute to Packer on his departure to Canada, John Stott noted
his 'major role in dragging the Anglican Evangelical movement out of its
former siege mentality', but said nothing on why his role diminished in
the 1970s. As Packer was a main apologist for the change heralded by
Keele he inevitably took a large share of criticism. Stott says in the same
place: 'He [Packer] has been misunderstood and misrepresented, especially
regarding his commitment to biblical theological renewal in the Church
of England.' *Church of England Newspaper* (CWN Series), 28 July 1978.

and Dr Lloyd-Jones. Dr Gerald Bray, in reviewing the McGrath biography of Packer, writes with reference to the 1960s:

> What Dr Lloyd-Jones saw clearly – more clearly, one feels, than either Dr Packer or John Stott did – was that Anglican Evangelicals were in danger of losing their cutting edge if they got too involved in the structures of the Church of England. This was a time when a younger generation of Anglican Evangelicals was beginning to feel that such involvement was both right and necessary, and in this they were supported by Packer and Stott. Trying to decide who was right in this debate is not easy, because so much depends on one's point of view. The Packer-Stott line would have had a good deal to commend it had Anglican Evangelicalism been united around a coherent Reformed theology, but it was not. Those who wanted to 'go into' the Church of England, as they put it, were often quite happy to ditch whatever theology they possessed, especially if they could get a bishopric. Whether Dr Lloyd-Jones realized this or not, subsequent events have shown that his was a prophetic voice. At the Evangelical Anglican Leaders' Conference in January 1995, for example, all the main speakers were bishops, but not one of them could be clearly identified with the evangelical wing of the church. A purple shirt was obviously more important to them than a committed soul, which is exactly what the Doctor could see coming twenty-five years before . . . In attempting to bring an Anglican neo-Puritanism into being, Dr Packer was heading for trouble, as this book makes perfectly clear. This is basically because modern Anglican Evangelicalism is thoroughly 'Arminian' in character, and is deeply marked by an amateur-ish do-it-yourself outlook which is its true uniting characteristic.[1]

What had happened in the ten years between Keele and Nottingham was surely something like this: Many younger

---

[1] Gerald Bray, in review of McGrath's biography of Packer, *Churchman*, vol. 111 (1998), no. 4, pp. 359–60.

evangelical clergy had interpreted the change advocated by their leaders as the Church at large had interpreted it, namely, that some of the old doctrinal distinctions were not so important after all. An impatience with 'doctrine' – even a boredom with it, according to John King[1] – began to surface, in part from the supposed greater importance of evangelism absorbed from the Graham crusades, and in part from the now burgeoning charismatic movement which was more interested in experience than theology. By the 1970s, it was said, the majority of younger evangelicals in the Church of England were charismatic in outlook.[2] The charismatic change was certainly in evidence at Nottingham where there was drama and dance but the public exposition of Scripture was no longer to the fore. In Michael Harper's opinion, 'The charismatic divide was given the last rites.'[3]

This whole discussion is far too serious to be reduced to a question of the respective reputations of Lloyd-Jones, Packer and Stott in the evangelical division of the 1960s. But one thing ought to be clear by this point. The often-repeated idea that Lloyd-Jones' position was dictated by his Congregationalism or by his Welsh nationality is untenable. The fact that the essential difference was not over denominational matters is proved by the testimony of the men – used in these pages – who remained Anglican and yet shared his conviction on the big issue. Dr Gerald Bray from the Anglican side can write: 'I can testify that Dr Lloyd-Jones was not anti-Anglican as such, because when he found out that I was going to seek ordination in the Church of England he came to see me and encouraged me in my vocation. The one thing

[1] *Evangelicals Today*, p. 11: 'Other things are more important.'

[2] Gavid Reid believed that the Anglican evangelicals were divided into four groups: Protestant, Keswick, Eclectic and Charismatic. 'Only the fourth category, in his view, contained anything like a large proportion of the younger Evangelicals.' Manwaring, *Controversy to Co-Existence*, p. 208.

[3] Capon, *Evangelicals Tomorrow*, p. 63. Capon notes the contrary opinion of Gerald Bray who believed that the issues raised by the charismatic movement were 'swept under the carpet with a dexterity which must excite the envy of even the totalitarian Church of Rome.'

he warned me about was the danger of becoming an ecclesiastical politician!'[1]

As we have already noted, Lloyd-Jones' concerns were over
what he believed would be the *spiritual* consequences of the
new Anglican evangelical policy.

* * * *

It may be inferred from what I have quoted above that
there was a change in the policy advocated by the evangelical leadership between 1967 and 1977, for how else could
Packer be committed to the policy in 1967 and no longer be
so by the time of the Nottingham Congress? It is certainly
Jim Packer's view that a change did indeed take place *after*
1967. In a personal letter he wrote to me on 8 June 1989 he
said:

> Like you, I am old-fashioned enough to see a confession of
> essential doctrines as the *sine qua non* of recognisable Christian
> identity, though unlike you I do not see Keele as implying
> otherwise; I hold rather that Anglican pietism betrayed Keele,
> so that NEAC 2 and 3 are out of line with Keele.

My own assessment is that there were diverse elements at
Keele and that it would be a mistake to suppose that a
unified, coherent policy was then put in place. In fact, the
Keele policy (which Gerald Bray calls 'the Packer-Stott line')
was more vague and by no means unified. It understood
more about what it was leaving behind than what it was
going towards. It might not be unfair to liken the indefiniteness of the policy to what General Slim said of the British
Army's battle in Burma in World War II: 'All would be conditioned by the overriding object of the campaign. What that
was we did not know. Indeed, it was never, until the last
stages, clear, and I think we suffered increasingly in all our
actions for this.'[2] Packer, as noted, thought that there was a
policy agreed at Keele which took a turn with which he did

---

[1] Bray, review of McGrath's *Packer*, *Churchman*, 1998, p. 360.
[2] Ronald Lewin, *Slim: The Standard Bearer, A Biography of Field Marshall
the Viscount Slim* (London: Leo Cooper, 1976), p. 96.

not want to be identified ten years later. The agenda had been hijacked by the 'activists'. Roger Beckwith, his associate at Latimer House, has made the same point more definitely, although he sees these same persons as already influential in 1967. Instead of the focus at Keele being on the platform addresses, all of them given by 'men of some maturity', he says, these

> took quite second place to the task of preparing the Keele Statement. The draft of the Statement, which was prepared in advance, had been drawn up at the insistence of certain young activists of unconventional views who prepared three of the six sections of the draft themselves. Ten years later, it was the same young men, and people of like mind, who largely organ-ized the Nottingham Congress and who both produced much of the draft statement and were prominent on the platform.[1]

One of the 'young activists' in question was Colin Buchanan of whom we have already written. His recent book *Is the Church of England Biblical?* confirms what Beckwith has written. 'Originally,' Buchanan writes, 'the Congress [that is, Keele] had been planned to reproclaim Evangelical fundamentals, and various big guns had been placed in position to fire their salvos from the platform. Then the younger clergy started to show signs of restiveness, which came to a head in November 1966 at the Eclectics Confer-ence at Swanwick.'[2]

As a result of this 'restiveness' it was decided that the addresses of the 'big guns' would be printed in advance and, 'The congress instead would write a Statement of Contem-porary Policy for Evangelicals.'[3] Given the 'swirling dynamics'

---

[1] 'Keele, Nottingham and the Future,' in *The Evangelical Succession*, pp. 104–5.

[2] *Is the Church of England Biblical?* p. 10. The Eclectics were a fraternal of evangelical clergy who met regularly in London under the chairman-ship of John Stott. See Dudley-Smith, *John Stott*, pp. 304–8; Saward speaks of the Eclectics as 'the single most significant influence on my ministry' (*Autobiography*, p. 249). The wisdom of the decision to restrict its membership to the under-forties age group has to be doubted.

[3] *Is the Church of England Biblical?* p. 10. The addresses were published as *Guidelines: Anglican Evangelicals Face the Future*, ed. J. I. Packer (London: Falcon Books, April 1967).

which Buchanan describes, it is not difficult to see why the 'Statement' did not represent a well-thought out and coherent policy. Buchanan's observation, made in another context, is relevant: 'People act under pressure of events in history, form groupings almost by instinct (and/or by conversions) and only later attempt rationalising ecclesiologies.'[1]

* * * *

I have sought to indicate in these last two chapters how the policy of the evangelical Anglican leadership from the mid-1960s constituted a major reversal of earlier evangelical thinking. A summary of the evidence for the change may be set down as follows:

1. The Thirty-Nine Articles were no longer used as a test of what Anglicans held to be the teaching of Scripture. Although the Articles had been, since 1572, the one standard of the Church's teaching, the Keele policy required that they be abandoned as the boundaries of belief permitted in the Church. In the seventy-eight pages of the *Nottingham Statement* of NEAC 2 the Thirty-Nine Articles are not once mentioned. At that congress a statement drafted by Jim Packer and others which began, 'We thank God for our heritage of fundamental divine truth in the Articles', was turned down at committee stage. 'It stands out like a sore thumb,' someone objected.[2] A decision to end the special authority of the Articles had been taken in the Church's General Synod in 1975 and the majority of evangelicals were no longer concerned to make a stand on that issue.[3]

It may be said in reply that although evangelicals acquiesced in the displacement of the Articles nevertheless they affirmed at Nottingham, as one identifying mark of the Church of England, 'Commitment to Christian truth

---

[1] *Is the Church of England Biblical?* p. 35.

[2] From 1 September 1975, 'general consent' to the Articles was no longer required of clergy. Henceforth they were only to be regarded 'as one of the historic formularies through which the Church of England has borne witness to Christian truth'.

[3] Capon, *Evangelicals Tomorrow*, p. 34

expressed in the acceptance of the Scriptures as the revelation of God to Man and the Creeds as the historic expression of the Christian faith.'[1] But which creeds? Article VIII of the Thirty-Nine Articles was specific, not only in naming three creeds, but more important in asserting *why* they should be received: 'For they may be proved by most certain warrants of holy Scripture.' It was against the binding authority of Scripture on doctrinal issues (well expressed in the Articles) that both liberals and Anglo-Catholics had combined; the former wanting *less* than Scripture and the latter wanting *more* (that is, Scripture plus tradition). The blander statement of Nottingham did not meet the need of the hour. If assent to the Articles, Ryle had said, ceased to be required of clergy, then we will 'concede that a Churchman may be anything or everything in opinion, and may even be a Papist!'[2] This is exactly what happened.

2. At no point was effect of this change more clearly seen than with regard to the way the church was to be defined. Whereas Article XIX begins: 'The visible church of Christ is a congregation of faithful men', the Nottingham Statement on 'The Church and Its Identity' begins, as already noted, with, 'The Church on earth is marked out by Baptism'. This was to put sacrament before faith, and the unity of church order before what the New Testament makes the real basis of Christian unity. This reversed the order of priorities set down in the Articles. In the composition of the Articles, gospel doctrine (Articles I–XVIII) was very deliberately placed *before* statements on church and sacraments. It is from the earlier Articles that we are to learn what 'faithful men' in Article XIX means. This justified Philip E. Hughes in writing in 1957 that, in the view of historic Anglicanism, '*faith*, agreement on *doctrine*, has always been given precedence over considerations of order.'[3]

---

[1] *The Nottingham Statement* (London: Church Pastoral Aid Society, 1977), pp. 19–20.
[2] Ryle, *Principles for Churchmen*, p. 29.
[3] *Christianity Today*, 22 July 1957, p. 39.

When evangelicals capitulated to the ecumenical insistence that issues begin with agreeing on 'church and unity' several consequences followed. Not the least of these had to do with the understanding of schism. For the New Testament unity is in order to preserve the faith, not something which can exist irrespective of doctrinal purity. But the price of recognition for evangelicals was that they had to accept quietly that church (that is, denominational) unity is the *first* priority and that its preservation is an overriding interest. So no circumstances were to be recognized where the absence of 'faithful men' and of 'the pure word of God preached' (Article XIX) would warrant secession. At Nottingham, evangelicals agreed: 'As Anglicans, holding to the Church of England's historic reformed stance, we also believe that to attempt to gather a "pure" church is not only impossible as a task but also contrary to our biblical understanding of the visible church.'[1] Similarly, Packer, Beckwith and Duffield, speaking of evangelical Anglicans, wrote in 1977: 'Their concern that the Church's purging and renewing should not bring fresh division makes them willing to endure for the moment grave doctrinal disorders, in the confidence that these will yet be dispelled through God's blessing on appropriate means.'[2]

Something had happened to evangelical convictions when unity could thus be treated as more important than 'grave doctrinal disorders'. It was this kind of thinking which brought David Watson and Julian Charley at Nottingham to speak of the division caused by the Reformation as a 'tragedy', and which also led Manwaring to praise Canon

[1] *Nottingham Statement*, p. 40.

[2] *Across the Divide*, p. 31. The Church is almost assuming the place of Christ in the simile which Packer uses in the following: 'When asked, as they sometimes are, under what circumstances they [evangelical Anglicans] would leave the Church, they find the question so remote from reality, and therefore hard to answer, as a husband working hard and fruitfully at his marriage would find it were he asked under what circumstances he would divorce his wife' (*Identity Problem*, p. 30). Yet the evangelical continues to speak in that document when he says, 'The Church of England is under judgment in these days for multiple unfaithfulness', and 'Evangelicals' first loyalty is not to the Church of England' (pp. 39, 37).

Michael Green who, at the same congress, 'grasped the nettle of real unity, rather than a mere spiritual unity, and Anglican oneness, rather than Evangelical unity.'[1] This was all a far cry from the words of J. C. Ryle:

> Divisions and separations are most objectionable in religion. They weaken the cause of true Christianity . . . But before we blame people for them, we must be careful that we lay the blame *where it is deserved*. False doctrine and heresy are even worse than schism. If people separate themselves from teaching which is positively false and unscriptural, they ought to be praised rather than reproved. In such cases separation is a virtue and not a sin . . . The old saying must never be forgotten, 'He is the schismatic who causes the schism' . . . Controversy in religion is a hateful thing . . . But there is one thing which is even worse than controversy, and that is false doctrine, allowed, and permitted without protest or molestation.[2]

3. Whereas evangelicals had previously deplored the presence of unfaithful men in the ministry of the Church, an accommodation with other 'views' was now justified. There was no call for the discipline of clergy unfaithful to Scripture at Keele or at Nottingham. Buchanan writes of such concerns as belonging to history. His thinking is predictable: 'In an avowedly (though perhaps inadvertently) comprehensive

---

[1] Manwaring, *Controversy to Co-Existence*, p. 201. This is a major denial of the teaching of the older evangelicals whose position is well stated in the words of Canon Christopher: 'There is amidst all the apparent divisions of Christendom only one Church of Christ, the Church of all true believers, the Church of all those who are "born again not of corruptible seed, but incorruptible by the Word of God which liveth and abideth for ever". Can anyone who knows the truth of the Gospel, and abhors the erroneous teaching which keeps people from real union with Christ, desire that a visible unity should be produced by the sacrifice of the spiritual unity of true believers?' (Reynolds, *Canon Christopher*, p. 251). Alan Stibbs had stated the same position well in the volume which Packer edited, *All In Each Place,* in 1965. To speak of 'real unity' over against 'mere spiritual unity' would have been unthinkable to such men.

[2] Ryle, *Warnings to the Churches* (London: Banner of Truth, 1967), p. 109–110.

Church, to find someone guilty of heresy and thus deprived of his or her post is in fact to flout the toleration factor in the life of the Church.'[1] He tells us that he prefers a diluted Christianity to any attempts at discipline.

The approval of doctrinal 'diversity' has become the hallmark of one-time evangelicals who have risen to high positions in the Church and left definite convictions behind them. Thus Donald Coggan (in his early life an Inter-Varsity worker), as Archbishop of Canterbury, in his Preface to *Christian Believing*, praised 'the variety of gifts and outlooks of the various contributors' as a 'source of enrichment'. Speaking of the commission responsible for the document (headed as we have noted by one who denied the deity of Christ), Coggan wrote: 'Each generation needs men who in honesty and devotion are prepared to undertake exploration into God, to press beyond the confines of what we hitherto have grasped and to move away from places that have become too narrow for us in the light of modern knowledge and experience.'[2]

Precisely the same sentiments come from another former evangelical, George Carey, the present Archbishop of Canterbury. 'I do not pretend our church is the only one worth joining', he has said. 'But I remain convinced it is a broad church combining the catholic, evangelical, charismatic and liberal in joyful harmony – even if at times we get the balance wrong.'[3] Elsewhere Carey wrote: 'For many of us in the Church, liberalism is a creative and constructive element for exploring theology today . . . It would constitute the end of

[1] *Is the Church of England Biblical?* pp. 9, 270–1.

[2] Quoted in *Unity in Truth: Addresses given by Dr D. Martyn Lloyd-Jones at meetings held under the auspices of the British Evangelical Council*, ed. Hywel R. Jones, p. 173.

[3] *Bath and Wells Diocesan News*, March 1988, p. 5. This was the issue recording the 'enthronement' of Carey as bishop of the diocese. Another page speaks of his leading 'a pilgrimage to the Shrine of Our Lady of Walsingham' – a shrine since the alleged appearance of 'the Blessed Virgin Mary' there in 1061.

Anglicanism as a significant force in world-wide Christianity if we lost this vital ingredient.'[1]

This is unity being given a higher place than the scriptural doctrines of salvation.[2]

* * * *

In review of all the above we conclude that there was no way forward for Keele comprehensiveness if evangelicals were to remain evangelicals. Yet the upholders of that policy appeared to have ruled out alternatives. The Keele and Nottingham statements disowned both 'the old days of entrenched "party" isolationism' within the denomination and the possibility of secession from it. The door was shut on any going back.[3] What choice then is left other than lending reluctant support to the official 'unity' required by the powers that be? This is the predicament which the decisions of the last thirty years have brought about. When Dr Packer, spoke on 'Unity in Truth: the Anglican Agony' at Latimer House in 1997, he lamented that tolerance of the intolerable had become the Anglican way, yet 'felt that there was no alternative but to take G. K. Chesterton's advice and "Go on gaily in the dark!"'. These words, said the reporter, were given 'with tears in his eyes'.[4]

* * * *

John Capon, the authorized reporter of the Nottingham Congress, noted: 'There was clearly a small but influential

[1] Quoted in *Church of England Newspaper*, 9 April 1998, p. 8, from 'Parties in the Church of England', *Theology*, July 1988. 'I owe much to the "Liberal" tradition for its commitment and passion for truth.' Quoted in Steer, *Guarding the Holy Fire*, p. 255.

[2] How different were the words of Bishop Daniel Wilson: 'We best advance the prosperity of our various bodies, when we seek the honour of our great Master, and the salvation of souls; and make our ecclesiastical platforms entirely subservient to these great aims.'

[3] Yet as Bray has indicated, faithfulness may compel Anglican evangelicals to go back to being 'a church within the Church', and even 'to form partnerships with ministries which are not subject to episcopal oversight' (*Churchman*, vol. 108, no. 4, p. 292).

[4] *English Churchman* (Canterbury, Kent), 20 & 27 June 1997, pp. 1, 4.

group at Nottingham who felt the present generation of evangelicals were "selling the pass".[1] Matters came to a head for this group when *Churchman*, for many years the theological journal of Anglican evangelicals, published articles on 'The Authority of Scripture' in 1982. The writer was James Dunn and he offered what he called 'a radical evangelical view of Scripture'. Evangelicals who still held the traditional evangelical position on inspiration were strong enough on the council of Church Society (who owned *Churchman*) to call a halt. They enforced a major change in the journal's editorial board, including the appointment of a new editor. Thereafter, for the first time for some years, a serious commitment to Scripture controlled what was published under the editorship of Gerald Bray. At the same time Dr David Samuel, an advocate for the older evangelical Anglican position, was appointed as the new secretary of the Society. Unprepared to accept the loss of this platform, the men who had figured as the managers at Nottingham launched their own journal. It came out with the title *Anvil* in 1984. The leading article, from which we have quoted above (p. 131) was by Buchanan, and Saward became a regular book reviewer. The disruption of *Churchman* was in Saward's view, a 'coup' executed by a group of 'hardliners' and 'extremist Protestants', whereas he and his friends were the 'mainstreamers'.[2] Referring elsewhere to these same 'numerically few Protestants', Saward has written: 'Whether they can recapture their lost ground (and they have lost huge tracts in the past thirty years) is very doubtful.'[3] He does not pause to consider the possibility that if these Church Society men had lost so much ground

[1] Capon, *Evangelicals Tomorrow*, p. 181.

[2] Saward, *Autobiography*, p. 427. By the time of the Caister Congress in 1988, he believed, there were three groupings of Anglican evangelicals. One wanted Christianity to be relaxed enjoyment with 'noisy, undemanding worship', while at the other extreme there was the 'hostile recrudescence of the old-style, hardline ghetto kind of Evangelicalism'. The 'mainstream' stood against both and stood for 'sane, open-mided moderation' (pp. 450–1).

[3] Saward, *Evangelicals on the Move* (London: Mowbray, 1987), p. 71.

they might themselves once have been the mainstream. Times were indeed changed when even the word 'Protestant' could be used in a pejorative sense by professed evangelicals.

To illustrate the differences among Anglican evangelicals by the 1990s I will close this chapter with quotations from two very different assessments. In Colin Craston's autobiography, published in 1998, he writes of 'substantially different perceptions' on the state of the Church of England:

> On the one hand, there is talk of serious doctrinal drift, of failure of Evangelicals to stand for the truth in synodical structures and especially in the House of Bishops, of unhealthy centralisation and burgeoning bureaucracy, and capitulation to liberal standards in faith and moral issues. Speaking for myself, on the other hand, and I believe for many other, I just don't see the same picture.[1]

But our confidence in Canon Craston's judgment is taken away by what follows. He writes, 'So far as doctrinal standards are concerned I see much to encourage', and goes on to refer to the latest report of the Doctrine Commission of the Church of England entitled *The Mystery of Salvation,* which, he believed, 'deserves wide acclamation'. Its authors, including such reputed evangelicals as Colin Buchanan and John Taylor (Bishop of St Albans), tell their readers of 'the unanimous support of the entire Commission' and affirm, 'We can all live with, endorse and happily commend the agreed text.'[2] But to compare the contents of *The Mystery of Salvation* with evangelical belief plainly confirms the very drift which Craston cannot see. Among its statements are the following:

> The idea of the fall does not require a prior paradise and the claim that physical death is the result of the fall of Genesis 3 is 'impossible' (p. 53).

---

[1] Colin Craston, *Debtor to Grace: A Journey in Faith and Ministry* (London: Silver Fish Publishing, 1998), p. 112.

[2] *The Mystery of Salvation: The Story of God's Gift* (London: Church House Publishing, 1995), p. x. For the sake of simplicity I will give the page references within the main text for the quotations which follow.

Jesus did not 'presume to know the reason behind the death he sees rapidly approaching' (p. 92).

'Theories of the atonement are secondary, necessarily diverse and all to some extent inadequate' (p. 92–3).

'Traditions . . . drove Paul to formulate the view that Christ died for us while we were helpless' (p. 96).

Salvation, for the writers of the New Testament, 'is not a theological concept but a present reality' (p. 100).

'For many Christians today the idea of God offering himself as a substitute for our sins is deeply repellent' (p. 122).

'In baptism . . . instead of being subject to such "original" sin, all the sin that is prior to any reflection on our part, we are granted the presence of the Holy Spirit in our lives, there to conform us to the image of Christ, the definitive human being, will we but let him' (p. 135).

'Baptism projects us into the ecumenical enterprise, for we all belong together in Christ' (p. 136).

In their views of the Eucharist, Catholic and Protestant are both right (p. 139).

The salvation of non-Christians is an open question – Schleiermacher 'saw a common essence within religious experience' (p. 152).

'The richness of other faith-traditions' is 'not to be lost' (p. 204).

'Juridical theories of the atonement tend to make legal considerations primary and moral ones secondary. In the realm of law a debt must always be paid and a penalty must always be enforced. But in the moral sphere there is no such necessity . . . The great weakness of juridical theories or models of the atonement is that they appear to eclipse moral considerations by legal ones. This runs counter to our best theological instincts' (p. 211–2).

For evangelicals who believe that Scripture controls all truth these beliefs represent the very opposite of biblical Christianity.

As a representative of an outlook very different from the above I quote from David Samuel who has written on the difference between the old evangelicalism and the new. What the old was he states in these words:

> True comprehensiveness, such as our Reformers envisaged, is based on a coherent and recognisable system of doctrine. It may be generous in its interpretation; wide and charitable with regard to things not essential or things indifferent; but it must be one, and consistent with itself . . . never a patchwork – a mere toleration, or accommodation, or juxtaposition of contradictory views.[1]

The interests of 'ecumenical fellowship', Samuel argued, could never be made compatible with the constitutional position of the Church of England and so the latter had to be abandoned in order 'to accommodate evangelicalism to the new unbiblical ecumenism in the church'. Yet this change was introduced in such a manner that it could scarcely be seen to be happening. 'It was rather like one of those party tricks, in which a man's shirt is removed without taking his jacket off. Outwardly everything looked the same – evangelicals seemed to be what they had always been; but there was something very important missing – and that was their insistence upon theological principle.'[2]

The leaders at Keele still professed to be constitutionalists but it was under their aegis that the position of the older evangelicals who had held firmly to the Articles position was undermined, and that to such an extent that the very memory of the former generation was too often caricatured. Samuel continued:

> By the renunciation of the so-called pietism of the past, evangelicals were, in fact, writing off evangelical history as well. To describe all evangelicalism prior to Keele as pietist was both unjust and untrue. Such a rash judgment was bound to

[1] *The Evangelical Succession*, p. 99.
[2] *Ibid.*, p. 97.

set up an alienation of contemporary evangelicals from their heritage and a separation from their history, which was to have the most serious and damaging results.[1]

The significance of Keele was to cut evangelical moorings ... it has left evangelicalism a prey to novelty and passing fashion. It is for this reason that the charismatic or neo-Pentecostal movement has made such marked inroads into evangelicalism. That, I believe, would have been impossible prior to Keele, for the fundamental principles and teachings of classic evangelicalism would have acted as a bulwark against it ... There is now among younger clergy a sense of incomprehension – sometimes impatience – when the names of Ryle or any of the Reformers are mentioned ... since Keele there has been the steady erosion of principles of churchmanship and doctrine which were common amongst previous generations of evangelicals.[2]

[1] David Samuel, 'Evangelicals and History', *Churchman*, vol. 106, no. 3, p. 235.
[2] *Ibid.*, pp. 236, 240.

6

Retrospect:
A Different
Approach

When the two thousand members of the second National Evangelical Anglican Congress, which met at Nottingham in 1977, had dispersed, and the wording of its Declaration had been published, one of that number drew attention to what seemed to have been missed. The Rev. Colin Bedford of Liverpool wrote:

> Many Evangelicals in all churches would agree with the Declaration and are seeking to share the Bible and to talk with Roman Catholics. But for many the basic problem remains, 'What is a Christian?' Nowhere in our statements do we face the basic concept of the new birth or conversion, or the reality of spiritual experience, which has united Evangelicals of all persuasions in the past.[1]

The omission of the question to which Bedford drew attention can hardly have been an oversight. Presumably the clergy at the second NEAC would have addressed it often in

[1] Smout, 77 *Notts Untied*, p. 98.

their churches. But the Congress was a different context and for a gathering committed to denominational and ecumenical involvement the subject was not seen as a necessary part of the agenda. The explanation has already been before us. The governing principle laid down since Keele was that the best interests of evangelicalism lay within the comprehensive setting. The alternative would have been a return to the 'ghetto' of isolationism and to a retreat from real Christian influence. These were the only available choices, or so, at least, it was generally assumed, and the opinion was supported by non-evangelical churchmen. Adrian Hastings, for instance, knew of no other course for evangelicals:

> It may well be the case that in England there remains no real alternative for Evangelicalism between an intellectually archaic and fundamentalist sectarianism on the one hand and absorption as a Conservative and biblically conscious wing within an ecumenical Catholicism upon the other.[1]

But what if the great issue of the hour was not the one which absorbed so much time and thought at these congresses? What if the first need of the Church and the nation was not Christian unity but the recovery of Christianity itself? In that case the question, 'What is a Christian?' demanded a very different order of priority. The fact seems to be that the prevailing outlook among Anglican evangelicals did not see the question which Colin Bedford missed at the Nottingham Congress of 1977 as the right starting-point in facing the contemporary situation. It was similarly absent from the mainstream of evangelical discussions and writing at this period. Men who were, for the most part, enthusiastic for evangelistic crusades aimed at the unconverted somehow moved to a different wavelength when it came to denominational and ecumenical discussions. It was not, as I have said, that they *intended* to down-play what made them distinctively evangelical, but the idea had been accepted that the gospel would ultimately be best served by the NEAC agenda.

[1] Hastings, *English Christianity*, p. 618.

Retrospect: A Different Approach

The case I want to set out in this chapter is that the either/ or of comprehensiveness or isolation was an understandable but wrong presentation of alternatives. There *was* another choice open. It is the course to which the New Testament's own definition of Christianity points and the one which has been repeatedly followed at the great turning points of church history. When churches lose their influence, when the Christian message ceases to arrest the indifferent and the unbelieving, when moral decline is obvious in places which once owned biblical standards – when such symptoms as these are evident, then the first need is not to regroup such professing Christianity as remains. It is rather to ask whether the spiritual decline is not due to a fundamental failure to understand and practise what Christianity really is.

To think in this way leads very quickly to a subject which has always been unpopular with the world and which is now far from popular in the church.

Is it not offensive and intolerant to suppose that anyone can distinguish true Christians from others? Are there not, it is said, many kinds of followers of Christ and does not love demand that we regard them all as 'fellow Christians'?

This objection often proceeds on the basis of another argument – usually unstated – namely, that the New Testament itself does not give us enough light to be definite. And if Scripture does not resolve the question, 'What is a Christian?' then we must tolerate and justify a breadth of opinion on the subject. But if the New Testament *does settle the question* then we have no liberty to redefine 'Christian' in terms which neither Christ nor his apostles ever authorized. Evangelicalism has historically been distinguished by its conviction that Scripture speaks plainly on this fundamental issue; it gives us all the light we need to discern between the true and the false, between the nominal and the real.

We turn, then, first to Scripture. There we read one common theme: to become a Christian is to experience the power of Christ in the forgiveness of sin and in the receiving of a new life. It is a change accomplished by God and

[151]

altogether apart from human effort or deserving, for the very faith which is the instrument in uniting the sinner to Christ is itself a gift: 'By grace you have been saved through faith, and that not of yourselves; it is the gift of God' (*Eph.* 2:8). Further, while obedience and love result from the gift of faith, these graces *follow* rather than contribute anything to our acceptance with God. It is Christ's finished work alone which secures for ever the believer's status of righteousness and of 'no condemnation'.

Scripture shows various ways in which an individual gives evidence of having been thus brought 'from death unto life'. The foremost has to do with the content of the faith which is exercised, for true faith rests on knowledge. 'To be saved and to come to the knowledge of the truth', is one and the same thing in apostolic Christianity (*1 Tim.* 2:4). To be 'saved', according to the New Testament, necessarily involves believing a *message*. Thus Luke sets it down as the first mark of the infant church at Jerusalem that 'they continued steadfastly in the apostles' doctrine' (*Acts* 2:42); and he tells us that it was through knowledge of the same message about 'the Lord Jesus' that 'the disciples were called Christians first in Antioch' (*Acts* 11:26). Christianity means knowing and trusting Christ as a living Person; it is a relationship which so captures both the mind and the heart of the believer that henceforth to know Christ, to esteem him and his words, becomes the very object of existence: 'To you who believe he is precious' (*1 Pet.* 2:7) – more precious certainly than all earthly goods or even life (*Luke* 14:26). A Christian is someone who no longer lives for himself but understands, with Paul, why Christ is his righteousness, his life, his all.

Opinions already stated in these pages express the possibility of a person not receiving the Christian message, or even being opposed to it, and yet being judged to be a Christian.[1]

---

[1] This attitude, it should be said, did not originate in the nineteenth century. At the time of the ejection of the Puritans from the Church of England in 1662 Thomas Case spoke of 'indifference as to matters of faith and doctrine . . . We have accounted it no matter of what opinion or

This is surely contrary to the New Testament. The first and invariable result of the new birth, according to Christ, is 'sight' (*John* 3:4). By this rebirth an individual comes to belong to the number of whom it is written: 'They shall all be taught by God' (*John* 6:45). He possesses an enlightenment which sets apart the teaching of God from all the teaching of men; for this person the promise 'You shall know the truth' is a reality (*John* 8:32).

This is not to say that becoming a Christian is primarily a change of opinion: it is far more profound. The Christian has received a new nature. Included in that nature is a capacity for truth, an affinity with truth, and a love for truth. He has been given 'the Spirit of truth; whom the world cannot receive' (*John* 14:17), with the result that his understanding of salvation no longer depends upon himself or upon the thinking of other men: 'But the anointing which you have received of Him abides in you, and you do not need that anyone teach you' (*1 John* 2:27). 'He who believes in the Son of God has the witness in himself' (*1 John* 5:10). What Jesus said to Peter is therefore true of every Christian, 'Blessed are you, Simon Bar-Jonah, for flesh and blood has not revealed this to you, but my Father who is in heaven' (*Matt.* 16:17). Or, as Paul wrote to believers at Ephesus, 'You were once darkness, but now you are light in the Lord' (*Eph.* 5:8).

On the basis of these facts, the New Testament shows that one sure test of a Christian profession is how that person reacts to the Scriptures. Unregenerate men not only do not receive God's Word but they have no moral ability to do so. By nature they are at enmity both against God and against his truth. 'The natural man does not receive the things of the Spirit of God, for they are foolishness to him' (*1 Cor.* 2:14).

---

judgement men be in these latter times. 'Tis an universal saying, "No matter what judgement men be so they be saints"; as if *truth in the judgement* did not go to the making up of a saint, as well as *holiness* in the will and affections . . . as if it were no matter, if God have the heart, so the devil be in the head.' Sermon of 17 August 1662 in *Farewell Sermons* (London, 1663).

So Christ could say to Jewish unbelievers, 'Because I tell you the truth, you do not believe me ... He who is of God hears God's words: therefore you do not hear, because you are not of God' (*John* 8:45, 47). On the other hand, a believing acceptance of his words is proof of belonging to his kingdom. All who hear the voice of Christ are members of his flock (*John* 10:28). So Paul could write to the Christians at Thessalonica: 'For this reason we also thank God without ceasing, because when you received the word of God which you heard from us, you welcomed it not as the word of men, but as it is in truth, the word of God' (*1 Thess.* 2:13).

In distinction from contemporary claims that dogmatism means unchristian intolerance, Scripture thus gives us an antithesis which is sharp and definite. Saving faith requires the power of the Holy Spirit, and his presence or absence in an individual is to be known by the response or the absence of response to his words: 'They are of the world. Therefore speak they as of the world, and the world hears them. We are of God. He who knows God hears us; he who is not of God does not hear us. By this we know the spirit of truth and the spirit of error' (*1 John* 4:5–6).

* * * *

What happens when these fundamental truths are recovered and proclaimed with power in an age of ignorance and unbelief is not a matter of theory or speculation. The history of the Protestant Reformation of the sixteenth century is second only to the apostolic age as a demonstration of what may be expected to occur. The lives of the Reformers are examples of men who, no longer content to trust the teaching of the institutional church of their upbringing, went back to Scripture. What was said of Luther might have been said of them all: 'He strengthens himself each day in his convictions by a constant application to the Word of God.'[1] The definition of a Christian which they found there was startlingly new,

---

[1] Dietrich to Melanchthon, in speaking of Luther at Coburg, during the Diet of Augsburg.

first to themselves, then to others, and it divided them from Renaissance scholars (such as Erasmus) on the one hand, and from the upholders of the traditional theology of the Church of Rome on the other.

Against the scholars who viewed Christianity largely in terms of a discussion on opinions and morality, and who objected to all claims to certainty, the Reformers asserted the sufficiency and finality of the truth which they had been taught by Christ. They saw the difference between the Renaissance and scriptural Christianity as the difference between natural and supernatural. Thus Luther could respond to Erasmus:

> Leave us free to make assertions, and to find in assertions our satisfaction and delight; and you may applaud your Sceptics and Academics – till Christ calls you too! . . . The truth is that nobody who has not the Spirit of God sees a jot of what is in the Scriptures. All men have their hearts darkened, so that, even when they can discuss and quote all that is in Scripture, they do not understand or really know any of it.[1]

Philip Melanchthon elaborates on the same point when he states what it means to be a Christian in the Preface to his *Loci* of 1521:

> If a man know nothing of the power of sin, of law, or of grace, I do not see how I can call him a Christian. It is there that Christ is truly known. The knowledge of Christ is to know his benefits, taste his salvation, and experience his grace; it is not, as the academic people say, to reflect on his natures and the modes of his incarnation. If you do not know the practical purpose for which he took flesh and went to the cross what is the good of knowing his story? . . . He is given us as our remedy, or, in the Bible's phrase, our salvation. And we must know him in another way than the scholars. To know him to purpose is to know the demand of the conscience for holiness, the source of power to meet it, where to seek grace for our

---

[1] Luther, *The Bondage of the Will*, eds. J. I. Packer and O. R. Johnston (Cambridge: James Clarke, 1957), p. 70.

sins's failure, how to set up the sinking soul in the face of the world, the flesh, and the devil, how to console the conscience broken. Is that what any of the schools teach? . . . How often Paul declared to his believers that he prays for them a rich knowledge of Christ. He foresaw that we should one day leave the saving themes and turn our minds to discussions cold and foreign to Christ.[1]

The same principle of the sole authority of Scripture bore equally against Roman Catholicism. For the traditional religion, salvation was an external, objective thing, which the disciple could never know with any personal certainty this side of purgatory. All that could be done was to trust the teaching of the Church and submit to her ceremonies. Against this the Reformers preached that by repentance and faith in Christ there was full and immediate acceptance with God, and that the Holy Spirit himself testifies to the reality of this acceptance in the heart of the believer. United with a risen Saviour, the Christian has the joy of pardon and assurance in present possession.

To the universal objection of Roman Catholicism that the Protestants had fallen into such beliefs through lack of the guidance of the Church (the only true interpreter of Scripture) the evangelicals replied that an understanding of Scripture comes from the Holy Spirit. William Tyndale prized Scripture so highly that he lost his life in giving it to his fellow-countrymen. But he knew that far more than the possession of New Testaments was needed to make men Christians. Nor could any church supply what was necessary. As he told Sir Thomas More, his Roman Catholic opponent:

Though the Scripture be an outward instrument, and the preacher also, to move men to believe, yet the principal cause why a man believeth, or believeth not, is within: that is, the Spirit of God teacheth his children to believe; and the devil blindeth his children, and keepeth them in unbelief, and

[1] Quoted by P. T. Forsyth, *The Person and Place of Jesus Christ*, (London: Independent Press, 1948), p. 220-1.

maketh them consent unto lies, and think good evil, and evil good . . .

It is impossible to understand either Peter or Paul or aught at all in the scripture, for him that denieth the justifying of faith in Christ's blood.[1]

For the Reformers the Reformation was no mere controversy or doctrinal dispute. The Church of Rome, in her opposition to the way of salvation clearly taught in Scripture, was demonstrating her lack of the Spirit of God. This is not, of course, to say that the Reformers believed that the teaching of the Holy Spirit makes the thinking of Christians identical in every respect. But the Spirit teaches every Christian what is essential to salvation. The Roman system, by putting faith in the Church, and its sacramental system, in the place of the finished work of Christ, gave sure proof that she was not being taught of God. Her adherents, commonly, did not know the testimony of the Holy Spirit.

On this same theme John Calvin wrote:

They who strive to build up firm faith in Scripture through disputation are doing things backwards . . . Since for unbelieving men religion seems to stand by opinion alone, they, in order not to believe anything foolishly or lightly, both wish and demand rational proof that Moses and the prophets spoke divinely. But I reply: the testimony of the Spirit is more excellent than all reason. For God alone is a fit witness to himself in his Word, so also the Word will not find acceptance in men's hearts before it is sealed by the inward testimony of the Spirit. The same Spirit, therefore, who has spoken through the mouths of the prophets must penetrate into our hearts to persuade us that they faithfully proclaim what has been divinely commanded . . . By this power we are drawn and inflamed, knowingly and willingly, to obey him, yet also more vitally and more effectively than by mere human willing or knowing

---

[1] *An Answer to Sir Thomas More* (Cambridge: Parker Society, 1850), p. 139, 169.

... I speak of nothing other than what each believer experiences within himself.[1]

* * * *

When we turn to the Evangelical Revival of the eighteenth century the parallel with the Reformation is immediately noticeable. That is not surprising because the men who were raised up for that work adopted a fundamentally similar approach to that of the Reformers. John Wesley had been a fellow at Oxford and a curate in the Church of England while, in his own words, 'I had no more of true love of God than a stone.'[2] When he and Whitefield were awakened to the real nature of Christianity they found themselves immediately opposed on that very point. 'Sir, if this be Christianity,' said one astonished hearer of Wesley's, 'I never saw a Christian in my life.'[3] William Warburton, Bishop of Gloucester, was sure the new evangelical teaching was *not* Christianity and objected: 'Why do you talk of the success of the gospel in England, which was a Christian country before you was born?' To which Wesley replied:

Was it indeed? Is it so at this day? . . . If men are not Christians till they are renewed after the image of Christ, and if the people of England, in general, are not so renewed, why do we term them so? 'The god of this world hath' long 'blinded their hearts.' Let us do nothing to increase their blindness; but rather recover them from that strong delusion, that they may no longer believe a lie.[4]

Wherever he spoke Wesley now pressed the necessity of a true conversion. Given the opportunity to preach in the

[1] John Calvin, *Institutes of the Christian Religion*, trans. Ford Lewis Battles, vol. 1 (Philadelphia: Westminster Press, 1960), pp. 79–80. See also pp. 580–3. This does not mean that the Holy Spirit supplies directly to each individual the evidence necessary to salvation. That evidence is already in Scripture but the Spirit's work is necessary that we should see it.

[2] 'A Farther Appeal to Men of Reason and Religion', *Works of John Wesley*, vol. 8 (London: Wesleyan-Methodist Book Room), p. 61.

[3] *Ibid.*, p. 11.   [4] *Ibid.*, vol. 9, pp. 163–4.

university church of St Mary's, Oxford, his subjects were 'The Almost Christian' and 'Scriptural Christianity'. For the challenge of the latter sermon he was permanently barred from speaking there again. A Christian, he told all men, is one who so knows Christ that all things are secondary to his Saviour. To prove it he would quote such texts as: 'He that loveth father and mother more than me, is not worthy of me' (*Matt.* 10:37); 'If any man cometh to me and hateth not [in comparison of me] his father and mother and wife and children, yea, and his own life, he cannot be my disciple' (*Luke* 14:26). Wesley represents his hearers listening to such texts and responding:

> 'O, but this is not a parallel case! For they were heathens; but I am a Christian.' A *Christian!* Are you so? Do you understand the word? Do you know what a Christian is? If you are a Christian, you would have the mind of Christ; and you would walk as he also walked . . . Are you inwardly and outwardly holy? I fear, not even outwardly.[1]

The clergy immediately complained that such preaching was disturbing the baptized members of the Church. As early as May 1742 Wesley and Whitefield were required to present themselves before the Archbishop of Canterbury. Despite their attempts to avoid causing needless offence, this was only the beginning of trouble. Given the situation, they knew that opposition was inevitable. Whitefield believed: 'It is every minister's duty to declare against the corruptions of that church to which they belong.'[2] Thus when the Bishop of London accused him of saying that he preached 'a new gospel unknown to the generality of ministers and people', far from modifying his words, Whitefield replied:

> 'Tis true, My Lord, in one sense, mine is a new gospel, and will be always to the generality of ministers and people, even in a christian country, if your Lordship's clergy follow your Lordship's directions.

---

[1] *Ibid.,* vol. 8, p. 123.   [2] *Works* (London, 1771), vol. 1, p. 140.

Whitefield then went on to quote the bishop's counsel that a preacher should 'leave no doubt' in their hearers 'whether good works are a necessary condition of your being justified in the sight of God'.[1] Referring to this opinion the evangelist continued:

Was the great apostle of the Gentiles now living, what anathemas would he pronounce against such *Judaizing* doctrine? . . . This is the great fundamental point in which we differ from the church of Rome. This is the grand point of contention between the generality of the established clergy and the Methodist preachers: we plead for free justification in the sight of God, by faith alone, in the imputed righteousness of Jesus Christ, without any regard to works past, present, or to come.[2]

In Whitefield's eyes the bishop's counsel on the need for good works in justification was as needless as it was false because the people already believed in salvation *by good works,* and not surprisingly, for 'our pulpits ring of nothing more than doing no one any harm, living honestly, loving your neighbour as yourselves, and to do what you can and then Christ is to make up the deficiency.'[3]

Wesley contended over precisely the same issue with the Archbishop of York. His lordship, opposing the new preaching, quoted the twelfth canon of the Council of Trent with its denunciation of evangelical belief:

If any man shall say that justifying faith is nothing else but a confidence in the divine mercy, remitting sins for Christ's sake, and that this confidence is that alone by which we are justified, let him be accursed.

The Archbishop declared his approval of these words. He was confident, 'Our Church holds no such scandalous and disgraceful opinion.'[4] To which the evangelical leaders

---

[1] *Works*, vol. 4, p. 15.   [2] *Ibid.*, p. 116.

[3] Whitefield, *Sermons on Important Subjects*, ed. J. Smith (London: Baynes, 1825), p. 197.

[4] Quoted in *Works of Wesley*, vol. 8, p. 73.

replied by showing that the Articles and Homilies of the Church of England themselves taught the very thing which Trent condemned. In the words of Whitefield:

> The generality of our clergy are fallen from our Articles, and do not speak agreeably to them, or to the form of sound words delivered in the Scripture; woe be unto such blind leaders of the blind! how can they escape the damnation of hell? It is not all your learning (falsely so called), it is not all your preferments that can keep you from the just judgment of God.[1]

Again, however, as at the Reformation, the difference went far deeper than articles of faith. For the evangelicals, saving faith was no mere right belief: it was faith wrought in the individual by the power of the Holy Spirit.[2] A Christian is someone into whose heart the Spirit of God has come to reside, to teach and to make a temple for prayer and praise. It was on the subject of true Christian experience that opposition was strongest. The generality of the bishops and clergy were united in the charge that the evangelicals ('Methodists' was the usual derogatory term) were fanatics – 'enthusiasts' was the common term. They regarded them as claiming promises about the Holy Spirit which were only for the apostolic age, and protested that to be anointed with the Spirit, to be led by the Spirit, to preach 'in demonstration of the Spirit and of power', were not experiences intended

---

[1] *Sermons on Important Subjects,* p. 390. John Berridge, who was a clergyman before he was a Christian, agreed: 'There was scarce a clergyman to be found, but who preached contrary to the articles he subscribed. . . . Do you ask how all the clergy came to fall into this pernicious doctrine? I answer, very easily. Every man, whilst he continues under the power of the carnal mind, is naturally disposed to embrace this doctrine.' *Works of John Berridge* (London: Simpkin and Marshall, 1838), p. 362.

[2] On this truth Wesley is as strong as any Calvinist: 'The author of faith is God alone. It is he who works in us both to will and to do . . . There is no more of power than of merit in man; but as all merit is in the Son of God, in what he has suffered and done for us, so all power is in the Spirit of God. And therefore every man, in order to believe unto salvation, must receive the Holy Ghost.' *Works of Wesley,* vol. 8, p. 49.

for the eighteenth century. On which assertion Wesley commented:

> Accordingly, whenever we speak of the Spirit of God, of his operations on the souls of men, or inspiring us with good desires and tempers; whenever we mention the feeling of his mighty power 'working in us' according to his good pleasure; the general answer we have to expect is, 'This is rank enthusiasm. So it was with the Apostles and first Christians. But only enthusiasts pretend to this now.'[1]

Against the Bishop of Lichfield who argued that the privileges of John's Gospel, chapters 14–16, are no longer possessed by Christians, Wesley pointed out that the promised comfort of the Spirit was given to the same number as received the command, 'If ye love me, keep my commandments. And I will pray the Father.'

> None surely can doubt but these words belong to all Christians in all ages. The following words are, 'Even the Spirit of truth, whom the world cannot receive.' True, the world cannot; but all Christians can and will receive him for ever . . . I assert that till a man 'receives the Holy Ghost,' he is without God in the world; that he cannot know the things of God, unless God reveal them unto him by the Spirit.'[2]

One reason why this teaching of conversion to Christ by the power of the Holy Spirit gave offence was that it appeared to ignore the sacrament of baptism. The Bishop of London complained of Whitefield that he and other Methodists made becoming a Christian sound as though it was a 'sudden and instantaneous change'. To which Whitefield replied that the bishop evidently had no such objection to a 'sudden and instantaneous change' when it came in connection with the popular teaching on the effect of infant baptism:

> For if the child be actually regenerated by the Holy Ghost, when the minister sprinkles water upon him in the name of

[1] *Ibid.*, p. 76.   [2] *Ibid.*, p. 81, 106.

the blessed Trinity, does it not follow, that if any change at all be wrought in the child at that time, it must be sudden and instantaneous . . . With what reason then are these itinerants upbraided for talking of a 'sudden, instantaneous change', upon which the very essence of baptismal regeneration, that Diana of the present clergy, entirely depends? . . . And do not the greatest part of the poor souls now in England, go on secure that they shall be eternally happy, and yet have no better foundation of comfort, and assurance of new birth, than that which is founded on the doctrine of a sudden and instantaneous change wrought upon them in baptism?[1]

Neither Wesley nor Whitefield would be drawn into a general debate on the theology of the sacraments. Nor did they attempt to explain how the teaching of the Articles was consistent with the language of other parts of the Prayer Book. They simply stuck to their witness as evangelists and scorned any idea that baptism was enough to identify a Christian. Wesley writes:

I tell a sinner, 'You must be born again.' 'No,' says you: 'He was born again in baptism. Therefore he cannot be born again now.' Alas, what trifling is this! What, if he was *then* a child of God? He is *now* manifestly a child of the devil; for the works of his father he doeth. Therefore do not play upon words. He must go through an entire change of heart. In one not yet baptized, you yourself would call that change, the new birth. In him, call it what you will; but remember, meantime, that if either he or you die without it, your baptism will be so far from profiting you, that it will greatly increase your damnation.[2]

Speaking of the opposition of the clergy on this same point Whitefield says:

The first quarrel many had with me was because I would not

---

[1] *Works,* vol. 4, pp. 161–2. 'Diana': the 'great goddess' of the Ephesians (*Acts* 19:27).
[2] *Works of Wesley,* vol. 8, p. 48–9.

say that all people who were baptized were born again; I would as soon believe the doctrine of transubstantiation.[1]

At the heart, then, of the eighteenth-century awakening was the question of what a Christian is. The evangelicals ('Methodists') believed that the clergy at large fell under the same condemnation as the false prophets of whom God said, 'You have strengthened the hands of the wicked, so that he does not turn from his wicked way to save his life' (*Ezek.* 13:22). Their opponents replied: 'Their doctrine is too strict; they make the way to heaven too narrow.' On which words, Wesley made the all-important observation: 'And this is in truth the original objection (as it was almost the only one for some time), and is secretly at the bottom of a thousand more, which appear in various forms.'[2]

It was certainly 'at the bottom' of the charge that the evangelicals were no true 'churchmen'. They were said to be 'undermining, if not openly destroying the Church'. They were 'dividing the Church'. Their duty, they were told, was 'to have a greater regard to the rules and orders of the Church'.[3] Such complaints were commonplace and to them all the evangelicals replied by asserting that an understanding of the church was not possible without first understanding what a Christian is. The real problem of their accusers was that they were wrong on that fundamental question. The Bishop of London, Whitefield warned, was treating nominal Christians as being in 'a very imperfect state', whereas the truth was that they were 'in no state of Christianity at all'.[4] 'Church or no Church,' said Wesley, 'we must attend to the work of saving souls.' And when challenged about his allowance of lay-preachers, he replied: 'Soul-damning clergymen lay me under more difficulties than soul-saving laymen.'[5]

---

[1] *Important Sermons*, p. 699, or again, see p. 229. 'The country swarmeth', said Berridge, 'with baptized rakes, baptized worldlings, and baptized infidels.' *Works*, p. 331.

[2] *Works of Wesley*, vol. 8, p. 215.   [3] *Ibid.*, pp. 30, 35, 119.

[4] *Works*, vol. 4, p. 6.

[5] J. H. Rigg, *The Churchmanship of John Wesley* (London: Wesleyan-Methodist Book Room, 1886), pp. 99, 88.

This was certainly a radical diagnosis of the state of so many of the clergy. For confirmation that it was true, Wesley appealed to the principle set down by Christ, 'The tree is known by its fruit' (*Matt.* 12:33), and he pressed its relevance on the opponents of the revival. He argued that, as a 'plain, demonstrable fact', God had poured forth his Spirit 'on the outcasts of men', and that 'this was not done in a corner'. Thousands who were previously irreligious and immoral were now transformed, and among these people, 'Cursing, sabbath-breaking, drunkeness, with all other (however fashionable) works of the devil, are not once named . . . Sinners leave their sins: The servants of the devil become the servants of God. Is this good or evil fruit?'[1] Across the land, he believed the fruit of the work of the Spirit was to be seen: 'Many began to show such a concern for religion as they never had done before. A stronger impression was made on their minds of the importance of things eternal, and they had more earnest desires of serving God than they ever had from their earliest childhood.'[2]

Despite all this, Wesley said to the clergy, when 'God begins a glorious work in our land',

> You set yourself against it with all your might, to prevent its beginning where it does not yet appear, and to destroy it wherever it does. In part you prevail. You keep many from hearing the word that is able to save their souls. Others who have heard it, you induce to turn back from God, and to list under the devil's banner again.[3]

For the evangelicals the reaction of their opponents was sure evidence that they were reading the situation correctly. Their insistence on saving faith in Christ was at the heart of the division. Therefore when faced with the complaint, 'They think none can be saved but those of their own way', they did not hesitate to reply: 'Most assuredly they do. For as there is but one heaven, so there is but one way to it, even the way of faith in Christ.'[4]

---

[1] *Works of Wesley,* vol. 8, pp. 41, 216.
[2] *Ibid.,* p. 203.   [3] *Ibid.,* p. 237–8.   [4] *Ibid.,* p. 216.

There are two observations arising from this retrospect:

1. The evidence shows that, just as true Christian teaching is the same in different ages, so is the nature of Christian experience. The parallel between the evangelicals of the sixteenth and the eighteenth centuries had nothing to do with any premeditated imitation on the part of the latter. It was that both went back to Scripture: it was evangelical truth, in the hands of the Spirit of God, bearing the same fruit. Of course, in many respects the children of one century will always differ from those of another, but when it comes to a saving experience of Christ there is a fundamental unity. A Christian is a person enlightened to believe the truth and to trust the Word of God. A Christian is one whose greatest pleasure is to see God magnified in Christ. A Christian ever has compassion for all men, recognizing that it is only the grace of God which has made him to differ.

Thus, for the evangelical leaders of the eighteenth century, fundamental biblical truths had universal and unchanging application. From those truths they deduced that their century's broad and polite definition of Christian was false. They also knew that the hostility of many academics and clerics was no cause for surprise or dismay, for what the New Testament taught on the nature of regeneration gave them a sound explanation. Thus when John Newton wrote to a friend he could speak as follows about one of the distinguished 'liberals' of their time:

Dr Taylor of Norwich told me, one day, that he had critically examined every original word in the Old Testament seventeen times; and yet he did not see those glorious things in the Scriptures which a plain enlightened Christian sees in them. The Doctor had not the plain man's eyes. Criticism in words, or rather ability to make them, is not so valuable as some may imagine. A man may be able to call a broom by twenty names, in Latin, Spanish, Dutch, Greek, &c. but my maid, who knows the way to *use* it, but knows it by only one name, is not far behind him.[1]

[1] *Letters and Conversational Remarks by the late John Newton, During the Last Eighteen Years of his Life* (London: Burditt, 1809), p. 167.

Newton returned to the same basic truth in correspondence with the Rev. Thomas Scott, a fellow-clergyman, whom he could not regard as a Christian. To a reply from Scott on the subject of Christian truth and experience, Newton responded:

> You quite misunderstand what I spoke of the light and influence of the Spirit of God. He reveals to me no new truths but has only shown me the meaning of his own written word; nor is this light a particular revelation – it is common to all believers . . . This (as you bid me to be explicit) is the one thing which I think you at present lack. And I limit my expression to *one thing*, because it is our Lord's expression, and because that *one thing* includes many.[1]

At the time Scott was irritated by this plain dealing, but it was to Newton's faithfulness that he would later attribute his conversion.

The light which is 'common to all believers' remains the same today. Thus when Professor Eta Linnemann became a humble Christian, she tells us how instantly she discovered a new Bible:

> God's inspired Word, which has many human authors but ultimately only one divine originator, exhibits a wonderful unity. As soon as I accept by faith the self-testimony of the Word of God regarding the inspiration of Scripture, I begin to realize this wondrous unity. How glorious is the framework of promises relating to our Lord Jesus Christ.'[2]

[1] Letter 6 to 'The Rev. Mr. S.', *Works of John Newton,* vol. 1 (Edinburgh: Banner of Truth, 1988), p. 588. Newton's faithfulness with Scott played a major part in the latter's conversion. John Berridge's conversion occurred in the same way. See his testimony below, pp. 321–2.

[2] Linnemann, *Historical Criticism of the Bible* (Grand Rapids, Baker, 1990), pp. 151–2. At the same time she came to believe that the condition of her distinguished mentor, Rudolf Bultmann, was the same as her own had been. He did not know the Holy Spirit (p. 87). Dr R. V. G. Tasker, Professor of New Testament Exegesis in the University of London, provides another twentieth-century example of a teacher of academic theology becoming an evangelical Christian. Thereafter he immediately began to write in defence of the authority of Scripture. See *Lloyd-Jones: The Fight of Faith*, p. 183. It is said that Tasker was cold-shouldered in the Common Room on affirming his new faith.

John Stott's words on how the Holy Spirit changed his view of Scripture is another identical evangelical testimony:

> Before I was converted I used to read the Bible every day but I did not begin to understand it. After I received Jesus Christ as my Saviour and Lord, one of the first ways in which I knew that something had happened to me was that the Bible became a new Book. As I read it God began to speak to me.[1]

My case in the above pages is that, whereas the vision of evangelicals in the sixteenth and eighteenth centuries was determined chiefly by fundamental beliefs, the policy of both Billy Graham in the United States, and of the Keele and Nottingham Congresses in England, was shaped too largely by other considerations. The idea that the Keele platform of Anglican evangelical comprehensiveness could claim the sanction of Whitefield's name (as has been suggested)[2] is to me incredible. Speaking of evangelicals in the Church of England structure Colin Bedford wrote after NEAC 2:

> We often exist at a superficial level in the deanery because we never dig down deep enough to find what really matters to us. As long as we keep away from discussion about what evangelism, mission, the new birth, conversion and commitment mean, we can survive together. But is that enough?[3]

Let that be compared with such an entry in Whitefield's *Journals* as the following for 29 January 1739:

> Sat up till near one in the morning, with my honoured brother and fellow-labourer, John Wesley, in conference with two clergymen of the Church of England, and some other strong opposers of the doctrine of the New Birth. God

---

[1] Dudley-Smith, *John Stott*, p. 99.

[2] McGrath, *Packer*, pp. 121–2, 289. Whitefield no more stood for 'full involvement in the Church of England' than did his friend John Berridge, condemned by Gervase Duffield above (p. 100). Anyone in doubt how Whitefield regarded non-evangelical clergy should read his 'Letter to the Clergy of Litchfield and Coventry', and his 'Observations on Some Fatal Mistakes' addressed to William Warburton, Bishop of Gloucester. *Works*, vol. 4, pp. 173–99, 285–302.

[3] *77 Notts Untied*, p. 103.

enabled me, with great simplicity, to declare what He had
done for my soul, which made them look upon me as a mad-
man ... I am fully convinced there is a fundamental difference
between us and them. They believe only an outward Christ,
we further believe that He must be inwardly formed in our
hearts also. But the natural man receiveth not the things of the
Spirit of God, for they are foolishness unto him.[1]

2. There is a prominent feature in the evangelical history of
the eighteenth century which may explain why many
evangelicals in Britain and the United States have taken a
different course in these last fifty years. As we have seen,
evangelical leadership today has been much concerned with
a matter about which their predecessors took a very different
view, that is, the approval and support of non-evangelical
clergy and denominational leaders. Wesley and Whitefield lost
any possibility of gaining the good opinion of their peers at
the very outset of their work. But, far from moderating
themselves in an attempt to win it back, they regarded the
very idea as a temptation to be resisted. In the midst of a
worldly church they saw the bearing of reproach as a necessary part of being a Christian. 'In our days,' said Whitefield,
'to be a true Christian, is really to become a scandal.'[2]

The church leaders of the eighteenth century did their
utmost to hinder other clergy from turning evangelical and
one of the principal threats was the certain loss of reputation
and preferment. Wesley said that 'great pains were taken' to
keep the number willing to take a bold stand few in number.
Any who did so 'could give up at once all thought of preferment either in Church or State; nay, all hope of even a
Fellowship, or a poor Scholarship, in either University'.[3]

For Wesley and Whitefield resistance to such threats was
the duty of all who do not live for the approval of man. To
clergy who failed to make such a stand as Scripture

---

[1] *George Whitefield's Journals* (repr. London: Banner of Truth, 1960), pp.
203–4. For similar references see pp. 350, 414, 478, 526.

[2] *Ibid.,* p. 32.

[3] *Wesley's Works*, vol. 8, pp. 217–8.

commands, Wesley said: 'You dare not: because you have respect of persons. You fear the faces of men. You cannot; because you have not overcome the world. You are not above the desire of earthly things. And it is impossible . . . till you desire nothing more than God.'[1]

Whitefield spoke in very similar terms to Christians who were fearful of how their good name would suffer if they risked the displeasure of their peers. One waverer was Dr James Stonehouse of Northampton who, while sympathetic, was afraid of the bold course which Whitefield was taking and wished to keep his friendship with the evangelist a secret. To him Whitefield wrote:

> I would have neither of you expose yourselves to needless contempt on my account. But then, I would not have my friends act an inconsistent part towards the Friend of all, that Friend of sinners . . . I do not believe God will bless either you or your friends, to any considerable degree, till you are more delivered from the fear of man . . . Whosoever renounces the world and takes up Christ's cross, and believes the doctrines of Grace, must be styled a Methodist, whether he will or not.[2]

There is reason to believe that evangelical policy of more recent times has not given due account to one of the most basic facts of evangelical Christianity. It has lacked due regard to the depravity and deceitfulness of human nature and to what Christ assures will happen when his truth meets the minds of unregenerate man. From apostolic times onwards, wherever the gospel has entered with discriminating power, it has been with disturbance, opposition, and personal

---

[1] *Ibid.*, p. 225.

[2] *Works*, vol. 2, pp. 182, 223, 263. When Samuel Davies and Gilbert Tennent were in Britain, seeking to raise money for the College of New Jersey, Davies recorded of Whitefield: 'He thinks we have not taken the best course to keep in with all parties, but should "come out boldly" as he expressed it; which would secure the affections of the pious people from which we might expect the most generous contributions.' Davies' Journal, in W. H. Foote, *Sketches of Virginia* (Richmond: John Knox Press), 1966, p. 247.

reproach for its preachers. 'As he who was born according to the flesh then persecuted him who was born according to the Spirit, even so it is now' (*Gal.* 4:29). Luther had biblical reason to say:

> Those who are in the teaching office should teach with the greatest faithfulness and expect no other remuneration than to be killed by the world, trampled under foot, and despised by their own . . . teach purely and faithfully, and in all you do expect not glory but dishonor and contempt, not wealth but poverty, violence, prison, death, and every danger.[1]

It has ever been the same. Understanding this the successors to the eighteenth-century evangelical leaders in the Church of England recognized the spiritual danger which respectability could bring upon them. Dr Joseph Milner, one of the leaders of that post-revival generation wrote to a fellow clergyman in 1794: 'I feel I need to pray continually, lest I be carried away by the the civilities of the world. We began as despised preachers of Jesus; in meekness and simplicity may we continue so to the end.'[2] In the same vein William Wilberforce warned his son, Samuel, of 'dread of ridicule' and 'the fear of singularity' as things which could 'greatly injure your advance in the Christian life'.[3]

Among the foremost Anglican preachers of the nineteenth century to learn this lesson was J. C. Ryle, with whose testimony I close this chapter:

> I have learned in the last thirty-two years that if a clergyman leads a quiet life, lets alone the unconverted part of the world, and preaches so as to offend none and edify none, he will be called by many 'a good Churchman'. And I have also learned that if a man studies the Articles and Homilies, labours continually for the conversion of souls, adheres closely to the great principles of the Reformation, bears a faithful testimony

[1] *Luther's Works*, vol. 12, pp. 220–1.
[2] *Life of Isaac Milner*, p. 100.
[3] Quoted in Newsome, *The Parting of Friends* (London: John Murray, 1966; repr. Grand Rapids: Eerdmans, 1993), p. 55.

against Popery, and preaches as Jewell and Latimer used to preach, he will probably be called a firebrand and 'troubler in Israel,' and called no Churchman at all! But I can see plainly that they are not the best Churchmen who talk most loudly about Churchmanship.[1]

---

[1] Ryle, *Warnings to the Churches*, p. 111–2. On the question, 'Wherein do evangelical Churchmen fall short of their great predecessors in the eighteenth century?' he answered: 'They fall short in doctrine. They are neither so full nor so distinct, nor so bold, nor so uncompromising. They are afraid of strong statements. They are too ready to fence, and guard, and qualify all their teaching . . . Only let the evangelical ministry of England return to the ways of the eighteenth century and I firmly believe we should have as much success as before.' *Christian Leaders of the Eighteenth Century* (repr. Edinburgh: Banner of Truth, 1978), pp. 430–1.

7

'Intellectual Respectability' and Scripture

I n previous pages I have sought to show how the inter-dependence of evangelicalism in the United States and Britain has led to common developments in both countries. Evangelicalism on one side of the Atlantic has resonated with that on the other and it is not accidental that the same patterns have emerged. I turn now to another feature which has marked evangelicalism in the English-speaking world since the 1950s, namely, a transference of leadership from preachers and pastors to evangelical intellectuals teaching in the academic world.

In the United States the change was led by Fuller Theological Seminary, with its emphasis on setting new standards of evangelical scholarship and competence. Referring to the goal in view, its president could write in 1957,

'Evangelicalism bids fair to capture the theological leadership in America.'[1] Harold Ockenga, chairman of Fuller's board of trustees could refer to the 'new respect for the evangelical position', and he was hopeful that this could be traced to 'a change in the intellectual climate of orthodoxy':

> The younger orthodox scholars are repudiating the separatist position, have repented of the attitude of solipsism, have expressed a willingness to re-examine the problems facing the theological world, have sought a return to theological dialogue and have recognized the honesty and Christianity of some who hold views different from their own in some particulars.[2]

A similar change was taking place in England. In terms of the wider world of scholarship, evangelical theology existed in a backwater in the 1950s. Speaking of the Church of England, Colin Buchanan has written of that period, 'The Evangelical colleges and their whole theological stance were dubbed "Stone Age" by the rest of the Church.'[3] The problem, it seemed, was the absence of professional theologians, and thus by the 1960s, as Alister McGrath notes, some evangelical Anglicans 'were advocates of the concept of the "career academic" – an idea which ran counter to the prevailing notion that the teaching staff of theological colleges were simple clergy taking five years out from their parish careers'.[4] Instead of the old practice of clergy teaching clergy it began to become common for bright students to go straight into teaching posts. David Stancliffe defended the change in this remarkable argument: 'Most people of middle age and beyond have not remained in touch with the academic subjects to the required level. And people coming out of

[1] E. J. Carnell to H. J. Ockenga, unpublished letter, 23 December 1957. I am indebted to the Ockenga Institute, Gordon-Conwell Seminary, Mass., for use in this chapter of unpublished letters between the two men.
[2] 'Resurgent Evangelical Leadership', *Christianity Today*, 10 October 1960. Solipsism is the view that self is all that exists or can be known.
[3] *Is the Church of England Biblical?*, p. 5.
[4] McGrath, *Packer*, p. 97.

college aren't sullied by the disillusionment of unfruitful parochial experience, nor by just having gone rusty and not being able to read.'[1]

Robert Horn, a Free Church minister, noticed the young academic leadership among evangelical Anglicans when he was asked to speak at two conferences of the Eclectics in 1968 and 1969. He wrote on his impressions of these conferences: 'Many individual parish ministers were deeply uneasy about the Keele direction, but hesitated to say so, feeling unable to handle debate with those (mainly bright theological college staff or academics) who were, it seemed to me, writing the agenda for Anglican evangelicalism.'[2]

These academics, of whom Horn spoke, were for the most part identifiable with the 'young activists' who started to take over at Keele and who set the pace ten years later at Nottingham. 'The new generation of younger evangelical leaders', wrote Capon in 1977, 'are primarily academics . . . and their contributions at Nottingham showed they are beginning to grapple seriously with issues previously almost beyond evangelical reach.' They were engaged, he believed in 'a continuing quest for a "respectable" theology'.[3]

Part of the influence behind this change certainly predated the 1950s and 60s. The IVF's Tyndale Fellowship for Biblical Research, founded in 1944, was a move to counter the image of evangelicals as people who did not believe in intellectual labour and who held blindly to traditions regardless of scholarship. By their failure to participate in the current theological milieu caricatures of this kind too easily succeeded while their real beliefs went unanswered.

With the coming of the ecumenical ethos of the 1950s and 60s, in which all disagreements were played down, a new opportunity had appeared to open. If evangelicals could gain attention in the Church of England why should it not be

[1] Carpenter, *Robert Runcie*, p. 158.
[2] 'His Place in Evangelicalism', in *Martyn Lloyd-Jones: Chosen by God*, p. 26.
[3] Capon, *Evangelicals Tomorrow*, p. 180.

possible for able men, with the same convictions, to attain positions of influence in the university world of academic theology?[1] With this prize in view, young scholars of IVF background were encouraged to set their sights on reaching senior posts in the British universities. Their success has become a matter of history. F. F. Bruce, a classicist, who turned to exegesis of Scripture, was one of the first to lead the way with his appointment to the Rylands Chair of Biblical Criticism and Exegesis in the University of Manchester in 1959. The numbers who subsequently followed him into university posts included James Barr at Manchester and Oxford; James D. G. Dunn at Durham; Ian Howard Marshall at Aberdeen; David Bebbington at Stirling (in his case teaching history); and Richard France at Wycliffe Hall, with its close association with Oxford. All were of IVF background and thus men who professed belief in 'the Divine inspiration and infallibility of Holy Scripture, as originally given, and its supreme authority in all matters of faith and conduct'.

Contrasting what he saw of evangelical participation in theological education in the universities in the 1980s with what he remembered it as being in the 1930s, John Wenham wrote, 'There were now fully thirty competent theologians who were from the evangelical stable.'[2] Others have subsequently quoted higher numbers.

* * * *

In this development the most crucial issue facing evangelical academics was the doctrine of Scripture, for here, more than anywhere, evangelicalism was distinguished by the teaching set down in the IVF basis quoted above. It was, as Ockenga wrote in 1960, 'the watershed' which divided theology.[3]

---

[1] It should be pointed out for non-UK readers that theological teaching goes on in most British universities independently of the theological colleges belonging to denominations.

[2] Wenham, *Autobiography*, p. 217.

[3] *Christianity Today*, 10 October 1960, p. 13.

'Intellectual Respectability' and Scripture

In Britain, at least, the number of scholars on the evangelical side of the watershed was small indeed and to appreciate this we must look briefly at preceding years. In the 1920s theological students were commonly told that 'the theory of the verbal inspiration of Scripture was as dead as Queen Anne'. As Oliver Barclay recalls, 'By the 1930s, evangelicals were effectively the only section of the British churches that held to this truth.'[1] 'The idea has got abroad', wrote Professor A. Rendle Short, 'that men of learning, and especially the scientists, have discovered facts which make the Bible impossible of belief for anyone with a modern education.'[2]

So pervasive was this assumption that a belief which had once been common to Christianity was almost without a spokesman in England's schools of theological training. Even at Ridley Hall in Cambridge, founded by evangelicals in 1881 to prepare men for ministry in 'the Protestant Reformed Church of England', a student in the 1930s found that the principal's 'favourite theologian was John Oman, who broadly followed in the footsteps of Friedrich Schleiermacher'.[3] Dr T. R. Glover in articles in *The Times* in 1932, wrote, 'To-day if you want a real old obscurantist college, you have to found one.'[4]

The Inter-Varsity Fellowship broke with the Student Christian Movement on this issue in the 1920s,[5] and for a time the IVF's testimony to the infallibility of Scripture was unique and alone in the universities. Frank Houghton, who belonged to CICCU (the IVF Christian Union at Cambridge) in the early 1940s, has recorded: 'I was at first amazed to meet very intelligent young people who believed

[1] Barclay, *Evangelicalism in Britain,* p. 10.
[2] A. Rendle Short, *Modern Discovery and the Bible* (London: IVF, 3rd ed., 1952), p. 230.
[3] Wenham, *Autobiography,* p. 72.
[4] Quoted by E. J. Poole-Connor, *Evangelicalism in England* (London: FIEC, 1951), p. 251.
[5] See Douglas Johnson, *Contending for the Faith: A History of the Evangelical Movement in the Universities and Colleges* (London: IVP, 1979), p. 131.

the Bible to be fully inspired and reliable. I had thought that
was only the old and unthinking.'[1]

As evangelical influence grew after the Second World War,
and noticeably among students, opposition centred on the
claim that evangelical Christianity *alone* was being true to
Scripture. A published address by Martyn Lloyd-Jones on the
subject, given at an IVF conference in 1952, drew a stinging
response from Nathaniel Micklem, Principal of Mansfield
College, Oxford. The IVF and Lloyd-Jones outlook, he
charged, was 'divisive, schismatic, obscurantist and quite
unbiblical'.[2] Controversy widened during the Graham
crusades of 1954–55 as clergy and academics noted with
dismay that the American evangelist was clearly a 'fundamentalist' in his view of Scripture. The hostile criticism of
Michael Ramsey and of others led to an emphatic response
from the hitherto-little-known James Packer. In his first IVF
book, *'Fundamentalism' and the Word of God,* published in
1958, Packer observed:

> There is one point, however, on which all 'anti-fundamental-
> ists' seem to agree; that is, that the doctrine of Scripture which
> they attribute to their evangelical brethren (whether they
> define it as dictation, literalism, inerrancy or anything else) is
> new, eccentric and in reality untenable. They note that the
> word 'Fundamentalism' is a twentieth-century coinage, and
> conclude that the thing is as new as its name.[3]

No matter how carefully evangelicals sought to distinguish
between what they believed and the aberrations associated
with some fundamentalists, as long as they held to the verbal
inspiration of Scripture the same label was given to them all.
Thus John Stott was a 'fundamentalist' according to some of
his fellow clergy, even although, as his biographer says, he

---

[1] Quoted in Dudley-Smith, *John Stott*, p. 132.

[2] The Lloyd-Jones address is in *Knowing the Times*, pp. 38–50; I give the
Micklem response in the second volume of my Lloyd-Jones biography,
The Fight of Faith, pp. 228–9.

[3] *'Fundamentalism' and the Word of God*, p. 11.

'had been taught in the best tradition of Cambridge liberal theology'. 'The trouble was,' as Archbishop Runcie once commented ruefully, 'he didn't believe it.'[1] In Stott's own words, in a letter written in 1960, he was 'a despised evangelical'.[2]

* * * *

It constituted no small problem how evangelicals could gain admission and prestige in the academic world if they carried with them such an outmoded belief. In brief, some solution to the difficulty seemed possible in the distinction between the divine and human sides of Scripture. Evangelicals noticed how the neo-orthodox Karl Barth gained credit by recognizing the full 'humanity' of Scripture and they believed that they could do the same without any compromise. Belief in the full inspiration of the Bible requires no weakening of the fact that God spoke through men. There need be no contradiction between the supernatural element and the human authorship. So evangelical scholars believed that they could compete with colleagues in researching the language, the motivation, the education and the cultural background of the biblical writers, without conceding the presuppositions which lay behind liberal scholarship. The human authors could be studied without any denial that what they wrote was also the Word of God. For liberals there was only one approach to the Bible: for evangelicals there were two and these would be complementary rather than conflicting. In the words of John Stott:

> The Bible is both divine and human in its authorship. Therefore we must neither affirm its divine origin in such a way as to deny the free activity of the human authors, nor affirm their active co-operation in such a way as to deny that through them God spoke his word.[3]

[1] Dudley-Smith, *John Stott*, pp. 393, 183.
[2] *Ibid.*, p. 357.
[3] Stott, *Evangelical Truth*, p. 61.

Applying this to the academic level, evangelicals would work with liberals on the human aspects, using the same critical tools, while retaining their own overall position. The immense cleavage of opinion over the actual authority of the Bible could be by-passed, yet with the ultimate intention of making the other side sit up and rethink the credibility of the conservative position. By not beginning with their 'personal beliefs', and by concentrating on the 'human', evangelicals hoped to dispel the prejudice which their position encountered.

How far this hope was fulfilled is now a matter of history and we must look at some of the evidence. Professor F. F. Bruce, as already noted, was one of the first evangelicals into the new field. In 1959, the same year that he began work at Manchester, the IVF issued his work *The Apostolic Defence of the Gospel*. In this he wrote:

> It may be part of our apologetic task to convince people of our day that (as Jesus said to the Sadducees) they are wrong, because 'they know neither the scriptures nor the power of God' (*Matt.* 22:29). It is necessary to inculcate a new aware-ness of the authority of the Scriptures as God's Word written, and a new awareness of the supernatural.[1]

But Bruce's ensuing years in teaching show that he meant to approach the authority of Scripture cautiously and indirectly. There was no question of asserting it as a matter of biblical theology. Instead, his method in teaching was that each part of Scripture has to be assessed without any prior determination to find it consistent with other parts and with-out any controlling belief which necessarily treats all as true. On this he has written:

> Occasionally, when I have expounded the meaning of some biblical passage in a particular way, I have been asked, 'But how does that square with inspiration?' But inspiration is not a concept of which I have a clear understanding before I come to the study of the text, so that I know in advance what limits

[1] F. F. Bruce, *The Apostolic Defence of the Gospel* (London: IVF, 1959), p. 12.

are placed on the meaning of the text by the requirements of inspiration.[1]

Despite the respect in which Bruce was rightly held, the effect of his method led to serious reservations on the part of some evangelical reviewers of his books. On his major work, *Paul: Apostle of the Free Spirit* (Exeter: Paternoster, 1977) an IVF reviewer said:

> There is a noticeable lack of any detailed consideration of such doctrines as the atonement, election, scripture and apostolic authority. He presents Paul's teaching as the developing thought of an apostle, formed out of his exceptional experience of Christ, rather than as the inspired truth of God. Whilst for the most part reaching conservative conclusions, he appears to proceed on largely liberal assumptions.[2]

It is hardly being ungenerous to Bruce to say that if his doctrine of Scripture was the same as that of IVF (of which he remained a vice-president) that doctrine was not proclaimed in his university work.[3]

The tendency which appears in Bruce is full-blown in a number of the professed evangelicals who followed him into the university world. It was James Barr, his one-time junior colleague, who launched a full-scale attack on the teaching to which he had once adhered in his book *Fundamentalism*, referred to above (pp. 98–9). Wenham notes how Bruce was excluded from Barr's criticism of evangelicals and comments, 'Barr reckoned that Bruce was a conservative liberal.'[4]

[1] Bruce, *In Retrospect*, p. 311.

[2] Quoted in Wenham, *Autobiography*, pp. 195–6.

[3] There has to be real doubt over his position on Scripture in view of statements in his autobiography. He regrets evangelical intolerance of the Barthian position. Of his continued assent to the IVF's doctrinal basis he writes: 'I have been signing the latter basis annually as a Vice-President of the IVF/UCCF for a long time now, but no one imposes its terms on me as a test of orthodoxy.' (*In Retrospect*, pp. 187–8, 310.) The implication of a number of statements in his autobiography is that he saw the IVF's position on infallibility as a 'party position' which he tolerated rather than positively supported.

[4] Wenham, *Autobiography*, p. 195.

This was not the last attack on evangelical teaching from its former friends. I have already referred to the 1982 articles on Scripture by James Dunn which led to disruption in *Churchman,* the journal in which they were published. Unlike Barr, Dunn, as a member of the Tyndale Fellowship, was still speaking from 'the inside'. What he wrote in *Churchman* had first been heard, apparently respectfully, by the 1981 Anglican Evangelical Assembly in London. With some subtlety and slight dealing with crucial texts, Dunn presented a case that the Bible does not teach that it is inerrant and that it is indeed more honouring to Scripture and to the Holy Spirit to recognize that fact. He also saw the text of the Bible as 'historically relative'. He argued that because some of its teaching was once true it does not necessarily follow that it is true for all time. Further, the Holy Spirit may give a text a meaning for us now which was not the original meaning, and to accept this, he claimed, is to 'exalt the Spirit' over the letter. Simply to be bound by 'the letter' is 'Pharisaic *legalism',* and when evangelicals attribute to Scripture the authority which belongs only to God they are guilty of 'bibliolatry'. As far as the teaching of Warfield and Princeton on Scripture was concerned, Dunn's language was unmeasured. It was 'exegetically improbable, hermeneutically defective, theologically dangerous, and educationally disastrous.'[1]

One of the most disturbing things concerning the statements of Barr and Dunn on Scripture is the absence of response from all the many other men supposedly upholding the evangelical position in the universities at that date. One of their number was Richard T. France, a well-known IVF/UCCF author and Principal of Wycliffe Hall, Oxford. This was the Anglican evangelical theological college in the city in which Barr taught after leaving Manchester. Dr France appeared to justify the lack of response to Barr from the evangelical academic professionals in these words:

[1] The *Churchman* articles of 1982 are reprinted in Dunn, *The Living Word* (Philadelphia: Fortress Press, 1987), pp. 89–136.

Professor Barr's target was not evangelical scholarship in general (indeed he uses the term 'evangelical' favourably, to denote the Christian tradition which he hopes to rescue from 'fundamentalism'), but those tendencies within it which are founded on 'inerrancy, infallibility, and the other accompanying features' spelled out in his book, one of which is an innate hostility to modern critical study of the Bible, where it appears to lead in a direction incompatible with a doctrine of scriptural inerrancy. 'Conservative evangelicals' who do not exhibit this tendency (he singles out F. F. Bruce for honourable mention) are therefore not included in the book's strictures.[1]

On these words John Wenham has commented:

Barr's attack on fundamentalism was particularly an attack on inerrancy; on the idea, that is, that the Scriptures were the direct product of the God of truth and therefore to be accepted in their entirety. Dick France's response to this was that he hardly ever met a fundamentalist, which presumably means that few of his acquaintances would now defend inerrancy.[2]

---

[1] France and McGrath, *Evangelical Anglicans*, p. 48. France also notes that the writings with which Barr takes issue 'are in many cases those on which the present generation of evangelical biblical scholars has been brought up'. He is reluctant to say plainly that he and others no longer believe what they once did. On Barr's statement that there had been a 'slide towards a liberal position' among evangelicals, he simply says, 'If evangelicalism were to be defined in terms of historical continuity, that might be so.' *Ibid.*, pp. 51–2. France appears to believe that evangelicals teaching academic theology have to show that they do *not* 'follow standard critical method only so far as our evangelical tradition, and the expectations of the evangelical constituency, will allow'. *Ibid.*, p. 49. It is to Packer's credit that he finds no favour with Barr who treats him as a 'hard-liner' and writes, 'It is not probable that the newer current of evangelical opinion will follow Packer' (*Fundamentalism*, p. 228).

[2] Wenham, *Autobiography*, p. 218. The evidence is incontrovertible that, as Bruce said, the basis of faith had ceased to be a test of orthodoxy, in other words, it was not enforced. R. T. France says: 'In the early days of the Tyndale Fellowship, the lines seemed fairly clearly drawn between

It is evident that Dunn's teaching was acceptable at Wycliffe Hall before France became its Principal in 1989. Two years earlier the Durham professor had been there to give the W. H. Griffith Thomas Lectures and had taken Scripture as his subject. In one of these lectures Dunn argued that Jesus was a 'liberal' rather than a 'fundamentalist' in his view of Old Testament Scripture.[1]

All this was no small change. For these men the former position of evangelicalism on Scripture had gone and those who still adhered to it were likely to be caricatured and to receive the same disdain which formerly came from avowed liberals. For 'the Fundamentalist', Michael Saward can write, 'what "the Bible says" is all that matters and its application is no more than the wooden repetition of the words, whatever the circumstances. Such an exposition is no longer acceptable to most thinking Anglican Evangelicals.'[2]

We are faced then with the question how the evangelical endeavour to gain influence in the universities had come to such a position within twenty years? Part of the answer has to be that the idea that the 'human' side of Scripture can be addressed without insistence on divine revelation was mistaken from the outset. While the human element and the divine may be distinguished in words, in reality they are so miraculously conjoined that the human cannot be truly understood without giving full weight to the supernatural. Certainly God did not obliterate the individual personalities and gifts of the writers, but he so controlled and directed

those who might be regarded as evangelicals and those who might not ... A survey of the contemporary situation shows that matters have for some time stood otherwise ... Members of the Tyndale Fellowship will in fact divide over many, perhaps all, of the issues which were once regarded as touchstones of orthodoxy. Evangelical theological colleges, too, embrace the same diversity.' *Evangelical Anglicans*, p. 38.

[1] Dunn, *The Living Word*, pp. 46–55.

[2] Saward, *Evangelicals on the Move*, p. 44. There was no objection from Saward and his colleagues (who started *Anvil*) to the Dunn articles in *Churchman*.

them that their words are those of the Holy Spirit.[1] There is therefore no possibility that the 'human' part of Scripture can rightly be studied separately. On this subject Dr Griffith Thomas, one-time principal of Wycliffe Hall, Oxford, wrote:

> Divine truth was given to, through, and for man, and when we accept the book as a record of the Divine revelation it will be found that it is not the 'human element' that impresses, but the Divine element ... By all means let us discover all that we can about the 'human element,' but let us never forget that it is not the human but the Divine element that constitutes the Bible, the Word of God.[2]

The academic approach to Scripture treats the divine element – for all practical purposes – as non-existent. History shows that when evangelicals allow that approach their teaching will sooner or later begin to look little different from that of liberals.

On this point Dr Oliver Barclay, from long familiarity with the university scene in Britain, has made the following perceptive comment:

> University theology in the twentieth century has been both highly reductionist and also very rationalistic ... Academic scholars delight to find differences between the various authors [of the Bible], and, if possible, between an author's

---

[1] 'The very words of God' (*Rom.* 3:2; *Acts* 7:38); 'the Holy Spirit spoke by the mouth of David' (*Acts* 1:16; 4:25), 'by Isaiah' (*Acts* 28:25), and by all the prophets (*2 Pet.* 1:20–21). Expressions such as 'the Lord said' are used some 3,808 times in the Old Testament. What Scripture says is what God says, and 'it is written' is always conclusive argument for Christ (*Matt.* 4:6–10, etc.). Further, what belongs only to God is attributed to Scripture: Scripture 'foresees' (*Gal.* 3:8); controls events (*Mark* 14:49), 'cannot be broken' (*John* 10:35), and will 'endure for ever' (*1 Pet.* 1:25).

[2] *Principles of Theology*, p. 118. As Packer has written, belief in inerrancy does not negate the need for the careful interpretation of Scripture, but 'it commits us in advance to harmonize and integrate all that we find in Scripture teaching . . . and so makes possible a theological grasp of Christianity that is altogether believing and altogether obedient.' 'Encountering Present-Day Views of Scripture' in *The Foundation of Biblical Authority*, ed. James M. Boice (Grand Rapids: Zondervan, 1978), p. 79.

earlier and later writings. (How else can one find something original to say for a thesis?) The Bible is then treated as bits and pieces of a mosaic that do not fit together . . . Theological study has been highly rationalist, and this has produced a tradition of believing only what can be rationally justified. Evangelicals working in this milieu have followed the tradition and argued for a conservative position on exclusively rational grounds. They have been pushed into this policy by the desire to defend biblical teaching in the only way that others will accept . . . Christianity has always been a matter of divine revelation rather than what can be argued for by human reason. No university in Britain would now boast that for them 'the fear of the Lord is the beginning of wisdom'. One wonders if any university theology department could rightly claim that motto today. Training for the ministry surely ought to do so, and not to ape the university faculties, which have increasingly different aims and intellectual foundations . . . Theology in the rationalist tradition is really philosophy and not theology because it depends on what the human mind can find acceptable. If evangelicals continue to teach theology in this tradition (even in evangelical colleges), they must expect to sterilize the preaching of many of their students . . . We cannot continue to teach theology through a rationalist methodology and expect to produce anything other than liberal evangelicals.[1]

John Wenham was an evangelical Anglican clergyman who spent most of his life in the university cities of Cambridge, Durham and Oxford. As one of the founders of the Tyndale Fellowship he was an eager supporter of the plan to get evangelicals into the theological departments of the universities and I have quoted above the figures he gives to show its numerical success. But by the 1980s he had serious misgivings. He had come to believe that it is 'difficult for evangelicals in high places to stand out clearly; they tend to be indistinguishable from the liberal establishment'.[2]

[1] Barclay, *Evangelicalism in Britain*, pp. 128–9, 131
[2] Wenham, 'Fifty Years of Evangelical Research: Retrospect and Prospect', *Churchman*, vol. 103, no. 3, p. 214..

Later Wenham went further and wrote that 'conservatives had largely abandoned their role as an opposition to the current liberal criticism of the Bible and had become part of the establishment'.[1] And in his judgment of how this had happened he concurs with Oliver Barclay: 'It increasingly became the practice to regard biblical inspiration as something slightly peripheral, not to be defined too closely. Criticism came to be thought of as something neutral.'[2]

* * * *

The quest for intellectual respectability shows the same pattern in the United States. It led to an irresolvable tension in the life of Edward Carnell as already partially indicated above.[3] Carnell's career at Fuller had begun with high expectations for the seminary's nation-wide influence. He was convinced that the policy of intellectual competence, combined with an effort to work within the mainline denominations, could succeed: 'If Fuller Theological Seminary rises to its full potentialities, seeking to please only the Almighty, a hungry world will beat a path to our door.'[4] For

---

[1] Wenham, *Autobiography,* p. 266. Dr Carl R. Trueman of the University of Aberdeen, and the current editor of *Themelios*, has stood out in repeating the same warning from within the academic world. In an article, 'The Impending Evangelical Crisis', *Evangelicals Now*, Feb. 1998, he wrote of 'the collapse of doctrinal consensus in the world of scholarly evangelicalism over recent years' and continued: 'One need only look at many of the works emerging from contemporary evangelical scholars to find that the notion of scriptural authority as understood in any of its classical, orthodox ways has in general been replaced either by the concepts of neo-orthodoxy or simply by silence on the most prickly issues. The enemies are too often Charles Hodge, B. B. Warfield and Carl Henry ... The saddest thing in this context is that few of the elder statesmen of evangelicalism are prepared to point out what is happening, apparently happy to allow the heirs presumptive to overthrow their legacy.'

[2] *Ibid.*, p. 218.

[3] See above, pp. 37–9.

[4] Carnell to Ockenga, 15 December 1948 (unpublished).

Westminster Theological Seminary, with its 'come-out-ism' belief, there was scarcely such a possibility.[1]

But if Fuller's men were to gain acceptance in the denominations at large the Seminary needed accreditation from the American Association of Theological Schools (an agency under liberal direction), and to that end Ockenga and Carnell had to act on principles which were ultimately incompatible: On the one hand they needed to demonstrate that Fuller exemplified the 'openness' axiomatic for academic recognition; on the other they were committed to upholding the inerrancy of Scripture. To advance the first of these Carnell sought to show – as we have seen above – that evangelicals were not averse to self-criticism and that fundamentalism was not to be taken as at all points identical with biblical Christianity. But when he did this in his *Case for Orthodoxy*, and sometimes in the columns of the liberal journal the *Christian Century*, he downplayed the irreconcilable nature of the difference with liberalism in a way which alarmed close colleagues.

On seeing the proofs of *Case for Orthodoxy*, Ockenga had told his friend that 'this self-criticism is wholesome.'[2] But by the spring of 1960 the Boston pastor (who continued to be chairman of Fuller's trustees and was the seminary's 'final authority in all its major matters'[3]) had changed his mind. He wrote to Carnell at Pasadena:

[1] 'There is no seminary in the land, including Westminster, that is equipped to do this, outside of Fuller.' Carnell to Ockenga, 22 October 1954 (unpublished). Westminster, of course, was far from being 'fundamentalist'. When John Murray, its professor of systematic theology, gave special lectures at Fuller in 1955 Carnell reported to Ockenga: 'We had a splendid time. I think that many of the members of the faculty had the impression that a professor from Westminster would appear on our campus with an overweening personality and a stuffy Calvinism. Mr. Murray's personal humility and his sublime and majestic devotion to the Scriptures proved to be a refreshing experience for all.' 30 March 1955 (unpublished).

[2] 9 December 1958 (unpublished).

[3] Wilbur M. Smith, *Before I Forget*, p. 293.

While I think you have said many things that needed to be said in the book and in these articles,[1] I nevertheless feel that you are making a mistake in waging a running battle against the fundamentalists when our real enemy is the modernist. During my whole ministry the *Christian Century* has been the mouthpiece of modernisn in its denial of the Trinity, the authority of the Word of God, of the supernatural, of the resurrection of Christ and of the atonement. Therefore in your second article, I would have expected you to level your big guns against modernism as much as you did against any errors or aberrations of fundamentalism, but this you certainly did not do.[2]

In an immediate but brief response to this letter, Carnell thanked his friend for 'gracious, forthright advice,' and concluded with this significant question: 'In the beginning you said that Fuller Seminary should train men to return to the major denominations. Have you changed your mind?'[3] Ockenga replied:

No, I have not. I believe this is the most effective strategy for our day. I would not overlook the fact, however, that in spite of our record at Fuller it is practically impossible to get a man into the Los Angeles, the Redlands, the San Jose, the Seattle and the Portland Presbytery. I am afraid if it were not for my own influence in the Boston area of Congregationalism, we would not be able to get them into the Congregational Church . . . My only concern is that we do not forget in the great modernist controversy the men who suffered were these true evangelicals.[4]

At this point Carnell had already laid down his office as president at Fuller. The tensions of the situation were too much for him. He concluded the above exchange with

[1] The Carnell articles in the *Christian Century* to which he referred were 'Beyond Fundamentalist Theology', and 'Orthodoxy: Cultic vs. Classical' (30 March 1960).
[2] 6 May 1960 (unpublished).   [3] 9 May 1960 (unpublished).
[4] 14 May 1960 (unpublished).

Ockenga with the suggestion 'we wait the verdict of history. It is too soon to tell.'[1] But as far as Fuller was concerned the resolution of conflicting principles came sooner than either man expected and in a way which neither desired.[2] Daniel Fuller, son of the founder, became dean of the Seminary, although sympathetic to a broader view of biblical authority. Supported by sufficient members of the faculty and the trustees, David A. Hubbard was made president in 1963, despite the fact that he also needed to reinterpret the seminary's stated position on Scripture. Under Hubbard, Fuller Seminary moved into the mainstream of the American churches and, as Marsden writes, he implemented 'Ockenga's earliest vision that the school had been unable to sustain in its fundamentalist-evangelical days'.[3] But it was at the cost of Scripture. Hubbard came to represent his predecessors' beliefs on inerrancy as 'the gas-balloon theory of theology. One leak and the whole Bible comes down.' By 1982 it is said that only about 15 per cent of the student body in the School of Theology held to the conviction of the seminary's founders on inerrancy.[4] In Carl Henry's words, Fuller Seminary 'moderated its initial biblical commitments and became infatuated with numbers'.[5] Carnell, not yet fifty years old, died in 1967 while the change was still in its early stages. Ockenga touched on his disappointment at developments when he wrote in 1976:

> Because no individual carried the banner of the new evangelicalism and no one developed a theology or a definite position, many younger evangelicals joined the movement and claimed the name, but did not confess the doctrinal position

[1] 14 May 1960 (unpublished).

[2] I have commented above (p. 38, note 1) on how Carnell's position on Scripture has been misrepresented. James Barr also does this when he says of Carnell, 'Inspiration for him is not an answer, rather it is a problem' (*Fundamentalism*, pp. 223–4). The truth is that in a critical faculty debate on inerrancy in 1962 Carnell argued, 'If we come to the Bible as the verbally inspired word of God we find we have fewer major problems with our system than with any competing system' (Marsden, *Reforming Fundamentalism*, p. 212).   [3] *Ibid.*, p. 266.   [4] *Ibid.*, p. 268.

[5] Henry, *Confessions*, p. 383.

of orthodoxy. This brought neo-evangelicalism into criticism and often, unwisely and unfairly, transferred these criticisms to the original leaders of the movement.[1]

A more recent example of the same kind of process as occurred at Fuller can be seen in the writings of Dr Mark Noll, Professor of History at Wheaton College. In his book *Between Faith and Criticism* (1986), Noll argued that evangelicals ought to secure a 'place in the wider academic world'. But he believed that this would require 'a new maturity among evangelicals', and even a readiness to leave 'secondary preconceptions about the Bible'. In this way, he hoped, 'evangelicals may yet exercise a creative role in scholarship that, in America, has been mostly absent since the dawn of the critical age'.[2]

An obstacle to the advancement of this agenda which Noll (and his British associates) foresaw was how it should be presented without alarming evangelicals and 'the ordinary Christian'. As an example of the trouble that can arise, he instanced a book written by J. Ramsey Michaels of Gordon-Conwell Seminary which led to the termination of his teaching appointment at that theological seminary after twenty-five years' service. Noll quotes Dr Howard Marshall of Aberdeen in praise of Michaels' book. Marshall wrote, 'He has brought the figure of Jesus to life in a new way'[3]; but the problem was that the basis of faith at Gordon-Conwell asserts that the Bible is 'free from error' and Professor Michaels who was terminated evidently did not agree.[4] He taught that some of the actions and words attributed to Jesus never occurred.

[1] Preface to Harold Lindsell, *The Battle for the Bible* (Grand Rapids: Zondervan, 1976), p. 12. This book was dedicated by Lindsell to the four colleagues who had taught with him at Fuller Seminary (Gleason Archer, Edward Carnell, Carl Henry and Wilbur Smith) and who 'stood or stand steadfastly for biblical inerrancy'.
[2] M. A. Noll, *Between Faith and Criticism: Evangelicals, Scholarship, and the Bible in America*. (Grand Rapids: Baker, 1991, 2nd ed.), p. 165.
[3] *Ibid.*, p. 171–2.   [4] *Ibid.* In Michaels' words, the dispute was over matters concerning 'the humanity and historicity of Jesus Christ, and the legitimacy of studying the Gospels historically. The issue is not inerrancy: we agree on that.' Quoted in James D. Hunter, *Evangelicalism: The Coming Generation* (Chicago/London: University of Chicago Press, 1987), p. 254.

Noll's own position on the inerrancy of Scripture is unclear. He regrets that 'evangelical scholars have not entirely broken free from a docetic approach to Scripture, which treats the Bible as a magical book largely unrelated to the normal workings of the natural world, or from a gnosticism which acts as if the key to interpreting Scripture belonged exclusively to one's own sect'.[1] A justifiable meaning may be given to this criticism, but when he goes on to characterize James Dunn as one who wants 'to substitute a better "high" view of Scripture for the one that has dominated conservative evangelicalism since its initial contacts with criticism'[2], there is good reason to be apprehensive. While Noll is prepared to say that Dunn's view 'has its weaknesses', he uses no such moderation in condemning the evangelical and especially the 'fundamentalist' for what he calls the 'scandal' of 'anti-intellectualism':

> When fundamentalists defended the Bible, they did so by arguing for the inerrancy of Scripture's original autographs, an idea that had been around for a long time but that had never assumed such a central role for any Christian movement. This belief had the practical effect of rendering the experience of the biblical writers nearly meaningless. It was the Word of God pure and simple, not the Word of God as mediated through the life experiences and cultural settings of the biblical authors, that was important.[3]

This is a repetition of the charge so often made by liberals that if Scripture is to be regarded as inerrant then no attention need be given to the human and historical elements which went into its composition. But that is not true.

---

[1] *Faith and Criticism*, p. 165. Docetism was an early heresy which undermined the humanity of Christ. Gnostics claimed the possession of a knowledge hidden from others.   [2] *Ibid.*, p. 174.

[3] Noll, *The Scandal of the Evangelical Mind* (Grand Rapids/Leicester: Eerdmans and IVP, 1994), p. 133. Of course, the presence of human factors has to be recognized, but the idea that Scripture cannot be understood unless we first learn all about the 'life experiences' and 'cultural settings' of the biblical authors from sources *outside* Scripture is a denial of what the Bible claims as to its clarity and sufficiency.

Background studies, with the use of other sources, may help to illuminate the text, or to assist in its interpretation, but they can never justly warrant its correction. To set those who believe in an inerrant Bible, over against those who hold to a Bible 'mediated through the life experiences and cultural settings of the biblical authors', is to depict all the upholders of inerrancy as 'fundamentalists'. It would include those who framed the IVF's statement on the infallibility of Scripture in their basis of faith, and yet Noll's book *The Scandal of the Evangelical Mind,* from which we have just quoted, was published by IVP in Britain.

David Bebbington of Stirling University has proposed a way in which the statement on Scripture in the IVF/UCCF basis of faith need not be viewed as upholding fundamentalism. He writes that the first clause in that basis 'affirmed not the inerrancy of the Bible but the infallibility of Holy Scripture, as originally given'.[1] In other words, he wants us to understand that 'infallible' does not mean 'inerrant'. It is true that some have spoken of an 'infallible Bible' when all they meant is that the general *message* is infallible.[2] But it is patently clear that those who drew up the IVF basis believed in the infallibility of the *words* of Scripture,[3] and how that differs from inerrancy no one has ever attempted to explain. The two expressions have long been interchangeable. Certainly

[1] *Evangelicalism in Modern Britain*, p. 259. Others are supposed to have deliberately made the same distinction: 'Even a conservative organization such as the Evangelical Movement of Wales preferred to confess only a belief in the "infallible Bible".' 'British and American Evangelicalism Since 1940', in *Evangelicalism: Comparative Studies*, p. 373.

[2] The most influential modern exposition of this view has been given by Jack Rogers and Donald McKim in their book, *The Authority and Interpretation of the Bible: An Historical Approach* (New York: Harper and Row, 1979). 'How an infallible "message" is carried by an errant text', comments John D. Woodbridge, 'Rogers and McKim never fully explain.' *Biblical Authority: A Critique of the Rogers/McKim Proposal* (Grand Rapids: Zondervan, 1982), p. 28.

[3] See, for instance, Douglas Johnson, *The Christian and His Bible* (London: IVF, 1953) pp. 118–23; and *Evangelical Belief: A Short Introduction to Christian Doctrine as Summarized in the Doctrinal Basis of the Inter-Varsity Fellowship* (London: IVF, 1951).

any distinction between them was as unknown to Packer when he wrote *'Fundamentalism' and the Word of God* as it was later to Barr in his *Fundamentalism*. It is very misleading therefore for Bebbington to imply that the founders of the IVF meant to avoid asserting the verbal inspiration of Scripture. The opposite can be shown to have been the case.

What can repeatedly be heard from professing evangelicals in academic posts are arguments first heard from non-evangelicals. Professor Alan Richardson, for example, argued in *Chambers' Encyclopaedia* in 1950 that belief in verbal inspiration was a novelty of modern times. Bebbington takes the same line in saying that it was a nineteenth-century phenomemon 'which had become common by the early twentieth century', though it held no attraction 'among the educated'.[1] 'In Britain,' he says again, 'inerrancy was seldom made a touchstone of evangelical orthodoxy.'[2] Historical evidence to the contrary is ignored.[3]

Still more significant in undermining the evangelical position on Scripture has been the liberal argument that divine truth cannot be precisely stated in words. Given all the limitations of human vocabulary, it is said, revelation cannot exist in 'propositional form'. God's thoughts so transcend our

---

[1] *Evangelicalism in Modern Britain,* pp. 189–90.

[2] *Evangelicalism: Comparative Studies,* p. 373. As though to give proof of this he writes in the same place, 'The Methodist biblical scholar Howard Marshall explicitly rejected inerrancy without losing the confidence of the evangelical community.'

[3] Nineteenth-century defenders of Scripture such as Dean Burgon (*Inspiration and Interpretation,* Seven Sermons preached before the University of Oxford in 1860-61), and J. C. Ryle (*Old Paths* [London: Thynne, 1898], chapter 1) demonstrate that the inspiration of all the words of Scripture was the historic belief of the church. Three centuries before them, Richard Hooker had written that the authors of Scripture 'neither spoke nor wrote one word of their own: but uttered syllable by syllable as the Spirit put it into their mouths.' See also John Owen, *A Discourse Concerning the Holy Spirit,* Book 2, Chapter 1. For recent books that go carefully into the evidence, see John D. Woodbridge, *Biblical Authority* (Grand Rapids: Zondervan, 1982) and John Hannah, ed., *Inerrancy and the Church* (Chicago: Moody, 1984).

capacity and language that it is a form of 'rationalism' to think
that *words* can convey revelation inerrantly. So it is affirmed.

This is an old argument from philosophy, and it was
adopted a century ago by those who wanted to retain faith in
God's redemptive acts but not in the infallibility of the text of
the Bible which records those acts. 'It is claimed', Douglas
Johnson wrote in 1953, 'that the Bible does not provide us
with definite propositions which would enable us to state
formally what God has been pleased to reveal, and from
which it is possible to draw up a creed.'[1] 'No propositional
revelation in Scripture' was the repeated objection raised
against evangelical 'dogmatism'. Thus, at the same period, we
find Lloyd-Jones responding to the claim that 'fundamentalism cannot be true because it claims that truth can be
reduced to a number of propositions'.[2]

Today professing evangelicals use this same argument
against the verbal inspiration of Scripture. Noll argues that
the shape of evangelical belief in the Bible, and the 'keen
preoccupation with the doctrine of biblical inerrancy' (as
seen at Princeton in the days of Hodge and Warfield), 'was
molded by the eighteenth-century Enlightenment'.[3] In other
words, it was a product of the 'rationalism' which entered
the English-speaking world during 'the Age of Reason'.
'Virtually every aspect of the profound evangelical attachment to the Bible was shaped by the Enlightenment.'[4] So
Noll writes, and he thinks that the retention of the outlook
which he criticizes is no part of Christian duty: 'What is
essential to Christianity, however, is a profound trust in the
Bible as pointing us to the Saviour.'[5]

Alister McGrath, successor to France as Principal of
Wycliffe Hall, Oxford, adopts the same thesis and expands on
it. He agrees that when the teachers of old Princeton

[1] *The Christian and His Bible,* pp. 36–7.
[2] Lloyd-Jones, *Authority* (1958, repr. Edinburgh: Banner of Truth,
1984). p. 8.
[3] Noll, *Scandal of the Evangelical Mind,* pp. 243–4.
[4] *Ibid.,* p. 97.   [5] *Ibid.,* p. 244.

Seminary thought they were upholding an inerrant Bible
they were in reality falling into rationalism. His case depends
on giving a new twist to that word. In the McGrath and Noll
connotation (and they are preceded by other authors) confidence that the human mind *is able to relate words to realities,*
and consequently to hold that the Bible gives us truth in
propositional form, is *rationalism.* Criticizing Charles Hodge
for falling into this, McGrath complains that the Princeton
divine thought

> that today's reader of Scripture can be 'assured of encounter-
> ing the very words, thoughts, and intentions of God Himself'.
> Yet this metaphysical idea has been borrowed, along with
> others of equally questionable theological parentage, from the
> Enlightenment. Hodge's analysis of the authority of Scripture
> is ultimately grounded in an unacknowledged and implicit
> theory of the nature of language, deriving from and reflecting
> the Enlightenment agenda.[1]

But if this criticism is just then it is not only verbal
inspiration which must fall. Evangelicalism is wrong all along
the line, for McGrath proceeds to argue that we must not

[1] McGrath, *A Passion for Truth: The Intellectual Coherence of Evangelicalism* (Leicester: IVP, 1996), p. 169. For a refutation of this line of
argument, see J. I. Packer, 'The Adequacy of Human Language' in
Inerrancy, ed. Norman L. Geisler (Grand Rapids: Zondervan, 1979), pp.
195–226. Douglas Groothuis responds to McGrath on propositional
revelation in 'The Postmodernist Challenge to Theology', *Themelios,*
November 1999, an article from his forthcoming book tentatively
entitled *Truth Decay: Defending Christianity Against the Challenge of
Postmodernism* (InterVarsity Press, USA, promised for April 2000). On the
Princeton position, see David B. Calhoun, *Princeton Seminary: The Majes-
tic Testimony* (Edinburgh: Banner of Truth, 1996), pp. 413–21. Also John
D. Woodbridge and R. H. Balmer, 'The Princetonians and Biblical
Authority' in *Scripture and Truth,* eds. D. A. Carson and J. D. Woodbridge
(Grand Rapids: Zondervan, 1983); and Woodbridge, *Biblical Authority,* on
the cover of which Packer has said, 'The unpleasant task of exposing
shoddy scholarship can rarely have been taken in hand with so much
gentleness and grace.' From McGrath's characterizations of the Princeton
Seminary men one can only wonder how much of their works he has
ever read. He asks us to believe that 'The strongly rationalist tone of this
philosophy is particularly evident from the work of Benjamin B. Warfield.'

identify *truth* with 'the propositional correctness of Christian doctrine'.[1] Frequently connected with this supposedly 'rationalistic' approach adopted by former evangelicals, he thinks, is

> a spiritual embargo on any kind of emotional involvement with Scripture . . . This has had a devastating impact on evangelical spirituality, and placed it at a serious disadvantage in relation to the spirituality of both Roman Catholicism and Eastern Orthodoxy. The Enlightenment forced evangelicalism into adopting approaches to spirituality which have resulted in rather cool, detached, and rational approaches to Scripture.[2]

This thesis rests on a fallacious definition. The *use* of the mind is not 'rationalism'; it all depends on whether that use is right or wrong. Rationalism is a use of the mind which trusts in its own ability to arrive at truth about God *without* his aid and *apart* from revelation: it treats the mind as a source of knowledge rather than as a channel. The Enlightenment was a classic demonstration of innate human pride in the exaltation of the human intellect. To equate that spirit with the teaching of the Princeton men, who believed that it is the grace of God alone which sets men free to understand, is to stand truth on its head.

There are other areas in which it could also be shown that current apologists for what professes to be evangelicalism have simply taken over arguments from men who were formerly regarded as opponents.[3]

* * * *

I turn now to the consequence which always follows a lowered view of Scripture. It is that biblical truth becomes a matter of possibilities or probabilities rather than of

---

[1] McGrath, *A Passion for Truth*, p. 177.   [2] *Ibid.,* pp. 174–5.

[3] The question of pseudonymity, for instance, which was effectively addressed by Packer (*'Fundamentalism' and the Word of God*, pp. 182–86). Yet the liberal view that parts of the New Testament were not written by the authors to whom the text attributes them is now argued by evangelicals as acceptable (for example, France and McGrath, *Evangelical Anglicans*, p. 52).

certainties.[1] According to liberalism this is an asset, not a defect, for it is 'dogmatism' and the 'closed mind' which are indefensible and incompatible with 'scholarship'. There was no complaint in the academic world when Keith Ward was appointed Regius Professor of Divinity at Oxford (in succession to Maurice Wiles) although he believed that, whatever the events which may lie behind the Gospel narratives, they are altogether uncertain and irrecoverable: 'The obvious conclusion', he thought, 'is that we should not try to get back to such objective historical truth, since the quest is impossible.'[2] Professor Dunn's scepticism differs only in degree. In his view, to insist on 'only one orthodoxy' is possibly 'the biggest heresy of all'.[3]

Here is a great divide. Harold Ockenga affirmed, 'The evidence that those who surrender the doctrine of inerrancy inevitably move away from orthodoxy is indisputable.'[4] Dunn, on the contrary, believed that the setting aside of inerrancy is the way to progress: 'It allows greater diversity, leaves more questions open, lets faith be faith in face of greater uncertainties.'[5]

While not writing as advocates of uncertainty, Noll, Bebbington and McGrath all speak of the greater academic or ecumenical freedom which is permissible where there is no insistence on verbal inspiration. 'Keen preoccupation with the doctrine of biblical inerrancy' has to be given up, Noll

[1] Richard Baxter's words are relevant: 'I observed, easily, in myself, that if at any time Satan did more than at other times weaken my belief of Scripture . . . I grew more indifferent in religion than before.' Quoted by W. G. T. Shedd, *Orthodoxy and Heterodoxy* (New York: Scribner, 1893), p. 97.

[2] Keith Ward, *A Vision to Pursue* (London: SCM, 1991), quoted in *Churchman,* vol. 106 (1992), no. 2, p. 177.

[3] J. D. G. Dunn, *Unity and Diversity in the New Testament* (London: SCM, 1990), p. 366. He says this in the context of criticism of 'early Catholicism' which he treats as only one of several justifiable developments from the 'enthusiastic apocalyptic sect' in which Christianity began (p. 364).

[4] Preface to Lindsell, *Battle for the Bible*, p. 12.

[5] Dunn, *The Living Word*, p. 135.

believes, so 'the life of the mind may have a chance'.[1] In the same way McGrath thinks that evangelicalism, revised at this point, 'is perfectly capable of mounting a sustained bid for a justified presence within the academic community, and for intellectual respectability as a serious option for thinking people in today's world'.[2]

Similarly, Richard Lovelace has argued that evangelicalism cannot hold together if there is continued insistence on inerrancy, and, further, that such insistence must work against efforts to reform the mainline denominations.[3] Bebbington agreed: 'Inerrancy, by positing doctrinal purity as a condition of fellowship, tended to encourage separatist convictions.'[4] Noll elaborates on this:

> Many modern evangelicals do show a commendable willingness to listen to other Christians who, only a few decades ago, would have been considered beyond the pale, and this willingness reveals a desire to think through differences . . . If evangelicals will listen carefully to each other . . . then it is possible to imagine that a way will be cleared to benefit from even broader Christian discussions, drawing in Roman Catholics, other Protestants, and the Orthodox, and still more expansive conversations including 'persons of good will' at large.[5]

What these views have in common is their insistence that in accepting them there will be benefit rather than loss for the Christian faith. Noll is sure that, with his opinions, trust in the Bible as 'pointing us to the Saviour' remains

---

[1] *Scandal of the Evangelical Mind,* pp. 243–4.

[2] *A Passion for Truth,* p. 9.

[3] Roger R. Nicole and J. Ramsey Michaels, eds., *Inerrancy and Common Sense* (Grand Rapids: Baker, 1980), pp. 36–47. Lovelace wrote: 'Mainline renewal groups contain some leaders who affirm total inerrancy, but many . . . have moved somewhat away from the Hodge-Warfield position.' He was concerned that biblical teaching on doctrinal purity could be so emphasized that Christian unity is lost and added, 'The New Testament records no heresy trials and no ecclesiastical separations.'

[4] *Evangelicalism: Comparative Studies,* p. 373.

[5] *Scandal of the Evangelical Mind,* pp. 245–6.

unimpaired. He means that it is the person of Christ and our relation to him, not any doctrine of inspiration, which is the great thing – 'not *what* I have believed but *whom*', as the phrase puts it. It is on the basis of this argument that evangelicals have often been accused of putting their 'theory of inspiration' in the place of the Lord himself, and so becoming 'bibliolaters'.[1] Yet the idea that what the Bible makes known on the person and work of Christ can somehow be separated from other aspects of its teaching has often been refuted. We do not know Christ apart from Scripture. In apostolic preaching the testimony of Scripture was integral with the facts of redemption (*1 Cor.* 15:3–4).

Not infrequently opponents of full inspiration seek to turn the tables on those who hold to it by representing them as possessing a weak view of Christianity. For it means, opponents argue, that the Christian faith is made to depend upon just one tenet, as though the whole must fall unless that one point is maintained – 'One leak and the whole Bible comes down'. Dr Anthony Thiselton, spoke approvingly of these words of Hubbard's at the Anglican Evangelicals' Nottingham Congress and warned that any return to the alternative view would mean 'putting the clock back to the 1920s'.[2] Others have referred to commitment to the verbal inspiration position as 'the Maginot line mentality'.

But however often this is repeated it always leaves one great question unanswered. If the Bible is only partly inspired and partly trustworthy, who is to determine which part is the authentic Word of God? Many have attempted to distinguish between parts of Scripture in this way. Sometimes the

[1] Lloyd-Jones, *Authority,* p. 36. Dunn repeats this old line. He fears 'that the heirs of Princeton theology are in grave danger of *bibliolatry*'. *The Living Word,* p. 106.

[2] Quoted in Capon, *Evangelicals Tomorrow,* p. 53. Similarly Dunn writes: 'Integral to the inerrancy position is the all-or-nothing argument, the slippery slope mentality, the repeated reasoning that if we cannot trust the Bible in all, we cannot trust it at all. That may be an argument which appeals to the over-simplifications of spiritual infancy; but it is hardly an appropriate expression of spiritual maturity.' *The Living Word,* pp. 106–7.

distinction is made between 'the form of Scripture and its substance', or between 'the words and the ideas', or between the alleged history and the essential doctrine. The object is always the same: to approve faith in one part and not in another. Yet no one has ever shown where a line can be safely drawn. The imagined line is constantly moving and that because, in the end, no such divisions are tenable, any more than inferences based on a division between the divine and the human aspects of Scripture are tenable. The only alternatives are an acceptance of the truthfulness of all Scripture or a questioning of the whole. Warfield is right: 'There is no standing ground between these supposed parts, between the two theories of full verbal inspiration and no inspiration at all.'[1]

Warfield's conviction is, of course, the 'gas-balloon' belief which Thiselton wanted to set aside at Nottingham. Instead, Thiselton urged that 'Evangelicals should be "where the action is", asking such questions as, "Do we have the words of Jesus in the gospels?"'[2] But he made no suggestion as to how such a question can be answered without taking the New Testament as it stands. The truth is that there is no answer, only multiplied uncertainties. This is well borne out by the writing of Gerhard Maier, rector of an evangelical study centre at Tübingen. In his work *The End of the Historical-Critical Method*, Maier reviewed a book of essays by leading German theologians and exegetes, written between 1941 and 1971 and compiled by Ernst Käsemann. The object of these fifteen writers was to make the kind of division

[1] B. B. Warfield, *Revelation and Inspiration* (New York: OUP, 1927), p. 423.

[2] Capon, *Evangelicals Tomorrow*, p. 53. The question is akin to that in Genesis 3:1, 'Did God say?' Are we to suppose that God sent his Son to live and die in this world and left us with no dependable revelation of his words? Or are we to believe that the disciples had to make up words they attributed to Christ because his promise that the Spirit 'will guide you into all truth' (*John* 16:13) was untrue? Were the apostles without revelation and simply dependent upon their own thoughts and memories? Close to the argument against inspiration lies unbelief in everything miraculous.

within Scripture on which we have commented above. They wanted to ascertain the original 'New Testament' lying behind what has been accepted as such – 'the canon within the canon'. Their method was the normal higher-critical one, 'according to which the Bible is approached from an extra-Biblical position and with extra-Biblical standards, with the objective of discovering the Word of God in the process'.[1] The result of the endeavours of these fifteen scholars was a total lack of unanimity. Maier concluded:

> It is becoming more and more evident that the higher critical method denotes a Babylonian captivity that hands the exegete over to a harmful degree of subjectivity . . . our examination of the exegetes has demonstrated that none of them was able to delimit or even to discover a convincing canon in the canon.[2]

* * * *

If it is the case that Scripture is sometimes true and sometimes erroneous, then a whole range of consequences follows

1. A proper understanding of the Bible passes from the hands of ordinary men and women to the professional scholar. 'We do not imagine, with some', Bishop Christopher Wordsworth once wrote, 'that the Bible is like a threshing-floor, on which wheat and chaff lie mingled together, and that it is left to the reader to winnow and sift the wheat from the chaff by the fan and sieve of his own mind.'[3] If such sifting was our responsibility, then it is immediately clear that most readers of Scripture would be disqualified from even making the attempt. It would also mean that the alleged clarity of Scripture is no more to be trusted. Instead extra tools would be needed for anyone to be sure of what he or she is reading. Understanding the Bible would thus become

---

[1] G. Maier, *The End of the Historical-Critical Method,* trans. E. W. Leverennz and R. F. Norden (St Louis: Concordia, 1977), p. 24. First published as *Das Ende der Historisch-Kritischen Methode* in 1974.

[2] *Ibid.,* p. 40.

[3] Quoted by Ryle, *Old Paths,* p. 20, from Wordsworth on *Inspiration,* p. 11.

the preserve of 'the scholars'. 'Many thinkers are now aware that we can read Scripture only in the light of hermeneutical history and the way the church employs the Bible.'[1] Criticizing what contemporary theologians have done in Germany in this regard, Maier has written:

> They have obscured the clarity by their 'proof' of contradictions in the Bible, and they have clung to and deepened the obscurity by means of their fruitless search for a canon in the canon. They have undermined the sufficiency of Scripture by claiming that the historical-critical work was necessary in order to comprehend the Scriptures.[2]

2. It follows that, if Christian belief in Scripture is reduced to conjectures and uncertainties, then a broad toleration of almost all opinions is allowable. Any dogmatism over 'points of view' has to be unscholarly as well as uncharitable. William Barclay was a typical spokesman for academic theology when he wrote: 'I am not likely to condemn a man's beliefs, I shall only think him wrong if he refuses to extend to men the same sympathy that I extend to him.'[3] To 'live and let live' is the one option for anyone teaching in the university world. Even in many theological seminaries this holds good. Speaking of seminaries in the United States, Professor Thomas C. Oden has written: 'The very thought of asking about heresy has itself become the new heresy. The archheresiarch is the one who hints that some distinction might be needed between truth and falsehood, right and wrong.'[4]

---

[1] Stanley J. Grenz, *Revisioning Evangelical Theology* (Downers, Ill.: IVP, 1993), p. 96.

[2] Maier, *Historical-Critical Method*, p. 48.

[3] W. Barclay, *Testament of Faith* (London: A. R. Mowbray, 1975) p. 30.

[4] Thomas C. Oden, *Requiem: A Lament in Three Movements* (Nashville: Abingdon Press, 1995), p. 47. A Report by the Advisory Council for the Church's Ministry recommended that men should be preferred for the ministry of the Church of England whose faith is 'an active search for fuller insight; a restless quest for truth . . . certainty is therefore not to be had . . . and firmness is to be found, we suggest, not so much in credal statements . . .'. Quoted by David Holloway, *The Church of England: Where Is It Going?* (Eastbourne: Kingsway, 1985), p. 207.

There is good reason why the laying aside of an earnest contending for the faith has usually gone hand in hand with a cessation of belief in the full inspiration of Scripture. Once doubt about the words of Scripture is admitted, what is to be defended becomes a great deal less definite. But Scripture itself lays great emphasis on its *words*. It is words which have to be obeyed (*Matt.* 7:24; *John* 14:23); words about which we are not to be ashamed (*Luke* 9:26); words that are going to be fulfilled (*Luke* 21:22); words which the Holy Spirit teaches (*1 Cor.* 2:13); words that must be held fast (*2 Tim.* 1:13). Once allow that we cannot be sure of the words of Scripture, then it ought to be no surprise if there is no resolute defence of the faith. As J. C. Ryle has written:

> If the words of Scripture are not all inspired, *the value of the Bible as a weapon in controversy is greatly damaged*, if not entirely taken away. Who does not know that in arguing with Jews, Arians, or Socinians, the whole point of the texts we quote against them often lies in a single word? What are we to reply if an adversary asserts that the special word of some text, on which we ground an argument, is a mistake of the writer and therefore no authority?[1]

3. Finally, it follows that a denial of the full inspiration of Scripture leads to theological teaching and education which is destructive and futile rather than enriching and upbuilding in the faith. Instead of certainties, worthy to be preached and taught, students are introduced to what their lecturers trust are the latest results of biblical scholarship. The fact that this scholarship is so quickly out of date, and to be replaced by new 'insights', seems to cause these instructors no misgivings. Presumably they regard changes as the inevitable result of progress, and think that theology is no different from any other branch of learning.

The differing results of ministries which accept this principle of uncertainty and those holding a full commitment

[1] Ryle, *Old Paths*, p. 23.

to Scripture are readily verifiable, and yet they are little considered. I want to enlarge on this difference with some examples and contemporary testimony.

The ministry of J. C. Ryle, first Bishop of Liverpool (1880–1900), was devoted to teaching what Scripture says, and the result has been the abiding fruitfulness and relevance of his writings. By 1897 an estimated twelve million copies of Ryle's tracts and booklets had been sold and his writings continue to be read world-wide today. Compare this with the work of his son, Herbert Edward Ryle, Hulsean Professor of Divinity at Cambridge and ultimately Dean of Westminster. Herbert Ryle, in contrast with his father, believed that verbal inspiration was 'irretrievably shattered'. He probably agreed with his biographer that the tendency of the Evangelical Revival was towards 'bibliolatry'. From the year 1916, Herbert Ryle was at work on a *Commentary on the Minor Prophets* and much of the work was done by the time of his death in 1924. Yet it was never published. A professor of theology, asked to evaluate it, considered the manuscript 'the work of a tired man'.[1] It was probably already out of date. Today no one reads Dean Ryle of Westminster.

Another contrast with the first Bishop of Liverpool is the ministry of one of his successors, Albert A. David, who served the same diocese from 1923 to 1944. David was a man who 'saw it as his task to set minds and spirits free'. This 'freedom' included supporting euthanasia and Unitarian speakers in Liverpool. His biographer says:

> In an important and expressive pamphlet 'Who are Christians?' (1934) he contended that no men of Christian life and goodwill should be excluded from the fellowship 'because they cannot express their kindred faith in our terms'. 'Exclude no one' was his abiding conviction . . . He often quoted with approval some words that reflected his own life and belief, in

[1] M. H. Fitzgerald, *Memoir of Herbert Edward Ryle* (London: Macmillan, 1928), p. 350.

as much as:

> *Each year he dreamed his God anew*
> *And left his older God behind.*[1]

Some of the most telling testimony to the barrenness of the controlling spirit in modern theological education comes from those who have themselves supported the system. Dr Eta Linnemann was a student under Rudolf Bultmann and Ernst Fuchs in Germany and belonged to the same liberal school as her mentors. After successful training she entered upon a career as an author and professor of theology in West Germany. Of the prevailing type of theological teaching she has written:

> The undeclared yet working basic principle of Old Testament and New Testament science is: What the text clearly states can, by no means, be true. The exegete's task is to *discover and solve* 'difficulties' in the text of the Bible. The better the interpreter, the more ingenious this will be.[2]

Such was Professor Linnemann's own practice, until, as she said,

> bitter personal experience finally convinced me of the truth of the Bible's assertion: 'Whoever finds his life shall lose it' (*Matt.* 10:39). At that point God led me to vibrant Christians who knew Jesus personally as their Lord and Saviour . . . God took my life into his saving grasp and began to transform it radically. My destructive addictions were replaced by a hunger for his Word and for fellowship with Christians . . . Suddenly it was clear to me that my teaching was a case of the blind leading the blind. I repented of the way I had misled my students. About a month after this, alone in my room and quite apart from any input from others around me, I found myself faced with a momentous decision. Would I continue to control the Bible by my intellect, or would I allow my

---

[1] Michael Smout, *Four Bishops of Liverpool, 1880–1965* (Liverpool: Diocesan Centenary Committee, 1985), p. 51.
[2] Linnemann, *Historical Criticism of the Bible*, p. 149.

thinking to be transformed by the Holy Spirit? John 3:16 shed light on this decision, for I had experienced the truth of this verse. My life now consisted of what God had done for me.[1]

The consequence for Linnemann was that she labelled her former teaching 'poison', destroyed her published writings, and became a missionary in Indonesia.[2]

Thomas Oden was a student at Yale Divinity School in the 1960s, where he talked of receiving a diet of 'divinity fudge', and where he did his doctoral dissertation on Bultmann. Thereafter, as a minister in the United Methodist Church, he went into the work of teaching theology. Of his position on Scripture at that time he leaves us in no doubt: 'For years I tried to read the New Testament without the premises of incarnation and resurrection.' This was no problem in the 'liberated' circles where he worked because, 'Virtually all mainline Protestants are steeped in a tradition of tolerance and amiability.'[3] When Dr Oden at last came to a personal crisis of faith his eyes were also opened to the 'insolvency of theological education', and in his *Requiem* he elaborated on the whole theme:

After a lifetime of teaching in orthodoxly retrogressive seminary settings, I am very nearly convinced that the present system is practically irreformable . . . I truly regret having to make these symptoms a matter of public record. Why?

[1] *Ibid.,* pp. 18–19.

[2] In Bultmann's theology, Linnemann wrote, 'the Holy Spirit is pushed aside'. Bultmann denied Christ's incarnation and resurrection, yet Noll can say, 'It is the truly benighted evangelical who comes away from intensive study in, say Bultmann, without more than a little to inspire evangelical faith.' *Faith and Criticism,* p. 184.

[3] Oden, *Requiem,* pp. 15, 91. The intellectual ethos is only 'intolerant and uncharitable when it comes to traditionalists of any sort, all of whom are capriciously labeled "fundamentalist"' (p. 35). Oden does not name his own location (it was 'better', he believed, than 'old-line ecumenical seminaries . . . even with its quirks and follies'); his intention was rather 'to reflect generally on the broader scene of liberated ecumenism and on theological education the world over' (p. 18). He is currently Professor of Theology at Drew University.

Because I am describing an institution I have spent my life in trying to build, to nurse, and to some extent fundamentally repair. So there is a heavy sense of private failure and personal loss and principled emptiness in this discussion.[1]

Oden's book goes on to describe how he faced the issue of remaining in 'a seminary system that I think has drifted so far afield'.

A more careful and less personal statement has come from Dr John H. Leith in his recent book, *Crisis in the Church: The Plight of Theological Education*. After fourteen years in pastoral charges, Leith, a minister of the Southern Presbyterian Church, taught for thirty-one years at Union Theological Seminary, Virginia, of which institution he remains Pemberton Professor of Theology Emeritus. The crisis of which he writes is 'a crisis of belief. Many basic Christian doctrines are at risk on seminary campuses today'.[2] Institutions 'sponsor with believers' money those who are seeking to undermine the Christian church and faith'.[3] Leith's conviction is that 'the problem today is not primarily paganism, not doubt, not the Enlightenment, not the culture, but the corruption of the Christian faith.'[4] This has come about, he argues, from the wrong treatment of Scripture:

The recovery of the reading of the Bible as scripture, not as a piece of Near Eastern literature and not as a text for scientific study, must have priority in the seminary . . . The agenda and context for the study of scripture must be set by the faith of the worshiping, believing community that built seminaries to prepare pastors. The questions Christians ask of their scriptures differ significantly from those of secular scholarship . . . The Bible must be taught in seminaries so that students come under the power of the Holy Spirit to cherish it as God's Word to each Christian believer and to each Christian community. Professors cannot do the work of the Holy Spirit, but they

---

[1] *Ibid.*, p. 36.
[2] Leith, *Crisis in the Church*, p. 10. [3] *Ibid.*, p. xii. [4] *Ibid*, p. 36.

ought not create difficulties for the work of the Holy Spirit, much less a defiance of the Holy Spirit.[1]

The concern for 'up-to-dateness' Leith sees as a main part of the present tragedy. 'The plethora of theologies in the last fifty years has contributed to a *break* with the past. All the contemporary theologies have been more concerned with answering the questions of the present than with articulating the theological heritage.'

The result has been a failure to produce pastors and preachers ready to transmit the faith by which alone congregations can be built and society changed. He tells us that in his denomination, where as late as 1923 more than fourteen thousand could recite the *Shorter Catechism*, a biblical illiteracy now prevails, even among those who come as students to seminaries. Leith deplores what the present ethos in seminaries has produced at the parish level and asks how it is that teachers are so unwilling to face the history of what has already occurred elsewhere:

Theologies written in German universities and in the tradition that began with Schleiermacher fascinate many American theoogians today. This theology has many striking qualities: generally a wide philosophical background, an intellectual cleverness, and not infrequently a pedantic quality. Yet those who are fascinated with this theology have not, to my knowledge, taken seriously the ineffectiveness of this theology in Germany itself and in Europe. Why has this theology so little effect on the vitality of a declining church in Europe and so little impact on social and political life?[2]

[1] *Ibid.,* pp. 49–52.
[2] *Ibid.,* p. 38. Maier, as a German, makes the same point: 'Through the use of the higher-critical method we have been far removed from the directive of Jesus: "Search the Scriptures for in them ye think ye have eternal life: and they are they which testify of Me" (*John* 5:39) . . . The subtle net woven by the higher-critical method resulted in a new Babylonian captivity of the church. It became more and more isolated from the living stream of Bible proclamation, and therefore more and more uncertain and blind both as to its own course and also in relation to its influence towards the outside.' *Historical-Critical Method,* p. 48.

The main point of all the above is surely clear: evangelicals who step into situations where it is professionally unacceptable to teach the infallibility of Scripture come under immense pressure to show that the difference between them and their non-evangelical colleagues is not as great nor as serious as the Bible says it is. And where the desire to share the intellectual respectability associated with 'modern scholarship' is strong, we should not be surprised if a less 'rigid' view of Scripture soon comes to be espoused. In some cases, as we have seen, the process may well end with men criticizing the very evangelical Christianity which, it seemed, they once wished to see re-established.

The way in which the same pattern has emerged on both sides of the Atlantic is also unmistakable. Referring to a weakened doctrine of Scripture, Dr D. A. Carson of Trinity Evangelical Divinity School has commented: 'In evangelical academic circles, the change in the last decade and a half or two decades is remarkable.'[1] At more length, James Davison Hunter writes of the whole trend which has occurred:

> The irony in the Evangelical case is that the emphasis placed upon gaining intellectual credibility for the Evangelical position (from the late 1940s to the present) may ultimately have the unintended consequence of undermining the Evangelical position. What began as an enterprise to defend orthodoxy openly and with intellectual integrity may result in the weakening or even the demise of orthodoxy as it has been defined for the better part of this century. To come full circle, the weakening of the plausibility of traditionalist approaches to the Bible among Evangelical intellectuals appears to be foreshadowing a similar dynamic among the larger Evangelical population.[2]

It is not commitment to scholarship as such which has brought this reversal, for high standards of scholarship have

---

[1] K. S. Kantzer and Carl F. H. Henry, eds., *Evangelical Affirmations*, (Grand Rapids: Zondervan, 1990), p. 351.

[2] J. D. Hunter, *Evangelicalism: The Coming Generation*, p. 33.

frequently been present in church history without such consequences. The fault has been rather, as Hunter also says, that 'the theological tradition is conforming in its own unique way to the cognitive and normative assumptions of modern culture'.[1] This means in turn that the quest for respectability went fundamentally wrong in not giving its true weight to the biblical revelation on human depravity.

To suppose that because of their culture and their learning the universities are somehow neutral when it comes to the Bible is to deny that this whole fallen world is in a state of hostility to God. John Stott is right when in speaking of our Christian witness today he says: 'Either we are unfaithful in order to be popular, or we are willing to be unpopular in our determination to be faithful. I very much doubt if it is possible to be faithful and popular at the same time. I fear we have to choose.'[2] We wish the principle contained in these words had been more apparent in the church policy with which Dr Stott's name has been identified.

Evangelicals in academic circles have therefore no reason to be surprised when their teaching is given a reception very different from the tolerance which is shown to others. John Wenham, a long-time advocate for an evangelical presence in the theology departments of the universities, came to speak with dismay of how little had come from earlier hopes: '*We ourselves have scarcely dented the academic world.* People can write books about contemporary theology and not mention us at all . . . we are not considered as offering an alternative school of biblical criticism.'[3]

---

[1] *Ibid.,* p. 46.

[2] Stott, *Evangelical Truth*, pp. 99–100. 'Critical historical study and the secular university are never faith-neutral' (Leith, *Crisis in the Church*, p. 51).

[3] *Churchman*, vol. 103 (1989), no. 3, p. 214. He adds: 'We have gained some ground and lost some ground and could lose a great deal more if the liberals were to get their way' (p. 218). Referring to scenes familiar to him in the United States, Professor Oden writes: 'Evangelicals are marginalized, demeaned, and systematically cut out of significant representation.' *Requiem*, p. 97.

It was not a passing quirk of the first century that Christianity was 'everywhere spoken against' (*Acts* 28:22). Certainly
the gospel can penetrate academia. It has done so in the past.
But it has never done so by a quiet coalescence within
systems with which it is basically incompatible. Christians are
not to be sheep in wolves' clothing. The Christian faith is
rather at its strongest when its antagonism to unbelief is most
definite, when its spirit is other-worldly, and when its whole
trust is not 'in the wisdom of men but in the power of God'
(*1 Cor.* 2:5).

In this chapter I have not always maintained a distinction
between theology as taught in secular universities and as
taught in theological seminaries and colleges which are not
under secular control. The latter obviously have greater
opportunity to be biblical and some seminaries use their
freedom well. In general, however, the gap between seminaries and the universities has decreased to the point at which
one can speak, as Leith does, of 'the secularization of the
seminaries'. The pressure of secular accrediting agencies,
supported by the prestige of the great universities and their
famous teachers, is a very powerful one. Robert Yarbrough,
the American translator of Linnemann's book, is right to
observe: 'Evangelicals can ill afford to be complacent about
where their own scholarship, influenced as it is by the larger
academic world, is taking them.'[1]

As the theological seminaries have followed the universities
in making degree courses part of their curriculum, so the
marketing of degrees has become crucial in their appeal to

---

[1] Translator's Introduction, Linnemann, *Historical Criticism,* p. 12. In
Scotland the conservative Free Church of Scotland College in Edinburgh
took a decision to relate its courses to the degree programmes of
Edinburgh University, although, as its present principal has commented,
it was a difficult choice between 'conservative elements in the denomination' and accreditation which has 'to conform to criteria laid down by the
liberal-humanist establishment'. D. Macleod, 'The Free Church College
1900–1970,' in *Disruption to Diversity:Edinburgh Divinity 1846–1996,* D. F.
Wright and G. D. Badcock, eds. (Edinburgh:T. & T. Clark, 1996).

new students.[1] It is not insignificant that in these last fifty years, when this change has so widely occurred, the health of the churches whose pastors have depended on this system has generally steadily declined. As Linnemann tersely comments, 'Parishioners receive a condensed version of what was learned at college.'[2]

Speaking of the new emphasis on degrees since the World War II period, Leith has written, 'Many of the ablest teachers in seminaries and colleges at that time did not have Ph.D.s or any graduate training.' On the same point he noted: 'The ablest graduates of a theological seminary a generation ago went automatically into the pastorate or the mission field . . . When I went to university theological school I suddenly discovered that the ablest students were supposed to take Ph.D.s and become teachers. There is a subtle but a very real change.'[3]

It is beyond the scope of these pages to trace the source of this change but it has an evident close connection with Germany. For it was not only German theology which was adopted by so much of the English-speaking world but a good deal of the German university system also, as it related to theology. It was from there that the Ph.D. (as a qualification for teachers) was taken to the United States in 1861. More significant than that, it was in the German universities that the idea that theological teaching could be done from a 'neutral' standpoint was first established. And with that came a readiness to allow for appointments to theological chairs to belong to the state. No personal knowledge of the gospel was stipulated for professors any more than it was for theological students. In the words of R. L. Dabney:

> To require a credible profession of regeneration and spiritual life, as a prerequisite for joining a theological school (or for

[1] For comment on this in regard to the D. Min. as 'a lucrative product to sell', see D. F. Wells, *No Place For Truth* (Grand Rapids: Eerdmans, 1993), pp. 235–6.

[2] Linnemann, *Historical Criticism*, p. 95.

[3] Leith, *Crisis in the Church,* pp. 58, 92.

receiving ordination and a parish, even), would excite in Germany nothing but astonishment: it would be hard to tell whether the feeling of absurdity or of resentment would most predominate in the German mind at this demand.[1]

Professor Bruce described the very same situation when he wrote: 'In a British university it is quite irrelevant whether a man is conservative or liberal in theology; what matters is ability to teach.'[2]

To suppose that evangelical Christianity can be advanced by the acceptance of such a situation is to disregard what is fundamental to the message of the gospel.

What is most needed today is a renewal of the prayer of Thomas E. Peck:

Oh, that God would write in characters of fire on the hearts of his people those pregnant words, 'that your faith should not stand in the wisdom of men, but in the power of God.'

---

[1] R. L. Dabney, 'The Influence of the German University System on Theological Education', *Discussions: Evangelical and Theological,* vol. 1 (repr. London: Banner of Truth, 1967), p. 443. As Dr Leith has done more recently, Dabney, who wrote in 1881, deplored the failure of men to see the results of this procedure: 'While German scholarship has been busy with its labors, it has suffered almost a whole nation to lapse into a semi-heathenish condition.'

[2] Bruce, *In Retrospect*, p. 143.

8

Rome and
New Division

At the outset of the involvement of evangelicals in the ecumenical movement there was no question in their mind of reunion with the Church of Rome. Speaking at the Islington Conference of evangelical Anglicans in 1960, Maurice A. P. Wood attributed any idea of a Roman Catholic 'take-over' to the fears of 'gloomy prophets'. In 1964 Bishop A. T. Houghton was confident that, despite Vatican II, Rome would remain 'outside the movement for unity', for 'there is not the slightest sign on the part of the Church of Rome that its dogmas, which precipitated the Reformation, have been in any way repudiated or toned down'. 'Rome's idea of unity is still nothing less than the absorption of "separated brethren".'[1] The Keele Congress of 1967 had little to say on the subject. Its Statement was hopeful of 'signs of biblical reformation' but 'could not contemplate any form of reunion with Rome as she is'.

[1] Douglas, *Evangelicals and Unity*, p. 34.

The 1970s and 1980s saw a massive change in the evangelical view. The Lausanne Congress of 1974 heard one of its main speakers affirm the need for 'a catholic evangelicalism', and he went on: 'The time may be ripe around the world for the emergence of a thoroughly biblical evangelical movement that includes both Catholics and Protestants . . . The biblical and charismatic emphases within Roman Catholicism in the wake of Vatican II are rapidly invalidating many traditional Protestant criticisms.'[1]

The Anglican evangelicals' Nottingham Congress Statement of 1977 gave two pages to the subject and affirmed, 'Seeing ourselves and Roman Catholics as fellow Christians, we repent of attitudes that have seemed to deny it . . . We shall all work towards full communion between our two churches. We believe that the visible unity of all professing Christians should be our goal.'[2]

Following the Nottingham Congress, and in the same year, Latimer House, Oxford, sent out an Open Letter, signed by 130 ordained and lay Anglicans to the entire Anglican Diocesan episcopate, supporting the bishops' efforts for further co-operation with Roman Catholics and assuring them of their loyalty 'in seeking unity in Christ with all his people'. This Letter, its organizers went on to say, 'embodies the most striking change of stance' on the part of evangelicals 'in relation to the Roman Catholic Church'.[3]

[1] Howard A. Snyder, 'Co-operation in Evangelism', published in *The New Face of Evangelicalism: An International Symposium on the Lausanne Covenant*, ed. C. Rene Padilla (London: Hodder and Stoughton, 1976), pp. 141–2.
[2] *The Nottingham Statement*, pp. 44–5. 'Evangelicals are confused to hear of the 2,000 Evangelicals who, led by John Stott at Nottingham, April 14–18, 1977, endorsed the rapprochement of the Church of England with the Roman Catholic Church. English Evangelicals at this National Evangelical Anglican Congress were reported as rediscovering the nature of the church.' Johnston, *Battle for World Evangelism,* p. 356. Johnston's book really ends with the Lausanne Congress of 1974. NEAC 2 met while he was still writing. He was, it seems, as yet unaware of the extent to which the Graham organization was proceeding the same way.
[3] Beckwith, Duffield, Packer, *Across the Divide*, p. 14.

No one had yet given an account of why this 'change of stance' took place when and as speedily as it did. Almost overnight doubt whether Roman Catholics were Christians came to be regarded as a sad evidence of former evangelical mistrust and bigotry. One of the reasons for the change was the new evangelical belief 'that there is today a common readiness to hear and be led by what the Bible says'.[1] Another reason was the effect of co-operation with Anglo-Catholics in such things as the defeat of the Anglican-Methodist reunion scheme. The sacramental system came to be treated with new respect and, and as noted earlier, there was growing a view of baptism more akin to Roman Catholicism than to historic evangelicalism. That view figured largely in the unity which David Sheppard, appointed as an evangelical bishop to the diocese of Liverpool in 1975, forged with his Roman Catholic counterpart, Archbishop Worlock. In explaining their unity the two men affirmed: 'The break-through has at least been linked with a new approach to the understanding of baptism. For to recognize the bond of baptism is to acknowledge a common faith in Christ and makes it possible for the baptized to know each other as fellow Christians.'[2]

It is hard, however, not to believe that a chief factor in the Anglican evangelical change towards Roman Catholicism was the sheer pace of the developments going on around them. By the 1970s relignment with Rome had become one of the most popular ideas in the religious scene and it was being advanced by many increased links. 'Only a few more divine miracles', Michael Ramsey said in August 1978, 'will bring us all to that day of unity in truth and holiness, total unity in the Mass given to us by Jesus.'[3] Although Ramsey, by that date had been succeeded as Archbishop of Canterbury by

[1] *Ibid.*, p. 56.
[2] David Sheppard and Derek Worlock, *Better Together: Christian Partnership in a Hurt City* (London: Hodder & Stoughton,1988), p. 66. 'Our union with him through baptism' (p. 69), is a recurring note.
[3] Quoted by Hastings, *English Christianity*, p. 629.

Donald Coggan, the momentum for reunion was not lost. It is remarkable that before Robert Runcie was appointed to follow Coggan in 1980 the appointment was discussed with Cardinal Basil Hume (the Roman Catholic leader in Britain). Hume assured Donald Wright, the Archbishop's Patronage Secretary who visited him, that the Pope (John Paul II since 1978) 'was particularly interested in the Church of England and the Anglican Communion'. Wright noted that the cardinal believed that he would 'want to give reunion a big shove . . . so what [Hume] is hoping for in the new Archbishop of Canterbury is a man who will give reunion an equally large shove'.[1] Runcie, as a liberal Anglo-Catholic, was well able to do that. 'Of course I wouldn't have any difficulty in being a Roman Catholic', he told a friend.[2] His enthronement in Canterbury Cathedral was marked by the presence of several cardinals in the choir near him, the full use of Catholic vestments, a hymn in praise of Mary and Cardinal Hume reading a lesson.[3] Billy Graham was among 'specially invited' guests and gave a 'warm greeting' to the new archbishop.

Two years later Runcie welcomed the Pope himself to Canterbury Cathedral, and Sheppard welcomed him at Liverpool.[4] At this date there was still enough residual Protestantism in the Church of England for John Taylor, Bishop of St Albans, to seek to allay concern in much the same language as Maurice Wood had used in 1960. He wrote in *Home Words*: 'I do not think we need fear that Lambeth will sell our Protestant heritage down the river . . . Nor do I fear that a few days of papal over-exposure will sweep Anglicans unthinkingly into the arms of Rome: the Englishman is too canny to let that happen.' But reaction to Taylor's words

[1] Quoted in *Robert Runcie: Reluctant Archbishop*, pp. 232–3.
[2] *Ibid.*, p. 116.
[3] Hastings, *English Christianity*, p. 613.
[4] Tongue in cheek, no doubt, Runcie's friend, Hugh Montefiore, told him that the Pope's visit put him in 'something of a dilemma . . . before I was enthroned as Bishop of Birmingham . . . I recollect swearing an oath that "no foreign potentate or prelate hath any jurisdiction in this realm of England."' *Robert Runcie*, p. 236.

showed how times had changed since 1960. Archbishop
Runcie's biographer, who reports the quotation just given,
tells us: 'Catholic complaints about Taylor's phraseology were
received at Lambeth, and Runcie delicately administered a
rebuke.'[1]

The year 1980 had, of course, come and gone without the
reunion of the English denominations anticipated in 1964.
Yet, as Adrian Hastings has written, the ecumenical movement was not a failure:

> This was because it had in fact discovered a longer goal. All the
> conventional ecumenical planning hitherto had more or less
> left Catholics out but – however hard it must prove to bring
> them fully in – it was now becoming clear that really no
> significant Christian unity in England could be achieved with-
> out them. The principal achievement of the period was
> precisely this recognition.[2]

The words 'to bring them fully in' would increasingly
come to be seen as a misstatement. The Roman Catholic
understanding of the Church demanded that, not themselves,
but others needed to be brought in. This was demonstrated in
the prolonged discussions carried on in the Anglican–Roman
Catholic International Commission (ARCIC).[3] After the
work of eleven years the commission presented its Final
Report in 1981, representing, it believed, a major advance
towards full communion between the two denominations.
But while there was some use of the language of ambiguity
and obscurity, at no point was there any give in Roman
doctrine. The Final Report was approved by the General

---

[1] *Robert Runcie*, p. 245.

[2] *English Christianity*, p. 627. This was not simply an ecumenical
assessment. Gerald Bray in his first editorial in the reconstituted *Churchman* in 1984 could write: 'It has now become clear in discussion generally
that the major question at issue is, and always will be, reunion with
Rome.' *Churchman,* vol. 98, no. 1, p. 5.

[3] ARCIC had twenty members, eleven of them English. Among them
was Julian Charley whom Hastings calls 'a leading Evangelical'. Charley
had been put forward in the Evangelical Alliance Conference of 1966 to
answer the Lloyd-Jones case.

Synod of the Church of England in 1986; the Vatican delayed its response until 1991 and then, instead of thankful consent, it required that the Catholic teaching – especially on the Eucharist (the Mass) – be spelt out specifically. It wanted assurance that there was agreement on 'the propitiatory nature of the eucharistic sacrifice', applicable to the dead as well as the living; and 'certitude that Christ is present . . . substantially when "under the species of bread and wine these earthly realities are changed into the reality of his Body and Blood, Soul and Divinity"'. This confirmation was given from the Anglican side in *Clarifications of Certain Aspects of the Agreed Statements on Eucharist and Ministry* (1994). The Anglicans assured the Vatican that the words of the Final Statement – already approved by Synod – did indeed conform to the sense required by the official Roman teaching.

In the 1990s the approval of the ordination of women in the Anglican communion and the continuing absence of full agreement on the Pope's position in a reunited Church delayed further formal moves, but in the meantime a new approach to unity was being commended by evangelicals. In his 1995 publication, *Evangelicalism and the Future of Christianity*, Alister McGrath reported the growth of an 'unofficial ecumenism':

> It has two aspects; on the one hand, some individual evangelicals are exploring the attractions of Roman Catholicism; on the other, increasing numbers of individual Roman Catholics are being drawn to evangelicalism while generally remaining publicly loyal to their church. In the short term, this will probably lead to a growing warmth between individual evangelicals and Roman Catholics, despite the substantial official doctrinal divide between them.[1]

This change was probably more advanced in the United States where it had the support of IVP and other publishers. Ten years earlier, IVP in the States (but not in Britain) had

[1] McGrath, *Evangelicalism and the Future of Christianity* (Downers Grove, Ill.: IVP, 1995), p. 178.

published a work by Dr George Carey, which supported seeking reunion with Rome. Carey was the man responsible for steering the ARCIC documents through the General Synod. (These facts were undoubtedly known by those whose influence led to Carey's elevation to the bishopric of Bath and Wells in 1988 and to Canterbury in 1991.) He was confident that the resistance of a Protestant minority 'goes directly against God's will for his people'. He deplored that attitude and believed it failed to see 'that in spite of the differences between us we still belong to one family, the Christian church'.[1]

This whole discusion took a new and far more publicized form in the States in 1994 and, because of its bearings on evangelicalism, we shall look at it in some detail. In March of that year a twenty-five page document was published in New York and widely reported in the media: *Evangelicals and Catholics Together: The Christian Mission in the Third Millennium*. Prepared by a fifteen-strong group from both sides, and 'endorsed' by twenty-five evangelical and Catholic leaders, the ECT statement, as it quickly became known, aimed at promoting united action at the 'grass-roots' both on the social/moral front and in witness to the gospel. From one side of evangelicalism a critical response was immediate, varying from disquiet to downright opposition. Given Dr Packer's standing as an evangelical theologian and the presence of his name among the endorsers it was inevitable that he would become prominent in its explanation and defence. A first step in its explication was a statement produced by Michael Horton and Packer, 'Resolutions for Catholic and Evangelical Dialogue' (August 1994). This intended clarification, produced solely by evangelicals and for evangelicals, restated the traditional position on Roman Catholicism: it repudiated the existence of any consensus 'on all the essential elements of

---

[1] G. Carey, *A Tale of Two Churches: Can Protestants & Catholics Get Together?* (Downers Grove, Ill.: IVP, 1985), pp. 154–5. Foreword by J. I. Packer.

the Gospel' and named 'justification by faith alone an essential of the Gospel on which radical disagreement continues'.[1] But despite the fact that Packer, and two other evangelicals who signed ECT, gave their approval to the 'Resolutions' the controversy continued. Before the end of the year (1994) Dr John F. MacArthur was in print with a lengthy review and rejection of ECT in his book *Reckless Faith*. He was sure the endeavour was wrong: 'The Reformation was not a tragedy but a glorious victory for Christianity. The result of the Reformation was not a breach in the true body of Christ but the recovery of the Gospel of grace from the near obscurity it had fallen into under Catholic abuses.'[2]

Christianity Today, as could be expected, came to the support of ECT. Richard John Neuhaus, Lutheran turned Catholic and the prime mover from the Catholic side in ECT, had already appeared in its columns.[3] Alister McGrath, writing for the 12 December 1994 issue of the magazine, although 'somewhat uneasy about this emerging consensus', believed that evangelicals should be occupied with the need to confront greater dangers:

> The threats to Christian orthodoxy from mainline Protestantism, secularism, and Islam still remain, and evangelicals and Catholics indisputably have more in common with each other than with any of these movements. The question that needs to be addressed is this: Can feuds between Christians be allowed when non-Christians seem to be winning the cultural battles? A divided Christianity is simply a weakened Christianity.

[1] The Resolutions were first published in *Modern Reformation*, July–August 1994, and reprinted in *Evangelicals and Catholics Together: Towards a Common Mission,* eds. Charles Colson and Richard John Neuhaus (Dallas: Word Publishing, 1995).

[2] J. F. MacArthur, *Reckless Faith: When the Church Loses Its Will to Discern* (Wheaton, Ill.: Crossway, 1994), p. 148.

[3] 'A Voice in the Relativistic Wilderness', *Christianity Today,* 7 February 1994. 'The current pope is crusading for "moral truth". We should welcome his help.'

Rome and New Division

In the same issue of *Christianity Today*, Packer contributed four pages under the heading, 'Why I Signed It: The recent statement "Evangelicals and Catholics Together" recognizes an important truth: Those who love the Lord must stand together.'

* * * *

But the difference between evangelicals over ECT was now too wide to be healed simply by articles in the press. Charles Colson (original ECT leader on the Protestant side) accordingly invited ten key evangelicals to a private discussion at Fort Lauderdale on 19 January 1995. Most of the invited group were long-time friends although now divided into supporters or opponents of ECT. For this meeting Packer drafted a further five-point statement which asserted that, for its evangelical endorsers, ECT 'does not imply acceptance of Roman Catholic doctrinal distinctives or endorsement of the Roman Catholic church system'.[1] At the end of what was evidently a difficult and too hurried meeting, the endorsers of ECT seem to have believed that accord had been restored between them and the opponents. For their part they promised that the five points would be as widely distributed to the media as ECT itself had been, and one of those points gave assurance that 'the further theological discussions that ECT promised should begin as soon as possible'. It would appear that Packer and those who took his view supposed that, for the present at least, no further public opposition to ECT would come from brethren present at the meeting and that peace between them had been restored. It was a misjudgment. One commentator has written:

> Unfortunately, the peace began to unravel in less than 24 hours. As most of the leaders caught planes home, MacArthur and Sproul headed for a TV set [that is, studio] to fill a pre-scheduled John Ankerberg show critiquing the ECT statement. When this show went to air nationally, the ECT signers

[1] *Evangelicals and Catholics Together*, p. 161.

[223]

were shocked. They felt the show renewed the attacks on ECT just as though the Fort Lauderdale meeting had never happened. From that point on, relations have gone from bad to worse. It is a sad situation – not that the dispute continues, for there are profound and profoundly important theological issues at stake – but that evangelical leaders who share so much have become so alienated from each other.[1]

On the television programme referred to, John MacArthur, R.C. Sproul and D. James Kennedy did indeed criticize ECT but they also took care to present the motives of Packer and Colson in the best possible light and to express their distress over the division which had emerged among them. It is not easy to see how the broadcast could have caused personal alienation. Two things, however, were clear by 1995. First, there was now a fundamental difference among evangelicals, and second, the movement for evangelical and Catholic consensus to which ECT had given such publicized support was not about to end. 'I am convinced', said Dr MacArthur in the television broadcast, 'that this is only the beginning of a rather large movement which is going to continue to escalate; primarily because of the reigning cry for tolerance, because of the abysmal lack of discernment in the church and because of the tremendous impetus that this unity mentality has.'[2]

One evidence of the escalation occurred in Ireland in July 1998 when a revision of ECT literature was published in booklet form with the signatures of 130 Irish Catholics and evangelicals. Its sixteen pages begin with the assertion that

a billion Roman Catholics and more than 300 million evangelical Protestants represent world-wide the two most rapidly growing Christian communities. Yet in many countries,

[1] Tim Stafford, 'When Christians Fight Christians', in *Christianity Today,* 6 October 1997.
[2] Quoted from the video of the television discussion on ECT entitled *Irreconcilable Differences.* This has a running time of 135 minutes and is available from Grace to You, P.O. Box 4000, Panorama City, USA 91412, or 2 Caxton House, Wellesley Road, Ashford, UK TN24 8TH.

including our own, the scandal of conflict between them obscures the scandal of the cross (*1 Cor.* 1:23), thus crippling the one mission of the one Christ.[1]

At public meetings in Dublin and Belfast the chief speakers at the launch of the booklet were Dr James Packer and Father Pat Collins. Other support came from members of 'Evangelical Catholic Initiative', a group which is said to be backed by the European Programme for Peace and Reconciliation.

As the most able defence of ECT comes from Packer we must address his statements, the fullest of which is to be found in his chapter 'Crosscurrents Among Evangelicals' in the published volume, *Evangelicals and Catholics Together.* In quoting from this source (I will give the page reference within brackets) it is important for the reader to distinguish between the ECT *statement* and the *book* of the same name published a year later (1995). When I use the abbreviation 'ECT' I am referring to the statement. This is reprinted as pages xv-xxxiii in the book (and so all bracket references in Roman figures come from ECT itself). The remainder of the book is made up of six chapters, three from Protestant defenders of ECT and three from Roman Catholics. In distinction from their common endorsement of ECT, each of these contributors took no responsibility for the opinions of the others. Unless this is understood the reader will be confused in what follows.

Packer's starting point is to affirm that ECT is not another ecumenical effort at *rapprochement* with the Church of Rome: 'Co-operation with the Roman Catholic *Church* is not what ECT is about' (p. 165). Or again, 'I am not and could not become a Roman Catholic' (p. 161). He sets down the biblical issues over which evangelical Christianity has always opposed Rome and states that the unity which concerns him is 'with individual Roman Catholics who for whatever reason do not self-consciously assent to the precise definitions

---

[1] *Evangelicals and Catholics Together in Ireland: A Call to Christians in Ireland*, 1998 (ECT, 66 North Rd, Belfast, BT5 5NJ).

of the Roman Catholic magisterium[1] . . . but who think and speak evangelically about these things'. Such individuals 'are indeed our brothers and sisters in Christ, despite Rome's official position' (p. 159). The co-operation which ECT proposes is not one of *churches*. It is rather of evangelicals and 'believing Catholics', acting in the manner of a parachurch agency 'up to the limit of what divergent convictions allow' (p. 149).

The motive behind their alignment, Packer and his fellow Protestant endorsers of ECT argue, is the advancement of the gospel itself. He writes that evangelicals and Catholics who have worked together in supporting moral standards and Christian values, in opposition to humanism, have been brought to recognize that they must go further. They understand that for real moral change in society there has to be the reawakening of conscience, and that cannot be without the re-establishment of Christian truth and doctrine. This is the theme of Colson's impressive first chapter in *Evangelicals and Catholics Together,* and Packer strikes the same note when he writes, 'Adherents to the key truths of classical Christianity . . . should link up for the vast and pressing task of re-educating our secularized communities on these matters . . . domestic differences about salvation and the church should not hinder us from joint action in seeking to re-Christianize the North American milieu' (p. 172). Such co-operation, he is at pains to repeat, is not with theological liberals but with those 'who honour the Christ of the Bible and the historic creeds and confessions' (p. 171).[2] The Bible speaks clearly of the duties which fellow Christians have towards one another, and why should the fact that Catholics and evangelicals

[1] 'Magisterium' = the teaching office of the Roman Church. 'The task of interpreting the Word of God authentically has been entrusted solely to the Magisterium of the Church, that is, to the Pope and the bishops in communion with him.' To this 'Supreme Magisterium' infallibility belongs. *Catechism of the Catholic Church* (London: Geoffrey Chapman, 1995), pp. 28, 207, etc.

[2] 'Historic creeds and confessions', presumably a reference only to the ecumenical creeds of the early centuries of the Christian era.

cannot agree on everything hinder them from 'standing and working together to uphold Christian values and spread the good news of Jesus Christ' (p. 164)?

The opposition to this argument centres on one main objection. It is that the Catholic and Protestant framers and supporters of ECT have recognized one another as fellow-Christians without any agreement on the way in which anyone becomes a Christian. The New Testament presents a gospel which is to be believed *in order to* salvation, and it requires those who would teach that gospel to others to be clear and definite about its message. Yet ECT is blurred at this vital point. It states:

> We affirm together that we are justified by grace through faith because of Christ . . . All who accept Christ as Lord and Saviour are brothers and sisters in Christ. Evangelicals and Catholics are brothers and sisters in Christ (p. xviii).

This language is compatible with the understanding of both Protestant and Catholic. It avoids any indication that behind the agreed words lies a very major difference. The Catholic certainly believes in justifying grace. It is first received through baptism, and subsequently sustained by good works, including faith, confession, penance and the ongoing reception of Christ in the Mass:

> As regards those who, by sin, have fallen from the received grace of Justification, they may again be justified, when, God exciting them, through the sacrament of Penance they shall have attained to the recovery, by the merit of Christ, of the grace lost . . . [In Penance] are included not only a cessation from sins, and a detestation thereof, or, 'a contrite and humble heart', but also the sacramental confession of the said sins, – at least in desire, and to be made in its season, – and sacerdotal absolution; likewise satisfaction by fasts, alms, prayers and the other pious exercises of a spiritual life.[1]

[1] Chapter xiv of the Canons and Decrees of the Council of Trent, in Philip Schaff, *History of the Creeds of Christendom*, vol. 2, *The Creeds of the Greek and Latin Churches* (London: Hodder and Stoughton, 1877),

By such means every 'good Catholic' may be said to 'accept Christ'. The evangelical Protestant believes no such thing about the way of salvation. The grace that makes a person a Christian is not mediated through sacraments; it is the Holy Spirit's work in making a new creature and such a person, by faith in the gospel message, has the obedience (righteousness) of his Saviour reckoned as his own. For the Catholic, justification is a subjective process inherent in us and never so complete in this life that assurance of salvation can be certain; for the Protestant, the believer is righteous before God only on account of Christ's righteousness being credited to him by the declarative act of God; in which act a person, although ungodly in himself, is in the instant of believing freed from condemnation perfectly and for ever.[1]

The framers of ECT were perfectly aware of these distinctions but they by-passed them because, writes Packer, they could not 'be made foundational to partnership . . . so ECT

---

pp. 104–5. There is no major difference between the formulations of Trent and the latest statement of Catholic orthodoxy. The *Catechism of the Catholic Church* is approved by John Paul II as 'showing carefully the content and wondrous harmony of the catholic faith'. It says: 'Since the initiative belongs to God in the order of grace, *no one can merit the initial grace* of forgiveness and justification, at the beginning of conversion [that is, at baptism]. Moved by the Holy Spirit and by charity, *we can then merit* for ourselves and for others the graces needed for our sanctification . . . The children of our holy mother the Church rightly hope for *the grace of final perseverance and the recompense* of God their Father for the good works accomplished with his grace in communion with Jesus' (pp. 437–8). In Catholicism good works are part of the way to salvation. In Protestantism they are evidence that salvation has already been received. See Article XII, 'Of Good Works', in the Thirty-Nine Articles. In Catholicism good works and indulgences also remain a vital means for reducing the pains of purgatory, as the Papal Bull for the Millennium, *Incarnationis Mysterium*, issued on the first Sunday in Advent 1998, indicates.

[1] The words of Richard Hooker cannot be improved: 'The righteousness, wherewith we shall be clothed in the world to come, is both perfect and inherent. That whereby here we are justified is perfect but not inherent. That whereby we are sanctified is inherent but not perfect.' *Works of Richard Hooker,* 6th edition (Oxford: Clarendon Press, 1874), vol. 3, p. 485.

lets go Protestant precision on the doctrine of justification
and the correlation between conversion and new birth . . .
ECT shows skill here, and those who read it as an irrespons–
ible sellout of Protestantism have simply not appreciated what
it was up to' (p. 167).[1]

Packer's case is that it is simple faith in Christ himself, not
a commitment to the 'fine print' of biblical doctrine, which
makes a person a Christian, and he is personally satisfied that
there are many Christians in the Roman Catholic Church
who are in this position. Accordingly he answers the question, 'May ECT realistically claim that its evangelical and
Catholic drafters agree on the gospel of salvation?' with 'Yes
and No'. 'No,' he says, 'if you mean, could they all be relied
on to attach the same small print to their statement, "we are
justified by grace through faith in Christ".' But 'yes', if this is
understood to mean basic faith in Christ himself. 'What
brings salvation, after all, is not any theory about faith in
Christ, justification, and the church, but faith itself in Christ
himself.' [2]

In response to this it has to be said at once that there is no
disagreement over whether individuals may truly belong to
Christ and yet be only babes in understanding. That is not in
doubt, nor is the question how many such persons there may
be in the Church of Rome the issue. The question is
whether, for the ECT vision of 'the common task of evangelizing the nonbelieving world', its vague statement of the
gospel is legitimate and sufficient. 'Domestic differences
about salvation and the Church', Packer writes, 'should not
hinder us from joint action . . . propagating the basic faith

[1] At the same time he elsewhere repeats the Protestant conviction that
'Roman teaching obscures the gospel and indeed distorts it in a tragically
antispiritual and unpastoral manner' (p. 153). 'Rome's official doctrinal
disorders, particularly on justification, merit, and the Mass-sacrifice, so
obscure the gospel that were I, as a gesture of unity, invited to Mass . . . I
would not feel free to accept' (pp. 162–3). In the light of such words, is
it reasonable to complain that critics have not understood what ECT 'was
up to'?

[2] 'Why I Signed It', *Christianity Today*, 12 December 1994.

remains the crucial task' (p. 172). The only logical conclusion to be drawn from this and from his distinction between 'small print' and 'the basic faith' is that the teaching of justification by faith in Christ's righteousness *alone* is not an essential part of the gospel proclamation. Dr R. C. Sproul makes this same point:

> Packer argues that it is faith in Christ himself that brings salvation, not any theory about faith in Christ, justification, or the church. This is a red herring. What Reformed person ever asserted that justification is by faith in the doctrine of justification by faith alone? Who has maintained that doctrinal theory ever saved anyone? The sole point of *sola fide*, which Rome categorically rejects, is that we are saved by Jesus Christ alone. The issue is not, Does Christ save or does doctrine save? The issue is, What is the gospel that must be the basis of any shared mission of faith?[1]

Another implication follows from what is conceded by the evangelicals supporting ECT: If the doctrine of justification is not an essential part of a church's confession, then a foremost reason why Christians should leave the Church of Rome disappears. Despite the corruptions of that Church – on account of which he could not join her communion – Packer does not want to say that there is any basic inconsistency in belonging to Rome *and* believing the gospel. In his view the standing of the Church of Rome as a Christian church is apparently no longer in dispute.[2]

There is a strange inconsistency in Dr Packer's case. On the one hand, he wants to say that the evangelical unity in ECT is 'with individual Roman Catholics who for whatever reason do not self-consciously assent to the precise definitions of the Roman Catholic magisterium' [that is, to official

---

[1] R. C. Sproul, *By Faith Alone* (London: Hodder, 1995), p. 154.

[2] In earlier writing Dr Packer is crystal clear on why the Reformers so strongly opposed Rome, for example in 'What Did the Cross Achieve?' *Celebrating the Saving Work of God*, p. 115. The Reformers 'had to withdraw to save the gospel'. 'Divisions in the Church', *Serving the People of God*, p. 26.

Roman dogma].[1] On the other, he supports the statement
quoted above which is constructed to gain the backing of
Catholics *who do hold to the precise definitions of their faith.* Why
should the trouble be taken to exclude 'precise definitions'
from ECT if the support desired is only from inconsistent
Catholics, out of step with their own Church? The fact is that
it was because the Catholic participants did 'self-consciously
assent' to Roman Catholic teaching that the document could
not spell out in unambiguous form the way of salvation. How
many Catholic signatories would there have been to ECT if
the document had said that a Catholic can only be a faithful
Christian if he or she does *'not* self-consciously assent' to all
their Church holds? Maybe none; certainly not Richard
Neuhaus, Avery Dulles, John Cardinal O'Connor or Bishop
Sevilla. ECT was thus forced to craft its language so as not to
conflict with official Roman teaching. Neuhaus explicitly
rejects the spin put by Packer on Catholic support for ECT
when he criticizes 'Protestant theologians' of the past who
thought Catholics could only be Christians if, by 'felicitous
inconsistency', they did not actually believe what they
professed to believe, i.e., the official teaching of their Church
(pp. 194–5). Speaking of ECT, he writes: 'For evangelicals,
there would be little point in engaging in evangelical-
Catholic conversation with Catholics who are not authentically Catholic' (p. 179). When the short statement entitled
ECT II ('The Gift of Salvation') was issued in November
1997, the defence previously offered by Packer is abandoned
in the affirmation that the partnership is in fact between
'Evangelicals who thank God for the heritage of the
Reformation' and 'Catholics who are conscientiously faithful
to the teaching of the Catholic Church.'

This was a major change, yet Packer signed ECT II. What
can one conclude other than that he no longer holds to the

[1] The quotation is from the document, 'Resolutions for Catholic and
Evangelical Dialogue' which was drawn up only for evangelicals and,
though used by Packer in *Evangelicals and Catholics Together* (pp. 157–9),
was not agreed to by any Catholic signatories to ECT.

'no self-conscious assent' previously set down in response to criticism from evangelicals?

The extent to which the major Catholic contributors to ECT adhere to the official teaching of their Church is made very clear in their chapters in *Evangelicals and Catholics Together.* The ECT statement itself made no reference to 'believing Catholics'. The term was introduced *later* when the participating evangelicals sought to defend their position. The document rather talked in the broadest terms: 'Our mission includes many other Christians, notably the Eastern Orthodox and those Protestants not commonly identified as Evangelical . . . Our present statement attends to the specific problems and opportunities in the relationship between Roman Catholics and Evangelical Protestants' (p. xvi).

But while Colson and Packer subsequently spoke of ECT as representing a unity with *believing* Catholics, the Catholic contributors to *Evangelicals and Catholics Together* never use that qualifying word in referring to any who belong to their communion. And they do not do so because the whole weight of official Roman Catholic teaching enforces the conclusion that all who belong to the 'Church' (that is, the Church of Rome), and who are partakers of her sacraments, are Christians. Thus a sentence in the ECT statement reads: 'For Catholics, all who are validly baptized are born again and are truly, however imperfectly, in communion with Christ' (p. xxx). Any valid baptism, Father Dulles tells us (quoting *Unitas Redintegratio,* 22), 'causes the baptized to be "truly incorporated into the crucified and glorified Christ, and reborn to a sharing of the divine life . . . Thus baptism establishes a sacramental bond of unity existing among all who have been reborn by it"' (p. 131). To speak of a non-Christian, or an unbelieving, Roman Catholic is therefore a contradiction in terms. True to this teaching, Neuhaus insists that communion with the Church (the Roman Church) and communion with Christ are one and the same thing (pp. 214–20). So the Catholic contributors to this book want to speak of 'different ways of being Christian' (pp. 180,

219, etc.) rather than of 'believers' and 'unbelievers'.[1] In so doing they are repeating the language agreed in the original ECT statement – 'There are different ways of being Christian' (p. xxix); and different understandings of conversion, for it may be 'understood as having received the new birth for the first time or as having experienced the reawakening of the new birth originally bestowed in the sacrament of baptism' (p. xxxi).

We conclude that the qualification, 'only believing Catholics', with which the evangelical defenders of ECT propose to limit the proposed unity, is meaningless. Almost any Roman Catholic who is not an avowed liberal could be included, and such broad inclusion is precisely what the Catholic participants in ECT themselves approve.

All this is surely incontrovertible proof that a common mission in promoting 'the gospel' is impossible on the basis proposed by ECT. It should also be pointed out that there is a strange discrepancy in the view of the Catholic supporters of ECT: they profess to be able to adhere to their Church's official teaching *and* to treat teachers of evangelicalism as Christians.

Father Dulles and Father Neuhaus make a good deal of the permission given them by Vatican II to acknowledge the Christian status of non-Catholics. Such persons are said to be 'truly but imperfectly' in communion with the Church even although they do not know it (p. 204). But this hardly gives them the liberty to apply that allowance to Dr Packer. The modification of 'Outside the Church there is no salvation' allowed by Vatican II does *not* cover those who, 'knowing that the Catholic Church was founded as necessary by God through Christ, would refuse to enter it, or remain in it'. The charity extended is for those who 'through no fault of their own' remain non-Catholics, not for intelligent

[1] It is true that Dulles says 'Vatican II declared also that external membership is not sufficient for salvation' (p. 123). The inconsistencies in the Roman teaching are closely connected with her belief that to be a Christian is not necessarily to be saved.

Protestant theologians for whom there is no excuse for ignorance.[1]

* * * *

This brings us to what the supporters of ECT have recorded as one of their main motives for partnership, namely, the avoidance of needless proselytism. By this term is meant any attempt to evangelize and seek the conversion of those who are already Christians. Accordingly the signatories to ECT discourage evangelistic endeavour in each other's territory: 'We call upon Christians to refrain from such activity . . . it is neither theologically legitimate nor a prudent use of resources for one Christian community to proselytize among active adherents of another Christian community' (pp. xxix–xxx). Evangelical critics of ECT rightly saw that it is here that the practical consequences of a blurred definition of 'Christian' begin to emerge. How can a boundary be drawn between *who needs the gospel and who does not* unless there is agreement about what the gospel is and what a Christian is? If Roman Catholics are already Christians then any attempt to 'convert' them has to be 'proselytizing'.

Inevitably there was no unanimity among ECT supporters when challenged on this point. Packer says that for the evangelicals 'proselytism' only meant that they should not teach that people must leave the Church of Rome in order to be saved; it did not mean that church planting evangelism in Roman Catholic parts of the world had to stop. Neuhaus looked at it differently. He denied 'that ECT condemns the practice of evangelicals witnessing to Catholics, and vice versa', on the grounds that everyone is in need of further 'conversion': 'To take one another seriously as brothers and sisters in Christ means constantly calling one another to a deeper conversion to Christ' (p. 197). Avery Dulles, another Catholic contributor to ECT, in accord with his Church's teaching, affirmed that all 'justified by faith through baptism are incorporated in Christ', and then proceeded to say, 'To

[1] See *Catechism of the Catholic Church*, pp. 196-7.

enter into a saving relationship with God in Christ is the principal and all-embracing *goal* of the Christian life' (p. 124, italics added).[1]

In ECT II it is the Neuhaus/Dulles (Catholic) solution to this confusion over 'proselytising' which seems to have been adopted. The idea of not evangelizing those already Christian is dropped and this new wording introduced, 'In obedience to the Great Commision of our Lord, we must commit ourselves to evangelizing everyone . . . Evangelicals must speak the gospel to Catholics and Catholics to Evangelicals.'[2] The Irish version of ECT adopts the same words, while also saying, 'We reject proselytising among believing members of another Christian community.'

Perhaps it is this attempted elucidation which has something to do with the disappearance from ECT II of the senior Catholic signatories to the original ECT. The names of John Cardinal O'Connor and Bishop Sevilla no longer appear. They know perfectly well that it is not proselytism to urge people to turn to the Church of Rome because, as ECT noted, for Catholics the church is 'an integral part of the Gospel' (p.xxi), and it is the sacramental grace which she imparts which is bound up with becoming a Christian. We are back to the same basic point: the 'gospel' which an authentic Catholic has to 'speak' is not the same as that of the evangelical.[3]

[1] According to Roman teaching no one can be sure he is a Christian until he is dead.

[2] As ECT II, issued 12 November 1997, was simultaneously published in *Christianity Today* and many other places it is pointless to give page numbers. It is clear it was primarily intended to address the concern of evangelicals on the point of proselytism and on the absence of reference to justification by faith alone in the original statement. In our view it does not succeed.

[3] The absence of these names may also be connected with the fact that in ECT II (designed to reduce evangelical fears of a compromise) the wording 'justification by faith alone' is introduced although with the proviso that 'further and urgent exploration' needs to be given to 'the language of justification as it relates to imputed and transformative righteousness'. It is also observable that while Cardinal Edward Cassidy was

We must return now to Packer's distinction between the 'basic faith' and the 'small print'. In support of the conclusion which he wants to base on this distinction, he reasons that to make an acceptance of the full Protestant doctrine of justification essential would be to treat such Christians as Athanasius, Augustine, and Anselm as 'no real believers' (p. 170). If these men of far-off centuries were true Christians – and who doubts it? – why should we make it essential to formulate the Pauline doctrine of imputed righteousness precisely? So he concludes that, although Rome is defective in this truth, nevertheless she is a Christian church: those who adhere to her still have the 'opportunity and means for growth in Christian discipleship' (p. xxx). There is no duty to tell anyone to leave her communion (p. xxxi).

It is this argument based on history and Christian experience to which we must now turn. At the Reformation the doctrine of justification was recovered from the New Testament and for untold thousands the message it conveyed was the means of their becoming Christians.[1] That same truth demonstrated afresh the antithesis between all forms of church-salvation, or works-salvation, and salvation by grace through faith alone. The Roman Church both by its persecution of Christians and, more permanently, by its official teaching ratified at the Council of Trent (1545–63), determinedly took the unbiblical side of that antithesis.

---

present at the discussion which led to ECT II, his name also did not appear as a signatory. No figures on the Catholic side have given official status to continuing ECT discussions. A leading biographer of the present Pope says that he is little interested in ecumenical discussions in the West and regards thought in North America as particularly shallow (Jonathan Kwitny, *The Life and Times of Pope John Paul II*, New York: Henry Holt, 1997).

[1] It was recovered, not invented. Neuhaus repeats the traditional Catholic objection that to identify 'the formula "justification by faith alone"' with the gospel, would be to say 'the Good News is to be judged by a theological formula devised sixteen centuries after that reality came into existence' (p. 207)! The Epistle to the Galatians surely makes the very identification which he wants to reject.

Canon XI of that Council reads: 'If anyone saith, that men are justified, either by the sole imputation of the justice of Christ, or by the sole remission of sins . . . let him be anathema.'[1] In so speaking, the Reformers believed Rome was in direct contradiction of the gospel and was employing her power to prevent the salvation of men and women. That she was doing this unconsciously did not lessen the reality. She was misled, as the unregenerate are ever prone to be, by demonic deception.

Now it is perfectly true that by the grace of God men and women have become Christians who have lived in times or places where the full meaning of justification has been little understood. They have not known the 'small print'. But it is a very different thing for a professing church to pronounce anathemas against the doctrine when there is a flood of light from Scripture and the 'small print' of Romans and Galatians becomes big print for believers across Europe. That is what Rome did in the sixteenth century and it is where her teaching still stands today. The appeal to church leaders who had never seen the darkness of medieval Catholicism, nor the blessing which followed it, is no proof at all that the Christian standing of a church can *now* be determined irrespective of whether it believes or rejects New Testament teaching on how a sinner becomes a Christian. As John Frame has written, 'Views tolerable in the church in the year 200 are not necessarily tolerable in the year 2000, since God continually teaches his church new things out of the Scriptures.'[2] From the Reformation onwards an intelligent adherence to Roman dogma has commonly meant ignorance of, or opposition to, salvation by grace through faith. Defending ECT, Dr Packer has written: 'What is ruled out is associating salvation or spiritual health with churchly identity.'[3] This is to accord to the Church of Rome the same kind of status as any comparatively orthodox Protestant denomination.

---

[1] *Creeds of Greek and Latin Churches*, pp. 112–3.

[2] John M. Frame, *Evangelical Reunion* (Grand Rapids: Baker, 1991), p. 90.

[3] 'Why I Signed It.'

What has been nearly forgotten today is that the whole Reformation struggle centred – as all great controversies centre – on what it means to be a Christian. Evangelicals (literally, 'gospellers') left the Roman communion because the true way of salvation was not taught there. The experience of all the reformers across Europe was unanimous at this point. Luther writes:

> The state of the church was terrible under the pope. Then nothing was seen or heard which could encourage a heart in such distress, except that each year the story of the Passion was taught, though quite indifferently. This faintly indicated where pardon was to be sought. Everything else led away from the promise of forgiveness towards one's own righteousness. And so in many monasteries we saw stricken and despairing people passing the entire time of their lives and in the end wearing themselves out in the conflict by their worries and griefs. Because this doctrine was unknown, the rest of the brothers did nothing more than stand near by and try to obtain the protection of saints with their idolatrous prayers . . . Nothing is more terrible than to be in sin and yet to be remote from, or ignorant of, the forgiveness of sin or the promise of grace. But the pope was responsible for the concealment of the forgiveness of sins, because sound doctrine and true forms of worship were not maintained in the church. If some in faith were saved, it was the bare reading of the Passion of Christ accepted in faith which saved them, against the will and opposition of the pope.[1]

William Tyndale, the leading English Reformer, gives the same picture of the spiritual darkness of his country. Instead of teaching the faith which the biblical sacraments proclaim, Rome taught the people to put their trust in 'dumb ceremonies'. 'Antichrist's dumb ceremonies preach not the faith that is in Christ'.[2] When the priest of this 'false church'

---

[1] *Luther's Works,* ed. Jaroslav Pelikan, vol. 1 (St Louis: Concordia, 1958), pp. 179–80.

[2] Tyndale, *Works*, vol. I (Cambridge: Parker Soc., 1848), p. 283.

leadeth me by darkness of sacraments without signification, I cannot but catch harm, and put my trust and confidence in that which is neither God nor his word. As for ensample, what trust put the people in anoiling, and how they cry for it, with no other knowledge than that the oil saveth them; unto their damnation, and denying of Christ's blood.[1]

Such teaching, Tyndale constantly said, arose from the absence of the Spirit of God. Those taught of God see everything differently: 'I say, it is impossible to understand either Peter or Paul, or aught at all in the scripture, for him that denieth the justifying faith in Christ's blood.'[2]

Calvin, in replying to the charge that 'we have apostatized from the Church because we have withdrawn from subjection to the See of Rome', is likewise sure that salvation is bound up with this withdrawal:

So *Catholic* – so universal – is the mass of errors by which they have overturned the whole of religion, that it would be enough to destroy and swallow up the Church a hundred times over. We can never, therefore, extol, in terms so lofty as the matter deserves, the unbounded goodness of God, by which we have miraculously escaped that destructive whirlpool, and have fixed the anchor of our faith on the firm and everlasting truth of God. And, indeed, this Commentary will itself, I trust, be sufficient proof that Popery is nothing else than a monster formed out of the innumerable deceptions of Satan, and that what they call the Church is more confused than Babylon.[3]

---

[1] *Ibid.*, vol. 3, pp. 148–9. 'Anoiling' = extreme unction administered to the dying. Contemporary Roman teaching on this 'sacrament of those departing', says that it is to be 'given to those who are seriously ill by anointing them on the forehead with duly blessed oil': 'By the grace of this sacrament the sick person receives the strength and gift of uniting himself more closely to Christ's Passion . . . It completes the holy anointings that mark the whole Christian life.' *Catechism of the Catholic Church*, pp. 339–41.

[2] Tyndale, *Works*, vol. 3, p. 169.

[3] Calvin, *Commentary on the Gospel of John*, vol. 1 (Edinburgh: Calvin Translation Soc., 1847), p. 17. It is common today to say that the

In all the countries of Europe the united explanation why men opposed the truth of divine grace and faith in Christ alone was simply that they were not Christians. So Luther told Erasmus.[1] The Church of England's 'Homily of Justification', which is singled out in the Thirty-Nine Articles for special commendation, affirms:

> This doctrine advanceth and setteth forth the true glory of Christ and beateth down the vain glory of man: this whoever denieth is not to be counted for a true Christian man, nor for a setter forth of Christ's glory, but for an adversary of Christ and His Gospel.[2]

To such quotations the evangelical supporters of ECT might well reply, 'If God so broke into the situation in the sixteenth century why may he not do so today?' Indeed they would go further and say that God is already doing so. Packer writes: 'Despite the shortcomings of Rome's official teaching, there are many Roman Catholic Christians' (p. 163). Accordingly, he argues, 'the togetherness that ECT pleads for has already begun . . . ECT is playing catch-up to the Holy Spirit.'[3] We are repeatedly told that it is the 'discovery' which

---

hostility between Rome and Protestant teaching in the sixteenth century was due to a misunderstanding. Those living at the time believed that it was just because the Papacy *could* see how its whole position was challenged by evangelical doctrine that it reacted as it did: 'There is no other reason why the pontiffs rage with such madness against the reviving doctrine of the gospel, and stretch every nerve to suppress it; why they incite all kings and princes to persecute it – except that they see that their whole kingdom will fall and crumble as soon as Christ's gospel gains sway . . . since they cannot be safe until they have put Christ to flight, they strive in this cause just as if they were fighting for altar, hearth, and their very lives.' John Calvin, *Institutes of the Christian Religion,* ed. F. L. Battles (Philadelphia: Westminster Press, 1960), vol. 2, p. 1144.

[1] See p. 155.

[2] The Thirty-Nine Articles single out this homily for special commendation. Alister McGrath's statement that 'the birth of the Church of England is not linked directly with the doctrine of justification' (*Anvil,* vol. 4, no. 1, p. 68) is a reminder that assertions need to be checked at first-hand.

[3] 'Why I Signed It'.

has been made of many evangelically-minded Christians within the Church of Rome which has motivated the policy that is now recommended.

But how does Packer know that there are 'many Roman Catholic Christians'? Queried on this point he has replied that the issue is to be judged in evangelical terms: 'Our confidence that anyone is truly a brother or sister in Christ depends not only on the content of his or her confession but by our perceiving signs of regeneration in his or her life' (p. 161). So Packer by personal experience has come to the conclusion that many Catholics whom he has met are Christians. We hope he is right, but we know that the 'many' he has met are still only a fraction of the world's billion Catholics.[1] The personal experience of a some evangelicals is a very slender basis on which to base the impression given by ECT that Catholics generally are Christians. Even Charles Colson appears to support the view of the critics of ECT who believe 'Roman Catholics are not ordinarily Christians' (p. 154) when he reflects on the low morals of American Catholics (p. 18) and writes that 'the Catholic Church in America seems to many observers to be characterized by a

---

[1] It may not be as a result of personal experience, however, that Packer describes Pope John Paul II as 'a wonderful man who has done a wonderful job as a world Christian ambassador' (p. 162). The pope claims what belongs to Christ alone. As 'Vicar of Christ' he 'has full, supreme and universal power over the whole church'. By 1996 he had canonized 276 'saints'. In countless ways he hides or denies the glory of the Redeemer he is supposed to represent. He teaches that the faithful are 'to ask the Mother of God to intercede for us "at the hour of death" in the *Hail Mary*; and to entrust ourselves to St Joseph, the patron of a happy death' (*Catholic Catechism*, pp. 205, 231, etc.). He further upholds the anathema upon Packer and upon all who deny Trent's teaching on justification. On his world tours John Paul II has been faithful to the whole Roman tradition. It is the Mass – 'blasphemous fables and dangerous deceits' (Article XXXI) – and not gospel preaching which marks all his visits abroad. In *The gift of authority – Authority in the church III*, Anglican-Roman Catholic International Commission (ARCIC) (London: Catholic Truth Soc., 1999), the paragraph on how the Christian faith comes to the individual contains no reference to hearing the gospel preached. See Gerald Bray, *Churchman*, vol. 113 (1999), p. 207.

merely nominal faith' (p. 32). In Colson's own autobiography of more than twenty years ago he has told us that, at the time of his conversion to Christ, all that he had ever heard from his Roman Catholic wife in their ten years of marriage was what she 'felt about confession and Communion, the significance of the Mass'.[1] Christianity as a living relationship with Christ was evidently as new to her as it was to those who came to faith at the time of the Reformation.

Much weight is put on the alleged numbers of Catholic Christians at the present time, but before we see this as a repetition of the work of God in a new reformation we need to ask how these alleged numbers came to saving faith. Has an evangelical party arisen in the Church of Rome to challenge the official teaching? It has not. The only theological challenge has come from liberals whose hopes have dwindled before a tightened conservatism in the Vatican. The 'many' Catholic evangelicals in North America and elsewhere have appeared in connection with the charismatic movement. Packer makes this observation, as does George Carey. The latter writes of charismatic renewal:

> It is the only revival in history which has united evangelicals on the one hand, with their strong emphasis on the death of Christ and full atonement, and Roman Catholics on the other, with their emphasis on the sacraments. Somehow charismatic experiences have brought together people who on the face of it have little in common theologically.[2]

Certainly the doctrinal vagueness of the charismatic movement gives it a unifying ability.[3] It is neither Protestant nor

[1] Charles W. Colson, *Born Again* (London: Hodder and Stoughton, 1976), p. 135.

[2] Carey, *Tale of Two Churches*, p. 17. The ECT authors frankly recognize that the way was prepared for them by the charismatic movment (pp. xi, 97–8, 173).

[3] More than thirty years ago David du Plessis (1905–1987), catalyst for the charismatic movement, was advocating that the way to unity with Roman Catholics was to be found in shared experience rather than in any common understanding of biblical truths. He became the first non-Catholic to receive the Pope's 'Good Merit' medal for 'service to all Christianity'.

Catholic. But the evidence shows that it cannot stay like that. Sooner or later Catholic charismatics must take the Bible seriously or official Roman teaching seriously. Already there are many charismatics who have left the Church of Rome.[1] Others move in the opposite direction and treat 'evangelicalism' as a path to full submission to Roman dogma.[2]

Charismatic 'renewal' is a far too uncertain and changing thing to be made a justification for the partnership of evangelicals with 'believing Catholics'. If we suppose that charity and Christian tolerance requires us – as ECT requires – that we make no judgment on the consistency of being both evangelical and authentically Catholic then we can only exercise such charity by being a party to the blurring of essential biblical truths.

The danger of ECT is not that it encourages personal friendships between evangelicals and individual Roman Catholics. Nor is it that it urges co-operation with Catholics in opposing moral evils.[3] It is rather that it advocates a public policy which implies that there is no *vital and essential* difference between Christianity and Roman Catholicism. The real issue is not about numbers, or tolerance, or morals, it is about the way of salvation, and, if the gospel recovered at the Reformation is the truth, then love for the souls of men and women warrants a division now as it did then.

---

[1] The testimonies of several priests in this category will be found in *Far From Rome, Near To God, Testimonies of Fifty Converted Roman Catholic Priests*, eds. Richard Bennett and Martin Buckingham (Edinburgh: Banner of Truth, 1997).

[2] Thus the charismatic priest, Tom Forrest, says: 'Our job is to make people as richly and fully Christian as we can by bringing them into the Catholic Church. No, you don't invite someone to become a Christian, you invite them to become Catholics. There are seven sacraments and the Catholic Church has all seven.'

[3] The justification for such co-operation does not lie in Protestantism or Catholicism: it lies in the duty of all to uphold the moral law given to man at creation. That people will support moral standards and advance the welfare of others is part of the operation of common grace. Such action, however, can only act as a restraint upon evil and injustice. The power to change human nature is only in the gospel.

In *Evangelicals and Catholics Together,* Neuhaus, from the Catholic side, laid down a principle to which there has been no response from the evangelicals. With an emphasis unusual in the text of the book, he wrote: '*If at the end of the twentieth century, separation for the sake of the gospel is not necessary, it is not justified*' (p. 199). This is possibly the most significant statement in the whole book. If differences with his Protestant friends are not essential to the gospel – and ECT conceded that they are not – then what can justify their continued standing apart from the greater unity of the Church of Rome? If there is unity in 'fundamentals' why the continued separation? The only convincing answer to that question is to affirm that there are essential differences, and that Rome as an institution lies outside the unity of the body of Christ. Dr Packer has reasons, he tells us, why he cannot join the Church of Rome, but the ECT case which he supports has implications which others may well come to accept. The Keele policy led others further than he wanted to go. ECT may well do the same. The possibility is not imaginary. The Alpha course in London, of which Nicky Gumbel is a main author, gains Packer's public support; yet it is Gumbel's view that the differences between Protestant and Catholic are 'totally insignificant compared to the things that unite us'. If that is true, then evangelicals are left with no answer to the challenge of Neuhaus.

* * * *

There are two final points to make. First, that while we can believe that the evangelical supporters of ECT have genuinely sought to avoid the lowest-common-denominator approach to differences of belief, the ecumenical ethos is still here. There are the ambiguities, concessions and inconsistencies common to all such dialogue. Crucial differences are left untouched or postponed. As already noted, at the beginning of 1995 further theological discussions were promised but to date nothing has been forthcoming apart from the brief pages of ECT II in November 1997. At the time of ECT II a

further volume responding to criticisms of ECT was promised 'in the near future'; yet, again, nothing has apppeared to
date. The reason for such delay is not hard to imagine. In the
past thirty years numerous Catholic-Protestant groups,
official and unofficial, have sought a resolution of theological
differences. The only real 'success' has occurred where
supposedly Protestant negotiators have given way to Roman
Catholic teaching. This has happened in ARCIC discussions,
as already noted, and in Lutheran discussions with Rome.[1] At
the outset Roman spokesmen in such discussions adopt an
accommodating posture. In the course of discussions the
other side make all the serious concessions, and only in the
end is it apparent that nothing in official Roman teaching can
be the subject of change. The authorized pronouncements of
past centuries are not open to correction. In the words of
Neuhaus, 'the Church is not authorized to repudiate retro-
spectively a conciliar decree' (p. 209).

The Pope underlined the same lesson in his encylical
letter *Ut Unum Sint* in 1995 when he warned all Roman
Catholics engaged in ecumenical dialogue to 'stand by the
teaching of the Church'. What Rome has said she can never
unsay. This had been spelt out so many times, apart from
ecumenical dialogue, that one can only suppose that some
evangelicals never read or took seriously such books as
Cardinal Bea's *The Unity of Christians.* The infallibility of the
Roman Church and her head, the successor of Peter; the
inherent efficacy of the sacraments; the final authority of her
teaching (both Scripture *and* later revelation) 'by virtue of the
very special help of the Holy Spirit' – all this was clearly set
out by Bea, head of the Secretariat for the Promotion of

[1] The Lutherans removed their own historic condemnation of Rome
in the ecumenical interest, only to discover that Rome meant to uphold
the anathemas of Trent. Nothing had changed since John Owen wrote:
'The church of Rome lays claim to the very same authority over and
conduct of the consciences of men in religion as were committed unto
Jesus Christ and his apostles. It is as safe, as they pretend, for a man to cast
off the authority and institutions of Christ himself as to dissent from those
of the pope' (*Works,* vol. 14, p. 499).

Christian Unity. 'The evangelical side rejects all these tenets', he noted in his book of 1963.[1] He did not know how muted or non-existent those objections were to become.

The inescapable fact is that Roman Catholicism is an interlocking system – sacramental grace, a sacrificing priest-hood which 'guarantees that it really is Christ who acts in the sacraments',[2] an apostolic succession ensuring infallibility, these are key points which cannot be amended without a dismantling of the whole. There is no half-way position. Describing the concessions of professed Protestants to Catholicism, Bishop E. A. Knox once wrote, 'The good Bishops were like men trying to turn tigers into tame cats by feeding them on buns.'[3]

If, then, all the committees of the past thirty years have got nowhere in obtaining any doctrinal change, it is not unworthy to suppose that an inability on the part of ECT supporters to make effective doctrinal progress was perfectly predictable.[4]

A second and final comment has to do with an argument presented by evangelical supporters of ECT which is

[1] Augustin Cardinal Bea, *The Unity of Christians,* ed. Bernard Leeming (London: Catholic Book Club, 1963), p. 159. As Bea underlines, the difference is essentially a conflict over authority. Packer has agreed: 'The continuing controversies between "Reformed" and "Catholic" Christians . . . cannot in principle be settled until both sides agree that the appeal to Scripture, interpreted in terms of itself – in this sense, *sola Scriptura,* Scripture *alone* – is final.' *God Has Spoken: Revelation and the Bible* (London: Hodder and Stoughton, 1965), p. 82.

[2] *Catholic Catechism,* p. 257.

[3] E. A. Knox, *Reminiscences of an Octogenarian, 1847–1934* (London: Hutchinson, 1935), p. 311.

[4] We noted above that the discussion which secured ECT II was in the presence of Cardinal Edward Cassidy. Cassidy is one of the chief Catholic negotiators in ecumenical affairs, active in both the Anglican and Lutheran discussions. It was Cassidy who pointed out to Anglicans that their submission in the Final Report of ARCIC that Anglican teach-ing is conformable to the authoritative teaching of the Church of Rome must be understood to include such things as 'the propitiatory nature of the eucharistic sacrifice, which can be applied also to the deceased', and the adoration of 'Christ' in the bread of the reserved sacrament.

obviously a major part of their thinking. Given the humanistic society of the West, in which all 'truth' is relative, and
recognizing the strength of liberal theology in the main
Protestant churches, it was argued that closer links between
evangelicals and 'good Roman Catholics' (theological
conservatives or 'conservationists' as Packer prefers to call
them) has to be the way forward:

> It is the theological conservationists, and they alone – mainly,
> Roman Catholic and the more established evangelicals – who
> have the resources for the rebuilding of these ruins, and their
> domestic differences about salvation and the church should
> not hinder them from joint action in seeking to re-Christian-
> ize the North American milieu.[1]

In the same vein Alister McGrath writes of the Roman
Catholic Church: 'An important ally could be at hand in the
struggle for the restoration of doctrinal orthodoxy to the
mainline denominations.'[2]

The argument is that side skirmishes should be left and
forces joined to face the main battle against humanistic and
secular unbelief. At first sight this may sound a reasonable
case. It ignores, however, the fact that Roman Catholicism
owns the same dependence upon human reason which, in a
different sphere, produces humanism. As Bishop McIlvaine
once said, to elevate tradition 'is essentially rationalism,
because it sets up Tradition, which is simply *man's* reason, in
ecclesiastical raiment, in superiority to the Scriptures'.[3] In
other words, the Church of Rome partakes of the very same
spirit which is responsible for the human predicament and by
its ability to coalesce with forms of unbelief it has often

---

[1] Packer, 'Why I Signed It'.

[2] McGrath, 'Do We Still Need the Reformation?', *Christianity Today*,
12 December 1994. Elsewhere he has written that 'today the real threat
to the gospel of grace comes from the rationalism of the Enlightenment
rather than from other Christian denominations' (Quoted by Sproul, *By
Faith Alone*, p. 90).

[3] *Memorials of Charles Pettit McIlvaine*, ed. W. Carus (London: Elliot
Stock, 1882), p. 271.

shown itself to be a broken reed when it comes to upholding Scripture against the world. The last encyclical of Pope John Paul II, *Fides et Ratio* (September 1998), on the relationship between faith and reason, illustrates what I am saying.[1] The hope for the kingdom of Christ does not lie in any such alliance.

What this argument also forgets is that Scripture treats religious error as far more dangerous than open unbelief. William Tyndale knew this when he said, 'Antichrist will ever be the best Christian man.'[2] It is against the subtle pretensions of religious leaders, who believe they have the truth, that Christ's strongest warnings are given. The 'beast' of the book of Revelation is a *religious* power. In the modern dialogue this is usually wholly ignored. David Edwards, for instance, tells us that he finds it difficult to see why, 'as a conservative', Jesus should have been in so much dispute with such fellow 'conservatives' as the 'Jewish religious authorities' of his day.'[3] He says that because he has missed entirely what the Reformers well understood.

In the last century it was the belief of E. B. Pusey, the Anglo-Catholic leader in the Church of England, that the final conflict in history would be between Rome and Geneva. But by Geneva he did not mean the Reformed theology of an earlier day, he meant the liberalism which had captured the Swiss city in the French Enlightenment. The contest then, he supposed, would at length be between the divine authority of Rome and the combined forms of human error. He was wrong. His two contestants, while outwardly different, will both in the end be found to be against Scripture. Evangelical alliances with Roman Catholicism rest on the same mistake. An Anglican evangelical has written: 'I am very happy to work with Anglo-Catholics in fighting

[1] Further on this subject, see Herbert J. Pollitt, *The Inter-Faith Movement* (Edinburgh: Banner of Truth, 1996).

[2] Tyndale, *Works*, vol. 3, p. 107.

[3] Edwards and Stott, *Essentials*, p. 56.

battles against Liberalism, but the day will come when we will need to fight against the ritualism and the sacramentalism which they have introduced.'[1] The Bible presents us with a different alternative. If we sacrifice truth today for short-term influence we cannot guarantee what our conduct will be tomorrow. When the day to fight is postponed the very will to fight may go from us.

We close this chapter with the words of 'a respected evangelical theologian who wishes to remain anonymous' who wrote to a fellow evangelical engaged in the ECT discussions as follows:

> I pray that what you and your colleagues have done is pleasing to God. I cannot praise or condemn it. I expect that this may change for ever what generations of Bible-believing Protestants have thought was their mission in relation to Roman Catholicism. I pray that you are right. I tremble to think that you may be wrong.[2]

We scarcely know sadder words than these. They amount to the opinion that on an issue of momentous consequence Scripture can give no clear light.

[1] Donald Allister, 'Facing the Challenge of Liberalism', *Churchman*, vol. 107 (1993), no. 2, p. 168.
[2] *First Things*, 'The Public Square'. Aug./Sept. 1995, p. 2.

9

The Silent
Participant

In the preceding pages I have traced something of the doctrinal drift which has occurred within evangelicalism in the last forty years. From the mid-century position, where evangelical leadership was concerned to see no fundamental biblical truths compromised, a condition of indefiniteness with respect to teaching, and a readiness to tolerate the 'insights' of others, has come to gain wide acceptance. That this has happened simultaneously in America and Britain is the result, as I have argued, of common influences. And in both countries the consequences have been very similar. What George Marsden wrote of the United States might well have been said of England:

> By the 1970s . . . more and more evangelicals could be found trying to engage in the same kind of 'me too' that had become so disastrous for liberalism in the 1960s. It seemed as if the

evangelicals were as busy following the course of the liberals as offering an alternative to it.[1]

Typical of the changing mood in Britain are the words of Dave Tomlinson, who wrote in 1995:

> I am not saying that theology and doctrine are unimportant, far from it; but there is no evidence from the Bible that it is of ultimate importance. Doctrinal correctness matters little to God and labels matter less; honesty, openness and a sincere searching for truth, on the other hand, matter a great deal . . . God is ultimately unimpressed with our church pedigrees or our spiritual experiences or our credal affirmations. St Peter will not be asking us at the pearly gates which church we belonged to, or whether we believed the virgin birth; the word 'evangelical' will not even enter the conversation.[2]

This kind of thinking follows a policy of ecumenical comprehensiveness as surely as night follows day. When evangelicals turned from emphasizing the biblical truths basic to their position, the necessity for being distinctly evangelical began to pass out of sight. It proved impossible both to co-operate in the ecumenical ethos *and* to hold together a strong evangelical centre. For some, indeed, this combination of aims had become needless; they had come to regard all attempts to preserve a strong and distinct evangelicalism as akin to the promotion of sectarianism.

This is not to say that the toleration of indefinite and superficial teaching had been the policy of evangelical leaders. It was not. But, as Carl Henry noted of Billy Graham,[3] the strategy required them to be seen putting the wider religious unity before the evangelical cause, and consequences which they had not actually intended were the result. This can be illustrated from the teaching of John Stott who has increasingly urged upon fellow Anglican evangelicals

---

[1] *Evangelicalism and Modern America,* p. 45.

[2] D. Tomlinson, *The Post-Evangelical* (London: Triangle, SPCK, 1995), pp. 61–2.

[3] See above, p. 36.

the need for 'maintaining a distinct identity'.[1] But the reason
why that distinctness has come to be questioned by younger
men arises directly from his own policy. He approves
Anglican comprehensiveness in terms of the Church holding
'the fundamentals of the faith' while 'tolerating different
views on secondary issues'.[2] What constitutes evangelical
distinctiveness, however, he states as being 'faithful to the
unique glory of the person and work of the Lord Jesus
Christ'.[3] Is that not a 'fundamental'? And if it is, what need
can there be for an evangelical distinctiveness within the
Church of England, unless it be that such faithfulness does
not mark the denomination? While Dr Stott therefore does
not regard evangelical beliefs as 'secondary issues' it is logical
for others to deduce from the comprehensiveness apparently
approved that there is at least some doubt about it. Roger
Steer has no doubt about it. Writing (as he believes) apprecia-
tively of the evangelicalism of Stott, Packer and McGrath, he
concludes:

> Anglican Evangelicals get into difficulties when they grow too
> concerned to preserve the distinctiveness of their heritage. The
> notion of Evangelicals strongly identifying themselves with,
> and seeking to sustain, one particular wing of Anglicanism, or
> taking a partisan position as a guiding principle is unhealthy.[4]

The evidence points to the conclusion that the new
'openness' taken up by the Billy Graham Evangelistic
Association, and by Anglican evangelicals at Keele, could not
long co-exist with an insistence on evangelical distinctives. So
evangelicalism on both sides of the Atlantic lost its strong
centre. As David Wells has written:

> Those who had marched gladly under the banner of evangeli-
> calism and had affirmed the truths of historic Protestant
> orthodoxy now began to look sideways. As the theological

[1] As in his chapter, 'I Believe in the Church of England', in Gavin
Reid, ed., *Hope for the Church of England?* (Eastbourne: Kingsway, 1986),
p. 24.   [2] *Ibid.*, p. 28.   [3] *Ibid.*, p. 24.
[4] Steer, *Guarding the Holy Fire*, pp. 332–3.

centre began to give way, there arose a multitude of evangelical amalgams with, among other things, Catholicism, Eastern Orthodoxy, special interests such as feminism, the pieties of the World Council of Churches, and radical politics. The most important thing that this potential movement needed – theological unity – grew ever thinner and more insubstantial.[1]

People thought they saw an invincible religious army who claimed to have experienced spiritual rebirth poised to sweep before it all its cultural and religious opponents. But the perception was a mirage. The sea that looked a mile wide turned out to be only an inch deep.[2]

Dr Carl Henry, who himself was for so long close to the centre of evangelicalism, saw the situation which had developed in largely the same way. By the early 1970s, he tells us, he had begun 'to question the depth and stability of the stateside evangelical resurgence'.[3] He came to the opinion, 'The evangelical movement looks stronger than in fact it is.'[4] As 'ambiguities within evangelicalism' grew, so its identity became increasingly confused, and this situation, he believed, was brought on 'by some of the movement's own leaders'.[5] Instead of a strong evangelical unity of belief a new outlook had been popularized:

> Many evangelicals now measure growth mainly in terms of numbers; distinctions of doctrine and practice are subordinated in a broad welcome for charismatic, Catholic, traditional and other varieties of evangelicals. Theological differences are minimized by evangelical publishers and publications reaching for mass circulation, by evangelists luring capacity audiences and even by evangelism festivals seeking the largest possible involvement . . . Numerical bigness has become an infectious epidemic.[6]

[1] Wells, *No Place for Truth*, p. 9.
[2] Wells, *God in the Wasteland* (Grand Rapids/Leicester: Eerdmans/IVP, 1994), p. 18.
[3] Henry, *Confessions of a Theologian*, p. 353.   [4] *Ibid.*, p. 390.
[5] *Ibid.*, pp. 351, 362.   [6] *Ibid.*, p. 387.

Once more, the parallel with the United Kingdom is unmistakable. Michael Saward, surveying the evangelical scene in the 1980s, could say:

This is the disturbing legacy of the 1960s and 1970s. A generation brought up on guitars, choruses, and home group discussions. Educated, as one of them put it to me, not to use words with precision because the image is dominant, not the word. Equipped not to handle doctrine but rather to 'share'. A compassionate, caring generation, suspicious of definition and labels, uneasy at, and sometimes incapable of, being asked to wrestle with sustained didactic exposition of theology. Excellent when it comes to providing religious music, drama, and art. Not so good when asked to preach and teach the Faith.[1]

I will give one more quotation to support the fact of this common trend and it leads us into the main question which we have to consider. In his book on *Evangelicalism* of 1987, James Davison Hunter wrote:

In substantive terms, the continuity of conservative Protestant theology in America is plainly discernible. From a distance, it would appear as though little if any change has occurred in the past century. Evangelicals have, by and large, been successful in maintaining the cognitive boundaries which encompass theological orthodoxy as they have defined it. Yet upon closer scrutiny, one can see that the continuity is far from perfect. Qualitatively there are some noteworthy differences. There is less sharpness, less boldness, and, accordingly, a measure of opaqueness in their theological vision that did not exist in previous generations (at least to the present extent). A dynamic would appear to be operating that strikes at the very heart of Evangelical self-identity.[2]

What then is this 'dynamic'? I believe that all the evidence points in one direction. It is that evangelicals, while commonly retaining the same set of beliefs, have been

[1] *Evangelicals on the Move*, p. 92.
[2] Hunter, *Evangelicalism*, p. 46.

tempted to seek success in ways which the New Testament identifies as 'worldliness'. Worldliness is departing from God. It is a man-centred way of thinking; it proposes objectives which demand no radical breach with man's fallen nature; it judges the importance of things by the present and material results; it weighs success by numbers; it covets human esteem and wants no unpopularity; it knows no truth for which it is worth suffering; it declines to be a 'fool for Christ's sake'. Worldliness is the mind-set of the unregenerate. It adopts idols and is at war with God.

Because 'the flesh' still dwells in the Christian he is far from immune from being influenced by this dynamic. It is of believers that it is said, 'the flesh lusts against the Spirit, and the Spirit against the flesh; and these are contrary one to another' (*Gal.* 5:17). It is professing Christians who are asked, 'Do you not know that the friendship of the world is enmity with God?' (*James* 4:4) and are commanded, 'Do not love the world', and 'keep yourselves from idols' (*1 John* 2:15, 5:21). Apostasy generally arises in the church just because this danger ceases to be observed. The consequence is that spiritual warfare gives way to spiritual pacifism, and, in the same spirit, the church devises ways to present the gospel which will neutralize any offence. The antithesis between regenerate and unregenerate is passed over and it is supposed that the interests and ambitions of the unconverted can somehow be harnessed to win their approval for Christ. Then when this approach achieves 'results' – as it will – no more justification is thought to be needed. The rule of Scripture has given place to pragmatism. The apostolic statement, 'For if I still pleased men, I would not be the servant of Christ' (*Gal.* 1:10), has lost its meaning.

No Christian deliberately gives way to the spirit of the world but we all may do so unwittingly and unconsciously. That this has happened on a large scale in the later-twentieth century is to be seen in the way in which the interests and priorities of contemporary culture have come to be mirrored in the churches. The antipathy to authority and to discipline;

the cry for entertainment by the visual image rather than by the words of Scripture; the appeal of the spectacular; the rise of feminism; the readiness to identify power with numbers; the unwillingness to make 'beliefs' a matter of controversy – all these features so evident in the world's agenda are now also to be found in the Christian scene. Instead of the churches revolutionizing the culture the reverse has happened. Churches have been converted to the world. David Wells has written:

> The stream of historic orthodoxy that once watered the evangelical soul is now dammed by a worldliness that many fail to recognize as worldliness because of the cultural innocence with which it presents itself . . . It may be that Christian faith, which has made many easy alliances with modern culture in the past few decades, is also living in a fool's paradise, comforting itself about all the things God is doing . . . while it is losing its character, if not its soul.[1]

This same worldliness has come to affect the way in which the gospel is often presented to the unconverted. Leonard Sweet has pointed out that evangelicals and liberals are often similar in the inducements which they propose to their hearers why they should become Christians. Both offer such things as more success in life, a happier marriage, an integrated personality, more meaning to existence, and so on. In other words, the reasons for becoming a Christian are pragmatic and they are presented with stories of how it has worked for others. Neither the evangelical nor the liberal, says Sweet, is prone 'to provide the answer to the question that substantively engages issues of authority and identity,

[1] Wells, *No Place for Truth*, pp. 11, 68. Perhaps no modern author has written more powerfully on this subject. 'The world, as the New Testament authors speak of it, is an alternative to God. It offers itself as an alternative center of allegiance. It provides counterfeit meaning. It is the means used by Satan in his warfare with God . . . Today, evangelicalism reverberates with worldliness . . . it is offering the church a counterfeit reality with the power to destroy what the church is.' *God in the Wasteland*, pp. 54–5.

"Why should I become a Christian?" Because it is true.'[1]

* * * *

The subject of worldliness, however, has a deeper bearing. Human conduct is not capable of being understood so long as it is imagined that man is self-contained and insulated from any power other than his own. Worldliness, it is true, is the outcome of man's fallen nature, but the same fall which introduced that nature also brought man under the control of Satan and demonic powers. Worldliness is no accident; it is the devil's use of such idols as pride, selfishness, and pleasure, to maintain his dominion over men.[2] What he proposes for man's happiness is in truth the result of implacable malice towards the whole human race. He means to exclude God and to destroy men, and the system he has devised to do this is so subtle that man is a willing and unconscious captive: 'You are of your father the devil, and the desires of your father you want to do. He was a murderer from the beginning, and does not stand in the truth, because there is no truth in him' (*John* 8:44).

Scripture says a great deal on the reality of the demonic, and yet the subject is today largely passed over in silence. Human wisdom has no place for the very idea and diverges completely from the revelation in Scripture. The devil is a mere fable and superstition, so men believe; according to Scripture he is the unseen enemy who constitutes the greatest problem for men in general and for the churches in particular. For the New Testament, the world's readiness to judge its needs merely in terms of the human and the visible

[1] Marsden, *Evangelicalism and Modern America*, p. 45.

[2] 'It is the Devil which blows up in us the fire of lust, pride, covetousness, and all other vices. He lays before us evil baits, agreeable to our nature, and so seduces us. He enrages persecutors, he blinds idolaters, he seduces heretics, etc. If this were well weighed it would make us pity "flesh and blood" when it fights against us, rather than envy [that is, feel a grudge against] it; it would keep us from snarling like a dog at the stone which is flung.'William Gouge, *The Whole Armour of God* (London: 1619), p. 60.

EVANGELICALISM DIVIDED

is proof of its spiritual darkness. The reality is that man is in the midst of a supernatural conflict; and the adversary – 'the spirit who now works in the sons of disobedience'(*Eph.* 2:2) – is vastly superior to all the intelligence and energies of men.

While we may expect unregenerate men to have no discernment on this issue, it has to be a matter of concern when – given the prominent warnings of the New Testament – the demonic ceases to be a vital part of the belief of professing evangelicals. For the apostles, understanding the existence and wiles of Satan was essential to Christian living: 'Be strong in the Lord and in the power of his might . . . For we do not wrestle against flesh and blood, but against principalities, against powers, against the rulers of the darkness of this age' (*Eph.* 6:10, 12). This teaching determines the biblical view of human need. Non-Christians are in a condition of blindness and bondage. They are under a power greater than the will of man and from which only Christ can set them free. Here was the recognition which led the apostles to repudiate all the world's methods for winning disciples. Supernatural power had to be met with supernatural power: 'For though we walk in the flesh, we do not war according to the flesh. For the weapons of our warfare are not carnal but mighty in God for pulling down strongholds' (*2 Cor.* 10:3–4).

The biblical revelation on evil spirits is no less relevant to the way in which the church is to defend herself against the demonic. We are constantly warned that Satan works principally through doctrinal deception and falsehood.[1] He was the inspiration for all the false prophets of the Old Testament: 'He is a liar and the father of it' (*John* 8:44). His great intent is to bring darkness and confusion into the church as he did among the Jews. It was a lie of Satan which brought judgment into the infant church at Jerusalem (*Acts* 5:3). It was Satan who at Paphos opposed Paul on his first missionary journey by using a sorcerer 'to turn away the proconsul from

[1] See Appendix 3 below, p. 323.

[258]

the faith' (*Acts* 13:8). The church at Corinth was in danger of allowing 'a different gospel' to be unopposed because 'the serpent who deceived Eve by his craftiness' was working to mislead her (*2 Cor.* 11:3). False prophets arise within the church yet they do not appear as such, 'And no wonder!', writes the apostle, 'For Satan himself transforms himself into an angel of light' (*2 Cor.* 11:14).

The idea that Christianity stands chiefly in danger from the forces of materialism, or from secular philosophy, or from pagan religions, is not the teaching of the New Testament. The greatest danger comes rather from temptations within and from those who, using the name of Christ, are instruments of Satan to lead men to believe a lie and to worship what in reality belongs to the demonic (*2 Thess.* 2:3–9; *Rev.* 13:11). 'False christs and false prophets will arise and show great signs and wonders, so as to deceive, if possible, even the elect' (*Matt.* 24:24).

No one can rightly believe this without seeing the seriousness of error. Wrong belief is as dangerous as unbelief. To deny the deity and the work of Christ will shut men out of heaven as certainly as will the sin of murder (*John* 8:24; *1 John* 2:22–23). To preach 'another gospel' is to be 'accursed' (*Gal.* 1:6–9). Those who support heresies 'will not inherit the kingdom of God' (*Gal.* 5:20–21). This means that a large part of the preservation and defence of the church lies in resolute resistance to falsehood and in forthright teaching of the truth. Such warnings as 'beware of the doctrine of the Pharisees and Sadducees' (*Matt.* 16:12), for they 'shut up the kingdom of God against men' (*Matt.* 23:13), run right through the New Testament. 'Tax collectors and prostitutes' would enter the kingdom of God before such false teachers (*Matt.* 21:31). The apostles, filled with the Spirit of Christ, suffered no toleration of error. They opposed it wherever it arose and required the same spirit of all Christians.[1] Eusebius, the early church historian wrote of their outlook:

[1] For example, *Phil.* 1:27; *Col.* 2:8; *2 Thess.* 3:14; *1 Tim.* 1:3–7, 6:3–5; *2 Tim.* 2: 14–19; 4:2–4; *Titus* 3:9–11; *2 Pet.* 2; *1 John* 4:1–3; *2 John* 7; *Jude*.

Such caution did the apostles and their disciples use, so as not even to have any communion, even in word, with any of those that thus mutilated the truth, according to the declaration of Paul: 'An heretical man after the first and second admonition avoid, knowing that such a one is perverse, and that he sins, bringing condemnation on himself.'[1]

Yet today this kind of witness against heresy and error, if not altogether silenced, has become muted to an extraordinary degree. 'Even the mildest assertion of Christian truth today sounds like a thunderclap because the well-polished civility of our religious talk has kept us from hearing much of this kind of thing.'[2]

The explanation often given by evangelicals for the lack of confrontation with error is that a harsh militancy has done more harm than good. As Christians, it is said, we do not want to be party to the kind of strident controversy which has too often marred the faith. Dr Billy Graham has often blamed 'fundamentalists' for this fault. But the fact that what the New Testament says on love has been ignored is no reason why its injunctions against error should not be obeyed. That some have followed these injuctions in a contentious spirit is no excuse for others not to follow them at all. A biblical contending against error is fully consistent with love, indeed it is love for the souls of men which requires it. The command to contend for the faith is not abrogated because some have failed to speak the truth in love.

There would appear to be a far more probable reason for the contemporary absence of opposition to error. It is the way in which the instrumentality of the devil in corrupting the truth has been so widely overlooked. In this, as I have already said, we differ widely from Scripture. Instead of

---

[1] *Ecclesiastical History of Eusebius of Pamphilus,* C. F. Cruse, trans. (London: George Bell, 1884), pp. 130–1. He reports that the apostle John, entering the baths at Ephesus on one occasion, saw Cerinthus inside and exclaimed, 'Let us flee lest the bath should fall in, as long as Cerinthus, that enemy of truth, is within.'

[2] Wells, *No Place for Truth,* p. 10.

believers in the apostolic age being directed to listen to all views 'with an open mind', they were told how to 'test the spirits, whether they are of God' (*1 John* 4:1). For there are 'deceiving spirits and doctrines of demons' (*1 Tim.* 4:1); false teachers 'who will secretly bring in destructive heresies' (*2 Pet.* 2:1). There are words which 'spread as a cancer' (*2 Tim.* 2:17).

When churches have been in a healthy state they have always been watchful in this regard. In the great persecutions of the first three centuries, for example, Cyprian (c. 200–258), bishop of Carthage, is to be found writing as follows:

> It is not persecution alone that we ought to fear, nor those forces that in open warfare range abroad to overthrow and defeat the servants of God. It is easy enough to be on one's guard when the danger is obvious; one can stir up one's courage for the fight when the Enemy shows himself in his true colours. There is more need to fear and beware of the Enemy when he creeps up secretly, when he beguiles us by a show of peace and steals forward by those hidden approaches which have earned him the name of the 'Serpent'. . . Light had come to the gentiles and the lamp of salvation was shining for the deliverance of mankind, so that the deaf began to hearken to the Spirit's call of grace, the blind to open their eyes upon the Lord, the sick to recover their health unto eternity, the lame to make speed to the Church and the dumb to raise their voice aloud in prayer. Thereupon the Enemy, seeing his idols abandoned and his temples and haunts deserted by the ever growing numbers of the faithful, devised a fresh deceit, using the Christian name itself to mislead the unwary. He invented heresies and schisms so as to undermine the faith, to corrupt the truth, to sunder our unity. Those whom he failed to keep in the blindness of their old ways he beguiles, and leads them up a new road of illusion.[1]

---

[1] *St Cyprian: The Lapsed. The Unity of the Catholic Church,* trans., M. Bevenot (New York: Newman Press, 1956), pp. 43, 45.

The same note was prominent in the teaching of the Reformers and the Puritans. Satan makes havoc of the churches, writes John Owen, by 'filling the minds of men with prejudices against the truth, and turning them from it'.[1] For a long time this same note of warning was a characteristic of evangelicals in the Church of England. It was said of Whitefield:

> The warmth of his zeal disgusted many who make a mighty outcry about candour and charity, and are willing to extend it to every sentiment except the truths in which the Apostles gloried . . . He knew errors in the great truths of the Gospel are not indifferent, but dreadful and fatal; he knew it was not candour and charity to say that errors in judgment are not hurtful, but the greatest unmercifulness and cruelty; therefore he often reproved such sharply.[2]

Josiah Pratt one of the leaders of the original Eclectics in London in the nineteenth century was of the same spirit. He viewed the Romeward Tractarian movement with grave concern and wrote:

> Let us consider well how much and plainly our Lord himself, and his holy apostles, especially St Paul, speak of the devil's working on men by error. We shall dread and hate error more than we do, and be more keen than we are in detecting it in its even distant approaches, when we rightly estimate its power as an instrument of evil.[3]

---

[1] 'Nature and Causes of Apostasy from the Gospel', in Owen's *Works*, vol. 7, p. 141.

[2] D. Edwards preaching on 11 November 1770. Appendix to *Memoirs of George Whitefield*, J. Gillies (London, 1811), p. xv.

[3] J. Pratt and J. H. Pratt, *Memoir of the Rev. Josiah Pratt* (London: Seeleys, 1849), p. 341. Anglican evangelicals of this period often referred to this subject. John Newton wrote of the devil imitating God by a 'black inspiration', and thereby assisting men's faculties 'to be more assiduously wicked and more extensively mischievous than they could be of themselves. I consider Voltaire, for instance, and many others writers of that stamp, to be little more than secretaries and amanuenses of one who has unspeakably more wit and adroitness in promoting infidelity and

These quotations are in marked contrast with the total lack of suspicion which is today so commonly held up as a Christian virtue. To take everything at face value is often treated as the true Christian attitude. 'Beware of men', and 'Beware of false prophets', are among the least quoted of Christ's admonitions. 'Brethren, do not be children in understanding' (*1 Cor.* 14:20), writes the apostle. There is good reason to believe that we have been children in accepting the ecumenical agenda. In one of the first evangelical publications to recommend the new approach on openness, the Rev. M. H. Cressey could write in 1964: 'The real question in the whole discussion of the ecumenical movement is one of trust. Are we or are we not willing to trust the Christian sincerity of those who name the name of Christ?'[1] But far more than 'sincerity' ought to have been considered. Cressey, we do not doubt, was sincere when he saw no need for anyone to fear the 'blurring of theological issues, and a drift to compromise with the unreformed church of Rome'. He advised: 'Evangelicals need to realize that these trends are more apparent than real and that in so far as they have reality they are as actively opposed within the ecumenical movement as they are from outside it.'[2] Events have shown how sincerely wrong he was. The fact is that teachers can be used to mislead others without even being conscious that they are doing so.

Sometimes in the past forty years the use of deception has been intentional. Thomas Oden speaks of the practice of duplicity even being recommended to theological students.[3] More commonly people are misled by a careful and

---

immorality than they of themselves can justly pretend.' *Works of John Newton*, vol. 1 (1824, repr., Edinburgh: Banner of Truth, 1985), p. 508. Another contemporary Anglican wrote: 'I would rather meet a hundred devils roaring than one smiling.' John Owen, *Memoir of the Rev. Thomas Jones of Creaton* (London: Seeleys, 1851), p. 66.

[1] Douglas, *Evangelicals and Unity*, pp. 29–30.
[2] *Ibid.*, p. 26.
[3] Oden, *Requiem*, p. 28.

deliberate non-disclosure of information which might be prejudicial to ultimate objectives. No one knew at the time, for instance, that Archbishop Ramsey had gained clearance from the Vatican on the scheme for Anglican-Methodist reunion which he was backing. With a greater reunion in view, he wanted to be sure that the scheme's proposals did not contravene Rome's teaching on apostolic succession. Nor, as already mentioned, was it disclosed that, when a new Archbishop of Canterbury had to be appointed in 1979, Cardinal Basil Hume, leader of the Roman Catholics in England, was consulted.

Leaders who have preached 'openness' as a great virtue have often been singularly lacking in that characteristic when it came to informing people accurately of their own beliefs. The 'assent' to the Thirty-Nine Articles, 'solemnly' required of all Anglican clergy until 1975, is a striking example. For so long had this assent been a charade that, as *The Times* wrote at the time of Robert Runcie's enthronement at Canterbury, 'The Articles have been virtually unusable as a norm of faith for many years.' The last archbishop who believed them would be hard to name. Michael Saward, immediately prior to his ordination in 1957, tells us how he heard Geoffrey Fisher, the Archbishop of Canterbury, 'explaining how we could give assent to the Thirty-Nine Articles "without meaning it"'.[1] This is akin to a story told by Runcie. When an agnostic philosopher at Cambridge (to the surprise of all his friends) was to be baptized, 'it was alleged that he made a pact with the Bishop of Ely – this was gossip – that he could say *sotto voce* before the Creed: "I agree to act as if I believe in . . ."' Gossip or not, it was advice the archbishop could appreciate. In the same conversation with his biographer, he was asked, 'If the church didn't tell you to believe in the resurrection, would you?' To which Runcie replied, 'I don't know.'[2]

[1] Saward, *Autobiography*, p. 164.
[2] Carpenter, *Runcie*, pp. 96–7, 99.

It was Runcie who wrote the Foreword to the House of Bishops booklet, *The Nature of Christian Belief*. This thirty-nine-page statement appears to have been intended to allay growing fears about the state of belief in the Church of England. At the outset the bishops declared, 'We affirm our faith in the Resurrection of Our Lord Jesus Christ.' Yet if anyone reads to the end of the document they find the same bishops criticizing the wording of the Thirty-Nine Articles on the resurrection of Christ. The words 'physical' and 'bodily resurrection', they say, are 'an inadequate or even misleading term, which does not do justice to Scripture'. We are not then surprised when we go on to read that on the question 'whether Christ's tomb was empty . . . the divergent views to be found among scholars of standing are reflected in the thinking of individual bishops'.[1]

The Rev. Michael Harper has reported on the findings of a poll of thirty-nine diocesan bishops at this same period. Over thirty replied. Ten did not believe in the virgin birth of Christ. Nine did not believe in either Christ's bodily or 'spiritual' resurrection. To the question, 'Do you hold it is necessary for Christians to believe that Christ is God?', nineteen bishops replied that they did not consider it necessary.[2]

The plain fact was that assent to the Thirty-Nine Articles was ended because liberals opposed the scriptural nature of the doctrine while Anglo-Catholics resented the rejection of Roman Catholic belief. Yet this was never openly admitted. Criticism of the Articles had always to be expressed cautiously

[1] *The Nature of Christian Belief: A Statement and Exposition by the House of Bishops of the General Assembly of the Church of England* (London, Church House Publishing, 1986), pp. 2, 23–4, 25. Yet by acknowledging on p. 2 the 'belief that Christ's tomb was empty . . . as expressing the faith of the Church of England', they were admitting that bishops did not hold the faith of the Church. The same document allows the legitimacy of thinking of 'the Virginal Conception as symbolic legend rather than history.' p. 32.

[2] Michael Harper, *The True Light: An Evangelical's Journey to Orthodoxy* (London: Hodder & Stoughton, 1997), p. 34.

by men who had assented to them at their ordination; it rarely went beyond the guarded words used by the Bishop of Aberdeen, 'The Thirty-Nine Articles do not reflect the faith other than in a narrow part of Christendom and at a certain time.'[1]

For a still more important example of how men have misled both themselves and others we need to return to the subject of the inspiration of Scripture. We have already discussed reasons why the rejection of verbal inspiration is preferred by some who otherwise profess orthodox Christianity. Again there is no need to question the sincerity of the many who advocated this change from the traditional evangelical position but, whether they recognized it or not, the change coincided with the destruction of doctrinal Christianity. That at least some have had that intention in mind when they questioned the inspiration of Scripture is beyond doubt. Dr Joseph Priestley, for instance, the eighteenth-century Nonconformist minister, sought to popularize the idea that the Scriptures were written 'without any particular inspiration'. But his opposition actually went much further than the subject of Scripture. As Donald Fraser, writing on the inspiration of Scripture in 1834, asked:

Why do the followers of that noted leader discover the same reckless confidence on this most essential article? The reason is clearly this, that whilst they cherish a determined hostility against certain prominent doctrines of the prophets and apostles, they are desirous to possess some specious pretext for receiving or rejecting their announcements at pleasure.[2]

[1] In a letter in *The Times*, 5 October 1985. Frank Longford, who quotes these words, tells us that in interviewing thirteen bishops, the Articles 'were mentioned in passing if at all and as providing no more than general guidance'. *The Bishops: A Study of Leaders in the Church Today* (London: Sidgwick & Jackson, 1986), p. 13.
[2] D. Fraser, *Essay on the Plenary and Verbal Inspiration of the Holy Scriptures* (Edinburgh: 1834), published in *Biblical Family Library*, vol. 2, (London/Edinburgh/Dublin: 1835), p. 468.

The same kind of influence was widely operating in Scotland at the end of the nineteenth century. It has been fashionable in recent years to contrast the position of Hodge and Warfield with that of certain Scottish teachers who, it is claimed, were as evangelical as the Princeton men although they did not believe in verbal inspiration. The names of James Orr and James Denney are most frequently mentioned in this connection.[1] Both men are praised by James Dunn in his attack on the Princeton teaching. But what we are not told is that, under the looser doctrine of Scripture taught by these Scots, biblical faith not only rapidly declined in their country but the very faith of the teachers themselves often suffered. In a letter of 1908, William Robertson Nicoll, editor of the *British Weekly,* wrote to Professor H. R. Mackintosh of his concerns over Denney who was their mutual friend. Dr Denney had just published his book *Jesus and the Gospel* in which he objected to the teaching that Jesus claimed to be God and instead presented a view of the person of Christ which any Arian or Unitarian would have been happy to accept. After noting this, Nicoll continued:

> I am clear in my own mind that I do not want to belong to a Church which contains Arians and Unitarians in its ministry, and I know quite well what the end of such a Church would be, for all history points it out. I have written to Denney, but I am in perplexity about the book. There is a singular vein of scepticism in him, for all his apparent orthodoxy. For instance, he does not believe in the existence of the devil and of evil spirits. Nor does he believe in the Second Advent.[2]

The same thing was even more marked in Dr Marcus Dods, another professor of theology in the Free (and United

[1] Dunn, *The Living Word*, pp. 90–1, 102; Craston, *Debtor to Grace,* p. 76 ('Even in pre-Keele days I knew very well Evangelical stalwarts who found these two theologians more convincing than Warfield.'). Notwithstanding his position on inerrancy, Orr was more conservative than Denney and contributed to the *Fundamentals.*

[2] T. H. Darlow, *William Robertson Nicoll: Life and Letters* (London: Hodder and Stoughton, 1925), p. 364.

Free) Church of Scotland at the same period. Dods described the doctrine of verbal inspiration as 'a theory of inspiration which has made the Bible an offence to many honest men, which is dishonouring to God, and which has turned inquirers into sceptics by the thousand.'[1] But his unbelief went further than his rejection of verbal inspiration. He also denied a substitutionary atonement and thought faith in the deity of Christ to be unnecessary for conversion. Part of Dods' defence for his unorthodoxy was that he was an 'evangelist', and that it was his kind of up-to-date and progressive Christianity which would bring a living faith to the nation. It has been said that Dods' significance in relation to the biblical issues and scholarship of his day lay 'in his open and optimistic acceptance of criticism'.[2] The optimism, however, was more in his public writings than in his private life. An apprehensive letter to a friend in 1902 gives a very different view of the religious prospects for Scotland under such teaching: 'The churches won't know themselves fifty years hence. It is to be hoped some little rag of faith may be left when all's done.'[3]

* * * *

Conclusions to be drawn from the above may be summarized as follows:

1. The idea that error and false teaching is only an innocent mistake and an inevitable part of scholarship is directly contrary to Scripture. 'Many deceivers have gone out into the world' (2 John 7) is the apostolic testimony, and this activity

---

[1] Henry F. Henderson, *The Religious Controversies of Scotland* (Edinburgh: T. & T. Clark, 1905), p. 238. When no effective action was taken against Dods in the Free Church General Assembly a Dingwall minister told them, 'Pass your motions and shield your professors; but let this House in any way degrade the Holy Word of God and you may bid good-bye as a Free Church to your influence in the Highlands.'

[2] Wright and Badcock, *Disruption to Diversity: Edinburgh Divinity 1846–1996*, p. 81.

[3] *Later Letters of Marcus Dods* (London: Hodder & Stoughton, 1911), p. 67.

is going to continue: 'Now the Spirit expressly [distinctly] says that in the last times some will depart from the faith, giving heed to deceiving spirits and doctrines of demons' (*1 Tim.* 4:1). The struggle in the future, as in the past, is to be with false religion.

2. The idea that knowledge is enough to make a Christian is false. The devil believes Scripture, knows Scripture, uses Scripture, and yet remains unholy and in love with all that God condemns. It ought therefore to be no surprise that scholarly men can be familiar with the text of Scripture (as the Jews were with the Old Testament) and yet remain unchanged. The corruption of the human heart is such that it needs more than knowledge. As the Puritan William Gurnall wrote:

> Take men of the greatest parts, natural or acquired accomplishments, who only want [that is, lack] an union with Christ and renewing grace from Christ: O what fools does the Devil make of them, leading them at his pleasure ... The Scriptures are like the Red Sea, through which the Israelites by faith passed safely, but the Egyptians attempting to do it, for want of that guide, were drowned. A humble believer passes through the deep mysteries of the Word safely, without plunging into any dangerous mistakes; whereas the sons of pride, who leave faith, and take reason for their guide, we see how they are drowned in many damnable errors.[1]

3. There is an irreconcilable enmity between Satan and Scripture. For it is the only book which reveals the perfections of God's character, the way of salvation, and the workings of the powers of darkness. The great opposition which he energized against Christ was because of the truth; as Jesus said to his unbelieving brethren: 'The world cannot hate you, but it hates me because I testify of it that its works are evil' (*John* 7:7). For the same reason evangelical

---

[1] W. Gurnall, *Christian in Complete Armour* (London: Fuller, 6th ed., n.d.), vol. 1, p. 54; vol. 3, p. 345.

Christianity suffers the age-long hostility of worldly men who can tolerate all forms of belief but not the truth. Those who 'keep Christ's word' will always be subject to Satan's special assault (*Rev.* 3:8, 12:17) and this has been true in every nation.[1] Luther could say:

> We are surrounded on every side by angry and raging bishops and princes who wish we were wiped out. Still this is nothing in comparison with that spiritual battle . . . Satan is grasping at us with all his powers . . . We are on the battlefront whenever we teach the Word, whenever we preach and glorify Christ.[2]

4. Scripture asserts that the destruction of man's best interests is brought about by the reception of error. This is abundantly demonstrated in history. The man is blessed whose 'delight is in the law of the Lord . . . The ungodly are not so, but are like the chaff which the wind drives away' (*Psa.* 1:2, 4). When countries embrace a lie rather than God's Word there will be an irresistible descent into moral and spiritual darkness. When Jerusalem listened to false prophets and rejected the Word of God through Jeremiah its overthrow was certain. The same prophet's words have been true of many subsequent nations: 'Cursed is the man who trusts in man . . . For he shall be like a shrub in the desert, And shall not see when good comes, But shall inhabit the parched places in the wilderness' (*Jer.* 17:5–6). 'While German scholarship has been busy with its labors,' Dabney wrote towards the end of the nineteenth century, 'it has suffered

---

[1] 'A plague on it, this book hath bred all the quarrel', persecutors of the Protestants said as they burned the Bible in seventeenth-century Ireland. J. S. Reid, *History of the Presbyterian Church in Ireland* (Belfast: 1867), vol. 1, p. 330. 'The Christians at Tse-kia chwang were attempting to hold their customary Sunday service; but Mrs Kwo (or the demon possessing her) was determined to prevent it. She raved wildly, and springing upon the table threw the Bible and the hymn-books to the floor.' John L. Nevius, *Demon Possession and Allied Themes* (Chicago: Revell, 1892), p. 33.

[2] Luther, *Works,* vol. 12, p. 227.

almost a whole nation to lapse into a semi-heathenish condition.'[1] Catastrophe followed. Spurgeon correctly anticipated the same thing happening to Britain. 'Modern criticism, like modern theology,' he knew, 'is like the sirocco that blasts and burns, it is without either dew or unction, it proves itself to be unblest of God and unblessing to men.'[2] Marcus Dods' thought of the mere rags of faith which would be left in a future Scotland was no imaginary fear. Demolished or empty churches, scarred lives, broken homes, and no hope of heaven, are the sure result of listening to Satan instead of God.

5. Despite all this, demonic power can never finally prevail over the truth or the church of Jesus Christ. In Gurnall's words:

> News may come that truth is sick, but never that it is dead. No, it is error that is short lived: 'a lying tongue is but for a moment;' but truth's age runs parallel with God's eternity. Wouldest thou but in thy thoughts wipe away tears and blood, which now cover the face of suffering truth, and present it to thy eye as it shall look in glory, thou couldest not but cleave to it with a love stronger than death.[3]

---

[1] Dabney, *Discussions: Evangelical and Theological*, vol. 1, pp. 447–8.
[2] Spurgeon, *Metropolitan Tabernacle Pulpit,* 1893 (London: Passmore and Alabaster), p. 266.
[3] Gurnall, *Christian Armour*, vol. 2, p. 60.

10

'Church' and the Unresolved Problem

When the third national gathering of Evangelical Anglicans (described as a 'Celebration' rather than a 'Congress') met at Caister in 1988 an Archbishop of Canterbury was again invited to speak. Presumably it was meant as an evidence of respect for denominational leaders. Robert Runcie was not accustomed to such gatherings, for his biographer writes of his 'distaste for those who are so unstylish as to inhabit the clerical ghettos of Evangelicalism'.[1] Despite all that had been said by evangelicals since Keele, the Archbishop evidently believed that the 'ghettos' were not yet empty, and so he proceeded to counsel his audience on the well-worn theme. He believed that there was a continuing absence of any 'developed evangelical ecclesiology', and advised the gathering that 'if the current evangelical renewal

[1] Carpenter, *Runcie,* p. 346.

[272]

in the Church of England is to have a lasting impact, then there must be more explicit attention given to the doctrine of the church'. John Stott, who quoted these words in his published 'Report' on NEAC 3, thought that Dr Runcie's criticism would 'form a useful basis for the domestic dialogue we need to initiate', although 'it raises painful problems for us as Evangelical Anglicans'.[1]

The charge that evangelicals are not 'churchmen' is at least as old as the sixteenth century. It was one of Sir Thomas More's complaints against William Tyndale.[2] Exactly the same objection was raised, as we have seen, against Wesley and Whitefield two centuries later. The basis for the charge has commonly been stated in this form: it is said that evangelicals put the 'invisible church' before the 'visible'; that they act as though there were two churches and that, while their commitment to the invisible church is strong, to the visible it is weak or even (as in the alleged case of Tyndale) non-existent. Stated in such a way the criticism looks simple and valid. For the New Testament surely contains no justification for anyone supposing that belonging to the 'invisible church' can be a substitute for commitment to the church as it is seen and organized in the world.

But the evangelical position on the church rests on no such understanding. It begins rather with what Scripture says on the nature of the church. The 'church' is the assembly of the 'called', 'the saints', 'the faithful brethren', those delivered 'from this present evil age', 'the household of faith', 'the church of the firstborn who are registered in heaven'. Such words describe people whose life comes from union with Christ and the abiding indwelling of the Holy Spirit. Without such life there is no church; yet what constitutes the essence of that spiritual life is not visible to the world, and her

[1] Quotations from the Archbishop and Dr Stott are from point (4) of *NEAC 3: 'What is the Spirit Saying . . . ?* (Church of England Evangelical Council, 1988). The Report was, in fact, Stott's closing address 'expanded and modified'.

[2] For Tyndale on 'church', see his *Answer to Sir Thomas More's Dialogue*, in his *Works*, vol. 3, pp. 11–42.

EVANGELICALISM DIVIDED

members are known with certainty only to God (*2 Tim.* 2:19). With respect to her inward life the church may therefore be said to be 'invisible'. In another respect, however, the church is visible – in her profession of the gospel, and in her obedience to Christ's commands and ordinances. So although there are not two churches, the church may be considered under the two aspects of invisible and visible.

Such a distinction is necessary to grasp the fundamental difference between the Protestant (evangelical) understanding of church and the Roman Catholic. According to the latter, to be in the membership of the Roman communion is to be united to Christ. But the evangelical holds that men may have a place in the visible who are not members of Christ and his church at all. The unregenerate may be *in* the church yet not *of* it: 'They went out from us, but they were not of us; for had they been of us, they would have continued with us (*1 John* 2:19). In the words of Augustine: 'Whosoever do dissent from the scriptures concerning the head, although they be found in all places where the church is appointed, yet are they not in the church.'[1] Defining the church issue over against Rome, a seventeenth-century divine wrote:

> So the question comes back to this, whether the essential form of the Church consists in the sole outward profession of faith, or is to be found in the inward genuineness of faith; whether if the godless and impenitent but outwardly unite themselves to the fellowship which professes Christ's teaching, although otherwise they are devoid of faith or holiness, they may be said to constitute the Church; whether it is not solely the godly and believing who not only profess faith but truly believe and are regenerate, who are presented with this title and enjoy this privilege. The former is the Papist claim, the latter our own.[2]

[1] Augustine, quoted by Samuel Lee, 'The Visibility of the True Church' in *Puritan Sermons, 1659–1689: Being the Morning Exercises* (repr. Wheaton, Ill.: Roberts Publishers, 1981), p. 80.
[2] Leonardus Riissenius, quoted in Heinrich Heppe, *Reformed Dogmatics,* trans. G. T. Thomson (Grand Rapids: Baker, 1978), p. 666.

The evangelical, then, does not put the external first, because Scripture does not put it first. The gospel comes first. It is by the gospel that election takes effect; that God adds to the church; and therefore where that gospel is obscured or denied, and where the biblical terms of admission and membership are no longer upheld, the external may become 'church' in name only. When that happens there *are* two churches: not the 'visible' and the 'invisible', but the true and the false.

Often, however, the issue is not black and white. The true and the false can be mingled together and, where the church neglects Christ's rule for the admission of men and women, such an outcome is certain. The number of non-Christians will then so increase that, in the proverb quoted by Nicholas Ridley, the Marian martyr, 'the greater part overcometh the better'.[1] Which situation, as John Foxe, another Reformer writes, brings 'great variance and mortal persecution, insomuch that sometimes the true church of Christ hath no greater enemies than those of their own profession and company'.[2] In the words of the Westminster Confession: 'The purest churches under heaven are subject both to mixture and error; and some have so degenerated as to become no churches of Christ, but synagogues of Satan' (xxv:4).

The visible church is glorious to the extent to which she corresponds with the invisible. For her spiritual glory does not lie in the possession of anything external – not buildings, nor numbers, nor place, nor succession of bishops. Wherever such external things are accounted highly, spiritual life has gone. As John Owen says, where men are unable 'to discern the glory of spiritual things, and, through their carnal, unmortified affection, do cleave unto and have the highest esteem for worldly grandeur, it is no wonder if they suppose the beauty and glory of the church to consist in them'.[3]

---

[1] *Works of Nicholas Ridley* (Cambridge: Parker Soc., 1841), p. 130.

[2] Quoted by V. N. Olsen, *John Foxe and the Elizabethan Church* (Los Angeles: University of California Press, 1973), p. 102.

[3] Owen, *Works*, vol. 8, p. 571. Conversely, 'When the mind is enabled

A church which supposes she can impress the world is no church at all, for she is denying a first principle of the gospel. Just as 'no one can say that Jesus is Lord but by the Holy Spirit' (*1 Cor.* 12:3), so no one can see the glory of the church until his eyes have been opened to spiritual things; which is what Luther meant when he wrote: 'It is not written: "I see a holy church," but, "I believe"; for it does not have its own righteousness but Christ's, who is its head.'[1] Foxe wrote on the same point:

> Although the right Church of God be not so invisible in the world that none can see it: yet neither is it so visible again that every worldly eye may perceive it. For as like as is the nature of truth, so is the proper condition of the true Church, that commonly none sees it but such only as be the members and partakers thereof. And therefore they which would require that God's holy Church should be evident and visible to the whole world seem to define the great Synagogue of the world, rather than the true spiritual Church of Christ.[2]

This points up another fundamental difference in the understanding of the church between Protestantism and Roman Catholicism. Rome ignores the difference between external appearance and inward life, and so treats salvation and an outward church membership as though they are one and the same thing. But that is not all. Because she claims to be the very church which Christ promised to build and preserve in all ages, she knows no possibility of defection from the faith. She must be secure, for if she fell – she who is the body of Christ and alone entrusted to administer sacraments unto eternal life – then there would be no church and

---

to discern the true beauty and glory of spiritual things, with their alliance unto that which is above, it will be secured from seeking after the glory of the church in things of this world, or putting any value on them unto that end.' When the true spiritual glory of the church has been corrupted so that it rests in the external, 'Many have been infatuated by it, and enamoured of it, unto their own perdition.' p. 570.

[1] *Luther's Works,* vol. 12, p. 235.
[2] Olsen, *John Foxe,* p. 113.

no salvation. Protestants reply that God made no such promise of permanence to any local church, or group of churches. The continuance of all churches depends on the presence of the Holy Spirit and the obedience of faith. Thus Paul warned the first church at Rome that what had happened to the Jews who professed to be God's people could happen to them: 'Because of unbelief they were cast off, and you stand by faith. Do not be haughty, but fear. For if God did not spare the natural branches, he may not spare you either' (*Rom.* 11:20–21). To no local church has the promise been given that she will always be kept from error and be a permanent part of the church which is 'one, holy, catholic and apostolic'. In the words of Article XIX of the Thirty-Nine Articles:

> As the Church of *Jerusalem, Alexandria* and *Antioch*, have erred: so also the Church of *Rome* hath erred, not only in their living and manner of Ceremonies, but also in matters of Faith.[1]

The evangelical, then, because he starts with the faith of the gospel, will not simply take the name of 'church' on face value. He knows that it is gospel doctrine, preached and believed, which alone gives the right to any assembly to be named as Christian. In the words of Calvin: 'Although they put forward Temple, priesthood, and the rest of the outward shows, this empty glitter which blinds the eyes of the simple ought not to move us a whit to grant that the church exists where God's Word is not found.'[2]

* * * *

The ecumenical movement has raised a different issue, although related to the above. In this last half-century it has

---

[1] 'Since accordingly the continuance of the Church rests solely upon the gracious operation of the Holy Spirit, in and for herself she is not visible and not the object of vision, but invisible and the object of faith . . . although particular parts of the visible church may disappear, a congregation of elect and called will always be preserved on earth.' Heppe, *Reformed Dogmatics*, pp. 660, 664.

[2] Calvin, *Institutes,* vol. 2, p. 1046.

been said that evangelicalism cannot provide an alternative to the 'one church' vision of ecumenism because evangelicalism is not after all a church movement. That assertion is true if 'church' is understood in the sense of denomination. Evangelicalism stands for the saving essentials of Christian belief. But it has never claimed that such a minimum of belief is all that is necessary for the full life and organization of churches. The whole counsel of God contains more than that minimum and how that counsel is to be understood at certain points has been the subject of prolonged disagreement among those who are united in accepting the rule of Scripture. Rather than ignore such conscientious disagreements, different Protestant denominations have often arisen to preserve, as they have understood it, a particular aspect of biblical truth. As far as their creeds and constitutions were concerned, evangelical belief was common to them all. Even when unbelief entered, evangelicals in the membership of these various denominations had therefore reason to justify remaining where they were.

This brings us back to the division which surfaced at the National Assembly of Evangelicals convened by the Evangelical Alliance, 18–19 October 1966, when, it was said, the 'peaceful coexistence within evangelicalism was now shattered by Lloyd-Jones'.[1] We have touched on this assertion already but the argument needs re-examining with respect to the church issue. I have said above that the discussion in 1966 was partly confused by the evangelical press.[2] There was,

---

[1] McGrath, *Packer*, p. 123.

[2] 'The situation was made more difficult by some journalistic-type treatment in the Christian press.' John Laird, *No Mere Chance* (London: Scripture Union, 1981), p. 174. Above I have criticized the Graham-influenced press in this regard but would-be advocates of the Lloyd-Jones position were not without some blame. Further, the fact that almost all of Lloyd-Jones' addresses of this period were not available until many years later hindered a better understanding of the disagreement. A brief synopsis of his Evangelical Alliance address was given in *Unity in Diversity: Ten Papers Given at the National Assembly of Evangelicals* (London: Evangelical Alliance, 1967) but the full text did not appear until 1989.

however, an additional reason for confusion and for this some on the Lloyd-Jones side bear a measure of responsibility. The Evangelical Alliance meeting had been preceded by a Commission on Unity, set up by the EA 'to study radically the various attitudes of Evangelicals to the Ecumenical Movement, denominationalism and a possible United Church'.[1] By the last phrase (so the Commission's subsequent *Report* stated) was meant a 'United Evangelical Church', and these words dominated the thinking of those who believed they were opposing Dr Lloyd-Jones' viewpoint. They conceived his proposal to mean the secession of all evangelicals from their different denominations in order to form one 'pure' church; and they saw this as a major departure from the long tradition of inter-denominational fellowship between evangelicals irrespective of denomination.

In fact it was not such a 'United Evangelical Church' that Lloyd-Jones proposed, as an examination of his address on that occasion ought to show; but, given the wording of the *Report of the Commission on Church Unity* (which was issued to coincide with the October 1966 Assembly), people might be forgiven for assuming that it was. Further, the idea of one United Church – as opposed to all 'mixed churches' (a Lloyd-Jones term) – suggested to its critics a 'perfectionist view' which would 'only lead to further division'. So the Rev. Julian Charley argued, in answer (as he thought) to the Lloyd-Jones address, in a session given to him for that purpose on the second day of the EA Assembly. 'How long', he asked, 'would a united Evangelical Church last before it was shattered into fragments? . . . It is absolutely certain that Anglican Evangelicals (with only a very few exceptions)

[1] This was the wording agreed after the first National Asssembly of Evangelicals (September 1965). Lloyd-Jones was not present on that occasion but some men sympathetic to his concerns agreed to the wording 'United Church' without realizing how it would skew subsequent debate. See *Report of the Commission on Church Unity to the National Assembly of Evangelicals, London, October 1966* (London: Evangelical Alliance, 1966), p. 3. The *Report* did not address Lloyd-Jones' main point, nor did he expect that it would.

would not join in such a scheme, fundamentally because it involves a false conception of the Church.'[1]

In ensuing years opposition to the 'pure church' idea was to become a staple part of the Anglican evangelical response to what they conceived to be the Lloyd-Jones challenge. Hence the words in the Nottingham Statement: 'As Anglicans ... we believe that to attempt to gather a "pure" church is not only impossible as a task but also contrary to our biblical understanding of the visible church.'[2] The 'pure church' idea, it had been argued at NEAC 2, relied on an 'unobtainable certainty'. 'It did not take fallible individuals, however faulty in behaviour or vague in belief, seriously enough as *the* constituents of the church.'[3] So 'the sacramental view of the church', as Buchanan called it, was to be preferred: he believed that it encouraged church attendance and thus increased the possibility of people 'gradually assimilating, accepting and responding to the gospel'. In a similar way McGrath represents the view of Lloyd-Jones, and others in opposition to Keele, as one which saw the church as 'by definition, a body of saints, not of sinners, so that only those who were publicly recognized as regenerate could be considered to be church members'.[4]

The text most often quoted to oppose the 'perfectionist view' was from Christ's parable of the wheat and the tares, with its command, 'Let both grow together until the harvest' (*Matt.* 13:30). But to use this text, or others, to argue that the New Testament is against the 'attempt to gather a pure church' is an extraordinary argument. It is patently clear that New Testament church members were meant to be true believers and separate from the world; the church is never defined in Scripture so as to *allow* the presence of the worldly and the unbeliever. That such persons entered the churches

[1] *Unity in Diversity*, pp. 20, 23.

[2] *The Nottingham Statement,* p. 40.

[3] Capon, *Evangelicals Tomorrow,* p. 67. Capon noted of Buchanan: 'He said that evangelical Anglicans had been struggling against this ecclesiology for fifty years.'

[4] McGrath, *Packer,* pp. 120–1.

even in apostolic times was not because Scripture permitted it. It was because God has given to men no infallible power to discern between the real and the nominal Christian. Real grace can be imitated. Admission to church membership does not rest on the certainty of the regeneration of the candidate (and Lloyd-Jones never thought otherwise).

To plead Matthew 13 and human fallibility as an argument against seeking the purity of the church is to break an elementary rule of biblical interpretation. No one Scripture is to be interpreted so as to deny many others. The New Testament churches were required to be distinct from the world; there was to be credible evidence of faith and repentance in those admitted to membership; they were to exclude as well as include – to 'put away' the immoral, and not 'to bear those who are evil' (*Matt.* 18:16–17; *1 Cor.* 5:13; *Rev.* 2:2). We read such directions as, 'A man that is an heretic after the first and second admonition reject' (*Titus* 3:10, AV); and warnings that if evils are condoned or tolerated, then Christ will remove his presence (*Rev.* 3:16). 'You are the salt of the earth; but if the salt loses its taste, how shall it be seasoned? It is then good for nothing but to be thrown out' (*Matt.* 5:13). Purity was clearly demanded of apostolic churches: 'As many as walk according to this rule, peace and mercy be upon them, and upon the Israel of God' (*Gal.* 6:16).

The parable of the tares does not contradict texts which require church discipline; it is rather a warning against excessive strictness in the exercise of such discipline.[1] To turn the warning of the parable into a permission for the church

---

[1] 'In *The Teaching of Jesus Concerning the Kingdom of God and the Church* Geerhardus Vos offers a most reasonable explanation of this parable. The disciples entertained the notion, so prevalent among the Jews of that day, that the very first work of the Messiah on His arrival would be the absolute separation of the good and the evil. Jesus here corrects that notion by telling them that the complete separation will not occur until the end of time, and that in the meantime the kingdom, which is the church, must partake of the limitations and imperfections to which a sinful environment exposes it.' R. B. Kuiper, *The Glorious Body of Christ* (London: Banner of Truth, 1967), p. 307.

to tolerate all and sundry in her membership is to change the whole nature of the church. Because the authenticity of what *appears to be* Christian faith and experience is not finally susceptible to human determination it does not follow that the church has no obligation to seek to be all that she professes to be. As already said, in the absence of that attempt she will sooner or later cease to be the church at all. As Calvin wrote:

> Those who trust that without this bond of discipline the church can long stand are, I say, mistaken; unless, perhaps, we can with impunity go without that aid which the Lord foresaw would be necessary for us.[1]

The understanding of all the Reformers is in harmony on this subject. In the reformed Church of England the presence of the nominal within the church is recognized. In the words of Article XXVI of the Thirty-Nine Articles, 'In the visible church the evil be ever mingled with the good.' But that did not mean that the definition of 'church' was to be lowered to justify the presence of such persons: rather the church is 'a congregation of faithful men, in the which the pure word of God is preached' (Article XIX).[2] Clearly by this definition the church is true as she corresponds with the invisible, that is, as she is made up of living members of Christ who have believed the gospel. Similarly in the Homilies of the Church of England (which belong to the same period as the Articles) we read such words as: 'The true church ... hath always three notes or marks, whereby it is known: Pure and sound doctrine; The sacraments ministered according to Christ's holy institution: and the right use of ecclesiastical discipline.'[3]

---

[1] Calvin, *Institutes*, vol. 2, p. 1232.

[2] 'The visible Church of Christ is therefore one, in outward profession of those things, which supernaturally appertain to the very essence of Christianity, and are necessarily required in every Christian man.' Richard Hooker, quoted by P. E. Hughes, in *Guidelines*, ed. Packer (London: Falcon, 1967). p. 166.

[3] 'Homily Concerning the Coming Down of the Holy Ghost and the Manifold Gifts of the Same.'

Yet while this discussion is important it is still not the main issue involved in the dispute of 1966. Dr Lloyd-Jones did not hold perfectionist views of the church. When he spoke of 'mixed churches' he meant churches where, in the words of the Homily, 'pure doctrine' and 'the right use of discipline' were not upheld. He was far from thinking that churches not so 'mixed' were perfect.

For whatever reason, some undoubtedly perceived the crux of the Lloyd-Jones message to be that evangelicals should leave mixed denominations and that, unless they did, he and others could not continue in fellowship with them.[1] But this was to miss his main thought. His evangelical critics were thinking in terms of static denominations where they could maintain their minority witness as hitherto. He argued that a momentous change was taking place in the denominational situation which would allow evangelicals no such option. Because of the success of ecumenical thinking, with its call to end denominational divisions and to seek 'one church', there was a new question before evangelicals; it was whether they would continue within *that* church? His point was that it would be impossible to do that and to remain a consistent evangelical. This was the unresolved problem which he addressed at the crucial meeting of 18 October 1966. To quote his words:

> I am here to suggest that we find ourselves in a new situation, which has very largely been caused by the arising and arrival among us of what is known as the ecumenical movement . . .
> Are we content with just being an evangelical wing in a territorial church that will eventually include, and must, if it

[1] It is true that the Westminster Fellowship of ministers, of which Lloyd-Jones was chairman, revised its principles of membership in 1967 to include the words, 'We see no hope whatsoever of winning such doctrinally mixed denominations to an evangelical position.' But, as Lloyd-Jones own example showed, this did not mean ending all fellowship with those who stayed in the mainline denominations. He did largely cease from public co-operation with Anglican evangelicals who supported the Keele position.

is to be a truly national and ecumenical church, the Roman Catholic Church?[1]

In the eyes of the evangelicals who listened to him unsympathetically in 1966 these were scaremongering words which envisaged a situation they regarded as utterly improbable. In Julian Charley's response to Lloyd-Jones on the second day of the Assembly, there was not so much as a mention of the Church of Rome. Yet thirty years later Lloyd-Jones' anticipation of events could be seen to be far from imaginary. In 1999 Charley was himself a member of the Anglican–Roman Catholic International Commission whose report endorsed the primacy of the Pope and expressed regret that 'for four centuries the Anglican Communion and the Catholic Church developed their structures of authority in separation from each other, and Anglicans lived without the ministry of the Bishop of Rome'.[2]

It is said that North American Indians when navigating a treacherous river could hear a cataract long before it came into view. Lloyd-Jones 'heard the cataract'. What then did he want evangelicals to do if it was not to form a 'United Evangelical Church'? McGrath thinks the answer is so obscure that, 'We shall never know what Lloyd-Jones intended his address to achieve.'[3] There is no such mystery. He wanted evangelicals to recognize that a situation was developing in which the need could not be met by inter-denominational societies and para-church organizations. Evangelicals had to stand and work together *as churches.* Some, gathering this much from him, complained that he did not say what kind of churches he had in view. His vision, they thought, was too vague, and his proposal could mean the loss of their valued denominational distinctives. To which Lloyd-Jones replied

[1] *Knowing the Times*, pp. 248, 251.

[2] The Commission published its report *The Gift of Authority*, from which I quote, on 12 May 1999. It was rejected by a statement of the Church of England Evangelical Council (29 June) but in Church Assembly evangelicals have entirely failed to prevent the acceptance of ARCIC reports.

[3] McGrath, *Packer*, p. 125.

that it was lamentable that men should be concerned to uphold secondary distinctives in denominations where the very foundations of the Christian faith had been undermined and in a day when the masses of the people were totally bereft of gospel preaching. What the evangelical churches needed was not a new solution to questions of church government to facilitate a new evangelical denomination. The situation was far more serious than could be met by any change in organization. The need was for new spiritual life, new devotion to Christ and his Word, and a new Spirit-anointed preaching to bring the indifferent masses of the population to conviction of sin and to joy in God.

This is not to say that Lloyd-Jones was indifferent to questions of church order; but he put his emphasis on the spiritual health of local churches. Greater unity would follow, not precede, renewed health. In this regard his thinking was akin to that of Spurgeon who wrote:

> You cannot, by Presbytery, or Independency, or Episcopacy, secure the life of the Church – I find the Church of God has existed under an Episcopacy – a form of government not without its virtues and its faults. I find the Church of God can flourish under a Presbytery, and decay under it too. I know it can be successful under an Independent form of Church government and can decline into Arianism quite as easily. The fact is that forms of government have very little to do with the vital principle of the Church. The reason why the Church of God exists is not her ecclesiastical regulations, her organization, her formularies, her ministers, or her creeds, but the presence of the Lord in the midst of her.[1]

It will not do to put down an emphasis on the health of the local church to independency, for it surely stands at the forefront of the teaching of the New Testament. Even such a

[1] Spurgeon, *Metropolitan Tabernacle Pulpit*, vol. 10, p. 163. Whitefield, another major evangelical leader, took the same view: 'I despair of greater union till a greater measure of the Spirit be poured from on high. Hence, therefore, I am resolved simply to preach the gospel of Christ, and leave others to quarrel by and with themselves.' *Works*, vol. 1, p. 376.

strong Presbyterian as Thomas M'Crie could write of local congregations: 'For the ordinary performance of religious duties, and the ordinary management of their own internal affairs, they may be said to be complete churches, and furnished with complete powers.'[1]

* * * *

Perhaps the strongest resistance to the Lloyd-Jones argument was connected with the ecumenical belief that Christian unity had to come from the uniting of *denominations*. For a time at least, many evangelicals seemed to believe this as much as non-evangelicals. It was said that it was only from within the main denominations that evangelicals could be heard speaking on Christian unity; and that if evangelicals were outside these denominations, they could exert no possible influence in the wider scene. Some professing evangelicals in the main denominations, it is true, began to doubt this, being disillusioned by the doctrinal disarray and the liberalism of their own communions. But their thinking remained so conditioned by denominational blocs that they turned to the Roman Catholic or Orthodox Churches. In contrast with what they saw of the absence of real church unity among evangelicalism, with its para-church personality-centred agencies, here were historic structures whose unity and long traditions, they hoped, would provide a more secure alternative to the unbelief prevailing in mainline Protestantism. It was in this way, for instance, that the North American teacher Dr Thomas Howard reasoned. Howard, who joined the Church of Rome in 1985, wrote in his autobiography:

The question, What is the Church? becomes finally intractable; and one finds oneself unable to offer any telling reason why the phrase 'one, holy, catholic and apostolic church,' which we all say in the creed, is to be understood in any way

[1] Thomas M'Crie, *Two Discourses on the Unity of the Church* (Blackwood: Edinburgh, 1821), p. 16.

other than the way in which it was understood for 1500 years.[1]

Similar thinking occurred in Britain. The Rev. Michael Harper, evangelical curate at All Souls', London, later an Anglican charismatic leader and a speaker at the Nottingham Congress, has written of his growing dismay at Anglican disbelief, indiscipline, and the ordination of women. These things led him to abandon a non-denominational evangelicalism for the security of the Orthodox Church. He now believed:

> The slogan *sola scriptura* is not sufficient. On its own it has led to the proliferation of denominations, each claiming to be faithful to the truth ... It is my view that Evangelicals can find their home in the Orthodox Church. Of course, adjustments are necessary. However, one can have a great deal more confidence in a Church that has stood the test of nearly two thousand years than in a comparative newcomer to the scene like Evangelicalism.[2]

This type of thinking includes the assumption that a large denominational bloc is more able to withstand error.[3] It makes another assumption which is still more significant, namely, that 'denomination' can be taken as synonymous with 'church', and that, the older and larger the denomination, the greater must be its claim to our allegiance. But 'denomination' does not equal 'church' in any biblical sense of 'church'. A denomination is neither a local church nor is it the church universal. As S. L. Greenslade, an Anglican and a Regius Professor of Ecclesiastical History at Oxford, has pointed out:

[1] Thomas Howard, *Evangelical Is Not Enough: Worship of God in Liturgy and Sacrament* (San Francisco: Ignatius Press, 1984), p. 157. Thomas Oden, in his reaction against liberalism, has also written of his admiration of the Pope. *Requiem*, p. 82.

[2] Harper, *The True Light*, pp. 160, 162. The Church of England, he writes, was his foster mother before he came home to the true church, his real mother.

[3] Owen refutes this point, *Works*, vol. 14, p. 525.

The application of the word 'church' to Christian denominations severally is at best the acceptance of a misnomer forced upon us by what has happened in history. The Orthodox and Roman Catholic communions, together with the Anglican, Lutheran, Presbyterian, Methodist and many others, are not, strictly speaking, churches but denominations.[1]

The recognition of this fact has important consequences. It means, for one thing, that no congregation can be credited with church status (biblically understood) simply because it belongs to a larger body termed 'The Church of . . .'[2] It means also that amalgamating denominations is not necessarily the same as uniting churches. Further, a correction of the misnomer has important implications for understanding the nature of schism. Because the New Testament says nothing about leaving 'the church', when 'church' is taken as the equivalent of denomination, the deduction is often drawn that the Bible gives no justification for leaving a denomination. But the two things are not the same.[3]

The consequence of what I am saying is not that denominations are illegitimate, nor that their extinction is the real solution to Christian disunity. Not at all. As already said, denominations have often arisen to maintain what Christians believed were aspects of biblical truth which could not otherwise be upheld and defended. While acknowledging that these aspects (forms of church order, baptism and the

[1] S. L. Greenslade, *Schism in the Early Church*, p. xviii. John Frame makes the same point in his stimulating book, *Evangelical Reunion: Denominations and the One Body of Christ* (Grand Rapids: Baker, 1991), p. 43. 'It seems that in our ecclesiological literature and in our usual thinking and speaking, we tend to equate the church with the denominations. When Jesus says that the gates of hell shall never prevail against the church, preachers routinely apply that text to the Free-Will Baptist Church or whatever.'

[2] I am not, of course, arguing that 'church' in Scripture is never used of more than one local congregation, but when the word is used in the wider sense it includes *all* the Christian churches of an area or region and is not therefore parallel to denominational usage.

[3] For good comments on schism and denominations, see A. A. Hodge, *Evangelical Theology* (repr. Edinburgh: Banner of Truth, 1976), pp. 181–3.

like) often constituted secondary issues among Christians, the founders of denominations have believed that their action was warranted on scriptural grounds. Such denominations only became schismatic if they limited Christian fellowship to their own people, and claimed a unique church status for themselves which all other Christians were expected to recognize. Protestant denominations (with very few exceptions) have always avoided such exclusiveness and recognized their oneness with all who hold to Christ regardless of secondary differences. Spiritual unity does not demand oneness in organization.[1]

But – and this is where Dr Lloyd-Jones' case comes in – for evangelicals to want to retain secondary denominational differences in denominations where the very essentials of the gospel are no longer maintained, is to give denominations an importance which no appeal to Scripture can justify. He argued that to put an external unity before essential truths (without which there is no church at all) is inconsistent with being an evangelical.[2] Such thinking could well lead finally to an acceptance of 'one Church' under the primacy of Rome. It was indeed such thinking which led the English Tractarians of the mid-nineteenth century into the Church of Rome, as it has led others more recently. 'I had learned', wrote Henry (later Cardinal) Manning in 1841, 'that unity is a first law of the Church of Christ.'[3] Today Archbishop Carey talks in the same way.

It was not a Nonconformist such as Lloyd-Jones but an evangelical Anglican who warned most clearly what this mindset could bring on. In one of the addresses published

---

[1] It was therefore an extraordinary thing for David Watson at NEAC 2 to join the ecumenical cry against denominations and say 'denominationalism was second only to apartheid in South Africa as a scandal to the church'. Capon, *Evangelicals Tomorrow*, p. 80

[2] This was also the reason why Spurgeon left the Baptist Union in England, as I have shown in *The Forgotten Spurgeon* (Edinburgh: Banner of Truth, 1973).

[3] Quoted in Newsome, *The Parting of Friends: The Wilberforces and Henry Manning*, p. 274.

prior to the Keele Congress of 1967, Dr Philip E. Hughes presented a very different scenario from the one which was to command popular appeal among his younger colleagues. Instead of sharing in the current optimism, he believed that they were seeing 'the rise and swift spread of antichristianity within the Church', and referred to such things as 'its merely human (and dead and buried) Jesus, its anticredalism, its secularism, its utter relativism, its antinomianism, and its free-for-all-ism'. All this was 'rapidly leading the Church into a state of crisis'. Hughes went on:

> This is the assassination of Christianity and its gospel. There is no juster way to describe this spirit which is now rampant in the Church than as the spirit of antichrist . . . Unless the ecumenical movement resolutely and explicitly sets its face against this antichristianity, the prospect of the organization on a worldwide scale of a vast and immensely powerful church of antichrist, embracing any and every form of pseudo-Christianity, paganism, and heathenism, is far from fanciful. And this will be a 'church' so incredible as to be unrecognizable as the Church of Christ, so totally assimilated to the image of the unregenerate world that the church and world will be indistinguishably merged into one. If and when this happens, it will mean the eclipse and disappearance of the visible church of the West.[1]

This was not a counsel of despair; it was a comparatively lone voice facing facts. Hughes believed with Lloyd-Jones that one had first to be negative if the positive solutions were to be the right ones. The first need was to see the church as a spiritual body. It is the possession of the inward qualities of truth and holiness and love, flowing from union with Christ himself, which make the church to be the church. The tragedy of the churches of the late twentieth century was that, in the absence of the power of the gospel, evangelicals were being drawn to remedies proposed by an alien tradition. Those remedies were directly contrary to the exclusiveness and the separateness which the gospel requires.

[1] 'The Credibility of the Church' in *Guidelines*, p. 178.

The ecumenical call was not for truth and salt; it was supremely for oneness: the greater the unity of 'the Church', it was confidently asserted, the stronger would be the impression made upon the world; and to attain that end churches should be inclusive and tolerant. But it has never been by putting unity first that the church has changed the world. At no point in church history has the mere unity of numbers ever made a transforming spiritual impression upon others. On the contrary, it was in the very period known as 'the dark ages' that the Papacy could claim her greatest unity in western Europe.[1]

The unity which leads to the conviction of the world – according to the words of John 17:21, 'that the world may believe You sent me' – is a unity of people who receive all Christ's words; a unity in truth which unregenerate men hate but which sanctifies those who believe; a unity in Christ which binds his members together in love (as the whole context of John 17 shows).

Such a conviction has often been given to the world when the church has been very small in number as it was during the Marian persecution in England in the mid-sixteenth century. Hugh Latimer could write from prison before his martyrdom along with Nicholas Ridley on 16 October 1555:

> 'The Lord knoweth them that are his; and let every man that nameth the name of Christ depart from iniquity.' Now how many are there of the whole catholic church of England which depart from iniquity? how many of the noblemen, how many of the bishops or clergy? how many of the rich men, or merchants? how many of the queen's councillors, yea, how

[1] Ian Henderson made this point in his book, *Power Without Glory: A Study in Ecumenical Politics* (London: Hutchinson, 1967). He argued that the ecumenical movement in Britain was primarily concerned with church leaders (often academics) looking for power. 'Churches [i.e., denominations] are power structures, the relations between churches are power relations, apostolic succession is a power mythos, the call for oneness has often been the demand for power.' p. 182. Dabney likewise thought the reunion movement was largely concerned with 'numbers, wealth, combination and power'. *Discussions,* vol. 2. p. 442.

many of the whole realm? In how small room then, I pray you, is the true church within the realm of England?[1]

To this suffering remnant Luke's description of the first Jerusalem church applied: 'None of the rest dared join them, but the people esteemed them highly' (*Acts* 5:13). And in the course of time it was the testimony of this small number of Christians in England, and especially of the less-than-three-hundred who were put to death, which was so owned by the Spirit of God that almost a nation seemed to turn from unbelief and Roman Catholicism. The world can amass mere numbers but when God convicts the world it is by something of a very different nature: 'God has chosen the weak things of the world to put to shame the things which are mighty' (*1 Cor.* 1:27).

Exactly the same lesson was shown to be true in the eighteenth century. Clergy such as Joseph Butler lamented that the people of England had come to treat Christianity as a fable, but they were helpless to change the situation. Then, in the words of Wesley:

> Two or three Clergymen of the Church of England began vehemently to 'call sinners to repentance.' In two or three years they had sounded the alarm to the utmost borders of the land. Many thousands gathered to hear them . . . How extensive is the change which hath been wrought on the minds and lives of the people! Know ye not that the sound has gone forth into all the land; that there is scarce a city or considerable town to be found, where some have not been roused out of the sleep of death . . . In what age has such a work been wrought, considering the swiftness as well as the extent of it? When have such numbers of sinners in so short a time been recovered from the error of their ways? when hath religion, I will not say since the Reformation, but since the time of Constantine the Great, made so large a progress in any nation, within so small a space? [1]

---

[1] *Acts and Monuments of John Foxe,* vol. 7 (London: Seeley, Burnside and Seeley, 1847), p. 415.

The great majority of professing Christians disparaged all this, and to do so they seized on the small number of the preachers involved: 'But there are only a few young heads.' To which Wesley replied:

What do you infer from their fewness? that, because they are few in number, therefore God cannot work by them? Upon what scripture do you ground this? I thought it was the same to Him, to save by many or by few. Upon what reason? Why cannot God save ten thousand souls by one man, as well as by ten thousand? How little, how inconsiderable a circumstance is number before God! Nay, is there not reason to believe that whensoever God is pleased to work a great deliverance, spiritual or temporal, he may first say, 'The people are too many for me to give the Midianites into their hands?' May he not choose few as well as inconsiderable instruments, for the greater manifestation of his own glory. Very few, I grant, are the instruments now employed; yet a great work is wrought already.[2]

It was in the same tradition as Latimer and Wesley that Lloyd-Jones was speaking at the Evangelical Alliance in 1966 when he appealed for faith that the Holy Spirit will bless his own Word and that, if evangelicals would stand together as churches, the great problems before them could be overcome:

We may be small in numbers but since when has the doctrine of the remnant become unpopular among evangelicals? It is one of the most glorious doctrines in the whole Bible. We are not interested in numbers. We are interested in truth and in the living God. 'If God be for us, who can be against us?' . . . If we stand for God's truth we can be sure that God will honour us and bless us.[3]

[1] *Works of Wesley*, vol. 8. pp. 203–5.
[2] *Ibid.*, p. 218.
[3] *Knowing the Times*, pp. 256–7. On this point John Stott replied that he thought the remnant was 'inside the church, not outside it' – a comment which both begged the question of the 'church' and took the main Lloyd-Jones point to be a case for secession.

11

From the Quarries to the Temple

The conflict between Christianity and all other forms of belief has invariably turned on those truths of divine revelation which are most offensive to human pride. The particular truths thus rejected have varied through history. In the first centuries it was the exclusiveness of Christianity which was especially attacked; then, more particularly, it was the deity of Christ; at the time of the Reformation the great division was over how God saves sinners; in the twentieth century opposition centred on the Bible as divine revelation. More fundamental and abiding, however, than all these several issues, has been the subject to which we have repeatedly returned in these pages: the question of who is a Christian lies at the very centre of disagreement. For if it was not for the existence of Christians, and what Scripture says about them, there would be no conflict at all.

All the major differences which have been the subject of controversy lead back to two irreconcilable starting points: either Christianity is just another variation of human thought and imagination, with no right to teach certainties; or it is the one God-given means by which sinners are brought to Christ and heaven. The practical consequences are equally antithetical: either one lives trusting in oneself or believing in Christ. The Scriptures know no other alternative. It is either, 'Cursed is the man who trusts in man', or, 'Blessed is the man who trusts in the LORD' (*Jer.* 17:5–7). 'He who believes in the Son has everlasting life; and he who does not believe the Son shall not see life, but the wrath of God abides on him' (*John* 3:36).

If the case I have sought to present in these pages is true, then the greatest failure of professing Christianity in the English-speaking world in the twentieth century has been the way in which this division has been confused. The chief human factor in this has been the unbelief of liberalism with its new definition of Christian: 'Christ is a wonderful person', was the message, 'whose example we must follow and whose life is to be reproduced in us.' Here was a Christ who did not confront men with questions or doctrinal demands; no longer needed were such admissions as those of Peter, 'Depart from me, for I am a sinful man, O Lord!' or of Thomas, ' My Lord and my God!' (*Luke* 5:8; *John* 20:28). In essence, liberalism was 'Christianity' harmonized with the moral aspirations of all men. It was truth modified to give offence to none. It required no commitment to the facts of Christ's incarnation, vicarious death, and resurrection. It proclaimed no good news of how the finished work of Christ is counted as the righteousness of the ungodly who believe on him. Rather it assumed the goodness of human nature and portrayed Christianity in terms of doing rather than of believing. In so far as it spoke of hope after death, it was with a promise of universal comfort – heaven not as the exclusive home of the redeemed but as the ultimate destination for all who pass through this world. It denied (along with the false prophets) that 'wide is the gate and broad is the way that leads to destruction and there are many who go in by it' (*Matt.* 7:13,15).

The health of the church has always been in proportion to the extent to which, in her teaching, the difference between Christian and non-Christian has been kept sharp and clear. Once the line is blurred spiritual decline is a certainty, and the blurring of the line has been the main cause of the decline of the English-speaking churches of the past century. No doubt liberals intended no such result but their thought was ideally suited to serve the interests of the tempter who deceived mankind in the Garden of Eden. From that time, when God began to form a new people for himself, Satan has ever endeavoured to intrude his own people among them. Genesis chapter 6 is a record of how he succeeded in doing this when 'the sons of God' were united with 'the daughters of men', so that the line between the offspring of the woman and the offspring of the serpent (*Gen.* 3:15) disappeared, and it took the judgment of the Flood to restore the separation. What occurred in the time of Noah was, in Luther's words, that

> the true church yielded to the seductions of the Cainite church . . . The Flood came, not because the Cainite race had become corrupt, but because the race of the righteous who had believed God, obeyed His Word, and observed true worship had fallen into idolatry, disobedience of parents, sensual pleasures and the practice of oppression.[1]

Satan used the same temptation against Israel on many occasions. It was the presence of his people among the leaders of the Jews which explains their great opposition to Christ (*John* 8:44). The same demonic strategy reappeared almost at once amongst the apostolic churches. No sooner were congregations established at Corinth and elsewhere than the devil sought to mix darkness with light, the unbeliever with the believer and idols with the temple of God. Such was

[1] On Genesis 6:1 in *Luther's Works*, vol., pp. 10–12.

the situation which led Paul to demand, 'What accord has Christ with Belial? or what part has a believer with an unbeliever?' (*2 Cor.* 6:15). Precisely the same situation was uncovered by the Reformation of the sixteenth century. Hugh Latimer boldly addressed it when, preaching to the Convocation of Clergy in the reign of Henry VIII, he said:

> It is to be feared lest, as light hath many her children here, so the world hath sent some of his whelps hither: amongst the which I know there can be no concord, nor unity, albeit they be in one place, in one congregation. I know there can be no agreement between these two, as long as they have minds so unlike . . . Wherefore it is well done in all orders of men, but especial in the order of prelates, to put a difference between children of light and children of the world, because great deceit ariseth in taking the one for the other. Great imposture cometh, when they that the common people take for light, go about to take the sun and the light out of the world.[1]

No one who reads the Bible seriously can doubt that the same policy was followed with great success in the twentieth century. Multitudes were brought into church membership, and often into teaching positions, without any acknowledgement of sin or any evident reliance upon a divine Saviour. The result has been that the most insidious opposition to the gospel has come from within worldly churches.

* * * *

In the remaining pages I will seek to draw some general conclusions from the material we have considered.

1. *The history of the new evangelicalism has shown how difficult it is to remedy the faults of one position without falling into dangers at an opposite extreme.*

As we have noted, before the 1950s evangelical Christianity in the United States and, to a lesser extent, in Britain, had

---

[1] *Sermons by Hugh Latimer* (Cambridge: Parker Soc., 1844), pp. 10–12.

been affected by a narrowness of outlook – 'fundamentalism' – which too often saw people as Christians only when they were of the same persuasion. In its central tenet, namely, that to be a Christian is to be a believer in the gospel of the Scriptures, fundamentalism was biblical; but in its tendency to add stipulations not foundational to Christian believing, it was prone to make the boundaries of Christ's kingdom too small. The mistake was not a new one. It existed in the time of the first disciples (*Mark* 9:38), and Richard Baxter in the seventeenth century complained of those who 'think that the commoner sort of Christians are the *world*, and the better and more zealous sort only are the church'.[1]

While fundamentalism often suffered from hostile misrepresentation, there can be little doubt that in its reaction to the prevalent apostasy its definition of Christian was too narrow. In its zeal against compromise it could forget that weak and inconsistent Christians belong to Christ as truly as do strong ones – a fact which the apostle Paul lays down as a rule to control all Christian relationships (*Rom.* 14).

My present point, however, is that in seeking to remedy an outlook which erred in unbiblical strictness, the new evangelicalism moved to an opposite danger. If a narrow sectarianism is contrary to Scripture, no less so is the inclusivism which would embrace all who adopt the Christian name. If belligerence is wrong, so also is a false charity. It is not enough for would-be fellow workers to profess, 'Let us build with you, for we seek your God as you do' (*Ezra* 4:2). Scripture calls for a higher standard: 'If anyone comes to you and does not bring this doctrine, do not receive him into your house nor greet him' (*1 John* 2:10).

The tendency of fundamentalism in controversy was to assume too readily that its critics were unregenerate, and that all opposition was part of 'the offence of the cross'. Here, too, the new evangelicalism moved to an opposite extreme. Its policy too largely seemed to ignore the innate hostility in

[1] Baxter, *The Cure of Church Divisions* (London: Symmons, 1670), p. 31.

man's nature to biblical truth, as though in openness to the truth there is no essential difference between the saved and the lost. It was optimistic that opposition could be disarmed by better information, by love and by cordial relationships. If separation came too easily in fundamentalism, the new evangelicalism dismissed the very thought. And in its anxiety to conciliate the critics of its evangelical beliefs it could employ stronger language against the teaching of fellow Bible-believers than against the downright anti-Christian errors of the critics.[1]

An old saying has thus been illustrated again in these last fifty years, 'Many an error is taken up by going too far from other men's faults.'[2]

2. *A great deal of the confusion which has divided evangelicalism has been related to the question, 'Who is a Christian?'*

It would be a mistake to think that this confusion is to be explained only in terms of a broad and charitable definition versus a narrow and suspicious one. The case of this book has been that for over a hundred years a sustained attempt has been made to popularize a definition of Christian which possesses no biblical authority at all. Disagreement over the extent to which this attempt has been successful has been a main factor in the division of evangelicals. Painful although such disagreement has to be, it will be ultimately beneficial if it leads to renewed concentration on the subject which is more important than any other.

There are two ways in which Scripture identifies a true disciple of Christ. The first is by the evidence of a person's faith in Christ, and the second by the insistence that the accompaniment of true faith is always a new life.

On the first evidence enough has already been said in these pages. Faith in Christ, according to the New Testament, is the

---

[1] See above, p. 189, for Ockenga's words to Carnell on this danger. The same thing is illustrated when John Stott, as far as all contemporary Christianity is concerned, applies the word 'heresy' only to what, he says, is the fundamentalist view of Scripture. *Evangelical Truth*, p. 61.

[2] Baxter, *Church Divisions*, pp. 224–5.

same as receiving the truth; not, that is, all truth, but certainly the truth of salvation from the guilt and power of sin through Christ alone. The Christian knows that he is a sinner, that Christ is the divine Saviour, and that his salvation comes entirely from what Jesus has suffered for him and in his place. Every such person has 'the light of the knowledge of the glory of God in the face of Jesus Christ' (*2 Cor.* 4:6). The content of that knowledge admits of unending progress, but where it does not exist at all there can be no salvation. All true Christian faith rests on the same foundation.

But the New Testament does not stop at identifying Christians simply in terms of what they believe. Orthodox belief alone will take none to heaven. Becoming a Christian involves a change of nature, and in this the Holy Spirit gives all true believers a common experience, whatever the words they use to describe it. Joseph Hart, an English Independent of the eighteenth-century, wrote of it:

> *The faith that unites to the Lamb,*
> *And brings such salvation as this,*
> *Is more than mere notion or name:*
> *The work of God's Spirit it is;*[1]

Thomas Scott, a contemporary of Hart's, filled it out in these sentences:

> I will not pretend to say, nor do I think any man can say exactly, how much explicit knowledge of divine truth is absolutely essential to salvation . . . But this I will say, that, whatever darkness there may be in a man's understanding, unless he feels and behaves as a sinner justly condemned for breaking a righteous law, and expects salvation of mere grace in God's way, and as reconciled to God, as loving his service, and longing after holiness – that holiness which the law requires, – and so living holily in sincerity and truth, he cannot be saved, according to the Bible.[2]

[1] Hart, *Hymns Composed on Various Subjects,* 7th ed. (London: Hawker, 1911), p. 120.

[2] *Letters and Papers of Thomas Scott,* ed. John Scott (London: Seeley, 1824), pp. 408–9.

Blaise Pascal, the seventeenth-century Roman Catholic author, would have agreed with Hart and Scott:

> True conversion consists in annihilating yourself before this universal Being whom you have angered so many times, and who can justly destroy you at any moment – in recognising that one can do nothing without Him, and that we have deserved of Him nothing but disgrace. It consists in knowing that there is an unconquerable repugnance between God and us, and that, without a mediator, we can have nought to do with Him . . . Do not be surprised at seeing simple people believe without reasoning, God gives them love of Him and hatred of themselves. He inclines the heart to believe. We shall never believe with useful and faithful belief unless God inclines the heart.[1]

Such descriptions of a Christian are neither broad nor narrow: they are biblical, and evangelical Christianity has been right to insist that nothing less than this warrants the name of Christian.

But the problem evangelicals have faced is deeper than a common acceptance of definitions. It is one thing to agree on statements, another to apply those statements in the current church scene when it comes to admission to full church membership and to the sacraments. Part of the difficulty here lies in the fact that it is beyond human ability to discern the reality of spiritual experience with certainty. While the Bible draws a clear line between the saved and the lost, this is not a line which the church can draw with the same accuracy. Wherever Christianity has been healthy this

---

[1] *Thoughts of Pascal,* trans. C. S. Jerram (London: Methuen, 1901), p. 141. How far Pascal can be taken as representative of the Roman system may be judged from the fact that Pope Alexander VII 'prohibited and condemned' his *Provincial Letters.* Thomas M'Crie has observed that Pascal 'was virtuous without being indebted to his Church, and evangelical in spite of his creed; that his piety, for which he is so much esteemed by us, was the very quality that exposed him to odium and suspicion from those of his own communion.' *The Provincial Letters of Blaise Pascal,* trans. T. M'Crie (London: Chatto and Windus, 1875), pp. xlix, lxvii.

has always been recognized. In the words of Hugh Binning, the Scottish Puritan,

> Charity hath much candour and humanity in it, and can believe well of every man, and believe all things as far as truth will permit. It knows that grace can be beside a man's sin; it knows itself is subject to such infirmities; therefore it is not a rigid and censorious judger.[1]

In his *Religious Affections* (possibly the most discriminating book ever written on the true and false Christian), Jonathan Edwards repeatedly gave similar warning: 'The saints have not such a spirit of discerning that they can certainly determine who are godly and who are not . . . It was never God's design to give us rules by which we may certainly know who of our fellow professors are His.'[2]

It is a very different thing, however, to deduce from the church's lack of full discernment that no standards of judgment are to be required and that no endeavour is to be made to keep the church pure.[3] If it is true that Satan's great endeavour is to mix the world with the church, then it

[1] Hugh Binning, *Christian Love* (repr. Edinburgh: Kennedy, 1844), p. 29.
[2] Edwards, *The Religious Affections* (repr. London: Banner of Truth, 1961), pp. 110, 120.
[3] On the subject of admission to church membership there are helpful words in R. B. Kuiper, *The Glorious Body of Christ*, p. 145. He concludes: 'In brief, the elders must do all that is humanly possible to determine whether or not the applicant is a Christian.' I have written on the outworking of this issue in *Jonathan Edwards: A New Biography* (Edinburgh: Banner of Truth, 1987), chapter 17, where the words of John Owen are quoted: 'The letting go this principle, particular churches ought to consist of regenerate persons, brought in the great apostasy of the Christian Church.' Anglican authors are noticeably hesitant to address this issue. Archbishop Temple hoped for 'the utmost liberty of thought compatible with maintenance of spiritual fellowship', only to add: 'But what is the precise point at which spiritual fellowship is endangered, and by what methods those who endanger it should be restrained, are questions that lie outside our province.' *Doctrine in the Church of England* (London: SPCK, 1938), p. 2. Quoted by David Holloway, *The Church of England*, p. 119. John Stott, after referring to the indecency of 'indiscriminate baptizing', at once adds, 'Not that Scripture authorizes us to stand in judgment on the reality of people's profession . . . some would say that

follows that it is his purpose which is served when churches treat as believers those whose lives show no evidence of any saving dependence on Christ. While the church cannot infallibly discern the regenerate she can and must recognize belief and conduct which is plainly incompatible with Scripture. Anything less is surely contrary to the New Testament.

Where there is no attempt to apply the biblical standard of Christian to individuals there is inevitable disobedience to the commands that both by preaching and church practice a difference is to be made between the godly and the worldly: 'Say to the righteous that it shall be well with them ... Woe to the wicked!' (*Isa.* 3:10–11). To teachers who make no such distinction the warnings addressed to false prophets may well apply: 'With lies you have made the heart of the righteous sad, whom I have not made sad: and you have strengthened the hands of the wicked, so that he does not turn from his wicked way to save his life' (*Ezek.* 13:22). 'He who justifies the wicked, and he who condemns the just, Both of them alike are an abomination to the LORD' (*Prov.* 17:15).

When churches have recovered from apostasy, as at the time of the Reformation and the eighteenth-century Evangelical Revival, it has always been by a return to such discriminating preaching and practice. Given the great decline in the English-speaking churches of the twentieth century, the chief need again was the re-assertion of the meaning of being a Christian; the tragedy has been that the ecumenical movement, with its axiom that all church members are to be regarded as Christians, has led many evangelicals in the opposite direction.

3. *The church cannot succeed in the same way in which political parties may succeed.*

Politics has to do with the art of the possible, and with such concessions and compromises as may give a party

<hr />

it must be a *credible* profession, but then we begin to make arbitrary rules by which to assess credibility.' 'The Evangelical Doctrine of Baptism', *Churchman*, vol. 112 (1998), no. 1, pp. 58–9.

maximum appeal and influence. But the cause of Christ has never advanced on such a basis. The church is wholly dependent upon supernatural aid and without that all success is short-lived and illusory. The biblical principle is clear: 'Those who honour me I will honour' (*1 Sam.* 2:30); 'Not by might nor by power, but by my Spirit says the LORD of hosts' (*Zech.* 4:6); 'My speech and my preaching were not with persuasive words of human wisdom, but in demonstration of the Spirit and of power' (*1 Cor.* 2:4). But the temptation for Christians to diverge from this principle is attractive and it presents itself as a means to obtain a higher good.

Liberalism gained its hold on Protestant churches because good men feared that unless concessions were made to the latest 'scholarship' the churches would lose their place in the modern world. Co-operation with non-evangelicals and participation in the ecumenical movement were promoted in the genuine hope of wider gains for the gospel and for an evangelical renaissance. Anglican evangelical alignment with Anglo-Catholics was justified as the best counterpoise to liberalism in the Church of England. Neutrality over whether the miraculous gifts of the apostolic era have been renewed in the charismatic movement was judged best for the preservation of evangelical unity. An acceptance of the basic Christianity of Roman Catholicism has been advanced as a sound way to strengthen protest against a secular materialism.

In our view, many, if not all, of these changes were brought on by 'political' or pragmatic thinking. I do not mean that the move away from principle was deliberate. The temptation was more subtle. The spiritual gains appeared substantial yet an ethos developed in which one concession led to another. No one thought that the sending of the names of those who made 'decisions' back to Roman Catholic churches would lead to Billy Graham being prepared to share a platform with the Pope, but it did. No one supposed that if members of Inter-Varsity gained recognition in the world of university theology they might begin to criticize the faith with which they began, but in a number of cases it has happened. No one thought that if evangelicals could be made bishops or arch-bishops in the Church of England there would be no stand against heresy, yet so it has proved.

More than one commentator on the contemporary evangelical scene has noted how a policy which was expected to lead to so much has instead produced so little.[1] The fundamental explanation has to do with the way in which scriptural principle has been sidelined. When that happens the church's course is bound to be downwards. In the words of Horatius Bonar, 'Fellowship between faith and unbelief must, sooner or later, be fatal to the former.'[2] The reason is not that error is more powerful than truth: it is rather that, without the Holy Spirit, spiritual weakness is a certainty. Therefore any alliance or course of action which does not put scriptural principle first is bound to grieve the Spirit of God and to lead to spiritual poverty. This is not to say that declining denominations are never recovered. Where men take the course of a Wesley or a Whitefield they may; but the spirit of such men has never yet been found among those who have lost the will to contend boldly with error. This was the concern of Dr Lloyd-Jones in the 1960s when evangelicals faced the call to join in the ecumenical enterprise. Speaking of the existing defection from biblical Christianity in the mainline denominations, he said:

We have evidence before our very eyes that our staying amongst such people does not seem to be converting them to our view but rather to a lowering of the spiritual temperature

[1] 'The more one studies contemporary evangelicalism, the more one senses the profound frustration that grips many of its leaders. The statistics say we should be powerful and influential, and we are not. The intellectuals think they should be followed, and they are largely ignored. The entrepreneurs and media stars act as if they will bring revival, and of course they don't . . . Theologians and historians and pastors alike continuously expand the definition of evangelicalism, but instead of drawing in a wider circle they are gutting what is central.' D. A. Carson, *The Gagging of God* (Leicester: Apollos, 1996), p. 488.
[2] H. Bonar, *Our Ministry: How It Touches the Questions of the Age* (Edinburgh: MacNiven and Wallace, 1883), p. 97.

of those who are staying amongst them and an increasing tendency to doctrinal accommodation and compromise.[1]

At the same date Francis Schaeffer made a similar observation with regard to evangelicals in mainline churches in the United States:

The tendency is to go from ecclesiastical latitudinarianism to co-operative comprehensiveness. Thus Christians may still talk about truth but tend less and less to practise truth. The next step comes very quickly, say, in two generations. If one stays in a denomination that is completely dominated by liberals and one gives in to the ecclesiastical latitudinarianism which becomes a co-operative comprehensiveness, there is a tendency to drift into doctrinal comprehensiveness and especially to let down a clear view of Scripture.[2]

It was with good reason that Martyn Lloyd-Jones, as already noted, warned Gerald Bray about 'the danger of becoming an ecclesiastical politician'. But as David Holloway has observed, the danger is that 'When a church is not agreed over fundamentals, all that is possible is for the "entrenched positions" to play politics'.[3]

4. *This period of history confirms the painful fact that there can be serious differences of belief and consequent controversies among true Christians.*

The reason for this is not that they differ over fundamentals. Those who differ over fundamentals are not Christians at all. But there are other truths besides fundamental truths, as is clear from the way Paul deals with the subject of teaching in 1 Corinthians, chapter 3. Speaking of those especially responsible for the building of the church, he indicates that the work does not end with instruction on the 'foundation, Jesus Christ'. More has to be built on that foundation, truths

[1] Lloyd-Jones, *The Puritans*, p. 147.
[2] Schaeffer, *The Church Before the Watching World* (Leicester: IVP, 1972), p. 97.
[3] Holloway, *The Church of England*, p. 208.

which he likens to 'gold, silver, precious stones'. But there is the real possibility that instead of truths men will inadvertently add errors, 'wood, hay, straw' – things without permanence which will not stand the final fire of God's judgment. So in warning of 'ignorant, mistaken, non-genuine teaching',[1] Paul affirms: 'If anyone's work is burned, he will suffer loss; but he himself will be saved, yet so as through fire' (*1 Cor.* 3:15). The reference is to error inadvertently taught, and taught by men whose salvation is not in question. The verses have nothing to do with heretics and false prophets who are not building on the foundation at all.

It may well be that as evangelicals we have been too prone to forget that to be right on the gospel – the foundation – is not a guarantee that there will be no additions of 'wood, hay, straw'. Scripture is full of warnings that the best of God's people remain fallible and defective in understanding. Reflecting on disagreements among believers, John Berridge consoled himself with the thought, 'The Lord washed our hearts here, and he will wash our brains in heaven.'[2] On a similar note, John Wesley, while defending Methodism in terms of God's witness to the truth of what was preached, added an important qualification:

> God cannot bear witness to a lie. The gospel, therefore, which He confirms must be true in substance. There may be opinions maintained at the same time which are not exactly true; and who can be secure from these? Perhaps I thought myself so once: when I was much younger than I am now, I thought myself almost infallible; but I bless God I know myself better now.[3]

[1] R. C. H. Lenski, *The Interpretation of St. Paul's First and Second Epistles to the Corinthians* (Minneapolis: Augsburg, 1963), p. 144. For an application of the passage to superficial evangelicalism, see R. L. Dabney, 'Exposition of 1 Corinthians 3, 10–15' in *Discussions: Evangelical and Theological*, vol. 1, pp. 551–74.

[2] *Works of John Berridge*, 2nd ed. (London: Palmer, 1864), p. 97.

[3] To the Countess of Huntingdon, 19 June 1771. *Letters of John Wesley*, vol. 5, p. 259.

One conclusion which Paul draws from the fallibility of men in 1 Corinthians 3 is the warning, 'Let no one glory in men' (*1 Cor.* 3:21). We do not take readily to the lines of George Herbert:

> *Man is all weakness; there is no such thing*
> *As prince or king . . .*

Like the Corinthian Christians we are prone either to idolize men or to be unduly critical. We too readily form parties behind men in forgetfulness of the direction, 'One is your teacher, the Christ, and you are all brethren' (*Matt.* 23:8). Because an eminent Christian is evidently right in some things, or owned of God in his work, we are liable to take him as the leader in all things and to treat any who disagree as opponents.

But the truth is that to different leaders in the church are given different gifts and different measures of grace. None has every gift; none has all wisdom; as Pascal says, 'There is light enough to lighten the elect, and darkness enough to humble them.'[1] Men who err in one field of work or thought may provide true help to the churches in another (as the last fifty years have again shown). Richard Baxter was surely right when he observed:

> I now see more good and more evil in all men than heretofore I did. I see that good men are not so good as I once thought they were but have more imperfections, and that nearer approach and fuller trial doth make the best appear more weak and faulty than their admirers at a distance think.[2]
> . . . It is a grand pernicious error to think that the same men's judgments must be followed in every case. And it is of grand importance to know how to value and vary our guides, as the cases vary.[3]

The differences among Christians often arise from disagreements over what is 'gold, silver, precious stones', and

[1] *Thoughts of Pascal*, p. 162.
[2] *Reliquiae Baxterianae* (London, 1696), Part 1, p. 130.
[3] Baxter, *Church Divisions*, p. 216.

what is 'wood, hay, straw'. To our eyes the two may sometimes look very alike. It is not that Scripture is defective in
light, the defect is in our own understandings. The deduction
to be drawn from this fact is not that all opinions on beliefs
not essential to salvation are to be laid aside as of small
importance. On the contrary Paul warns strongly against any
such minimalist attitude to truth (*1 Cor.* 3:10-17). What may
be called secondary differences among Christians are not of
no consequence and they may be sufficiently important to
prevent the formal unity of Christians in the same denomination. Freedom of conscience to interpret Scripture is far
better than an external unity imposed upon all.

At the same time it is essential to recognize, as evangelicalism has sought to do, that differences of understanding
among Christians are never to be allowed to transcend the
truth which makes them one in Christ. God would use our
defective understandings and mistakes to humble us and to
make us the more diligent in seeking to know the truth. The
devil would use the same weakness to alienate believers from
one another and to destroy Christian love and sympathy. He
would have us forget that Christians share a common desire
to see Christ's kingdom advanced even when they differ over
the best means by which it is to be attained. He would have
issues not foundational to salvation so elevated in importance
that the larger Christian unity disappears and contention
threatens to 'destroy the work of God' (*Rom.* 14:20). This
ploy Satan used with effect at the time of the Reformation
and again in the Puritan period, for it is not Laodiceans but
those with the strongest attachment to Scripture who are
most likely to be tempted in this way.[1] From the harm done
by the dogmatism of controversies over secondary issues the
devil then tempts other Christians, who observe it, to abandon contending for the faith altogether.

[1] See Appendix 5 below. 'While we wrangle here in the dark', said
Baxter, 'we are dying and passing to the world that will decide all our
controversies.' *Reliquiae Baxterianae*, Part 3, p. 89.

The best remedy then for divisions among Christians is for all to put first the living and teaching of the gospel. An all-round failure to do this by evangelicals in the last fifty years has undoubtedly played a part in divisions which have occurred. The old saying is true: 'The best ministers are those who take most with them to heaven.' David Wells is surely right when he says: 'The most urgent need in the Church today, even that part of it which is evangelical, is the recovery of the Gospel as the Bible reveals it to us.'[1] When Christ is put first, when making disciples of all nations is the first priority, division is far more likely to occur where it should occur, between believers and the world. As Wesley said when preaching on the death of Whitefield:

> Let us keep to the grand scriptural doctrines which he every-where delivered. There are many doctrines of a less essential nature, with regards to which, even the sincere children of God (such is the present weakness of human understanding!) are and have been divided for many ages. In these we may think and let think; we may 'agree to disagree'.[2]

J. C. Ryle was reflecting the same spirit when he spoke of the improbability of the union of Protestant denominations: 'I regard it as a beautiful castle in the air.' But he was careful

---

[1] Wells, *Losing Our Virtue,* p. 204.

[2] 'On the Death of Mr Whitefield', *Sermons on Several Occasions,* vol. 1 (London: Kershaw, 1825), p. 677. At an earlier date Wesley answered the charge of opponents that he and Whitefield 'anathematized' each other as 'shameless untruth . . . false and scandalous. I reverence Mr Whitefield, both as a child of God, and as a true minister of Jesus Christ'. *Works,* vol. 8, p. 108. This spirit was not always maintained in the eighteenth century, nor was it in the twentieth. Francis Schaeffer (a participant in the division which saw Machen and others leaving the Northern Presbyterian Church in the 1930s) noted in 1972: 'We must show forth the love of God to those with whom we differ. Thirty-five years ago in the Presbyterian crisis in the United States, we forgot that. We did not speak with love about those with whom we differed, and we have been paying a high price for it ever since.' *The Church Before the Watching World,* p. 58.

to add, 'Keep the walls of separation as low as possible, and shake hands over them as often as you can.'[1]

In connection with the need to emphasize fundamental truths, controversy has occurred over the rightness of including the verbal inspiration of Scripture among those beliefs. Certainly, as already noted, Protestant Christianity treated an individual's dependence on the divine authority of Scripture as evidence of the reality of their Christian experience.[2] The affirmation of Zacharias Ursinus was common to all the Reformers: there is 'a firm persuasion, wrought in the hearts of the faithful by the Holy Spirit, that the Scriptures are the word of God . . . it is experienced by all who truly believe, in whom it is also strengthened and confirmed by the same Spirit, through the reading, hearing and study of the doctrine delivered by the prophets and apostles'.[3]

A Christian has an inward revelation to his heart which harmonizes with the revelation written. He therefore trusts Scripture as the Word of God. 'But', it is said, 'there are Christians who doubt the verbal inspiration of Scripture, and therefore that tenet cannot be held to be foundational or essential to salvation.' In reply it can be conceded that grace and doubt may coexist in the same person. It ought not to be so – any more than unbelief ought to be in a Christian – but it is, and no one can say to what degree the existence of doubt is compatible with being in a state of salvation. Yet what should be clear to Christians is the *inconsistency* of affirming belief in the gospel and not in all Scripture.[4] For no

[1] Ryle, *Charges and Addresses,* p. 297. In the same context he wrote: 'I shall not touch the subject of reunion with the corrupt Church of Rome. The very proposal is monstrous.'

[2] See above, pp. 155–8.

[3] *The Commentary of Zacharias Ursinus on the Heidelberg Catechism,* trans. G. W. Willard (Columbus, Ohio: 1852), p. 9.

[4] B. B. Warfield uses this argument with effect in reviewing James Denney's work, *The Atonement and the Modern Mind. Critical Reviews* (New York: OUP, 1932), p. 102–5. Denney wanted to keep the orthodox doctrine of the cross but without dependence on the authority of Scripture. Referring to the title of Denney's work, Warfield makes a point

saving belief is possible without conviction concerning the underlying authority of Scripture as divine revelation. If we can trust Scripture only so far as our reason can accept it we are not Christians at all. Yet, due to all manner of influences and temptations, we are not always consistent as Christians, and in the late-nineteenth and twentieth centuries numbers were misled by the argument that the Bible is more easily defended if it is not necessary to accept the inerrancy of all its details. Those swayed by this thinking are not to be identified with those who paraded their disbelief and taught it to others; the doubt of the former did not necessarily invalidate their profession of faith in Christ, as evangelical leaders recognized.[1]

A person who believes the gospel and yet is uncertain about the whole Bible will get to heaven in spite of the inconsistency of thought. But we cannot stop there. That same inconsistency, if condoned, has the potential to undermine all saving Christianity. Belief in the trustworthiness of all Scripture is essential for the preservation of the Christian faith as a whole. Without verbal inspiration the church cannot sustain a dependable corporate witness. All authoritative exposition depends upon it. Without it, as Ryle has said, 'A fog has descended on the Book of God, and enveloped every chapter in uncertainty.'[2] There is therefore the strongest reason why commitment to the truth of verbal inspiration has to be kept among the fundamentals of Christian and

---

often forgotten: 'There is after all but one "mind" to be considered, and this is the human mind; and the human mind is fundamentally much the same in modern times as it has always been.'

[1] 'I freely grant that many excellent Christians think that the view I maintain is open to serious objections . . . they shrink from maintaining that inspiration extends to every word of Scripture.' Ryle, *Old Paths*, p. 24. 'Many earnest Christians', writes Machen, believe only 'that many things which the Bible says are true . . . and upon those things we may ground our hope for time and eternity.' *The Virgin Birth of Christ* (repr. Grand Rapids: Baker, 1974), p. 386.

[2] Ryle, *Expository Thoughts on John*, vol. 1 (Ipswich: Hunt, 1877), p. ix.

evangelical belief. To make concessions to doubt at this point has been a tragic mistake and grievous to the Spirit of God.

5. *The history we have covered shows how hard it is for leaders to look in different directions at once.*

There has been, as we have seen, an evangelical concern for greater unity amongst all Christians. In itself this was desirable and commendable but at the same time it had to be remembered that the great cause of division and weakness was unbelief over fundamental truth. More evangelical humility, more recognition that 'we all stumble in many things' (*James* 3:20), does not affect the fact that a major apostasy has seen a denial of the gospel very widely established in the English-speaking churches. That is not a situation to be changed by conciliation and cordiality. Liberalism has had all the marks of the false prophet. It promised a great growth in light and Christian influence for the nations where it was adopted. Instead there has been spiritual desolation. This is exactly what all who believe Scripture should have expected.

The biblical portrait of false teachers is a very clear one. While they profess to speak for God, they mislead people over their true condition in God's sight. They do not speak faithfully to the unconverted. 'They are all dumb dogs, they cannot bark' (*Isa.* 56:10). They are 'men-pleasers'. 'They have healed the hurt of the daughter of my people slightly, saying, "Peace, peace!" when there is no peace' (*Jer.* 8:11). 'They have spoken lying words in my name, which I have not commanded them' (*Jer.* 29:23). The long-term effect of such influence is certain: 'For from the prophets of Jerusalem profanity has gone out into all the land' (*Jer.* 23:15). The consequence is moral decay and, finally, judgment: 'They mocked the messengers of God, despised his words, and scoffed at his prophets, until the wrath of the LORD arose against his people, till there was no remedy' (*2 Chron.* 36:16).

The decay of Christianity in the west in the twentieth century is not the result of sociological and secular pressures.

Spiritual decline is not a mystery which Scripture leaves unexplained. It is the result of the presence of falsehood where there should be truth: 'I have not sent these prophets, yet they ran. I have not spoken to them, yet they prophesied. But if they had stood in my counsel, and caused my people to hear my words, then they would have turned them from their evil ways and from the evil of their doings' (*Jer.* 23:21–22).

The parallels in history are unmistakable. False teaching always brings the church into impotence and contempt. John Berridge learned this from the age in which he grew up:

> When the doctrines of regeneration and justification by faith become despised or deserted doctrines, the labours of the clergy will prove useless, their persons will grow cheap, their office seem contemptible, and they at length may be ashamed of their function and their livery.[1]

It was good that evangelicals forty years ago gave new attention to the subject of Christian unity, but, if the thesis of this book is true, there was failure to look sufficiently at the broader religious scene in which gospel truth, not unity, was the first need. Thus a grave situation in the churches still remains to be addressed. We can be sure that it will not be addressed effectively until there is a renewed anointing of power upon those whose only authority is the Word of God.[2]

6. *The struggles and hopes of Christians are not to be understood in terms of the present and the temporal.*

Supposing our prospects were to be assessed only by what we presently see, we would be 'of all men the most

---

[1] *Works of John Berridge*, 1838, p. 345.

[2] Arthur Johnston made this point in writing on the Lausanne Congress. He was concerned that a wrong priority was being given to church unity: 'Authority and the power of the Spirit are always related to the Bible. The Church was filled with the Spirit to preach the Word with boldness.' *Battle for World Evangelism*, p. 329.

pitiable' (*1 Cor.* 15:19). At every point in Christian life and labour it is the certainty of what is future which is to govern the present.

This is relevant to the disagreements among Christians upon which we have commented in these pages. I do not think that Scripture forbids such comment; we have to form convictions on such matters, but we are warned that all our convictions are only provisional and may be reversed in the day when Christ infallibly discerns between 'gold, silver, precious stones, wood, hay, straw'. The command therefore has to be before us: 'Judge nothing before the time, until the Lord comes, who will both bring to light the hidden things of darkness and reveal the counsels of the hearts; and then each one's praise will come from God' (*1 Cor.* 4:5). Speaking of the surprising evaluation of many Christian labours which will then be given, Lenski has written:

> Many great works shall thus go down in ashes in the judgment and be absolutely disowned by the Lord. Many proud build-ers who were acclaimed of men while they lived and were honored with great tributes when they were buried will hang their heads when all their work becomes nothing in the fire test. But many a humble preacher, of whom nobody made much in life, shall shine at that day because he wrought gold, silver, and precious stones.[1]

The same dimension has to apply to our thoughts of other Christians. We know far too little to begin to estimate who might be first and who last in the kingdom of God. The direction given to us is clear: 'In lowliness of mind let each esteem others better [that is, higher] than himself' (*Phil.* 2:3).

---

[1] Lenski, *1 and 2 Corinthians*, p. 144. On this subject, the words of A. W. Tozer are relevant: 'The American genius for getting things done quickly and easily with little concern for quality or permanence has bred a virus that has infected the whole evangelical church in the United States and, through our literature, our evangelists and our missionaries, has spread all over the world.' *The Incredible Christian* (Harrisonburg, Pa.: Christian Publications, 1964), p. 23.

If we see the mistakes of other Christians, we have therefore to think how much greater could have been our failure if we had been exposed to the same temptations; and in the light of our own privileges, we are faced with our own poor use of the opportunities we have been given. I have tried imperfectly in these pages to deal with principles and not to deal in personalities. I hope that I can admire and love all fellow believers with whom I have disagreed. Where differences exist, the direction how we should treat one another is very searching: 'Why do you judge your brother? Or why do you show contempt for your brother? For we shall all stand before the judgment seat of Christ . . . So then each of us shall give account of himself to God' (*Rom.* 14:10,12).

A little before his death, Luther confessed to Melanchthon that, in their disagreements on the sacrament, 'he had gone too far'.[1] All Christian ministers are conscious of similar failure. Warfield says of Augustine, 'Had he lived long enough, then he would have corrected the unevangelical element in his thinking.'[2] But life is short and imperfections are with us until death. 'I never did anything which might not and ought not to have been done better', said Baxter.[3] 'I will begin to begin to be a Christian', said Whitefield four years before his death.[4] A longing for that which is future is true Christian experience: 'We also who have the first fruits of the Spirit, even we ourselves groan within ourselves, eagerly waiting for the adoption, the redemption of our body' (*Rom.* 8:23). None now attains to what he would desire (*Rom.* 7:15). All

---

[1] Quoted in Samuel Bolton, *The Arraignment of Error* (London, 1646), p. 339.

[2] Warfield, *Studies in Tertullian and Augustine* (New York: Oxford University Press, 1930), p. 129.

[3] *Richard Baxter's Penitent Confession* (London, 1691), p. 28.

[4] Whitefield, *Works*, vol. 3, p. 343. Jonathan Edwards quotes the words of Luther: 'We reach after heaven but we are not in heaven. Woe to him that is wholly renewed, that is, that thinks himself to be so. That man, without doubt, has never so much as begun to be renewed, nor did he ever taste what it is to be a Christian.' *Religious Affections*, p. 249.

servants of Christ fail as well as succeed. All die as 'unprofitable servants'. All have reason to sing:

> *The highest hopes we cherish here,*
> *How fast they tire and faint,*
> *How many a spot defiles the robe*
> *That wraps an earthly saint!*

At almost all times in history the kingdom of God has appeared to be in confusion to the outward eye. It is faith in the promises of God which provides a different perspective. The Holy Spirit assures us that infinite wisdom and love are presently directing the life of the church and that eternity will be witness to their success when a multitude which no man can number will be glorified with Christ. What we see now is but the beginning.

Words on the church by the Swiss pastor Felix Neff remain as true and beautiful as when he preached them in 1826. He likened the 'living stones' which make up the church of Christ to the stones which were brought into Solomon's temple. But they were only placed there after they had been duly cut and prepared: 'The temple, when it was being built, was built with stone finished at the quarry, so that no hammer or chisel or any iron tool was heard in the temple when it was being built' (*1 Kings* 6:7). In Jerusalem all had to be perfect:

But, surely, it was not so in the marble quarries, or in Lebanon, where the cedars were cut; or in the glowing furnaces between Succoth and Zarthan (1 Kings 7:46) where they melted the brass for the sacred vessels. Thus, in heaven, this majestic sanctuary is erected without noise, without labour; every material is brought thither pure and perfect. The Bride of the Lamb has neither spot, nor wrinkle, nor any such thing. But in this impure and dark world, this obscure quarry, whence the Great Builder is pleased to take some stones for his edifice, what shall we find, but work-yards for a season, where everything appears to be in movement and disorder? What unshapen stones, what rubbish, what fragments! How many things fit only for temporary service! How many arrangements merely provisional! How many mercenaries and foreigners are occupied in these quarries, just as the servants of Hiram were, and who, like them, will never enter the sanctuary! How many dissensions among the labourers; how many conjectures and disputes about the final purpose of the Great Architect, and the several parts of the plan, which are known only to Himself! Shall we search in this chaos for the true church, the spiritual temple? Shall we endeavour to arrange, in one exact and uniform order, all those stones that we find in the various quarries opened in a thousand places in the world? Oh! how much wiser is the Master! While some are disputing about the excellence of this or the other department of the work; and while others are spending their strength in endeavouring to introduce perfect order, the wise Master-builder surveys, in silence, the vast scene of operations, chooses and marks the materials which he sees to be prepared amidst all this confusion, and causes them to be removed and placed in his heavenly edifice; assigning to every piece the place most proper for it, and for which he has designed it. Such, my beloved brethren, is the sublime idea which we ought to form of this universal church. Oh! how contemptible now will appear, in our eyes, those endless disputes which have at all times divided the believers, and continue to do so to the present day. Let us rather labour in the quarry where our work is assigned, to prepare as great a quantity of materials as possible; and especially, let us entreat the Lord to make us all lively stones fit for his building. Amen![1]

---

[1] *Life of Felix Neff: Pastor of the High Alps* (London: Religious Tract Soc., 1836), p. 214–6.

Appendices

1: The Scriptures
Joseph Hart

Say, Christian, would'st thou thrive,
   In knowledge of thy Lord?
Against no scripture ever strive,
   But tremble at His word.

Revere the sacred page;
   To injure any part,
Betrays, with blind and feeble rage,
   A hard and haughty heart.

If aught there dark appear,
   Bewail thy want of sight;
No imperfection can be there,
   For all God's words are right.

The Scriptures and the Lord
   Bear one tremendous Name;
The written and the Incarnate Word
   In all things are the same.

For Jesus is the Truth,
　As well as Life and Way;
The two-edg'd sword that's in His mouth,
　Shall all proud reasoners slay.

Why dost thou call Him Lord,
　And what He says resist?
The soul that stumbles at the word,
　Offended is at Christ.

The thoughts of men are lies;
　The word of God is true;
To bow to *That* is to be wise;
　Then hear, and fear, and do.

JOSEPH HART,
Hymns Composed on Various Subjects,
7th ed. (London: Hawker, 1911),
pp. 226–7

2: The Testimony of John Berridge
(Fellow of Clare College, Cambridge)

When I first came to the University, I applied myself diligently to my studies, thinking human learning to be a necessary qualification for a divine, and that no one ought to preach unless he had taken a degree in the University. Accordingly I studied the classics, mathematics, philosophy, logic, metaphysics, and read the works of our most eminent divines; and this I did for twenty years; and all the while was departing more and more from the truth as it is in Jesus; vainly hoping to receive that light and instruction from human wisdom, which could only be had from the word of God and prayer.

During this time I was thought a Methodist by some people, only because I was a little more grave, and took a little more pains in my ministry than some others of my brethren; but, in truth, I was no Methodist at all, for I had no sort of acquaintance with them, and could not abide their fundamental doctrines of justification by faith, and thought it high presumption in any to preach, unless they had taken holy orders. But when God was pleased to open mine eyes, about half a year ago, he showed and taught me other things. Now I saw that nothing had kept me so much from the truth, as a desire of human wisdom. Now I perceived, that it was difficult for a wise or learned man to be saved, as it was for a rich man or a nobleman: *1 Cor.* 1:26. Now I saw that God chose the foolish things of this world, to confound the wise, for two plain reasons; first, That no flesh should glory in his presence: *1 Cor.* 1:29. And, secondly, That faith did not stand, or was not produced, by the wisdom of man, but in the power of God: *1 Cor.*2:5. Now I discerned, That no one

EVANGELICALISM DIVIDED

could understand the word of God, but by the Spirit of God: *1 Cor.* 2:12. Now I saw, That every believer was anointed by the Holy Spirit, and thereby led to the knowledge of all needful truths: *1 John* 2:20; and, of course, that every true believer was qualified to preach the gospel, provided he had the gift of utterance. Now I saw that the Methodist's doctrine of justification by faith was the very doctrine of the gospel: and I did no longer wonder at the success which those preachers met with, whether they were clergymen or laymen. They preached Christ's doctrine, and Christ owned it; so that many were added to the faith daily.

JOHN BERRIDGE,
Works
(London: Simpkin, Marshall, 1838),
pp. 358–9

[322]

3: Satan and the Gospel
Horatius Bonar

L et us mark how, in these days of ours, he works, and tempts, and rages:–

He comes as an angel of light, to mislead, yet pretending to lead; to blind, yet professing to open the eye; to obscure and bewilder, yet professing to illuminate and guide. He approaches us with fair words upon his lips: liberality, progress, culture, freedom, expansion, elevation, science, literature, benevolence, – nay, and *religion* too. He seeks to make his own out of all these; to give the world as much of these as suits his purpose, as much as will make them content without God, and without Christ, and without the Holy Ghost. . . .

He sets himself against God and the things of God in every way. He can deny the gospel; or he can dilute the gospel; or he can obscure the gospel; or he can neutralize the gospel; – just as suits his purpose, or the persons with whom he has to do. His object in regard to the gospel is to take out of it all that makes it glad tidings to the sinner; and oftentimes this modified or mutilated gospel, which looks so like the real, serves his end best; for it throws men off their guard, making them suppose that they have received Christ's gospel, even though they have not found in it the good news which it contains.

He rages against the true God, – sometimes openly and coarsely, at other times calmly and politely, – making men believe that he is the friend of the truth, but an enemy to its perversion. Progress, progress, progress, is his watchword now, by means of which he hopes to allure men away from the old anchorages, under the pretext of giving them wider, fuller, more genial teachings. He bids them soar above creeds, catechisms, dogmas, as the dregs of an inferior age, and a lower mental status. He distinguishes, too, between theology and religion, warmly advocating the latter in order to induce men to abandon the former. He rages against the divine accuracy of the Bible, and cunningly subverts its inspiration by elevating every true poet and philosopher to the same inspired position. So successfully has he wrought in disintegrating and undermining the truth, that there is hardly a portion of it left firm. The ground underneath us is hollow; and the crust on which we tread ready to give way, and precipitate us into the abyss of unbelief.

HORATIUS BONAR
God's Morning: or, Thoughts on Genesis
(London: Nisbet, 1875),
pp. 365–6.

4: The Offence of the Cross Ceasing

Thomas Scott

Leave out the holy character of God, the holy excellence of his law, the holy condemnation to which transgressors are doomed, the holy loveliness of the Saviour's character, the holy nature of redemption, the holy tendency of Christ's doctrine, and the holy tempers and conduct of all true believers: then dress up a scheme of religion of this unholy sort: represent mankind as in a pitiable condition, rather through misfortune than by crime: speak much of Christ's bleeding love to them, of his agonies in the garden and on the cross; without shewing the need or the nature of the satisfaction for sin: speak of his present glory, and of his compassion for poor sinners; of the freeness with which he dispenses pardons; of the privileges which believers enjoy here, and of the happiness and glory reserved for them hereafter: clog this with nothing about regeneration and sanctification, or represent holiness as somewhat else than conformity to the holy character and law of God: and you make up a plausible gospel, calculated to humour the pride, soothe the consciences, engage the hearts, and raise the affections of natural men, who love nobody but themselves. And now no wonder if this gospel (which has nothing in it affronting, offensive, or unpalatable, but is perfectly suited to the carnal unhumbled sinner, and helps him to quiet his conscience, dismiss his fears, and encourage his hopes,) incur no opposition amongst ignorant persons, who inquire not into the reason of things; meet with a hearty welcome, and make numbers of supposed converts, who live and die as full as they can hold of joy and confidence, without any fears or conflicts. . . . What wonder if, when all the offensive part is left out, the gospel gives no offence? What wonder if, when it is made suitable to carnal minds, carnal minds fall in love with it? What wonder if, when it is evidently calculated to fill the unrenewed mind with false confidence and joy, it has this effect? What wonder if, when the true character of God is unknown, and a false character of him is framed in the fancy, – a God all love and no justice, very fond of *such* believers, as his favourites, – they have very warm affections towards him?

. . . I would not give needless offence. Let this matter be weighed according to its importance. Let the word of God be examined impartially. I cannot but avow my fears that Satan has propagated much of this false religion, among many widely different classes of religious professors; and it shines so brightly in the eyes of numbers, who 'take all for gold that glitters', that, unless the fallacy be detected, it bids fair to be the prevailing religion in many places.

THOMAS SCOTT,
Letter and Papers, ed. John Scott
(London: Seeley, 1824),
pp. 441–4.

5: Puritans on Church Unity

When the Devil would hinder the work of Jerusalem, he knows no way more likely than by dividing the hearts of those who are employed, if he can possibly, that thereby he might bring confusion . . . We are here as bees, flying up and down from flower to flower all day, but at night they come all into the same hive; that is a place where Luther and Zwingli will well agree.

JEREMIAH BURROUGHS
Irenicum, To the Lovers of Truth and Peace
(London, 1646),
pp. 197, 281.

There is no remedy now left but brotherly forbearance towards those that hold the foundation. It were to be wished that we could agree, not only in fundamentals, but in all other the accessories of christian doctrine. But this cannot be hoped for.

THOMAS MANTON
On John 17:11, in *Complete Works, Vol. 10*
(repr. London: Nisbet, 1872),
p. 331.

It is matter of amazement to consider what feuds, and what alienations of affection, are the products of *differences of opinion*: as if heaven were entailed to understandings of one complexion. There always were in the Church of God, and there always will be, different apprehensions in some matters of truth; and generally they have brought forth disorders (great disorders) in men's practice; each one hugging his particular opinion, as if he judged himself, and none but himself, infallible. And even Protestants, declaiming against an infallible Head upon earth, will yet arrogate an infallibility of judgment unto themselves. When as nothing is more demonstrable than that my brother has as much reason to quarrel with me for differing with him, as I have to quarrel with him for his differing from me; unless he will say, 'I cannot be deceived, but you may' ... Mistake not, the kingdom of heaven is not entailed to parties, but as in every nation, so amongst all parties, whoso believeth in Christ, feareth God, and worketh righteousness, is accepted of God.

JOHN COLLINGES
Several Discourses Concerning the Actual Providence of God
(London, 1678),
pp. 731–2.

Nor, therefore, is it scepticism, by any means that I would advise to; as if there were nothing to be thought certain:– but this; that whereas the greatest and most necessary things in religion are most plain, that is, either most plain in themselves, or most expressly revealed in the word of God, here let us be stedfast ourselves, without being severe towards other men. Other things, that are more matter of doubt and dispute, by how much the less plain they are, we should count so much the less necessary. In reference, therefore, to these less momentous things, about which there is most of jangling, there ought always to be great modesty, and distrust of our own understandings, and a continued readiness to receive information, with constant looking up to the Father of lights for further illumination, and a resolution wherein we, with others, 'have attained, to walk by the same rule, minding the same (agreed) things,' hoping God will reveal his mind to the otherwise minded in his own time.

JOHN HOWE
'The Carnality of Religious Contention',
Works, Vol. 3
(repr. London: Tegg, 1848),
p. 150.

Title Index

Biographies, collected writings and works by or about the principal authors cited are brought together under the individual's name. Other publications are listed alphabetically. Publication details are given on the page where the work is first mentioned.

Title Index

Title Index

General Index

Academics, influence of, 173-214
'Altar Call', 51-4, 57, 76, 78
American Association of Theological Schools, 22, 188
Amsterdam school for evangelists, 70
Anglican Evangelicals,
and Graham Crusades, 40, 49, 131, 135
attitude to denomination, 40, 42-3, 45, 48, 83, 90-102, 107-9, 113-28, 134, 140-8, 168-72, 252
Anglican-Methodist reunion, 85-8, 92, 264
Anglican-Roman Catholic International Commission (ARCIC), 219-21, 241 n, 245, 246 n, 284
Anglo-Catholics, 40, 85-7, 90, 92-4, 103, 105, 107-8, 118, 121-4, 139, 217, 248, 265, 304
Ankerberg, John, 223
Anvil launched, 144
Apostles' Creed, 13, 73 n
Augustine, 236, 274, 316
Ayer, W. W., 75

Baillie, John, 12-13
Banner of Truth Trust, 132 n
Baptism, as basis of unity, 99-107, 139, 163, 217
Barby Moravian Seminary, 4
Barclay, Oliver, 110, 177, 185-7
Barclay, William, 203
Barr, James, 98, 176, 181-3, 190 n, 194
Barrows, Cliff, 24, 30
Barth, Karl, 179
Baur, F. C., 16 n
Baxter, Richard, 82, 198 n, 298-9, 308-9, 316

Bea, Augustin, Cardinal, 245-6
Beavan, Jerry, 30 n, 54, 99 n
Bebbington, David W., 108 n, 176, 193-4, 198-9
Beckwith, R. T., 89, 137, 140
Bedford, Colin, 149-50, 168
Bell, L. Nelson, 26-8, 30 n, 35, 67 n
Ruth, *see* Graham, Ruth
Berridge, John, 100, 161 n, 167 n, 168 n, 307, 314, 321-2
Bevan, Aneurin, 13
Beveridge, William, 101 n
Bible, *see* Scripture, doctrine of
Billy Graham Evangelistic Association, 25, 30, 32, 34, 40, 47, 49, 52-3, 57, 59, 66 n, 67, 72-3, 76, 78, 252
Binning, Hugh, 302
Bishops, evangelical, 127-8, 134, 305
Blanch, Stuart, 109
Bonar, Horatius, 305, 323-4
Bray, Gerald, 104 n, 118, 127-8, 134-6, 143 n, 144, 219 n, 306
Breslau, Poland, 7
British Council of Churches, 80
British Weekly, 56, 267
Brown, John, 329
Bruce, F. F., 80 n, 176, 180, 183, 214
Buchanan, Colin, 93, 99-102, 108, 114, 122, 131 n, 137-8, 141, 144-5, 174, 280
Bultmann, Rudolf, 167 n, 206-7
Burgon, J. W., 194 n
Burroughs, Jeremiah, 327
Butler, Joseph, 292

Caister, *see* National Evangelical Anglican Congresses, NEAC 3
Callistus, Pope, 116 n
Calvin, John, 10, 80, 106, 157-8, 239, 277, 282

[335]

General Index

Litton, Edward A., 106
Lloyd-Jones, D. Martyn,
  influence on British evangelical
    ism, 81-3, 178
  on crusade evangelism, 75-7
  on doctrinal compromise, 305-6
  on ecumenism, x, 43-8, 87, 97-
    8, 283, 305-6
  on evangelical unity, 45-8, 96, 278-
    93
  public breach with J. I. Packer,
    94-6, 110-1
  supposed isolationism of, 48,
    126-7
Longford, Frank, 266 n
Los Angeles, Calif., 24
Lovelace, Richard, 199
Luther, Martin, 64, 154-5, 171, 238,
  240, 276, 296, 316
Lutherans, 245, 246 n

MacArthur, John F., viii, 222-4
Machen, J. G., 16-18, 310 n, 312 n
Macleod, D., 212 n
Magnin, Edgar, 68
Maier, Gerhard, 201-3, 209 n
Mandela, Nelson, 62
Manning, Henry, Cardinal, 289
Manton, Thomas, 327
Manwaring, R., 91, 108 n, 113, 127,
  133, 140
Marburg, Germany, 16
Marsden, George, 22, 36, 190, 250
Martin, William, 29 n, 35, 55, 59 n,
  63 n, 65, 67, 68 n, 75
Marshall, I. Howard, 176, 191
Mascall, E. L., 93, 121
McCall's magazine, 73
M'Crie, Thomas, 286, 301 n
McGrath, A. E., 47 n, 88, 115, 118,
  126-7, 130, 174, 195-9, 220, 222,
  247, 252, 278 n, 280, 284
McIlvaine, C. P., 247
Melanchthon, Philip, 155-6, 316

Methodists, 19, 58, 161-4, 170; see
  also Anglican-Methodist reunion
Michaels, J. R., 191, 199 n
Micklem, Nathaniel, 178
Milner, Isaac, 104-5
Milner, Joseph, 171
Mitchell, Curtis, 52 n, 62-3, 69
Montefiore, Hugh, 125
More, Sir Thomas, 156-7, 273
Morgan. G. Campbell, 44 n
Mott, John R., 49
Muggeridge, Malcolm, 60-1
Murray, John, 19 n, 188 n

National Assembly of Evangelicals
  (UK), 44-8, 278-9, 284, 293
National Association of Evangelicals
  (USA), 20
National Council of Churches
  (USA), 70 n
National Evangelical Anglican
  Congresses (UK):
  NEAC 1, 42-4, 89, 92, 97, 99,
    107, 112, 117, 121-2, 127, 131 n,
    132-41, 143, 147-8, 168, 175,
    215, 272
  NEAC 2, 100-1, 108-9, 123,
    127, 131 n, 132-41, 143-4, 149,
    175, 200, 216, 280
  NEAC 3, 136, 144 n, 272
Neff, Felix, 317-8
Nelson, Rudolph, 38 n, 65 n
Neuhaus, Richard John, 71 n, 222,
  231-6, 244-5
Nevius, J. L., 270 n
New College, Edinburgh, 10 n
New Evangelicalism,
  beginnings, 20, 26, 33
  criticized by fundamentalists, 31
  criticized by liberals, 32
  decline, 39, 51, 72, 190-1, 297-9
Newton, John, 103, 166-7, 262-3 n
Nicoll, W. Robertson, 267
Niebuhr, R., 20 n, 55, 70-1

[339]

Ryle, H. E., 205
Ryle, J. C., 81, 103 n, 105, 129,
    139, 141, 148, 171-2, 194 n,
    204-5, 310-2

Samuel, David N., 89 n, 144, 147
Saward, M., 101, 144, 184, 254,
    264
Schaeffer, Francis, 50 n, 76-7, 306,
    310 n
Scharf, Kurt, 67
Schleiermacher, F., 3-11, 16, 23, 42,
    66, 146, 177, 209
Schuller, Robert, 73-4
Scott, Thomas, 38, 167, 300, 325-6
Scripture, doctrine of, 20-1, 37-8,
    156, 176-204, 266-8, 311-3,
    319-20
Self-Esteem movement, 73-4
Separatism, 18, 27-31, 35, 174
Shedd, W. G. T., ix-x, 198 n
Sheen, Fulton, 68
Sheppard, David, 217-8
Sims, J. A., 20 n
Slim, Field Marshall, 136
Smith, Wilbur, 36 n, 188 n
Smout, Michael, 101, 109, 130, 206 n
Southern Presbyterian Church, *see*
    Presbyterian Church US
Southwark, 40, 118-9
Sproul, R. C., 223-4, 230
Spurgeon, C. H., 23 n, 271, 285,
    289 n
Stancliffe, David, 174
Stewart, J. S., 6 n, 66
Stibbs, Alan, 110, 141 n
Stonehouse, James, 170
Stockwood, Mervyn, 14, 40, 118-9
Stott, John R. W.,
    and broadening of evangelicalism,
        49-50, 119-20
    calls for doctrinal discipline, 126
    life and conversion, 44, 168

    on Anglican evangelicalism, 42,
        100, 114, 133 n, 273
    on evangelical distinctives, 105 n,
        211, 251-2
    on evangelical unity, 44, 111
    on Scripture, 179, 299 n

Student Christian Movement (SCM),
    50 n, 177
Sunday, Billy, 24
Sun Oil Company, 25
Swanwick, 89, 137
Sweet, Leonard, 256

Tasker, R. V. G., 167 n
Taylor of Norwich, 166
Taylor, John, 145, 218-9
Temple, William, 12, 302 n
Templeton, Charles, 53 n
Tennent, Gilbert, 170 n
Teresa, Mother, 61
Themelios, 120, 187 n, 196 n
Thirty-Nine Articles, 12 n, 37, 65,
    71 n, 84-5, 90, 93, 105 n, 107,
    114, 122, 138-40, 147, 161, 228 n,
    240, 264-6, 277, 282
Thiselton, Anthony, 91, 200-1
Thomas, W. H. Griffith, 115, 117,
    185
Thompson, E. T., 10-11
Thompson, Mark D., 128
Thornwell, J. H., ix
Tinker, Melvin, 123 n
Tomlinson, D., 251
Tozer, A. W., 315 n
Trent, Council of, 160, 227-8,
    236-7, 241 n
Trueman, Carl, 187 n
Tyndale, William, 1, 156-7, 238-9,
    248, 273
Tyndale Fellowship, 175, 182, 184 n,
    186
Tyndale Hall, Bristol, 82, 118

Universities and Colleges Christian
Fellowship (UCCF), 13,120 n, 193
Union Theological Seminary, Va.,
10, 208
United Presbyterian Church, 48 n
Ursinus, Zacharias, 311

Vatican Council, Second, 79,
215-6, 233
Vietnam War, 62-3
Vos, Geerhardus, 281 n

Warburton, William, 158, 168 n
Ward, Keith, 198
Warfield, B. B., x, 182, 187 n,
195, 199 n, 201, 267, 311 n, 316
Watergate scandal, 63
Watson, David, 100-1, 140, 289 n
Weatherhead, Leslie, 34, 55, 58
Welbeck, B., 34 n
Wells, D. F., 72 n, 74 n, 109, 213 n,
252-3, 256, 310
Wenham, David, 120
Wenham, John, 88 n, 176, 183,
186-7, 211
Wesley, John, 158-65, 169, 273,
292-3, 307, 310
Westcott House, Cambridge, 124
Westminster Abbey, 13

Westminster Central Hall, 111
Westminster Chapel, 44, 76-7, 81,
110 n
Westminster Fellowship, 110 n,
283 n
Westminster Theological Seminary,
16, 18-19, 21, 47 n, 18ffl8
Wheaton College, 26, 28, 191
Whitefield, George, 158-64, 168-
70, 262, 273, 285 n, 310, 316
White House, 62-3, 65, 68
Wilberforce, William, 105 n, 171
Wiles, Maurice, 113, 198
Wilson, Daniel, 143 n
Wilson, T. W., 59 n, 68 n
Women, ordination of, 128
Wood, M. A. P., 87, 215, 218
Woolley, Paul, 18
Wordsworth, Christopher, 202
World Council of Churches, 3,
41, 55, 253
World Congresses on Evangelism,
Berlin, 32 n, 67, 75-6
Lausanne, 50, 57 n, 60-1, 216,
314 n
World Missionary Conference, 2
Worldliness, 169-72, 255-8
Wycliffe Hall, 82, 128, 184, 195
Yarbrough, R., 212